Finding My Little Red Hat

From Medicine Show, to Miss America, to Mountaintop

Jo-Carroll Dennison

D1528726

Finding My Little Red Hat

The events and conversations in this book have been set down to the best of the author's ability.

First edition: September 2021

ISBN: 9798517776662

Designed, edited, and produced by Evan Mills, Mendocino, California, USA. evanmills1@gmail.com

Available on Amazon.com

To my mother, who is belatedly much appreciated.

Contents

Foreword

Born in the Florence Arizona men's prison in 1923, Jo-Carroll Dennison learned to walk (and dance and sing) on a medicine show and later taught herself to trick-ride horses in the circus. She spent her childhood on the road and on the stage.

The huckster snake-oil salesman who ran the medicine show tried to rape her at age 12 — she fended him off.

Crowned Miss America in 1942 (at the age of 18), Dennison (aka "The Texas Tornado") shows us the underbelly of the Miss America organization at the time. She spoke up about the questionable year-long indenture of Miss America winners, and was the first to protest appearing for the organization in a bathing suit.

That was just for starters.

Her story goes on to provide an unvarnished view — from inside, looking out — of a starlet's life in Hollywood in the 1940s at 20th Century Fox. Among her films were *Winged Victory* and *The Jolson Story*. Her later work in front of television cameras included the *The Frank Sinatra Show*, *Ed Sullivan Presents*, *Kraft Theater and Omnibus*, *Abbott and Costello*, and *Dick Tracy*. Fan mail continues to arrive into her late 90s, complete with requests for signed glossy photos.

During World War II, she entertained at defense plants, hospitals, and service camps. A mixed blessing, her *LIFE* magazine bathing-suit photo series was the second-most popular pin-up among servicemen after Betty Grable's.

Her first love was young Blackie Sherrod, who became a famous journalist and sportswriter. He testified that her eyes were speckled like those of a trout. She was invited to dance by Howard Hughes and had a deep love affair with Sydney Chaplin (son of Charlie).

In Hollywood, it was rarefied air. "Normal" life revolved around the party scene at the homes of Frank Sinatra, Bing Crosby, Danny Kaye, and Gene Kelly. The crowd at Kaye's parties was stimulating. Groucho and Harpo Marx, Ira Gershwin, and George Burns were regulars, but the highlight was being part of the core group for weekly gatherings at the Kelley's, infused with music (including impromptu piano and song with Andre Previn and Paul Robeson). These evenings of "radical liberal intellectualism" also included occasional drop-ins like Garbo (to a Tupperware party, of all things), Garland, and Monroe.

Dennison's other inspirations included Norman Corwin, Yip Harburg, Dalton Trumbo, Howard Fast, Heywood Broun, and Ray Bradbury. In these circles, having been Miss America was more a stigma than an asset. But these people gave her a chance, and many served as matchmakers with the literature she'd missed in school, and helped forge her into an avid writer and thinker. She became a staunch liberal, as she watched friends persecuted under McCarthy's Red Scare and witnessed the ravages of blacklisting on her cultural world.

Unseduced by the glitter of men in power and their infamous "casting couches," Dennison shows us that superstars and power brokers are mere mortals, and often worse. Eighty years before the *Me Too* movement, Dennison endures her own version of inhumane treatment of women by boys, men, and institutions: among them charlatans, producers, directors, therapists, and husbands. Of particular note, these included Darryl Zanuck and Harry Cohn ("a tarantula of a man"). Orson Welles had more depth, but was unkind.

In Hollywood of the 40s and 50s, she also finds warm refuge and creative stimulation in close-knit circles of entertainment and literary friends — many of them also men. In magical moments, she encounters mentors that inspire and change the course of her life. Actors like Lew Ayres and Gregory Peck were honorable and encouraged her. Edward G. Robinson invited her to Jewish Seders at his home.

She had marriages to Phil Silvers ("for laughter") and to CBS producer and director Russell Stoneham, with whom she had two children. The second marriage inspired the storyline for Redford and Streisand's dilemma in Arthur Laurents' *The Way We Were*. She was the free-spirited liberal and he was he conservative pragmatist.

Following her intuition and inspired by poignant experiences in Europe and Israel, rather than being drawn further in by the flame of the entertainment industry, she ultimately steers away from film roles that would have propelled her to a higher level sf stardom — including an invitation from Chaplin to be the lead woman in *Limelight* — but would have required some form of existential compromise. She also screen-tested for *Singin' in the Rain* and was invited by famous Italian director Vittorio De Sica to be in his films.

She was reborn in the magical Greenwich Village of the 1950s. Working in the offices of friends Rogers and Hammerstein and later behind the camera as a production assistant for *Lux Video Theater* in Los Angeles — the first live television drama — proved far more creatively satisfying than being on the screen. Were it not for the pressure to defer to the needs of men, she would have become the first female producer of live television.

From a young age, Dennison cultivates and respects the guardian angels that seem to always emerge when needed most. She first meets God while climbing a tree as a child and again while stuck overnight in a snowy mountain pass, but never meets him in a church. She refers to one preacher "as phony as a circus barker for a Freak Show."

Among the books her mother read to her as a child, Lassie stood out as fearless, valiant, and trustworthy and a superb "moral arbitrator." When really in a pinch, she asks herself: "What would Lassie do?"

Years later, in confronting compromises she had made, she realized was that "to annihilate one's real self, to stifle one's natural impulses, is to eventually destroy oneself."

In search of her little red hat of courage — worn as a child to ever-changing schools while on the road with her parent's medicine show — in 1976 Dennison decamps to picturesque Mexican town of San Miguel de Allende, returning repeatedly over the following four years. This book was born and nurtured during those retreats, set aside to mellow, resurrected in the mid-1990s, and then, from her home perched on a mountainside in mile-high Idyllwild, California, tied together and supplemented with new reflections during the global pandemic of 2020-2021. Just as we ponder and tell our own stories, the flow of this one doesn't follow a tidy straight line. Dennison's writing dances back and forth across decades as she decodes her life and times.

Whether stroking poisonous Gila monsters, being unexpectedly hoisted high in the air while curled in the trunk of a circus elephant, or finding soulmates among her many domestic four-legged companions, a common thread through her life is a sublime connection with nature. Here she finds her truth and equanimity, both as a child on the road and then again, beginning in the 1980s, in Idyllwild. In those years, mentoring local schoolchildren learning the power of voting and then helping hospice patients find peace and connection in their final days were among the most meaningful experiences in the tapestry of her life.

Serendipity and intuition are everything in this story. For Dennison, key forks in the road, however small, made all the difference. Through choices born of being true to herself, she crafts a life entirely worth living while threading the needles of anger and fear with love and fearlessness.

Knowing Jo much of my life and working on this project together over the past few years has not only been like having a time machine; it's been like having a time machine complete with a learned guide. Helping her weave together disparate chapters she'd written over nearly five decades, and sifting through boxes of old black-and-white photos together, triggered additional recollections and stories upon stories that we could add to the fabric.

The resulting tapestry has a tight and beautiful weave.

Having passed more years than many regal trees — and as the oldest currently living Miss America — Jo continues to consistently rise above adversity, while caring to improve herself, living life to the fullest. As a woman of the 20s (the 1920s, that is), I find her completely at home in the moment (the 2020s, that is), web-savvy, culturally current, and able to draw uncanny connections between current events and social trends to old lessons that humankind hasn't yet learned.

Evan Mills, Mendocino, California, September 2021

The "Little Woman"

Russ and me by my yellow Buick.

"You have to understand that the wonderful things that happened to you in your teens and 20s are not going to happen to you in your late 50s," said the psychiatrist benignly. I was on my second box of tissues and couldn't seem to stop blubbering during my second visit to the Director of the Psychiatric Department of the University of California at Los Angeles (UCLA). He was an imposing, freshly barbered and manicured man in a gray, exquisitely tailored suit, with the austere, authoritative manner of a bank president. I was instantly intimidated by him. On my first visit, I had walked into his office in a kind of haze of unhappiness under an outwardly calm demeanor, but I had no sooner sat down in the large, maroon leather chair across from his shining, immaculate mahogany desk than I started crying. Unexpectedly, I was completely overcome with total sorrow. With what seemed to me a slight disdain, the doctor had indicated a box of Kleenex on a small table near my chair, and I had worked my way through it completely by the time I had finished the first installment of my sob story.

It was my husband who was going to this illustrious doctor for psychiatric counseling, and he had told me that his socialite sister had to use her considerable influence to get him an appointment. As my husband was very private about his physical and mental feelings, I always wondered what reasons he had given his beloved younger sister as to his need for a psychiatrist. He didn't tell me anything about his several visits until the doctor had asked to see me. I was astonished but pleased that Russ, my husband of 24 years, could admit he needed this kind of help and was glad to go and lend a hand, so to speak. I had diligently trained myself since a child not to cry, so my racking sobs had taken me by surprise. But between sobs, I managed to tell this august personage that I had been planning to get a divorce for two years, after I finally had found out that our "forsaking all others" vow, which I had taken seriously in thought and deed, had not lasted more than a few months for my husband after we were married. That, and the fact that our interests, enthusiasms and passions were by now almost diametrically opposed, had convinced me that once our two sons were out of school I would have to get a divorce. It shamed me dreadfully to find that old cliché of staying together for the sake of the children was also true for me, I who had such high hopes of beating the game of marriage, but there it was.

The cruel irony was, however, that once the time had come that our younger son was about to graduate from high school and the elder about to graduate from college, I seemed to have been caught in a dingy, gray cocoon of inertia which I was unable to break through. I pulled at the strands obsessively, but they seemed to reform into an even tighter web as soon as I got one strand loose. We had talked divorce of late, had even both agreed to it, my husband saying it was up to me if that was what I wanted, but then I couldn't seem to gain the strength of resolve to actually *do* it. At night I would look at this charming, handsome, beautifully-groomed, intelligent man across the dining table or sitting beside me in the den or at a party, and I wanted to bash my head against the wall and silently scream, "*We are not suited!*" until a wave of grief would reach up from my innards and grab me by the throat. I supposed, in a way, I still loved him as the father of my children, but I didn't *like* him anymore. The knowledge that I must get a divorce from Russ or sink into a kind of oblivion would repeatedly force me to make up my mind to call a lawyer the next morning and get divorce proceedings started. Then, I would wake up in our familiar bed, in our familiar lovely bedroom and that resolve became unreal and amorphous. The man sleeping next to me was my *husband.* We were *married.* This was my *reality!* How could I change that, how could I crack all that apart? So I did nothing. My butterfly cocoon was suspended in a space of the known without the possibility of breaking out to flutter off into the unknown. A butterfly seemed too fragile a thing in which to place my trust for the future.

Thus it was in January of 1976 in my 54th year as I tottered into the elegant office of this top-of-his-profession psychiatrist at one of the most prestigious universities in our country for succor and support. Embarrassed that I had been such a soggy mess on my previous visit, I was determined to be cool and mature this time, but no sooner had I sat down than I dissolved into tears once more. Seemingly from a great distance in an impersonal tone, the doctor began to describe my situation. "You see," said he, "based on early childhood trauma, your husband long ago found a behavior pattern that was comfortable for him, a defense mechanism to avoid emotional pain that has worked for him in his daily life, and consequently, he is set in concrete as to change. Since he *cannot* change, you will have to adjust to him. You have a lovely home, are well provided for, and your children are doing fine. At your age, this is more than many women have, and you must learn to appreciate and enjoy your life as it is."

Well, I was confident *my* childhood trauma would outshine anyone's! Gulping down sobs and struggling to make him understand my position, I cried, "But I no longer enjoy *being* with Russ, *sleeping* with him, you know? I mean, when we were first married we had a very satisfying sex life and I felt close to him, but that feeling just hasn't been there for a very long time."

With his own face seemingly set in concrete, he said, "You mean you no longer have orgasms?"

"Well, no, I never really *have* had an orgasm, but, anyway, I used to enjoy sex and just being with him."

Leaning forward into a lecturing position, he said soberly, "My dear lady, all these magazine articles and books for women about sex that began appearing in the 50s have misled the American woman severely. Biologically, it is not important that the female have an orgasm, only the male. There is nothing wrong with you or your sex life, if you can just accept it for what it is and not wear yourself out expecting more because of what you might have read or been told. Most of it is just nonsense. Anyway, as you have already entered menopause, and have had a hysterectomy, you will find that your sex drive lessens considerably. You have a good life and at your age you must learn to adjust and make the best of it."

"But I am not *happy*! I used to be *happy*! I know I seem weak to you crying all the time this way, but I am really very strong. I have *always* been strong. I have gone out and gotten jobs for myself ever since I was 11 years old. I've supported my mother since I was 18. I have always gotten everything I wanted all on my own, and I can do it again. I just have to get my strength back somehow. And I am lucky, too. All my life I have been lucky. Miraculous, wonderful things have happened to me right out of the blue ever since I can remember. When I was seven, a man I didn't even know gave me a horse. Creampuff was a beautiful palomino 2-year-old and changed my whole life. Things like that were always happening to me. And I was always winning things, like I won a Miss America Pageant when I was 18, and I hadn't even tried for it. I have had fascinating jobs all over the world, and people who were really interesting and talented have done great things for me, really for no reason I could see, and, well, miracles have just always happened to me when I least expected it. I know that if I can just get my strength back, I can get a divorce and I will be all right again."

Settling back in his chair and peering at me over his glasses, the doctor said, "Have any of these miracles happened to you lately?"

A tightening in my stomach foretold bad news, "Well, not just lately."

Gratified, he said, "You see? That is my point. Wonderful things that happen to a young girl do not often happen to a middle-aged woman. You can no longer count on that. That is why the saying goes that "youth is wasted on the young." You think that a miracle will happen and the joy of youth will come back to you if you get a divorce, but please believe me, it will not. You like to think that you are a strong woman and that miracles will keep happening to you, but that is just unrealistic, wishful thinking, and under all that defensive pretense I can hear a little girl crying out for help."

If he had thrown a bucket of ice water in my face, I could not have had a stronger reaction. Every muscle and cell in my body jumped to full alert like I had been stuck with a cattle prod, and I was instantly in a boiling rage. "Oh? Really? And just who is going to help that little girl? My husband? You, with all your talk of helpless middle-aged women? Not likely! All my life I have had to help myself, and I can still do it! I am *not* a helpless little girl!"

The image of me as a helpless little girl pushed a button that was at the most painful part of my nerve center. I couldn't tolerate it. As though a steel rod had suddenly been thrust up my spine, I strode out of his office, and — in a way — into a new life. The doctor's attitude had blown away the self-imposed cover that had been stifling my self-pride, that essential and defining part of my very being that I had lost track of somewhere along the way in my marriage. The determined commitment I had made to my marriage had so over-shadowed my commitment to myself that, without noticing, I had become a different and lesser person. A stranger, really, to everything I had believed about myself and worked toward all the time I was growing up. In a way he had not intended, the doctor had in one session cleared my mind of all the dross I had been stuffing it with all during the years of my marriage.

It was the strangest thing. The psychiatrist's condescending words had popped the cork off all my bottled up anger, and the re-pressed rage spewed out with volcanic force. Moments of holding my tongue to keep peace in the family, making up when I thought *Russ* was in the wrong, belittling *myself* to make him feel good about *himself*, a multitude of such remembrances flew vividly through my mind and curdled my blood with shame and torment. I felt all fizzy inside.

The doctor was right about one thing, however, I did have a lovely home. All my adult life, I had been able to find marvelous plac-es to live, always with grand vistas. The house I went home to from the doctor's office was just up the road from UCLA on Westridge Drive in Brentwood, and was a spectacular place to live. Set high on a mountain ridge, it overlooked the whole Los Angeles basin from downtown to Santa Monica; its view encompassed the Will Rogers State Park, the lights of the city, and the wide stretch of ocean. The den, one son's bedroom, and an enormous playroom looked out on a rather formal garden with a fountain spraying into a reflecting pool, a slate-tiled bridge leading over it to the front door. The nearly-solid glass walls of the spacious living room, dining room and kitchen/breakfast room overlooked the glass-fenced patio, gardens and swimming pool, and offered a fabulous view of the city, mountains, and ocean. The master bedroom suite and second son's bedroom had their own private garden and mountain view. My sons loved the pool and a patio large enough to play ball in and made good use of the sound-proofed playroom with its multitude of playthings, and my husband loved his den and all the comforts of home; in addition it was a great house for all the entertaining he so enjoyed. I loved my early morning and late night swims, and I loved the whole beautiful house filled with elegant furniture and "things" we had collected over the years. It was mostly this marvelous place we lived in, and the enormity of the boys' reaction to our having to sell it if we got a divorce, that shrouded my view and weakened my willpower.

But as I walked in the house that fateful morning and faced my image in the huge antique-framed mirror hanging in the foyer, I looked at myself for awhile and realized that I could do it. I could let it go. It was only a house.

Looking in the mirror, I felt as though I had spent years living inside a fully automated plastic mannequin which the psychiatrist's words had shattered into bits, revealing a much diminished and blurry me. I don't know what I had expected from that doctor. A little compassion or supportive understanding would have been nice. But to categorize me as the middle-aged loser who should be grateful for a roof over her head, the "little woman" who had to have a man to take care of her, and the one whose needs, sexual or otherwise, weren't as important as her husband's, riled me into a froth of fury. The most armor-piercing thought was that he dared *pity* me. That "crying little girl" thing, more than anything else he said, was the catalyst that woke me from the illusory dream I had been living and truly brought me back to the reality of who I was. I *wasn't* a loser. Never had been. It wasn't like me, not who I *really* was, to be terrified to make the move of jumping off into something unfamiliar.

When I was a child of seven, I learned that I was on my own, and that, if I was to survive, I had to learn to be as courageous as the heroes in the books I read. When I started to go to school, I wore a little red hat to give myself the courage to face down the room full of strange staring little faces. Now, I needed that courage again to face down those fears of the future. I decided that I must search for that little red hat of courage from my past.

Since I was a little girl, I had prided myself on being fearless; over and over, I had proven to myself that I could overcome any fear: pet a fierce dog, ride a rodeo horse, and have the guts to learn how to take care of myself when there was no one else to do it for me. Without trepidation, I went to Israel by myself as assistant to the producer to set up a television unit for a TV series starring Maria Riva, when I didn't really know what I was doing. I went to Paris as assistant producer to set up a television unit for a TV series starring Jean-Pierre Aumont, when I could hardly speak French, and got a similar job on a *Flash Gordon* TV series in Berlin when I couldn't speak German at *all*. Some people might call it chutzpah, but I call it brave. I had been a *contender*, by George, and a *winner* in many arenas. For years.

How had this paralysis happened to me? How and when had I let myself become this stupefied mannequin of myself? Tracing it back, I remembered that back in the early 50s when my husband and I first met, he was an assistant director on live TV shows at CBS, and I was a production assistant on *Lux Video Theater* at CBS for the advertising agency, J. Walter Thompson, and as such, I made more money than he did and was half-a-step higher than he on the TV hierarchy scale. We were on the same level financially, socially (although in quite different social circles), and in our station in life. I struggled to remember how and when that had changed. Why had I, of all people — an independent, self-supporting, enthusiastic world traveler — turned myself into the "little woman"?

A clear-as-a-bell memory clicked in: Clear in time, place, and depth of emotion. Surely, this was the starting point. It had happened like this: I loved my work, and, after Russ and I were married in 1953, had continued with it until two weeks before our first son, Peter, was born. Thinking I must do so in order to be a good mother, I had quit my job to stay home with him. I reached deeper than I had ever needed to reach before in order to make a go of being a housewife and mother, an occupation for which I had no experience and very little innate talent. I loved Peter with all my heart and soul, thought he was terrific, colic and all, but my mother had always acted the role of the housewife for me, so I had never had to learn to cook or clean a house and had never even *seen* a dirty diaper. Endearing and fascinating as Peter was to my maternal heart, staying home all day trying to learn how to succeed at this new occupation wasn't always a lot of fun, even after two years of diligent effort. I found I needed more support and comfort from my mate than I had previously. A different kind of communication between Russ and me had begun to matter greatly. I felt I was missing some kind of necessary adult warmth and contact. I had always had a strong, healthy ego and took it for granted that I was loved by those I loved, but somehow now, during my struggle to adjust to this life I was living, when we were out to a party, or even alone at home, I had this powerful *need* to be touched, to be *connected*. Not necessarily hugged or kissed or made over, but just a pat on the shoulder, a hand held, affirmative eye contact, a wink or something like that which said, "We are together, and I am glad, and I love you." For the first time since I was a child I badly needed an affirmation of worth, a physical manifestation of togetherness, of being *cared* for. Not flowers or presents or daily phone calls (though that would be nice), but just that when we were together, I wanted him to make some kind of overt gesture of affection, of support, and caring. Also, I wished we could talk together about something other than television.

So, one night when Peter was in bed, I tried to put into words what I had been feeling — to communicate! My husband was sitting in the corner of the lanai in his favorite chair reading *Newsweek*, and I was standing in the doorway of our bedroom close to him when I delivered my prepared communiqué. He didn't say anything or stop looking at the magazine, so I soldiered on and on, repeating myself as I tried to make my feelings and needs clear, until eventually I floundered to a stop. Without looking directly at me, he put down his magazine, stood, and firmly closed the bedroom door in my face.

I felt as though I had run full tilt into a brick wall in the dark. I hadn't seen it coming. The shock of his response was so unexpected that I was literally stunned. I had to admit that he was succinct. I mean, we could have discussed this issue at great length for weeks and his viewpoint would not have been as fully expressed as by the closing of that door. *He didn't want to talk about feelings, and he wasn't about to change his behavior.* It was such an overtly hostile act that I couldn't make up my mind what to do about it. As it happened, I was going out with a best friend to a seminar on *The Impressionists* at UCLA that night, so I just went down the hall and out the front door without another word. Needless to say, my friend and I never made it to the seminar, but went to our favorite bar where I rather hysterically told her what had happened. We sat face-to-face and puzzled over his attitude, swore at men in general and at Russ specifically, and discussed my bleak future options for several hours over several martinis. Even so, the shutting door was a disturbance of the peace that was beyond our pale of understanding, no matter how long we discussed the differences between men and women, and their needs and attitudes. Nor could I come to a conclusion about the pros and cons of leaving hearth and home, so eventually I went home determined to make a major decision I could act on in the morning, after sleeping on it and sobering up.

The next morning, my husband behaved as though nothing out of the ordinary had happened, and was exceedingly cheery. Trying to hold head and stomach together while enduring a fierce hangover, I just managed to speak. Our 2-year-old Peter was all excited as we were going out for the day with another friend of mine to go water skiing in the ocean on our 24-foot power boat. The *Toy Tiger* was my husband's pride and joy; it seemed to give him an important sense of power and control and he took meticulous care of it. I had decided on an attitude of calm and pleasant for the time being, but when we stopped for our picnic lunch, knowing I couldn't swallow a bite and be sure of keeping it down, I stretched out on the bow away from the others to think it over. It was time to make this momentous decision. The slam of the door had cracked wide open any illusions I'd had about Russ. For the first time, I could see that I had fashioned him in my own image of the perfect husband. When I had originally met this articulate, witty, handsome 33-year-old man from a wealthy, upper-class family, educated at Choate and Yale, he had just knocked my socks off. I thought he was beautiful. With his clean, crisp, good looks, reddish-blonde hair, light-blue eyes, immaculate clothes, and genteel air, he completely fulfilled my idea of a gentleman. And he wore garters to keep his socks up! Coming from a background that was about as far on the wrong side of the tracks as one could get, with very little formal education, I was secretly in awe of those who were well-educated, of those who were "up town." Instinctively, I was drawn to liberal, Bohemian "downtown" type intellectuals, but still I had a bit of subterranean yearning for the refined. He fit my image of a class act like a suede glove.

Never mind that, on closer acquaintance, I found that we were direct opposites. I acted and reacted from a purely emotional, subjective point of view; he was cerebral, analytical and objective. I left the top of my yellow convertible down in the rain; he kept his tightly closed. But I thought that "opposites attract" because it helps the gene pool and our gene pool should certainly cover all bases. It excited me when I found he had no taste for art, classical music, literature, ballet, theater, or opera because I figured it would be great fun to teach him to share my enthusiasms. I even took Dostoyevsky's *Crime and Punishment* on our honeymoon to get a start on shared joys. (He never did read it.) I refused to be concerned that his conservative well-thought-out ideas on civil rights and politics were diametrically opposed to my passionate, ultra-liberal commitment to *all* rights: civil, women, worker or animal. He was intelligent, so I figured I could soon show him the error of his thinking.

Now, shorn of the Emperor's clothes I had adorned him with, I took a good, clear look at the reality of the man I had chosen to marry. Finally I could see that, while feelings and emotions were the language that was natural for me, for him feelings and emotions were somehow fatally threatening and must be hidden deep under cheerful, charming manners and behavior. I realized that expressed tenderness, responsibility for the feelings of others, and openly showing or speaking of buried pain held a terror for him that I could not begin to understand. I had no idea who this man I had married really was. And I realized how incredibly naive I had been to ever think that I could change him! Lying there on the bow staring into the water, the image of the two of us going through life together made not a pretty picture. As the boat moved under me, the sun cast golden hieroglyphics on the surface of the ocean and I watched them thoughtfully, looking for an omen from the spirit of the deep, searching for a sign that would help me make the right decision. I said to the flashing writing on the sea, "Oh, great spirit of the deep, all-knowing wise and benevolent one, what shall I do? I need your help here. Shall I take my son and leave? Should I try to make it work out? What is the best choice, tell me, please."

And the moving letters on the water danced and changed and finally spelled out, "What choice can there be?" And it became apparent then that there was no choice but to leave. I couldn't live with that closed door.

Later, at home in the shower, I began to make plans. I would leave Peter at my mother's (they adored one another), while I went to New York and got a job to support the two of us. Most of the people

I knew in television were headquartered in New York, and, anyway, New York was always lucky for me. I could stay with a friend and start making the rounds. Such was my old sense of self that it never occurred to me that *my husband* should move out and pay alimony and child support; I just assumed that it was I who wanted to leave and therefore I should get out and take care of my child and myself. My plans were beginning to make sense and sound good to me when little Peter pulled back the shower curtain and said in a tearful, quavering voice, "Where's Daddy?"

I said, "Honey, he went to take the boat in for repair."

Tears beginning to really roll, he sobbed, "Isn't he coming back?"

As I looked down into those big, stricken hazel eyes, a mirror image of my own, I simply could not bear the fright and anxiety in them. I said, "Of course, he's coming back. He just took the boat in for a tune-up. He'll be back very soon, honey bunny." With a cold jolt of reality, I thought, "This is my child, my responsibility. Somehow he has sensed what is happening and I have to do everything I can to take that expression out of his eyes and never let it come back." Peter, as a person, had not been figuring in my thinking, but now his eyes had made me realize that he and *his* feelings had to be my first consideration. He didn't ask to be born, I asked for him. He was not just some piece of luggage I could drop off at my mother's to be picked up when I got around to it. He loved his father and needed him around. Obviously, I was going to have to rethink this whole thing.

Back when I had hit 30, my proverbial time clock had tocked, and suddenly my desire to get educated and see all those far away places had changed to one of an urgency to have children. Obeying the dictates of my era, I had to get married to do that and had chosen Russ as the man I wanted to be the father of those children. It was my decisions that had gotten us to where we were; therefore, it was my responsibility to make those decisions good ones. Leaning against the wall of the shower with the water slowly growing cold on my back, I made another decision. It wasn't Peter's fault that I had chosen the wrong man for the long haul, it was mine. If I believed that a child was better off with two parents, as my own experience had proven, I must stay with his father and do everything in my power to make Peter a happy and peaceful home. I could see that in order to do that I must never talk to Russ about *feelings* again, that was clear. I must constantly be on the alert to make my husband feel good about himself, whether I thought it was justified or not. I must keep a smile on my face and my big mouth shut. I must devote myself only to my children, my home, and my husband — and learn to be a good cook. I, who had prided myself on being prematurely anti-fascist and pro-feminist, must now stop being who I was and change myself into my placating, submissive mother.

To annihilate one's real self, to stifle one's natural impulses, is to eventually destroy oneself. It is sacrilege, actually, for one's inner core is sacred. I now think the genes given at birth have a will and rights of their own, and to realize their every potential is what life is all about. But at the time I speak of, when I made up my mind to do something, I let nothing stand in my way, so, with all the considerable will of my personality, I went about turning myself into the self-sacrificing, all-pleasing, geisha girl men dream of in order to make what I thought of as a good home for my son. I worked hard and consistently at it, and for the most part was able to pull it off. I am not saying there was not a lot of good along the way. We had lots of interesting friends, lived in great places in Los Angeles and New York, and had a comfortable, better-than-average life. And, as long as we stayed superficial, never quarreled or raised our voices to one another, and played a good game of "Let's pretend we're happy" — our friends all said we were the golden couple and envied us. We got along better than most married couples. Actually, when I studied the other marriages of which I had knowledge, I never saw another husband I would rather be married to; none of them had that tenderness and caring and respect for their wives that I instinctively yearned for, so it seemed best to make the best of what I had.

To make it more worthwhile, I tried mightily to have another child, but it took another three years before John was born. I *loved* being pregnant. Morning sickness and physical discomfort was nothing compared to the self-satisfied bliss of knowing I was going to have a baby, and the joyous awe of feeling the living kicks of my baby inside me. And I always thought making a home for my children *was* worthwhile. Peter and John were such a joy and satisfaction to me that never for one moment did I ever regret having stayed married until they were grown. I knew they were better off having the two of us together and that is what really mattered. I know it is not true for all women, but my whole being *had* to have children, and it had to be *these* children. I *knew* that Peter and John were meant to have been born into this world, and that made sense of everything.

By the time we had been married for over 20 years, however, the effort of trying to be who I was *not* had naturally dried up my joyous juices, withered my sense of self to the point that I had actually *become* the middle-aged zombie housewife that the UCLA psychiatrist had revealed to me. I had forced myself to live in a pleasant, unreal world, without realizing that doing what is wrong for one's self can never be right. Being married, as the psychiatrist had so succinctly said, was scary. I realized that the only miracle that had come to me after I married was that, because of the recognition of my work on *Lux Video Theater*, I had been asked by a producer to be the first woman to direct a live television show. The daytime soap, *Matinee,* was very successful, and to direct it was a very big deal indeed to me, a major coup for the women's side. I had rejected that miracle because I knew it would be threatening to my husband if I made director before he did. I had submerged myself in order to make Russ feel good about himself for a very long time and had been overtly enthusiastic about every good turn his career or interests took. It was easy to see that he was glad and relieved when I quit working and stayed home to look after Peter.

When Russ and I first started going together, we were members of quite different groups. My friends were all show-biz and my closest friends were the Gene Kelly group, all extremely talented, free-spirited, fun-loving, radical liberals. His family and friends were old wealthy Pasadena society types or young, on-their-way-up, Republican conservatives. It makes me laugh to think of the politely combustive collision between these two diametrically opposed groups when Russ and I attempted to commingle them. Over the years, this form of water torture wore away important parts of my sense of self.

The playwright, Arthur Laurents, was a friend while Russ and I were living in New York during his stint at CBS producing Leonard Bernstein and other projects. Anita Ellis was also a great friend of mine, and of Arthur's. He told Anita that the wife's character in *The Way We Were* (book and movie) was inspired by Annie Mostel – from the standpoint of a dedicated liberal – and me, married to the college-favorite Russ (played by Robert Redford), and the problems in our marriage due to the differences in our thinking and our politics. Russ was a handsome WASP from a wealthy family. Some people said the wife's character was modeled after a Cornell student Arthur knew when he went there, but that was just for show. My liberal causes and social conscience embarrassed him. We thought so differently. Streisand, who played the wife in the movie, was a liberal girl – it was a good part for her. She even had a yellow convertible, like me!

In the beginning, I thought I was so strong and secure within myself that his negative comments would just roll right off harmlessly — but you can't pretend to be the "little woman" for too long without becoming *little*!

As I read and reflect on this today, in 2021, it is stunning how poorly women have been treated in the American culture. I am so proud of the "Me Too movement" and the women who have been brave enough to come forward about the male sexual abuse they have suffered, and grateful I have lived long enough to see it. Maybe the "little woman" syndrome will be next!

To fulfill my commitment to Peter to make him a good home, and to appease my husband's desire to entertain a lot, I took cooking classes of all kinds, and, somewhat to my surprise, I eventually became a good cook. And, though I do say so myself, I was a good hostess and threw great dinner parties. That accomplished, however, after we could afford full-time help, and the boys were both in school, I found that I *needed* to get out of the house and do something for myself, dammit! Just keeping my head barely above water became the same as drowning and I knew I had to get out there and *swim* a little.

One of my most interesting experiences was when I volunteered, along with a group of my women friends, to spend three hours twice a week at the Sawtell Veteran's Hospital in West Los Angeles teaching ballroom dancing to catatonic patients. We were each assigned four patients with the objective of trying to break through their total rigid withdrawal by guiding them through the basic box step. These men had been so severely wounded in their minds by the horror of their wartime experiences, that they had retreated completely into their deepest core where they could not be reached or hurt by outside stimuli. Catatonics will not voluntarily make a move but they will allow themselves to be moved about, to walk, eat, or sit when guided. But if you hold one arm up in the air, for instance, the arm will stay rigidly as placed until someone moves it down again. Their slack, drooling, unseeing faces above their thin, steel-like bodies in loose, ill-fitting hospital pajamas and naked, vulnerable feet encased in dirty slippers broke my heart. They were vanished personalities. But with that great recorded music of the swing era as impetus, we drew them up from their chairs and held their arms and talked to them as we tried to get them to move their feet in rhythm to the music.

It was intensely rewarding to see some of these damaged, unfocused, speechless young men begin to trust and respond to me by beginning to pay attention to their shuffling feet and the music as I guided them around the floor. One day a young man, a boy, really, in whom I had taken a special interest, said an unintelligible word to me. I was so startled and elated that I wanted to jump up and down and yell with joy, but I was terrified that I would scare him back into his silence. I stayed very still, gave him soft, encouraging words, and desperately tried to understand when he finally put an unintelligible sentence together.

Gradually, under our encouragement, several of the patients began to say a word or two until they began to talk freely. At that point, they were released from the hospital into the custody of their families, and it was heartwarming to think that they would be able to live a real life again. It was heart*breaking*, however, when some of them were brought back a month or so later in a catatonic state again, unable to cope with life outside these walls. The important thing, though, was that the doctors told us that helping the patients to ballroom dance did more to bring them out of their catatonic state than any other method they had tried. Later, the program was so successful that the University of Southern California took it over as part of their social science work.

I was proud of that accomplishment, but Russ thought it was all a great waste of my time and seemed to resent my involvement and never wanted to hear about it. How can you explain that?

When we lived in New York, I volunteered as a teacher of Conversational English for non-English speaking children at P.S. 84, an elementary school on the upper West Side, which police records showed was the toughest neighborhood in Manhattan. This was in the sixties when Puerto Rico was made a commonwealth of the U.S., and Puerto Ricans had arrived in New York by the thousands, most of them speaking only Spanish. The public school system was overwhelmed, and a well-known, wealthy community leader (whose name I have unfortunately forgotten) came up with a program of volunteers to help these children, we brought boxes of small toys and interesting objects to be used as English teaching tools while worked one-on-one with selected children. It was almost incredible to see how these seven- to 12-year-olds blossomed under this kind of attention. Because of overcrowding, without this volunteer program, many of these children would have been judged unteachable and just put at the back of the class with coloring books, while the person there to teach them spoke to the class in a language incomprehensible to them. With our form of individual encouragement, however, after an astonishingly short time, they could speak rudimentary English and often they went to the front of the class, so eager were they to learn. It was fascinating. Another dividend of this program was that some of us took the children with the worst learning problems to retirement homes to meet with practically comatose elderly people in wheelchairs. It filled my heart with wonder as we found that involving the older with the younger in teaching English made a most amazing difference in the attitudes and abilities of both ages. The younger ones rapidly learned to speak English and the older ones rapidly learned to feel alive.

Though he fathered my sons, we ate at the same table and slept in the same bed, and I eventually learned some of the bare bones of the traumas he endured as a child, still I never knew what dark fears motivated Russ' disapproval of my work outside the home. How was he threatened? Why would a man *want* a robotic "Stepford Wife" anyway? I'll never understand it. Whatever, remembering it now, I felt his overall medieval attitude about my outside activities and political thinking was designed to put me down and keep me down, and I wondered grimly if the UCLA psychiatrist would have thought that was the proper position for me. Now, I was deciding finally that it was not.

One night after dinner, I spent a long time in the bath with foam and bath oil up to my ears. Looking around the luxurious bathroom, I felt a beneficent, soothing relaxation of tension and indecision. The boiling cauldron of rage had solidified into a firm resolve. Reviewing my past had the desired strengthening effect, and I could feel myself getting taller, straighter, and filled with a renewed sense of self. Even though I had played a submissive, placatory role for so many years, I knew that I was the stronger. He had taken my support for granted all these years and had no idea, I thought, of just how much he needed that support.

My husband was in bed reading his new *Sports Illustrated* when I came out of the bath. I sat cross-legged on my side of the bed and said, "Listen, we have to talk. I had an extremely revelatory session with your psychiatrist, and I have come to a very important realization. I simply cannot go on with the kind of marriage we have now. I know it bothers you to talk about feelings, but if we can't talk, I can't stay. I am not asking you to change completely, but we have to meet and open ourselves to one another on a much deeper level than we ever have or it's just no longer worth it to me. I don't like who I am any more. And I'm telling you, if I leave you, I will be OK, but you will not."

Without looking up, he said, "I know that."

I thought, "He *knows* that!" But I mushed on, "Well, can we talk about this or can we not?"

No response.

Now, if I had to make a choice between the cruel and annihilating actions of one person to another, silence as a response to a plea would be right up there with brutality. I *hate* it! Withdrawal without explanation should be a capital offence in my book. But in this case, it was the perfect reaction to goad me to action. Almost exultantly, I said, "OK then, I hereby divorce you. You and I are no longer husband and wife." I got up, took my pet pillow, went into Peter's empty bedroom (Peter was off at college now) and went to bed. Lying there in the single bed in the clean, crisp sheets, I stretched out with a grand feeling of being myself again. Of being *by* myself again, and it was delicious. He was not "my man" and I was not "his woman," any longer. I thought gleefully, "Not *this* time, Buster! You got away with that silent stuff before — *but not anymore.*"

After having made the move into Peter's bedroom, however, the exultation began to wear off in a few days when I was fully into the logistics, guilt, and actuality of what I was finally going to do. Our younger son, John, had to be aware of the situation, but he didn't mention it. Sadly, I realized that he had been well trained in the if-you-don't-talk-about-it, it-will-go-away syndrome, but was feeling rotten inside. It hurt me. The thought of having to tell Peter hurt even more; I knew he would take it harder.

One late night, I was lying in a deck lounge, gently rocking back and forth as I looked at the path the full moon made down the center of the pool, when I was suddenly overwhelmed by a vast feeling of failure and depression. Here I was at 54 having failed at staying with a promising career, failed at a happy marriage (the one thing I had tried hardest to achieve), had failed my children after all, and failed to fulfill the promise and potential given me at birth. I had been given many marvelous opportunities, could have had an altogether different life if I had made different choices, but now it was too late. My life was almost over — and I had blown it. I had *blown* it! I desperately wanted another chance to get it right, I wanted to scream at the gods, *"Let me go back and do it over again!"*

Then the remembrance of Peter and John made me reject that thought, but still the beauty of the shimmering, golden reflection of the moon in the pool somehow filled me with an aching sorrow of something missed. Russ came out to say good night and was startled by the tears streaming down my face. "What's wrong?" he asked. In answer to his question, I blurted out, "No man will ever love me," and was astonished at the sudden revelation of *this* hidden fear — the worst failure of all.

There it was, the shame that had humbled me for a good part of my life: the quietly devastating feeling that I could not be fully complete as a woman, and therefore never truly at one with a man, physically, mentally, and spiritually. The shock of the depth of despair indicated by that humiliating admission galvanized me into action. Or rather, the search for the right kind of action. It became an immediate necessity to find the courage to hoist myself up out of this morass of self-doubt and fear into a new (and old) way of thinking. I used to be brave. How did I lose that bravery? When and how could I get it back again? It was time to find my little red hat.

23

Searching for my Little Red Hat

*During my cold-stern period in Hollywood,
my Mother commented that "You were such a
sweet girl."*

When I was in the process of divorcing Russ, Peter was graduating from college and John was graduating from high school. I had
waited until then to take this giant step — and to my dismay — I
found that I was afraid of a single future. It was as a young child that
I first had to learn about courage. My parents had a small medicine
show and we traveled constantly from one little town to another so
I only went to school one or two weeks at a time. To give myself the

courage to face a room full of strange, gawking kids, I wore a little red hat with a little red feather to school on the first day. I felt it made me individual and different, as no child ever wore hats to school in those days. Of course, as a singer/dancer/actor on a traveling show, I was already different enough from these small-town kids, but somehow the little red hat gave me the poise and assurance to face them down. It was my red badge of courage, you might say, and in it I felt I was strong enough to prevail over any situation.

I realized now, so many years later, that I had lost that little red hat somewhere during my marriage. Where had it gone?

In the days that followed that abysmal moment by the moonlit pool at our home in Brentwood, I decided that I should try to write a book about my childhood in order to uncover the answer to that imperative question. A good part of my childhood was a complete blank to me. I had been to a couple of psychologists off and on, had even tried hypnosis, but was never able to find the *source* that caused my fear of complete intimacy and the shame of feeling incomplete. I was not stupid enough to think that the blame for our troubled marriage lay solely with my husband. I knew in my heart that I had brought a dead weight of my own to our relationship.

When I was a child, my parents had made me feel I was the most perfect person possible and surely destined for great things. My mother's adoration I took for granted; my father was the sun around whom my world circled. He and I had an almost romantic (in the platonic sense!) relationship; I was his beloved princess, he my courtly knight. Everything I did or tried to be was to please him. Then when I was seven, my 62-year old father left my 42-year old mother and me and ran away with an 18-old blonde, who was working on our show at the time. That breakup of my world left me with shattered pieces and defensive barriers that shaped the rest of my emotional life. Through the help of a psychologist I had recognized those barriers, but had never been able to break them down. Eventually, I had thought that when it was the right time, with the right circumstances, and the right man whom I was able to *love*, those defensive fears would naturally dissolve and I would be the complete woman I wanted to be. It didn't happen. So now, I felt it was necessary to understand the forces of the past that had made me into the young adult I used to be before I could understand the fearful, "middle-aged" adult I had now become. It seemed to me the only way I could do that was literally to dig up the shrouded past with its whys and wherefores by writing it out.

Of course, the brave thing to do would be to get a divorce and get an apartment to start my writing challenge, but my heavy backpack of guilt was like a giant leech draining the blood from my resolve. Knowing my difficulties in taking the leap, a friend called me one day to read a quote she'd found in an article in the *New York Times* about John Milton, the great, blind English poet who wrote *Paradise Lost*. The article said Milton had been very influential in bringing about the Reformation by arguing that subjects may depose and put to death an unworthy king, and Cromwell had given him high office. Most important to me, in his *Radical Address on the Doctrines and Disciplines of Divorce* to Parliament in 1643, he'd said, "In God's intention a meet and happy conversation is the chiefest and nobelest end of marriage," and he went on to say that divorce is not only necessary but *right* when that special conversation fails.

I said, "Beautiful! Right on!" Imagine a man thinking that a happy conversation with his wife was the most important and noble purpose of marriage! Just imagine the difference that would make in most marriages.

It was truly thrilling to hear such a statement from a man of that stature, but after a brief moment of feeling vindicated and inspired, I thought that he hadn't said anything about its effects on what the uneducated wife of that period would do to support herself. Also, the report of Milton's speech didn't say how the all-man parliament responded to that poetic declamation of the importance of man-woman communication. I would bet they responded much as my husband had. Be that as it may, that this understanding of the need for men and women to have "meet and happy conversations" had been around for several hundred years was encouraging. Except it made me sad, too. It reminded me of one day when I was sitting out by the pool after an early morning swim and a tiny bird came and perched on the deck wall near me and began the most beautiful "Ode to Joy" I had ever heard. I didn't know what kind of a bird he was, but he threw back his little head and soared out his own personal *joie de vivre* to the heavens, and my soul reached out to absorb the glory of his song. Suddenly, he stopped singing and darted in full flight straight into the glass wall of the living room and broke his neck. As I stood looking down as this broken wisp of a lifeless thing, I wondered where his glorious song had gone? Did it just evaporate into thin air — like love? Or did it still resonate somewhere in the universe continuing to send out lovely waves of inspiration and hope — like Milton's words?

These thoughts were, however, a spur to action, so summoning all the determination I possibly could, I bought an electric typewriter, lots of paper, a paperback dictionary, a thesaurus, and I was ready to turn Peter's room into my writing place. I didn't feel ready to get a divorce immediately, thereby having to sell the house and the disruption that entailed, but I felt if I could find the perseverance to really write a book, at least I would have found my courage and strength again. Never having tried to write much more than my name before, however, I was apprehensive that it was going to be very time-consuming to find just the most impressive, the most erudite and graphic words for what I wanted to say. Having had practically no formal education at all, I was vastly proud of how well-read I was now, was in fact conceited because in my 20s I had gorged on the Great Books and Modern Library lists, and had always continued to read ravenously. How would a reader know how articulate and well-read I was if I didn't use all the big words I knew? I mean, if I was going to do this thing, I wanted to be sure to do it right!

I talked to some writer friends of mine about that problem, and *three* of them (Ray Bradbury, Walter Newman, and Irwin Shaw) each gave me Strunk and White's *Elements of Style* to read. Its whole theme was *not* to use big words, rather to use the most clear and simple words possible. It was a blow to my desire to impress a reader, but I had to admit it made things easier. Or, at least *so I thought at the time!* My other problem was that I was greatly intimidated by the skill and imagination of my favorite writers, but my darling friend, Ray Bradbury, the sweetest and most imaginative Peter Pan of them all, said earnestly, "Just use your own words and experience, Jo, and tell *your* story. No other writer can be better than you if you write from your own heart and experiences. Just write, write, re-write, and have faith in yourself."

Gathering up all my available resources, I started out on this big adventure of seek and ye shall find with a firm grip on the idea of a faith I didn't have. And right away a miracle happened. Liz, one of my writer friends, suggested that I would find it easier to write away from my present situation and offered me the use of her charming "getaway" house in San Miguel del Allende, Mexico. She and her family lived in Malibu, but she had built herself a writing place high in the mountains of central Mexico some years before and wasn't intending to be there much in the near future. It *was* difficult to focus and concentrate on writing with the nerve-stretching circumstances in my home, but picturing dirt floors and no running water, I couldn't make up my mind to go to *Mexico*, for heaven's sake. Then Liz showed me photographs of her absolutely delightful house and its gardens, and immediately the whole thing made sense. I could leave my husband, begin the journey in search of my lost strength, test my character in private, and still not have to sell the house and disrupt my family. Although my husband had not become the director he'd wanted to be, he had prospered very well as executive producer on such CBS shows as *Front Row Center, Playhouse '90, The Mary Tyler Moore Show,* and others. He was greatly relieved that I was not rushing off to get a divorce and generous with money, so I was all set with traveler's checks.

Following my first trip to San Miguel in 1996, I returned many times in the following four years, picking up the threads of my life and weaving this book.

Ever since John was born, we had in our lives as friend and housekeeper a wonderful woman, named Flora, who had taken care of us in many ways. She was Black, from the South, lived in Watts, and was one of the finest human beings I had ever known. Now I arranged for her to cook dinner for my husband and John (Peter being away at the university) and take care of them in general.

As I was working out the remaining logistics of going to Mexico for an undetermined length of time, one day I was standing at the sink looking out the window at my beloved black lab, Wardwell (John had named him after Mrs. Wardwell, a 90-year-old woman he was fond of), who was lying out by the pool in the sun. I couldn't take him with me, my husband was away all day, and never took him for walks, anyway; John was working after school and weekends at Datsun Motors as a clerk, and Wardwell was a very sensitive dog who needed lots of attention. He and I had formed a strong bond and I knew he would grieve for me, so I decided that I would ask my friend, Charlotte, to take him home with her while I was gone. As I was thinking this, Wardwell roused himself and scratched at the sliding glass door of the kitchen to get in. After I let him in, I went back to the sink and he followed me and wedged himself between my legs and the cabinets and kind of moaned deep in his throat. He had never done something like this before and it dawned on me that he knew what I was thinking and was asking me not to do it. It is interesting how intuitive and unconditionally loving dogs can be. I wonder why those qualities are so natural for dogs and often not for people.

Charlotte and I had been good friends in New York in the '60s, but the previous year, when her husband died, she had come to California to live with her widower brother in the San Fernando Valley. She adored Wardwell and had a big fenced-in backyard, and I knew she would take good care of him. But when she came to pick him up, he didn't want to go with her. He hunched up and jerked his lead out of Charlotte's hand and ran back to look up at me with eyes begging not to be sent away. He *knew* what was happening. It nearly broke my heart. I bent down and held his muzzle and told him that I loved him, but he had to go with Charlotte and I would be back someday to get him. He turned, and without a backward look, went to Charlotte and jumped in her car. Remorse, guilt, and love for him flooded over me like a 7-foot ocean wave and I wanted to run after the car and get him back. Wardwell died the next year and I never saw him again.

As I stood there in a vise of indecision, the image of a painting I had once seen in a window abruptly flashed before my eyes. About 10 years earlier when we were living in New York, I was walking down Sixth Avenue when I noticed a large painting that almost filled the window I was passing. The import of it stopped me dead in my tracks. The painting was of a man and a woman sitting in a small row boat in the foreground of a large lake. The lake was an irregular circle of leaden, motionless gray water through which dead, shattered, gray tree trunks and broken off limbs stuck up grotesquely here and there. The row boat was a weather-beaten gray with splinters of peeling paint. The man and the woman, in their 40s, were seated on planks at opposite ends of the boat facing away from one another, their arms folded across their chests in a withdrawn, rigid posture. They were painted unnaturally large and vividly colorful in contrast to all the gray desolation surrounding them. She was wearing a pretty, brightly colored, flowing dress, and he wore a beautifully tailored navy-blue suit with a red tie. They were exceedingly good looking physically, but their rigid posture and angry, frozen faces strongly indicated an irreversible rejection of one another.

The painting had taken my breath away. Here I was in the city I loved best, living at prestigious 116 Central Park South in an apartment whose huge windows overlooked the most wonderful park in the world, surrounded by the richest cultural wealth in the world, my husband director of specials at CBS, my children in arguably the best schools in the world, with everything I wanted that money could buy. But my instant identification with the two disconnected people in the painting took my breath away like a blow to the solar plexus.

That memory of the man and woman in the rowboat put things back into perspective for me, I had to get out of that rowboat or perish — so I let Wardwell go and got busy. Within the week, I was flying off to the mysterious lands south of the border to find my little red hat.

During my wild and wonderful youth, I had been to Mexico City and Acapulco several times, and indeed, had taken my husband to the places I had loved best in those cities on our honeymoon. San Miguel del Allende, however, was in an altogether different part of Mexico. You couldn't even get there by plane! It was a 4-or-5-hour bus ride from Mexico City (depending on which bus you took), high in the mountains halfway to Guadalajara. Liz had warned me to be sure to get a *Tres Estrellas* bus, as the others were overcrowded and stopped at every crossroads. What the others must be like, however, was beyond my imagination as it would not have seemed possible to get more people, boxes, shopping bags and animals on board than were jammed into this large bus. Having traveled abroad a good deal, I was alert to the necessity of getting a good seat on public transportation so I stood long in line in order to be one of the first to board and grab myself an aisle seat near the front, to little avail. I had seen those movies about overcrowded South American buses with the goats, crates of chickens, crying babies and many-too-many people, but they in no way prepared me for the reality. The man in front of me let his back cushion all the way down, skewering me flat into my seat, the woman next to me held a child in her lap who constantly leaned over into my face while eating and dropping God knows what all over me. The man standing in the aisle beside me with his crated chickens leaned down over me to peer out the window. Within minutes, I was totally encapsulated by the odors and warmth of humanity and chickens during the seemingly endless hours it took this wobbly, brake-screeching conveyance from hell to get to San Miguel. It was dark by the time we arrived, and my rudimentary Spanish almost deserted me when it came to getting a taxi. But through the written word and desperation, I was finally delivered to 18 Calle Santo Domingo, and into one of the best periods of my entire life.

Liz had arranged to be there to welcome and get me started for a couple of days before she returned to Malibu. Her generous spirit and supportive encouragement had taken much of the anxiety out of my trip, but even so, looking up at this house in which I was to make or break my immediate future was a daunting experience. Like many of the better houses in Mexico, the property was surrounded by a high stone wall with the entryway barred by a beautiful, tall, wrought-iron gate. The headlights of the taxi revealed a blue and gold tile on the wall which bore the address, Santa Domingo 70, and "Architecto L. de la Canal."

Entry to my San Miguel sanctuary, with the "Arcos" through the old town wall behind. Drawing by beloved friend and artist Carol Mills.

I had heard much from Liz about her friend, Leonardo. They had met when she was renting a house at 70 Domingo in San Miguel years before, as he was about to graduate from the University of Mexico with a masters in architecture. Years later, he had been the architect of this house she was loaning me. His was an old Spanish family which had been given an extensive land grant in the 1700s by the King of Spain that included a good part of San Miguel and the surrounding countryside, with its lucrative silver mines. Although Leonardo was 20 years her junior, he and Liz had become best friends and always kept in touch, so I wasn't surprised to find the two of them there when I had dragged myself and my rather large suitcase up the steep winding walk to the front door. When Liz introduced me to this tall, dark, and very handsome man, however, I was instantly and painfully aware of being disheveled, dirty, and a little smelly. The fact that he was extraordinarily charming made me feel gauche and awkward and uncertain as to what to do with my hands. I had not the slightest premonition that he was to be the means of breaking physical barriers I had suffered from most of my life.

The home Leonardo designed and where I lived and wrote in San Miguel.

Leonardo had just come up from Mexico City, where he lived with his wife and two sons, to spend a couple of days with Liz before he drove her back to the airport. During dinner, I could sense that they had a lot to talk about together, he evidently wanting her advice about his desire to separate from his Catholic wife, so I excused my-self as soon as possible and fell exhausted into bed in the guest room.

The next morning, I awoke in this strange bed to a room filled with golden sunshine, hearing strange birds singing in strange trees, with a sense of being caught in a time warp. Even the air smelled strange. The bus trip seemed as though it was a nightmare that I had only dreamed, and I had the feeling I should touch my face and body to make sure the dream had ended. I found the guest bathroom had amazing little orangey-red tiles covering every wall and floor surface, even in the huge shower. The hand sink had ornate bronze fittings, and the mirror had a large, intricate vine and flower bronze frame, and somehow it all seemed exotic and fun. Blissfully, it had a bidet! No question I was in a foreign country.

Liz was having her first of many cups of coffee when I found her at the kitchen counter. The kitchen seemed to be made of sun-shine; its walls and counters were covered in little buttercup-yellow tiles, and, although small by California standards, it was extended at one end by a wall-to-wall window. The window was framed with banks of flowers and low-hanging branches of pepper trees, with little yellow birds flitting about to match the tile. It was enchanting.

Liz was a tall, slender, blonde with rather sharp features in her early 60s. Her husband was a wealthy rancher in Malibu, owning thousands of acres of prime cattle land in the mountains above the ocean, but Liz was not happy in the ranching business and had built this get-away house to write in for months at a time. She seemed sad to me in some way that I didn't understand. She was reticent about her private life and only wanted to talk about the show business she longed to be a part of by writing plays and screenplays. Several of her plays had been done by little theater companies, which is how I had gotten to know her. She seemed like a character out of a Chekhov play herself, with her husband and three children happy with ranch life, while she yearned for the romance of the theater and the bright lights of movie premiers. I could see that Leonardo played a romantic part in her life that was very satisfying, albeit a purely platonic one.

It was fascinating to me to put these two friends together in the building of this house. I could imagine the two of them spending hours planning it in just such a way as to provide Liz with the privacy, quiet, and beauty that she needed for her writing. The deep, hillside lot had been terraced into three distinct levels. Behind the gate on the first level was a parking place for two cars and a laundry-storage room; a stone retaining-wall and a rock and cactus garden ran up beside the walkway to the next level on which were the main house and wrap-around patio and gardens. And on the third level, concealed from the main house by trees and shrubs, was a vegetable garden. The house was E-shaped without the crossbar, built of white stucco, with dark-stained wooden beams or *Vigas*, and a red tiled roof with wide overhangs furnishing shade to the interior and patios. The walkways and patios were covered with small, earth-toned round stones which softened and warmed the stark white of the stucco walls. The landscaping was truly a work of art. The differing levels of trees, shrubs, cactus, flower beds, and large rocks were placed with meticulous care so that they brought a joy and peacefulness to the spirit. Sitting on one of the patios was like being in a marvelous live painting.

Except for the kitchen and bathrooms, the walls of all the rooms were white with very little decoration, the custom-made furniture was hand-carved, light-stained wood with beige cushions on chairs and sofa, and the shining floors were the typical Mexican large, brick-red tile. The whole effect was of light and airy simplicity and uncluttered comfort and stillness. Outside every window and sliding glass door, abundant brilliant flowers diluted the intense sun on the patios and the overhangs gave a cloister-like feeling to the interior.

The whole place was predicated on privacy. There was no doorbell by the gate, which was usually kept locked, and the walls and plantings were so high that no one could see in; there were no phones, radio or TV, and no neighbors close enough to be seen or heard. It was just a perfect place for a writer to concentrate and look for inspiration. Liz liked to garden for relaxation, so she grew zucchini, eggplant, tomatoes, several kinds of lettuce, chard, and cucumbers on the upper level, which thrived with wild abandon. She had a year-round gardener/handyman/house cleaner named Luciano who helped out in general and kept things going when she wasn't there. He was an extremely short and round, always smiling, lazy rogue whom she adored.

That first morning in this strange house, which was to become so much a part of me that I would dream about it for the rest of my life, had a sense of quivering newness with a kind of inner quiet that made me want to talk in whispers. It was clearly another miracle happening that would bring me to the place I needed to be and give me a jump start on my new beginning. "No more miracles," the psychiatrist had said. Ha!

Liz said that today she wanted to take me around to familiarize me with San Miguel and to meet some of her friends whom she thought I might like, and who could be helpful to me when and if I needed it. Leonardo, who also had a house in San Miguel, would meet us for lunch and drive us around later before taking Liz back to Mexico City to catch a plane home the next morning. I wish I could think of a brand new word to describe the village of San Miguel del Allende, with its cobblestoned streets, light-tan stucco buildings with arches everywhere, and its plaza square or *jardin* with wrought-iron benches under rows of sculptured trees. Picturesque, quaint, enchanting, old world, colorful, all those words were applicable, but they didn't really sum up its unique charm. It was like a child's giant sandcastle village. The large flattened stones comprising the sidewalks were barely wide enough for one person; cement gutters ran between them and the dusty, cobble-stoned streets, most of which were too narrow for two cars to pass one another. As there were few parking places around the city center, cars generally had to park blocks away so that there was a relaxing kind of quiet as you walked around the square. San Miguel was designated a national historical monument; new construction was prohibited in the city center and crumbling old buildings were carefully restored. Much like Santa Fe, New Mexico, where by law new architecture has to conform to long-ago established design, and signs have to be small and unpretentious, San Miguel retained much the same appearance as it had a couple of hundred years ago. At 6,000 feet, its dry, moderate heat and clear blue, blue skies with puffy white clouds were also much the same as Santa Fe, as were the large number of artists, artisans and writers who chose to live there. Like New Mexico, it was a village of enchantment.

Walking around the center you saw intricate stone carvings adorning windows and doors or forming a crèche or a statue at unexpected corners, sometimes little corner basins were planted with flowers. Most of the shops were gathered in a 2-or-3-block radius of the plaza, and many formed a wall of one-storied stucco buildings with narrow wooden doors of primary colors opening into the shops. Inside various ones, you'd find rows and rows of beautifully hand-colored pottery, some of which were of primitive, centuries-old designs, but all a work of art; a multitude of delightful, intricately hand-carved wooden animals, birds and flowers or trays of lacquered imaginative design; gorgeous hand-crafted opal or turquoise silver jewelry of very crafting; and top Mexican designer's blouses, skirts and dresses of the most exquisite embroidery and lace. The Mexicans are truly inspired artisans. The arched doorways of larger buildings often revealed a tantalizing glimpse of inner patios filled with fountains, flowers, sculptured trees and hedges.

Liz told me that San Miguel was originally a mission founded by a Franciscan monk, Juan de San Miguel, in 1542. The Allende was added when it became a city after the revolution to honor Ignacio Allende, a famous local freedom fighter. As we walked around, it seemed that almost every other large, imposing building Liz pointed out to me had been built long ago by one of Leonardo's ancestors. The main street around the plaza was Calle Canal. The parish church, the pink, many-spired, baroque La Parroquia just across from the plaza, had been underwritten by an early ancestor of Leonardo; the sprawling Bellas Artes building with large Sequerios murals had been built as a nunnery by a great, great aunt; the ornate church of Iglesia de la Concepcion was funded by another aunt. The Casa Maxwell, a huge building in the center of town with a multitude of upscale shops, had been the original Conte de la Canal's townhouse, while their country hacienda, which was only a mile or so away, was now the Allende Instituto where students from all over the world came to study languages and art. Just imagine living in a place where most of the whole village and its surrounds had belonged to your family before the revolution! Leonardo met us for a late lunch at a restaurant in the building that had been his family's original home, and the head waiter greeted him like he was still the grande señor. The waiters also made much of him as though they might kneel and kiss his hand at any moment, but he received these attentions with a pleasant, detached manner as though they really had no meaning. Leonardo was the most unpretentious person I had ever met. He dressed casually in khaki pants and jacket with an open-necked, crisp madras shirt, but otherwise, with his tall, slender body, black, curly hair, fair skin, long, narrow sculptured face, and elegant, long-fingered hands, he could have stepped right out of an El Greco painting of a Spanish grandee. Liz had told me that he wore a white adhesive patch over his right eye because he had pierced it irreparably with a mango knife as a child and they never could get a false eye to fit properly in a growing boy. She bragged that he saw more with his one good eye than any 10 people with two eyes and was an excellent painter with a wonderful sense for color and style. He liked to travel around the world, so besides the pure Castilian Spanish he spoke, he was fluent in French, English, German and Italian, and he liked to be with older women. Boy!

I'd been told years ago that all good *manners* are is *kindness*, thoughtfulness of others." I'd thought surely there must be more to it than just kindness, but Leonardo proved the truth in that statement. He was consistently thoughtful of the welfare and feelings of others, and took quiet care that their needs and comforts were fulfilled. He listened intently to what one had to say, and behaved as though it was very interesting. In his laid-back way, he taught me a lot about what "good manners" really meant. The word "courtly" kind of summed him up. And he had a great laugh and thought I was funny. I was dazzled.

After lunch, Liz wanted to visit a member of her writer's class before Leonardo took her back to Mexico City. Mr. Levitt and his wife owned a lovely home in San Miguel in which they spent six months of the year, spending the other six months in their apartment on Park Avenue in New York City. I took an instant dislike to him. I was partial to most New Yorkers, but this self-made-business-tycoon type, who aggressively indicated he knew everything better than anyone else, quickly tapped into the immense reservoir of boiling anger the psychiatrist had uncovered. While Debbie, his quiet, little wife, smiled wanly at Leonardo and me, Mr. Big Mouth devoted himself to discussing his important writing problems with Liz. Bored with this after too long a time, I butted in and said, "I am working on being a writer, too."

Irritated at the interruption, he turned and snapped at me, "Yes, yes, I know. Miss America and all that," and resumed his monologue with Liz while I fumed, wanting to hurl one of the exquisite Indian pots on the table at his round head to see which would break first. Eventually, having said all he could think of about himself, he turned to Leonardo and said, "Listen, Leonardo, you are a native here. We have to go back to New York next week and dummy there (indicating his wife with a brusque nod of his head) made bus reservations on the 16th, which would put us right in the middle of the holiday. Isn't that a stupid idea?"

In his calm, beautifully accented voice, Leonardo said, "Well, I wouldn't be as rude as you are, but, yes, traveling is sometimes more difficult during the holidays."

I wanted to throw my arms around him and smother him with thankful kisses. I had never heard a more civilized put-down to a bully, and I felt he was like a knight in khaki armor who had deftly sprung to the defense of two rather middle-aged maidens. When we were back in his car, I said, "Leonardo, you have earned my undying gratitude for skewering that fat, chauvinist pig like that. You are my hero!" He quietly laughed it off. But he *was* my hero, and remained so forever after.

And then it was time for them to go, and I was left alone. Once the final farewells were said, and the sound of the car had disappeared, I walked slowly through all the rooms of what was now *my* house, kind of establishing our relationship, seeking to bond with the spirits that lived there and make them my friends. I was going to need a lot of help from them during these next scary, critical months. Liz had said she wouldn't be coming back for six months or so, and I was determined to stay here until I had a complete first draft of the book I wanted to write. I had read somewhere that Socrates had said that the un-examined life was not worth living — well, I was going to *examine* mine until the universal question of "Who am I?" would be answered definitively.

I was exhausted from all the turmoil and excitement of the past few days, so I went to bed in the master bedroom early that night, every atom in my body thankful to be here alone in this comfortable, queen-sized bed. At 11 o'clock, I was abruptly awakened by a barrage of gunfire coming from somewhere down below. Through the yells and intermittent bursts of shots, I desperately searched my memory for anything about a brewing revolution or upheaval in Mexico on the news, but couldn't remember any. Finally, too tired to try and escape, I pulled the covers over my head and said aloud, "You'll just have to start the revolution without me," and went back to sleep. Of course, I later learned that each of the many barrios of San Miguel had its own special fiesta day, and all I had been hearing was a cheerful celebration, fireworks and all. It was, I later thought, an appropriate beginning to this marvelous part of my life.

The First Act - 1923

Born 1923

At 6:30 the next morning, I was awakened by the sound of a local rooster's salute to the day. For the rest of my life, a rooster's crow would momentarily transport me right back to that special moment in Mexico. I bounded out of bed, did my half-hour yoga stretches, had my breakfast, then sat down at Liz's typewriter and wrote, "I was born in the Arizona State Men's Prison on December 16, 1923."

It is possible that this extraordinary start fueled my desire to be unusual, as my father always told me I was. I have always been proud of that beginning.

I was raised on a traveling medicine show. The home-on-wheels I grew up in was not much larger than a prisoner's cell. It was built on the flat-bed of a truck, and was called a house-car. Nowadays, they call them an RV. The large wooden platform carried on its side was called a stage. The medicine show my father ran at that time comprised one house-car, a Model-T Ford, and two performers – my mother and my father.

They were working in Texas when they learned of my unexpected imminence and, thinking it more glamorous, Dad aspired for me to be born a Californian rather than a Texan. They had begun to slowly work their way to the Pacific Ocean when fate intervened in favor of Arizona, as Mother developed premature labor pains in the little town of Florence. At 35, and much against her heart's desire, Mother had no previous personal practice at giving birth. But luckily, she had witnessed her nine sisters do it many times, so, as money was short, she was confident she could manage this miracle of producing a child all by herself. However, it soon became apparent to Dad that the birth was too long and agonizing for her and he went in search of a doctor. Since Florence was primarily a service community to the prison staff and inmates, Dad had to persuade the prison doctor to come help. The doctor soon found he could not do his job adequately in the limited space provided by our house-car, needing more sophisticated equipment than hot water and clean towels, so thus it was that I made my first public appearance in the infirmary of the Arizona Men's State Prison. I like to think that the prisoners cheered at the news: "It's a GIRL!"

Our portable medicine show stage and seats, next to the Ford Model T, 1929.

You might say that I was a headliner from the first moment I set foot on a stage before a live audience. My performance of *"Mary Had a Little Lamb"* was perhaps minimal in content, but consideration would need to be given that the occasion was on my second birthday. It was never the applause from an audience that put iron in my determination to be a successful performer, it was the feel of the muscles in my father's arms as he held me up to receive it. From birth, I was stimulated to ever-increasing feats of derring-do by the source of courage I got from my father. Pictures of me at six months old show a naked, bald-headed baby (back stiff, chest arched, arms out wide to the side, face tight with effort) stretching straight in mid-air while a beaming father holds me firmly by the ankles. I am straining every fiber to remain erect because my father said, "Go on, Baby Jo, you can do it!" If he had wanted to shoot me from a bow I would have done my utmost to make myself into an arrow. It seems to me that my first memory is of that supreme effort to please my father. I can re-experience it even now, 97 years later.

My first trick.

It was a natural progression to "Go on, Baby Jo, you can say it," and "*Mary Had a Little Lamb*" was just the curtain raiser. By the time I was four, Dad passed out handbills with my name on them and persuaded store owners to put posters their windows.

Later, Mother made me a costume like a ballet dancer with a rhinestone, red velveteen top and stiff white crinoline fluffy bottom, white long stockings and black Baby Jane tap shoes. The sharp points of the rhinestones poking through the velveteen made wearing it a misery, but Dad assured me show folk didn't pay attention to little things like that.

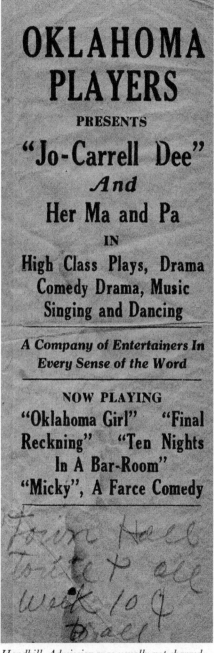

Handbill. Admission was usually not charged,
but this night it was 10 cents.

My father was born on April 6, 1869, to well-to-do Ohio farmers, but while his two older brothers became a successful stockbroker and engineer, respectively, my father had wanderlust and romance in his genes. He had to put his dreams aside for a bit, however, as at 18 he had to marry a farmer's daughter. There was a shotgun involved there somewhere, I believe, but anyway, he and his much older wife had five children before he took off and went to Hollywood to be in the movies. I have old photographs of him as a prop man and extra on a set and costumed as an Indian with Francis X. Bushman in *The Squaw Man* — Cecil B. DeMille's first film and one of the first feature films made in what is now Hollywood. But in ways I am not clear about, he wound up owning a vaudeville theater and a hotel in Odessa, Texas, around 1917, and it was there he met my farmer's-daughter mother.

The Squaw Man, *1914. My father, a prop man and extra, enters the scene from the left.*

Mother was escaping from an abusive husband she had married at 14. From him she had her first kiss, and she thought she had to marry him because a kiss would make her pregnant, and her father would otherwise kill her. She ran away from him when she was 21 when his abuse had become unbearable. She got a job as a chambermaid in my father's hotel, at a time when his wife had died and his children were settled on their own in California. Though she never seemed to think so, Mother was quite beautiful. She had shiny black hair and shiny black eyes, shiny creamy skin, and teeth so white and shiny you could almost see by them at night.

Mother's teeth were her one vanity, and she was forever breaking off twigs to make tiny toothbrushes to keep them clean. It was probably her figure that first brought her to Dad's attention, for it was a very good one, but mostly I imagine it was the fact that his bookkeeper and his girlfriend/secretary had just run off with all his money and he needed some female solace and revenge. Dad arranged for Mother to get a divorce and asked her to marry him two weeks after she first caught his eye. The oil boom town of Odessa, Texas, had done well by my father, and he soon had enough money to fulfill one of his dreams by selling the theater and hotel and buying a complete traveling tent show — a much larger operation than the one-car medicine show I was to later be born into. He changed Mother's name from Elizabeth Melissa Lemand Brownd to Miss Carroll LaRue, and told her she would make an excellent "straight woman."

In Mother's mind, God had reached out to touch her twice: once when my father asked her to marry him and much later when she finally had a baby. These two somewhat related events brought her nightly to her knees in gratitude. It was always a wonder to her that she had been so blessed. And what a wonder indeed my father must have been to an unsophisticated Texas farm girl. He was 54 when I was born, 20 years older than my mother, but he was still a splendid-looking man with his thick reddish-blonde hair going gray with a flair, piercing light blue eyes, and a strong, slender face and

Mother   *Father*

figure. Even more appealing was his manner. It wasn't only that he dressed differently from ordinary men in the little towns we played with our show, or that his speech and diction were beautiful and his attitude courtly; there was something indefinably high-class about him, even on a run-down show. In his three-piece suits, thin dark ties, white starched shirts, and gray felt hats, he looked as if he had just stepped out of a bandbox, as my mother would say. His name was Harry Arthur Dennison, but he believed that changing the name was changing the game, so he called himself Mr. Ennis.

In the heyday of the tent show.

Tent shows were movable vaudeville houses. In those days, they carried anywhere from 10 to 20 performers, some of which were specialty acts — dog acts, acrobats, trick musicians — but the stars of the show were the comics, straight man, and straight woman. Tent shows normally played the larger towns throughout the country for

2-or-3-week stands. They set up on big vacant lots near the center of town, and in those towns without vaudeville houses, they created almost as much excitement as a revival meeting. They made almost as much noise, too.

In the late afternoon, the more musical of the troupe, dressed in full costume and make-up, crowded on the afternoon "bally-hoo" wagon and paraded through town singing and shouting the news of that evening's performance. The bally-hoo wagon, which transported the tent and seats on a move, was a big, gaily painted trailer truck with huge banners on its side announcing the time and location of the show. Just before dark, flaming torches were lit all around the entrance to the tent box-office, and musicians played rousing songs to attract a crowd. The "Wild Man from Borneo" was a sure draw in his blackface make-up, long black underwear, grass skirt, feathered headdress, and noisy arm and ankle bracelets running the length of his chain. He yelled gibberish at the delightfully frightened children while the Pitchman in his little pulpit encouraged the gathering town folk to come on in and enjoy the show. And 100 to 200 people a night usually did. (In those days, blackface on performers was common, and white performers sadly failed to recognize or acknowledge that it was denigrating.)

Barking at the crowd; my half-brother at right with inappropriate blackface.

My father did not make a success of his tent show in the long run. I don't know if it was his hot temper in managing people, his grandiose ideas, or the changing times, but all his life something al-

ways seemed to go wrong with the projects he entered into so enthusiastically. By the time I was born in 1923, he was down to running
a 4-person medicine show.

Medicine shows presented the same sort of entertainment as
tent shows, but they took place in the open air. Admission was free,
and "medicine" was sold to make money.

We didn't set-up on large lots like a tent show or a big medicine
show; our little outfit usually fit in a small space between buildings
or on just one end of a lot. Measuring about 10 by 16 feet, the front
end of our house-car consisted of a 10-gallon water tank, a sink and
a gas cylinder stove, with kitchen storage overhead. On one side was
storage for the boxes of medicine, props, and musical instruments; on
the other a fold-down table and wooden fold-up chairs, while at the
back end a bed filled all the space. Over the bed was storage for our
clothes and costumes, and under it was my pull-out bed, a chamber
pot, and my father's treasure chest. This black tin trunk held a large
make-up box/mirror, boxed wigs, and my dad's carefully hoarded
collection of sheet music, sketches, plays, and monologues. My father
pored over his collection like they were gold pieces.

Fastened up for traveling, a wooden stage folded down from one
side of the house-car for the performances. It had attached canvas
"wings" which opened out as the stage came down. The planks and
cross bars for the open-air seats were carried under the house-car and
set up and taken down each time we moved, which was usually once a
week. Dad's outfit resembled a peddler's pushcart compared to most
medicine shows, but it fulfilled his most basic need — on it he was
The Star. That small, shabby stage with its dingy, frayed, unpainted
canvas wings had the essential glamorous ingredient of show business:
people came to watch the performers and applauded.

Mother did not come happy-hearted onto the stage. One of 14
from a dirt-poor West Texas family, she was a natural musician, sang
harmony, and could play any instrument by ear, but she was never
comfortable before a strange audience. When she and her large family
were together, most of them played guitars, banjos, and fiddles, sang
their hearts out, and had a whale of a time. But on a stage, Mother
stood with her head and shoulders well back, while she did her dead-
level best to "act" the way my father told her. My father ate it up to
be straight man, but Mother found it easier to pick a whole load of

cotton than to perform as straight woman, singer of songs and sales lady. She did it, though.

Sometimes Dad's eldest son, Joe, and his wife worked on the show. Joe was tall and thin, a couple of years older than Mother, and had a permanently soured disposition, but with his sad, long face, he did very well as the blackface comedian. Dad hired two or three other performers if business was good, but business was bad during the Depression when they learned of my anticipated arrival; so just the two of them were working little towns in Texas.

Medicine shows' direct ancestry were the mountebanks, often called quacks or charlatans, of the early 17th-century in Europe. Charlatans depended largely on extravagant rhetoric and airy chatter for selling their various kinds of restoratives, be they for hair, bowels, or skin. Before and during the "come-ons" came music, comedy and tricks of many kinds, including exotic animals, contortionists and jugglers. It is not recorded when the first charlatans came to the colonies, but early in the 18th century, the quack with his pills and elixirs, sold most often from a buggy, were a common sight. By 1773, both New Jersey and Connecticut had passed laws suppressing the mountebank's ability to practice medicine which "threatened the health and morals of the populace." Unsuppressed, however, by the late 1800s, the Hamlin Brothers of Chicago, Illinois, made a fortune manufacturing a patent medicine called "Wizard Oil," a concoction similar to Lydia V. Pinkham's Vegetable Compound, which was composed largely of alcohol and iron, and sold particularly well in "dry" states. The Hamlins sold this medicine on their own traveling shows in the east and midwest, and shipped it to shows like my father's all over the nation. John Hamlin put some of his millions into founding the Grand Opera House in Chicago. The most famous of the firms who made their own concoctions and sent traveling shows all over the country was the Kickapoo Indian Medicine Company of New Haven, Connecticut. The medicine came in large, cardboard boxes which made excellent playhouses for me when there were no good secret places to be found near our house-car. The boxes had a clean, pasty smell that I can still detect in big boxes now and then. Today, the smell of cardboard gives me a small puff of pleasant remembrance.

I had a happy childhood. Held securely in the hammock of my father's love and waited on hand and foot by a completely adoring mother, I grew up extremely self-confident, and held myself in high esteem. My father always told me that I was special and that there was nothing I couldn't do. I believed him. I took my mother's loving care and comfort for granted, but I felt my father's love required constant effort. I thought his approval had to be consistently earned by my actions and reactions and, mostly, by how well I performed on the stage. I greatly enjoyed earning my father's approbation and worked hard to achieve it. And too, there is a lot of satisfaction in being the star of the show. Performing on a traveling medicine show was far from boring, there is an excitement that goes along with the applause you get working on a stage, following that yellow-brick road is a come-hither call to see new places that is both stimulating and addictive. It was for my father, I know. I thought it should be for me, too.

Flo, my half-brother's wife, in the door of their housecar. I never forgave Joe for sneaking off in the middle of the night, my father died in his housecar, leaving me and my mother with just the clothes we had with us and the debts for the rooming house, doctor, funeral and grave site.

But as far back as I can remember, I was aware of being divided into a public and a private self. The public self was focused outward trying to please my father and the audience. That public self was always "on." But I had a completely different inner self that had innate enthusiasms and attitudes of quite another kind.

After exchanging the infirmary of the Arizona State Men's Prison for the glories of California, our medicine show played for a week or two in small towns all up and down the northern and southern coasts of California — and the wonders of nature became my playground. Unencumbered by siblings or playmates, by the time I was four or five, I was free to wander far from the lot where we were set up in search of adventure. Mother would say, "Now, don't go out of sight of the house-car, Josie." But Dad would say, "Let her go, Carroll, she knows how to take care of herself. An empty lot is no place for a little girl to play." My solitary adventures were exploring in shady, tree-sheltered, heavily-bushed places where – if you stayed very still – the lives and personalities of ants, strange insects, and small critters like squirrels or chipmunks were fascinating to observe for hours at a time. Just examining how plants grew was endlessly engrossing. I found that each tree or bush had individual, perceivable personalities, and I felt they had an inner life similar in some ways to my own. Perhaps best was climbing carefully to the very highest branches of a friendly oak tree, again sitting very still, I felt I could join in the lives of the winged creatures, and laugh at their twitchy and abrupt antics.

There is a certain sense of personal power when you are sitting so high above the ground. Becoming queen of all you survey. Of course, one of the most fascinating places, though hard to find, was a stream. I could lose all sense of time watching the movement of the water over the rocks and the darting little fish or still-sitting frogs. Holding a slippery, jello-like polliwog in your hand is one of the most delicious feelings I know. The sound of running water is still the most soothing music there is. But, most importantly, I could drop all the pretense involved in being Daddy's special little girl or the star of the show and really be myself at those times — Baby Jo and the stage disappeared and I became what I thought of as the "real" me in my own sanctuary. My revved-up inner motor slowed down to a quiet, contented purr among big trees, rocks, plants, insects, and animals. They were to me individual and sentient beings with whom I could become friends and carry on conversations, and even ask advice. I connected with nature in a very real way and in certain private places occasionally I experienced the awe and exultation of the sacred. In those lovely little California coast towns, in some secret place, I could always find, I was completely happy in a way I would remember and search to replicate for the rest of my life.

Rather than a hardship, I thought I was lucky not to have other children around to play with. I much preferred animals to people, and enjoyed being an only child. From earliest memory, anything with fur, feathers, or scales was delightful and all I ever needed for companionship. My father even brought me an orphaned baby fox one time, and I loved him dearly until he grew up and we had to let him go. I had nothing but contempt for dolls and playing "house."

I must have been about four or five when I made the acquaintance of God. My father was non-committal about nature and God; the books he constantly read sitting in our Model T didn't include the Bible. But Mother had a complete and simple faith. She taught me my nightly prayers and talked about God while she showed me religious pictures. This particular day, while watching the sun-streamers shifting through the leaves from an especially high perch on a tree, I had the heart-stopping, almost blinding impression that beyond the branches, beyond the sun, was the shapeless presence of GOD. I could see His cloudy face. Since God and nature were somehow intertwined, I wasn't startled or frightened, but with vast astonishment I realized that He also could see me personally, knew me, and was looking out for me. I knew that in some way He and I were one. That was my first miracle.

I had this experience of seeing God only once, but the knowledge that He was there became an important part of my life, and the experience always remained vividly clear in my mind. That knowing of God always remained in the back of my head like a soft, little cocoon of security. As opposed to the relaxed, tangible, hands-on connection I had with nature, however, the connection I felt with God was mystifying and nebulous and I thought that in order to maintain this vital connection, I would have to BE something, DO something, very specific. I instinctively felt He had shown himself to me because He wanted me to know that He was there, but that there were certain rules I must follow in order to keep in His good graces. After considerable thought, it became clear to me how to judge what those rules must be. For my second birthday, as a reward for my first professional appearance, my father had given me an Illustrated Junior Library set. Since performers can never go right to sleep after a show, and until I had learned to read the books myself, Mother had suffered through

nightly demands for "Just one more chapter," with Pinocchio, Dorothy and Toto, Mogli, King Arthur, Tarzan, and the rest until she literally went to sleep while reading. The rules of behavior, of which I was
confident God would approve, came from Albert Payson Terhune's
"Lassie." This magical dog overcame every obstacle because she was
fearless, valiant, and trustworthy. I had no respect for "Black Beauty"
because he let himself be the victim of circumstance, whereas Lassie
got out there and bravely made things come out right. Clearly God
would be pleased and continue to care about me if I followed Lassie's
example. It was such a comfort to know I had found the secure and
righteous path, and I strove mightily to religiously follow my set of
principles. There was no moral question or physical challenge that
could not be resolved by asking, "What would Lassie do?" But I never
told anyone about this experience; instinctively I thought it was just
between me and God, and nothing that I could or should share with
anyone else. And I knew I mustn't pester God with lots of requests
for help. I knew He wanted me to be self-reliant like Lassie and only
come to him when I was in dire need.

At four, I had learned to read by memorizing scripts, had long
blonde curls, a wide, gap-toothed smile, could sing all my father's
sheet music songs and, since every small town had a tap-dancing
teacher in those days, I was a fairly accomplished dancer. My big
show stopper was a number the three of us did together called, "Tie
Me to Your Apron Strings Again." It was a song about motherhood,
and we ended it like this:

"I thought that I was right, but I was wrong,
Please take me back tonight, where I belong,
Sing to me a cradle song, and then,
Oh, won't you tie me to your apron strings again?"

Then I stepped forward, curtsied, and said, "She's my ma and
he's my pa and I'm their children." (Big laugh.) While Mother and
Dad played their guitars, I did a soft-shoe dance and we were off to
good applause.

By the time I could walk and talk, I was no longer my father's
little girl — I was his leading lady. It seemed there was always an
orchestra playing a waltz when I worked with my father. When we
performed together, rehearsed together, or just were together, to me
we were not separate people but different parts of the same whole.

For one of my favorite numbers, Mother made me a long white, ruffled organdy dress with a tiny matching parasol. In his white suit, leaning on a black lacquer cane, Dad would tip his straw hat to me and sing: "Tell me, pretty maiden, are there any more at home like you?"

Twirling the long skirt and peering flirtatiously from under the parasol, I'd reply : "There are a few, kind sir," and between the continuing stanzas of the song we did a short minuet, ending with him kneeling as I sat daintily on his knee.

One day Dad had said to me, "Baby Jo, how would you like to do a sketch dressed like a boy? That Jackie Coogan is a big star now working with Charlie Chaplin where he gets in all kinds of trouble and breaks your heart when he cries. You could do that just as well as he can. We'll fix you up with some boy's clothes and you'll be a show stopper."

Mother said, "Harry, Josie is so pretty in her little dresses, I don't think she wants to look like a boy."

But Dad said, "Sure she does, don't you Baby Jo?"

Me as the boy character "Skippy".

"Yes."

So, an important part of our show became sketches with me as "Skippy." Mother made sure that my boy's clothes were nice and not raggedy like Jackie Cooper's.

It was easy for me to pretend to be a boy. My public life was all pretend anyway. The only time I felt in harmony with what was real was when I was alone with nature. My father told me I was born perfect and as talented as Shirley Temple, seemingly the highest possible praise. I preened under his admiration, but it was a heavy responsibility to be perfect and as talented as Shirley Temple all the time, and being alone with an undemanding, supportive tree was a blessed release from the tension of my father's high expectations.

When I was about five, I discovered my first passionate earthly love — the horse. In the little towns we played, many kids had access to a horse and would curiously ride up to or near our lot. Knowing my father wouldn't like me to ask a "townie" for a favor, it required finesse to get offered a ride.

"That's a good-looking horse you've got there."

"Yeah."

"Is it fast?"

"Yeah."

"I ride a lot. I know how to do tricks on a horse,"

"Yeah?"

"Want me to show you?"

With courage born of burning desire, I tried to do everything I had seen Tom Mix or the Indians do on a horse: hang on one side from the saddlehorn, ride in one stirrup, crouch on its rump while trotting. My objective in this derring-do was to keep the kid interested until I could get one fast run. It wasn't the tricks I enjoyed, it was the thrilling sensation of speed on horseback that I craved.

If everything I learned about nature or animal behavior was a joy to me, it was not so with human behavior. Especially that of little boys. If I didn't keep a vigilant eye out, they were always trying to torment the animals I kept around in cages or tied up. They'd twist a sharp stick into the fur of my rabbit and pull it up, or give my raccoon a piece of bread with broken glass in it. I defended the animals with rock and foot, but sometimes there wasn't anything I could do.

One day, I was sitting in the woods high in my favorite tree of the moment, when some boys came along with a fishing pole and began casting toward the squirrels I was watching. Before I could understand what they were doing, a squirrel had grabbed the nut on the end of the fishhook and was jerked dangling into the air while the boys danced around it shouting with laughter and making it swing. I jumped out of the tree and went at them yelling bloody murder, but they cut the line and ran off. I chased them until I was breathless and cramped up. It wasn't clear what I would do if I caught them, there were three of them and each bigger than I, but I felt fanatically they must be punished for what they had done. The thought of the squirrel starving to death because of the painful fish-hook in its mouth made me desperate to pound their heads on a rock or something. They ran from me as if they were seriously afraid of what I would do if I caught them.

Riding Creampuff in the show.

Sometimes boys like Tom Sawyer did bad things in books I'd read, but it was shocking to see these boys actually causing such pain to animals. I knew it wasn't possible for me to do something like that, so I decided it was because they were boys, therefore, boys were different from girls and not to be trusted. It became more apparent how different they were one day when I was involved in some fantasy or other in my favorite place under the house car when a little boy came by and said,

"Would you like to play marbles?"

"What's marbles?"

"Here, I'll show you. This is an aggie, this is a steelie and these others are just marbles. First, you make a circle and then — here, you can have my aggie — then you try to knock as many marbles as you can out of the circle."

He was very patient in teaching me how to hold my thumb and forefinger and, since he'd been so obliging, when he said, "Let's go over there under that building and I'll show you something pretty." I went.

It was dark and smelly under the building, filled with old lumber and spider webs.

The little boy had his back to the light and I couldn't see what he was talking about when he said, "Look. Here. Look at my thing."

As he got nearer, I could see he'd unbuttoned his pants and was holding a boneless, thumb-looking object in his hand. He had a silly-looking smile on his face as he flapped it at me and said, "Take down your underpants and show me your thing." Something in his attitude sickened me, as though I'd opened a can marked peaches and found a putrid mass of worms in it. I shoved him back so hard he fell over some lumber, and I scrambled out from under the building. As I started back to the house car, the boy yelled after me, "Fuck you!"

Mother flew out of the screen door where she'd evidently been watching for us and yelled at him, "Get on home, you little dickens. Get! You better not let me catch you around here ever again."

Then she turned on me in a rage, her eyes as black and hard as coal. "What were you doing under there with that boy?"

I was thunderstruck. She was mad at me! I had never seen Mother yell at anyone, much less at me. Something utterly horrible must be wrong for my timid, gentle mother to turn into this fire-breathing demon. I was flooded with the first personal sense of shame and guilt I'd ever known. I was afraid to tell her what the boy had said and done. "Nothing. We weren't doing anything."

With unrelenting eyes, "Why did you go under there with him?"

"To play marbles."

"You weren't playing marbles under there." Savagely grabbing my arm and giving me a hard shake. "Now, you listen to me. Don't you ever do a nasty thing like that again. Do you hear me?" She gave my arm such a hard pinch that I screamed with pain. "Don't you ever do that again or you'll get worse than that," and she shoved me violently away and went back in the house car.

I couldn't have been more traumatized if I had been branded on the forehead with a burning scarlet letter. I felt both the boy and I had done some shameful thing that didn't bear thinking about. I never saw the word "fuck" written on walls later without quickly averting my eyes with a stab of guilt. At age six, it didn't take the story of Adam and Eve to give me a sense of original sin — a nameless sin unrelated to any direct action of my own. A little boy with his "nasty" surprise had done it for me in an instant.

Perhaps it was because I had lived such a sheltered life that I had no concept of what it was all about. Although I slept on a trundle bed pulled from beneath the bed my parents slept in, I never saw them undressed. We changed clothes behind a screen, and Mother and I used a slop jar covered by our nightgowns for our personal needs when my father was out. My parents never used swear words or told dirty jokes, and Dad never allowed any kind of "smut" on the show. But I was able to make the connection between what was "good" and what was "bad," and became firmly determined never to let something "bad" be said or done to me again. And, clearly, I couldn't trust boys.

I turned seven in the winter of 1930 as the whole country was beginning to feel the effects of the Great Depression. It is difficult for those who didn't live through it to know the depths of economic distress it brought to so many people. That winter my father bought a 100-pound sack of pinto beans and we ate them three times a day. We had beans with onions, with chili powder, and sometimes on Sunday with cheap chopped meat for a treat. People simply couldn't afford to buy medicine for their ailments, and my dad was in a constant scramble to make enough money for us to exist. Dad had to resort to putting on "home talent plays," which were kind of a comedown for him, but I enjoyed them. A church or the chamber of commerce would pay him to produce a play with a cast of locals, which would be put on in the local auditorium for a few nights. I was always the star.

My favorite was "Ten Nights in a Barroom," which was a melodrama about a drunkard whose heartbroken, impoverished wife sends her little girl to the barroom to entreat her father to come home. The little girl stands outside the swinging doors and sings:

"Father, dear Father, come home with me now.
The clock in the steeple strikes one."
And so on.

One night, the father gets into a drunken brawl and hurls a bottle at his adversary, only to miss — and the bottle flies through the swinging door and strikes his beloved daughter off stage in the head. She screams, and the father rushing out is stunned with horror to find his ketchup-stained daughter dead at his feet. He picks her up in his arms and carries her on stage weeping, as her recorded song echoes behind him. You can be sure there was not a dry eye in the house, and I loved the drama of it, but soon it became hard to find a little town that could afford even a home talent show.

That winter, during the rainy season, we were holed up in Santa Barbara, California, when Dad came up with a great idea which he sold to the local radio station. Radio was big in those days, partly because people couldn't afford any other form of entertainment, and Dad sold the manager of the local radio station on a half-hour children's program. Dad said, "We'll call it 'Baby Jo-Carroll's Story Time.' I'll write a new story every week and Baby Jo will tell it. She can sing a song and recite a poem, and by the time you throw in your commercials you've got a sure-fire hit. The children are bound to love Baby Jo. The manager said they didn't have a budget to pay much, but Dad's great idea was that I would ask the children listeners to send in a quarter for a photograph of me in my blonde curls and off-the-shoulder costume signed "I love you, Baby Jo-Carroll." The quarters that were sent in bought the onions, chili and meat for the beans we ate that winter.

By the time the quarters began to dry up, a circus had come to Santa Barbara and Dad had the great idea that I should become the star of a circus. He got me a job riding a trick horse in the opening and closing parades, and himself a job as a barker for the freak show. I had never seen a circus, as they never played the small towns we did, and for me it was a tremendous culture shock as I went from being the star of the show to a humiliating walk-on overnight.

The Opening Parade never stopped being a thrill, but the drop from the star of our show' to insignificant bit player was a sickening one. I didn't even do tricks during the parade, the horse did. The circus was as different from our dinky little medicine show as the sun is to the moon.

Trick riding on the big medicine show

I don't think there is anything else in show business that is quite like a circus. It looks different, smells different, and sounds different from anything else. It even looks totally different in the daytime than it does at night. By day, it looked like it should have a big CLOSED sign out front. The Big Top, the freak show tent, the animal tents and cages, the concession stands, and the multiple house cars had a kind of suspended silence. The shadowy figures going about their business on the lot were drab and colorless. The performers practicing their act under a single work light in the big tent wore plain, shabby clothes and spoke softly. A slightly stale, fetid, saw-dusty smell is unique to a circus. Overall, there was a feeling of shut-down power. I couldn't find a place to fit in. When I tried to pet the elephants or ponies, someone was sure to come flying over to say, "Don't do that, please. We don't want an animal to interact with anyone but its trainer." There was no question of asking for a ride on an elephant or even a pony. And the big cats in their cages broke my heart. They just contemptuously turned their head away when I tried to make friends.

I admired the way the handlers patted the elephants, or just shoved one over when cleaning around him. I picked out a favorite and decided no one would mind if I made friends with him, so I climbed over the rope behind which they were staked and tried to get him to take some hay from my hand. His big eye with the long eyelashes didn't appear to be looking at me as he reached out his trunk — put it around my waist — and lifted me high above his head. Having come in search of me at just this moment, Mother let out a shriek loud enough to start a stampede. Unperturbed, however, after a moment, the elephant slowly, but decisively, put me down on the other side of the rope. The elephants didn't want to make friends with strangers either.

I was astonished at the magnificent accomplishments of the circus performers. They practiced all the time. Their day was spent in becoming more proficient at their job; to know them was to understand the iron determination they had to get better each day. Even the clowns. I learned right there, no matter what my father said, that I didn't have their kind of talent, and nowhere near their drive to excel. I had been conditioned to think that I was the "best" performer on any given stage, and I had taken for granted that my whole life would be as a performer in show business. But when it became clearly apparent to me that I was not as good at what I did as the least of these circus performers, and knowing that no way did I have the motivation to work as hard as they did to be as good as they were, I began to change my mind about wanting to be in show business. It was my father's most fervent desire that I should be a star, but right there and then I realized that my own heart was not in it.

Of course, the freaks didn't have to practice, they usually just sat around all day outside their house cars. "Miriam, the 400-Pound Fat Lady," "Roscoe, the Alligator Boy," "Sunny, the Half-Man, Half-Woman," and "Tiny Tim, the Smallest Man in the World" were pathetic to me. I was embarrassed to look at them, and tried never to catch their eye if I saw them around the lot. I was embarrassed for them and thought that if I looked like they did, I would stay home and never want anyone to see me. I was too insensitive at the time to understand that the only time they were not embarrassed at the way they looked, the only time they were not freaks, was in a circus.

The metamorphosis that nightfall brought to the circus was totally magical. The smell of fresh popcorn, cotton candy and excitement in the nighttime air was captivating. The sounds of the band within the Big Top and the calliope outside of it created a popping electricity in the veins of the crowds, and the shadowy, drab, daytime circus performers were transformed into exotic creatures from a fantasy world. The performer's gorgeous costumes brought the immense interior of the Big Top into a brilliant kaleidoscope of whirling color and movement. Even the daytime's bored, restless animals — ponies, elephants, lions and tigers — became prancing, high-stepping, proud performers. It was magic, and it was the "Greatest Show on Earth."

But neither my dad nor I were happy working on the circus. Dad didn't really like being a barker for the freak sideshow, and I felt out of place all around. After a few months, my father had another great idea, and he wrote some people he used to work with and they got us a job in a carnival.

The circus had been a comedown for me, but working on the carnival made me feel cheap and tawdry for the first time in my life. In my mind, the people who worked the carnival were trashy, not like performers in show business at all, and I had nothing in common with them. My father and I were hired to run a "Knock-'em" concession, a stand where people paid 50 cents for five balls to try to knock down one of the dolls lined up in back for a prize. There was a lever you could press with your knee so that the dolls could not fall if a customer had too good an arm. I never thought my father would do a dishonest thing like that, but one night I saw him push the lever.

The carnival experience was demeaning for us all, but Dad stuck it out until he had saved enough money to buy some more Wizard Oil for us to take our medicine show back on the road. Then it turned out Dad had picked up something else besides money on the carnival. He said to Mother and me, "I hired this girl who plays a whale of an accordion to liven things up a bit. The California coast towns are about played-out for medicine shows, but I plan to go across the desert now. Those desert towns must be starved for entertainment and we ought to do good business, so we need an extra performer."

Miss Accordion was young and pretty and eager to please. She rode with Dad as we moved from one little town to another in the mighty Mojave Desert, and he taught her some of our numbers. I guess you are never too young to suffer the burning knife of jealousy. It was especially damaging because I thought such an emotion as jealousy was beneath unusual people like me. When Dad was often to be found with his hand on Miss Accordion's shoulder instead of mine, I had to pretend not to notice, but when he and I performed numbers together like "Tell Me, Pretty Maiden," I sat stiff on his knee and smiled at the audience instead of him. If he put his hand on my shoulder, I was quick to pull away.

It was a long haul between towns in the California desert, and Mother would tell me stories about her childhood to keep me from getting restless. One day she said, "You want to be careful when you go scouting around in the desert. They've got tarantulas about as big as my hand out here."

"Are tarantulas dangerous?"

"My land, yes. They can kill you as quick as a rattlesnake. Why, I knew a girl once got bit by a tarantula when she sat down in the outhouse, she swole up and died before night. Was just about to get married, too."

Mother was a good storyteller.

One night, we broke our move at a little town in the California desert called Wayside. The two signs announcing your whereabouts upon approaching and leaving Wayside were within sight of each other. The only large building was composed entirely of enormous gray and charcoal blocks of stone. It had a gas pump in front, and the sign on top said "Hotel Wayside." My father stopped for gas and asked if we could spend the night parked beside the hotel. I didn't notice a yellowed, flyspecked sign in the lobby window reading: "For Sale." The next morning, Dad got into a discussion with the pleasant, weather-beaten old man who owned the hotel. "I see you have your establishment up for sale. Tired of the hotel business, are you?"

"Yes," the man said, "The wife and I have been wanting to retire if the right buyer came along. We built this place over 40 years ago. Had all the rock cut ourselves."

"What are you asking for it?"

"Well, to tell you the truth, we might could see our way clear to let it go for just so much a month without asking for a down payment. We've already bought us a place in the next town to retire in."

Another pot of gold beckoned and we were in the hotel business. Dad told Mother, "Baby Jo is seven now and she needs to go to school. The hotel man tells me they have a fine one here, so you can cook and the girl can serve, and we ought to really build up the restaurant end of it. I always liked the hotel business."

As usual, Mother said nothing. Miss Accordion looked a little startled, but I liked the big, old place. One of the selling points was that the Ford Motor Company was testing its much-publicized new V-8 engine by trial runs in the desert to prove something or other, and was scheduled to stop for gas at this hotel. It was exciting when the goggled drivers in their dust-covered cars roared up, but they didn't buy anything other than gas and a container of coffee and then they roared away. The hotel turned out to be a little big for the four of us, and since we were about the only ones who stayed there, it was the "so much a month" that turned out to be the problem.

It didn't seem to bother Dad too much, though, for within a few weeks he took the house car and left — with Miss Accordion. And my whole world fell apart.

Mother and I were left totally dependent on the miniscule income from the hotel for cash and the garden for food, which was also miniscule. My first days spent in the pursuit of higher learning at the little school there in Wayside presented me with a test of moral fiber that shocked me out of my cocoon of pain and misery. Mother said that I had to go to school, and anything was better than sitting around in that big old hotel counting my miseries, so in order to face this new and difficult situation, I put on a little red hat that I had worn riding the horse in the circus and marched into the office to start school with all my tattered banners flying. Right away, I ran into trouble. The principal, looking admiringly at my little red hat I thought, informed me that I had to have a smallpox vaccination before I could enroll. I said, "What's a smallpox vaccination?"

The principal, who had a sour, scrunched up face and a personality to match, said, "The nurse here will just put a little injection into your arm to protect you and others from getting a terrible disease. It is a federal law that each pupil must have the injection before entering class."

A little girl who was in the office to render an absent excuse, said in a know-it-all way, "Here, look at my arm, I've already got mine," and she pulled up her sleeve to show me a horrible, whitish-looking, puckered place on her arm.

I said to the principal, "Oh, I couldn't possibly have something like that on my arm. I am an entertainer, you know, and I wear sleeveless tops all the time so I couldn't have a scar like that showing to the audience."

With thinned lips, the principal said, "You have no choice. The law says you have to have it."

"Well, I won't."

The kind of soft-looking nurse bent down to my level and said, "I'll tell you what we'll do. Since you're an actress, I'll put the injection up here on your thigh so no one will see it." And that is why I have a whitish-looking, puckered scar on my leg instead of on my arm.

Actually, I didn't find school worth the trouble it took to get enrolled. Coming into the first grade at age seven, when I could read and write and make a good sentence on a fifth-grade level and make change for a dollar at lightning speed, I couldn't see any point in the "Jack and Jill Went up the Hill" kind of thing they were teaching in first grade. Then, too, instead of being bowled over with all my professional accomplishments, some of the little girls giggled out loud together about the mayonnaise and tomato sandwiches which were all that my mother could make me for lunch. They laughed at ME, the star of the show, those fat little girls with their fried chicken and roast beef sandwiches!

To top it off, one day that particular bunch of girls got me aside and said, "Do you know where babies come from?"

Mother had given me a perfectly understandable explanation, so I informed them, "God sends them."

There was an outburst of derisive laughter, "God doesn't send them. The daddies put them there. Daddies have a long thing down between their legs that they put inside the mommies where they go pee pee, and they put the babies there where they grow until they're ready to come out of the mommies."

"What long thing?"

"Men have a long thing down between their legs like horses do."

Now, I had seen that long, black, snake-like thing that hangs down from horses sometimes and it was immense, so I said, "I don't believe it. You'd see it under their pants."

"They draw it up into their stomachs like horses do and only bring it out when they want to put babies into the mommies."

"In where they go pee? I don't believe it!"

"It is so true. My married sister told me so."

Their chorus of agreement made it too horrible to contemplate. I went home to ask my mother about it as fast as I could, breathing hard with the shock of what I had heard. I couldn't bring myself to accept what they said, all mixed up with the pee and everything. But they spoke with the authority of advanced knowledge and I was sick to think they may be right. When I walked in the back door I stopped dead in my tracks. Mother was sitting at the kitchen table with her back to me and her head in her hands — crying. Her whole body shook with deep, gut-wrenching sobs of grief and despair. As though stung by a hornet, I stepped back outside. I had never seen my mother cry. Dad teared-up easily but the only tears I had ever seen her shed were just little sniffy ones at something on the radio. These open, desolate, lost sounds pierced right through me. I knew she was crying because Dad left her and she was helpless and alone. Her despair absolutely terrified me. I realized this was not the first time Dad had done this to her. I forgot about the little girls and their awful news and recoiled like I had stuck my hand on a hot stove. I couldn't bear to think of myself hurting like she was, crying like she was. I made an instant vow that I would never, ever, cry about anything again. I hated my father for leaving us like this. I wanted to strike out violently against him, make a clear gesture of defiance and resolve that I wouldn't let him hurt me like he could hurt her.

And suddenly I knew what to do. I went upstairs and got a dollar out of our diminished "kitty." A few days before, I had seen a poster in the window of the barber shop showing women with different hair styles, and a sign: Haircuts – 50 cents. I told the barber I wanted a haircut just like the style that said, "boyish bob." He was incredulous because my curly blonde hair was almost long enough to sit on and was certainly the prettiest thing about me, but I said, "That is the one I want. Just like this picture. Here is my money." So he cut off all my crowning glory. Afterwards, he gathered up this mass of hair and put it in a paper bag. When he gave me a hand mirror and asked me how I thought I looked, I said proudly, "Like a boy." I got my fifty cents change and went home with my hair in the bag swinging against my leg. My head felt light and cool and peculiar.

Mother, who had dried her tears by the time I got home, burst into fresh wails when she saw me. But now I had no patience with her, "Don't cry, for heaven's sake. I guess I can get my hair cut off once in a while without you having a conniption fit. I'm sick of having to sleep on rolled up rags every night. Here, you can have what he cut off." Silently, she took the bag and went upstairs.

After Mother died, 30 years later, while going through her dresser drawers I found my blond, coiled up hair in a white satin bag tied with a pink ribbon — that slippery symbol of my clenched fist. At the time I couldn't explain to her why I had done it; I couldn't tell her that I hadn't meant to hurt her, only him. I didn't understand myself then that it was a visible rejection of the thought that I was helpless like Mother. An unconscious rejection of being a girl and all that went with it. Losing my father was a trauma that diminished all subsequent loving relationships. It crippled me emotionally, sexually, and as painfully as an ancient Chinese girl-child's bound feet. The thought that I had failed as a person, that my father found me worthless, was an abyss into which I dared not look for fear of falling forever. With Dad's departure, I felt forsaken, but at the same time mysteriously chosen. God became my real parent; a father with whom I would somehow connect more closely, someday, and in the meantime, He would look after me. That belief had given me the courage to learn to fight to protect myself, and long hair was a symbol of femininity, and femininity, as represented by my mother, was submissive, vulnerable and hurt. I didn't dare admit to myself that I was as vulnerable as she, and cutting off my hair was a sign that no man was ever going to hurt me the way my father had hurt her. Unlike Samson who lost his strength when his hair was cut, I felt I had gained mine.

Nice Tarantulas

Me and Mr. McCandless in the California desert.

After my father left with Miss Accordion, my mother and I were adrift, left with a hotel to run in the middle of nowhere. Mr. McCandless came over for gas one day, and became friendly with us. He took me out to ride his horses on his ranch near Rosamond, California.

Mr. McCandless turned out to be the trustworthy kind of man I wanted my father to be. He became my new idol. While living in Wayside, I spent as much time as I could at their place. He got in the habit of picking up supplies around the time school let out and taking me to the ranch for a horseback ride. Then he and Mrs. McCandless would come back and sit with Mother for a while in the evenings. They'd never had children, and I guess they were lonely.

Mr. McCandless taught me to love the desert, to discover what was hidden in the seemingly empty expanse, to know and love the changing colors, and how to hypnotize a "horny" toad. These tiny creatures, with fierce-looking spikes all over their heads and backs, can't run fast and are easy to catch. Mr. McCandless showed me how to rub one's stomach until it flattened out in a "sleep" that lasted for a few seconds even after it was put back on the ground. Then it shook its tiny horns as though to clear off a spell, and crawled carefully away. I learned that you can stroke Gila monsters and water dogs (both of which can be dangerous if you frighten them) in the same way and send them into a trance. Of course, you have to be very quiet and slow in your movements.

On one of these adventures I said, "Mr. McCandless, can a tarantula kill you?" He said thoughtfully, "Well, they can hurt you. But I never heard of anyone dying from their bite. And the only time I ever heard of someone being bitten was if a tarantula happened to crawl into a bedroll and got rolled on. You can't blame the tarantula for that. Folks should keep their bedrolls closed up tight when they are sleeping in the desert. All kinds of things like to get in where it's warm. Come on. We'll see if we can find a tarantula for you. I know where one lives and maybe he's home."

We went further out in the desert, and behind some rocks, Mr. McCandless showed me a round spot the color of the sand made of dry grass. He took a stick and lifted the spot up. It was like a tiny, flat, hinged bird's nest. He said, "This is a tarantula's hole, and he has made himself a little trap door for privacy. Let's see if he's welcoming visitors."

He left the trap-door open, and we sat down on a rock and watched the hole. I kept both my feet up on the rock just in case. Sure enough, after a little while, I could see something moving at the edge of the hole. Then the ugliest, hairiest, brownish-black thing imaginable crawled out into the sunlight. He wasn't as big as a man's hand as my mother had said, but he was big enough. His slow forward movement made him appear very ominous. Mr. McCandless held the back of his hand down in front of this monster spider saying, "He's come out to see who left his door open. Let's see if he wants to be friends." After a short pause, the thing continued its deliberate approach and came right up to his hand and put its front legs on it. I held my breath in fear, but after a moment he turned around on his long, fuzzy legs and slowly crawled back in his hole and closed the door. I loved Mr. McCandless. He was my Lone Ranger and I was his Tonto.

God Comes Through

I didn't forgive my father when he returned without Miss Accordion or an explanation a month or so later. He walked in as though nothing had happened, saying, "Let's pack up, Carroll. We can't make a living here, so we'll just turn this place back to those people. They misrepresented it in the first place. We'd best go on to Texas. I hear they're selling a medicine called Tate-Lax there that is really going over strong."

Mother took him back without a word, but when he tried to hug me I turned away from him, even when he gave me a white, curly-haired, six-week-old toy poodle he'd brought as a make-peace present. I fell instantly in love with her and named her Fuzzy, but even she did not remove the pain of what he had done. I burned with scorn for my mother for being such a ninny as to forgive him like that, and I swore vehemently that I would never forgive him, not ever. And for the rest of my life I never had. To forgive, to love, to trust, even to remember the good he had given me, would be to allow myself to be vulnerable again to that intense pain I was just recovering from, and its memory was too sharp for me to take that chance. I hugged the thoughts of his treacherous infidelity close instead of him.

My father always told me there was nothing I couldn't do, but he was wrong. I couldn't forgive him.

I wanted to stay with the McCandlesses, but father insisted that we move on and that I take care of my mother.

In October, 1930, two months before my eighth birthday, we three started out in a small house-car and Model A Ford to cross the high mountains about which Zane Grey wrote with awe. It was the infamous pass where the Donner Party met their demise. Early one morning, we got to the foothills and stopped at a filling station for gas. The man said, "You know what you're doing, mister, trying to go over these mountains with a trailer this time of year?"

Dad said with dignity, "My good sir, I've crossed these mountains many times."

"Well, I doubt it was this time of year. They weren't allowing trailers to go through the beginning of the week because of the snowstorm. It's died down now, but you can't never tell when it'll start up again. You got snow chains for your tires? You'll be hittin' snow soon."

"Ah ... no. I was just about to ask if I may purchase some from you and we'll be on our way. We want to get to the other side before dark, you understand."

As we climbed higher over the pass, I had my first sight of snow. I loved it. Seeing real mountain trees covered with snow was like breathing deeply for the first time. Dad was disturbed by the man's warning and told us to take something to eat in the car so that we wouldn't have to stop except to put on the chains. It was a good thing, for snow began to fall softly the higher we went, and the cars that went by whipped wet snow across the windshield. Around noon, it started to snow more heavily and the road dwindled to one lane. A car came up behind Dad and the driver kept blowing his horn so he could pass. The house-car engine was having a hard time making it up the mountain as we were near the top, and finally Dad pulled over on the elbow of a curve to let the car go by, and got stuck.

Mother and I pushed while Dad tried to rock the tires out of the deep snow back onto the roadway. But the chains spun through the soft snow, hit solid ice below, and couldn't grab. What Dad had thought a little promontory was actually a bush growing tenaciously at the edge of the mountainside supporting a patch of snow which made it look solid. In moving around to push the house-car, Mother dislodged the patch and it became clear that we were stuck on the edge of a sheer drop to the sharp rocks of the valley thousands of feet below. Our thin shoes and clothes soon became wet, and we shook from the bitter cold as the wind began to gather force.

Dad said, "You better get in the house-car to keep warm. I'll get Fuzzy."

By the time he got back, the sun seemed already to have gone down. It was unbelievable to me that what had started as a glorious, sunny, bird-singing day could suddenly become a dark, howling night. Mother lit the lantern and got the gas stove going while I hopped in bed with Fuzzy and covered up. Crawling in with me, Dad said, "It's lucky I filled the stove so we have plenty of gas, we'll be warm in a jiffy. There's nothing to worry about, it'll let up in a little while and then we can put some billboards or canvas under the tires and get out."

Mother heated a can of beans for us and some canned milk for Fuzzy, and we huddled together in bed to eat. We found the stove had as much chance to keep us warm as a candle in a typhoon with that wind finding all the cracks in our old house-car. Normally our stove made this little room suffocatingly hot in the time it took to cook dinner, but as the afternoon wore on we couldn't even feel it.

We were at the beginning of a sharp curve without any protection from the icy torrent which hurled its incredible force directly against the side of our house-car. It began to rock at each increasing gust. Perched high on its truck bed, it seemed easily possible the next gust could send it rolling down the side of the mountain.

Dad said, "We'll have to let the stove burn all night. I'd better siphon some more gas out of the tanks to refill it. Hold the door for me when I get back."

He was almost frozen and shaking violently when he returned. Mother said, "Get out of your wet clothes quick and wrap up in the blankets. Josie, get a pan of cold water to put his feet in. It'll stop frostbite."

While she was rubbing his feet, we noticed a peculiar little sound between blasts of wind. It was Fuzzy's teeth chattering uncontrollably like tiny castanets. It struck us all funny, but Mother and Dad's laughter sounded strange. None of us laughed long.

Dad said, "Her teeth are going worse than mine. We better put on all the clothes we can, and pile the rest on top of us and stay under the covers. Put canvas in the cracks around the bed, Carroll, and turn out the lantern. We want to save gas."

As we lay there in the roaring darkness, the storm appeared to have gathered strength. Mother said, "Harry, are we going to be all right?"

"Of course we're going to be all right. These mountain storms blow themselves out in a short while. It's bound to be clear by morning and the snow plow will be along."

I had never heard Mother call Dad "Harry" before, she always called him "Dad." I knew she must be terribly frightened. I also knew she couldn't trust him about anything much, and certainly not about the habits of mountain storms. With a new sickening feeling, I realized we were in serious trouble.

To me God was an overall, nebulous, protective power whom I acknowledged by good behavior, not a God I could communicate with directly on demand. But as the wind began a wild, high whistle which kept rising in pitch and volume like the unearthly shriek of a stuck pig, it seemed impossible for anything but a superhuman force to keep us from being blown over the cliff. I was terrified into making a private personal appeal.

"Oh, God. Help me. If you don't, we will be killed. Please listen to me, God. I need you to help me."

Almost immediately I felt a connection. A connective thought between God and me. I grasped it desperately, and felt if I could hold onto that thought we would not blow over. The wind stopped to catch its breath and I thought for an instant God had worked a miracle, but then the enraged screaming began again and, as the wind drove against the house-car, I clung to my thought with all my will. "Stay with me, God. Don't go away."

In my imagination God had no shape or form, but the storm took on a tangible identity, became a recognizable force with a face and personality. We all gasped as hail hit the house-car like machine gun bursts and I imagined a face as big as the mountain itself puffing up its cheeks and spitting giant nails at us; I could see them striking violently into the sides of the house-car until it looked like a big porcupine. If the storm continued its vicious attacks on us, I thought the house-car would have to fall apart like a shot-away target and be carried in pieces far out over the valley by the victorious wind.

I hugged Fuzzy, and kept thinking over and over, "God, don't let go. Don't let go, God." It seemed there was a rope stretching up from me into space which I had to hold firmly and constantly in order to resist the wind. I knew God was stronger than the storm, but the question was could I hang onto my connection with Him long enough? I was afraid I might go to sleep. It is some job to keep a house-car from blowing over when you are up against a powerfully determined wind.

Without knowing it, I went to sleep. The sound of Dad's whooping awoke me, and for a moment I couldn't recollect what had happened. There was a different awesome sound — the sound of stillness. Jumping to the window, I saw the same glorious snow scene of the morning before, the brilliant sun making dark blue shadows beside the stately, snow-covered trees. The storm was over.

Dad was jubilant. "I told you we had nothing to worry about. We've just had a little cold adventure, something to tell our grandchildren."

But I thought, "Thank you, God. Thank you." I knew it was only the power of my personal appeal to God that had saved us. It was a wondrous cosmic discovery to find I could talk to God.

We'd slept until almost noon, and about an hour later, we heard the distant hum of the snowplow. We were so happy to see the two men when they arrived, but they must have thought we were pretty stupid to have tried to come over the pass in that dinky house-car and didn't have much to say to us. They dug us out, pulled the house-car back on the road they had just cleared, and, with a wave of their hands in response to our eager thanks, went on making the snow fly in front of them.

When we got down to the foothills we stopped to get gas.

After the man had filled our tanks, Dad asked him for credit; he had spent his last dime on the chains, and we had burned up the gas he thought would carry us to the next town. The look on the man's face when Dad explained his desperate need nearly killed me.

The man said, "OK," and walked away.

Dad took out his note pad and pencil, saying, "I'm writing down the name of your station, mister. When we get to Texas, I'll send you the money we owe you by return mail. We sure do thank you, the little girl and I, and you'll have this money back before you know it — with interest."

The man called, "Yeah, OK. Never mind the interest."

He didn't believe my father would repay him.

The Miracle of Creampuff

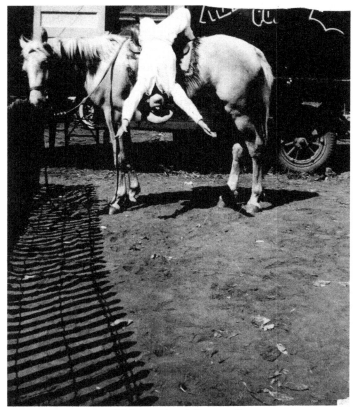

Tricks on a bored Creampuff.

I was never lonely. I found the company of animals or even a tree more reliable and satisfying than that of people. The ripping buzzsaw of my father's departure severed the vital connection I had with him and left a memory of a pain so intense that it constantly quivered just below my consciousness. Consequently, I had developed a protective outer life connected only to nature and the books I read. My protective inner life was connected through the instinctive need I had for something sacred, safe and powerful, only to God, and the father with whom I still danced a waltz and sang, "Tell Me Pretty Maiden." I didn't want to need real people. It was not something I actually thought about. I didn't say to myself, "You can't trust people, or this father you see every day." I didn't try to explain God or the young, golden-haired prince-father who was there inside my head to love and protect me. Not having a logical mind, I never tried to analyze or articulate what was real, I just relied totally on what I intuitively feel I needed — and didn't hurt anymore.

The beauty of California coast towns and the fascination of the desert were both lacking in barren, dusty West Texas, so I transformed it into Zane Grey's gold-tipped cathedral spires of rock and lofty crags where the tall pines whispered in the wind and spread the smell of wildflowers. One day I was sitting on one of the benches in front of our stage pretending it was a horse. As I was talking to my trusty four-footed companion while we rode the lonesome trail through the purple sage, an old man with white stubble on his face, wearing dirty jeans and a stained cowboy hat, came up and caught me at it. I ignored him until he said,

"What're you doin'?"

I was embarrassed to be found talking to a bench, but I said, "I'm talking to my horse."

"Where are you goin' on your horse?"

"Nowhere."

"Would you like to have a horse?"

I looked away. Such a stupid question really had no answer. He tried again.

"Do you like horses?"

"More than anything in the world."

"Well then, wouldn't you like to have one of your own?"

"Of course I would."

He sat down on the bench beside me. "How'd you like it if I gave you one?" ·

I backed up a little. "My father is right over there in our house-car and I think he wants me to come in now."

The old man got up. "Ask your father if you can have a horse and if he says yes, I'll give you one," and he ambled off.

I ran to the house-car and told Dad what the man said. He said, "You want to stay away from old men like that."

Mother chimed in, "He didn't mean it, honey, nobody gives horses away. You have Fuzzy, you don't need a horse anyhow."

What they said made sense, but the next day I kept a sharp lookout for the old man; visions of sugarplum horses had danced in my head all night. Sure enough, that afternoon, there he was.

"Did you ask your father about the horse?"

"Yes, sir."

"What'd he say?"

"I think you'd better come and talk to him about it."

The old man told Dad, "Your little girl seems to love horses. I don't know how you're fixed for carrying one with you, but I have a horse I'll give her if you want her to have it. I come into town every day, so if you decide you want the horse, I'll take you out and we can catch her."

Incredulous joy blew up inside me like a balloon.

Mother asked Dad, "How could we ever carry a horse with us?"

"I think I can fix up something that will do."

The next day, Dad and I rode out of town with the old man in his pickup. At a gate in a seemingly endless fence he turned in, then left the road to cut across an open bumpy pasture to a corral with a bunch of horses in it. Getting a rope out of the back of the pickup, he made a lasso and threw it accurately over the head of one of the milling horses in the corral and brought it over to us.

I couldn't believe my eyes. My joy had been undiminished by the thought that any horse to be given away couldn't be much of a horse, but on the end of the rope was the most beautiful thing I had ever seen. A Palomino. She was a pale cream color with white mane and tail, a white blaze down her forehead matched the two white stockings on her forefeet. She was fighting to pull away, but the old man held her with ease.

"She's a 2-year-old. Part of last year's crop that we just brought down from the upper pastures. Mr. Kleberg, the man who owns this King Ranch, raises Champion Gold Dust Palominos, but this here little filly's a throwback. She doesn't have the medallions or gold color Mr. Kleberg is breeding, so she's a cull. The fillies are destroyed and the colts are gelded if they aren't born true to the color line, but this one has such a good disposition I hated to put her down. So, seeing as how you folks'll be leaving town in a day or two, I thought I'd just slip her to the little girl here, kind of on the quiet, if you take my meanin'."

It came through to me that this wonder at the end of the rope was the horse he meant to give me, and there was something possibly terrible about "put down," so I eased over while he was talking to Dad, slipped the rope out of his hand and began cautiously to pull my horse away. "Gee, I sure do thank you, sir. I'll take good care of her." She tossed her head, but apparently sensed my desperate urgency and came along with me. "Dad, come on! Ah, thanks a lot, mister."

So Dad came on, and she came on, and I got us out of there before something terrible happened like the old man changing his mind, or men with guns suddenly appearing. I waved once to the old man, and then never looked back. I had to get my horse home.

Dad said, "Now, Baby Jo, you know you can't ride her until she's been saddle-broke. The man said she's not even halter-broke. We'll have to be very careful how we handle her until I can get a fellow to break her."

"I'm going to call her Creampuff!" I said.

When we got Creampuff back, Dad showed me how to make a slip-knot, and tied her to the Ford while he went off to get some hay. I sat on the running board and gazed at her while she tried to adjust to her new surroundings. She had spent her two years of life on the open range with a herd of other horses, had never seen a town, or even people on foot, never had a halter on, or felt a human hand. Dad said she was "green as grass" and I shouldn't try to touch her, so while she took a nervous look at civilization, I sat and sent her a steady beam of love to hold her quiet. Mother stood off and made running comments on how pretty and fine she looked. There were no words to express how she looked to me. Without a doubt, she was a miracle sent to me directly from God because I'd been good.

Dad got some old lumber and wheels and built a trailer. Behind it had a ramp, and in front was a two-sided covered partition; one side to hold hay, and the other a manger with a door folding up to give her head protection from sun and rain. I was surprised at Dad's ability to build a thing like this; I never thought of him as good with his hands, only with words. He also knew how to make a halter out of rope, but had quite a time getting it on her.

Mother had to serve my meals by Creampuff. She had big, brown, expressive eyes and we looked at each other steadily for long periods. By the second day, I could pet her. She shied when Dad came too near, but the gentle disposition the man had noticed wouldn't let her be afraid of the constant love I poured out to her.

I was eager to get away from that town before Mr. Kleberg found out one of his horses was missing. I willed Creampuff up into her first trailer ride with the aid of some precious oats, while Dad and Mother maneuvered her from behind. We got to the next town without mishap, and I breathed a sigh of relief thinking she was now safely mine.

But my breath was taken completely away the next morning when I awoke at dawn to go see how she was and found her gone. The halter had come loose. Frantically, I got Dad up, and we set out to look for her. We drove all around the town and wound up on the outskirts in the direction from which we had come, defeated by the vast, empty expanse of West Texas. There were miles of fences and cattle guards between us and the King Ranch, so we knew she couldn't find her way back there, but she was nowhere to be seen. She was lost.

I got hysterical, and Dad took me back to the house-car while he and Mother went off to look for her some more. As I lay on the bed in a paralysis of despair, I heard something outside by the trailer. A surge of hope shot up. I peeked out the door, and there she was nibbling around her manger for stray bits of hay. I cautiously walked out to her, and then realized that Dad had the rope and there was nothing I could tie her with. She might run away again before they got back. I didn't dare speak, and slipped quickly into the housecar to look for something to hold her. I kept thinking, "Oh, God, let me find something; don't let her get away again." All I could see in my frenzy of hurry was a piece of string and I ran out with it, for I was terrified to wait longer. She had finished up the last crumbs of hay and was looking around wistfully. I was sure she was going to leave. I crept up to her, still afraid to speak. I prayed, "Oh, God, let me put this string on her. Make her hold still while I get it on." I eased the string around her neck. "Oh, God, this string won't hold her if she tries to get away. Help me, God. Help me get her to stand here until my father gets back. God, I'll never ask you for anything again, I promise."

Then she turned her head around to me and, putting her nose up against my face for the first time, began to breathe on me, taking long in-and-out sniffs of my hair and ear. I could smell her sweet, warm breath and began to cry. I knew that God had heard me, and she was not going to run away again. When my parents returned, there I was with my head buried in her neck, crying, holding onto my piece of string.

My father said we had to get someone to break her. I could pet her all over and lead her around by the hour, but Dad was afraid to let me get on her back. One day a big, hard-looking man drove up in a pickup, and said he'd come to break this horse. He took out a huge saddle and blanket, along with a bridle which had a cruel bit on it, and sat down to put on a pair of spurs that looked like they had 10-penny nails on them. I immediately began to cry. He said, "Now, listen, little girl, I'm not going to hurt your horse. I've broken hundreds of horses in my time and I know what I'm about. You have to show them who's boss, and then that's all there is to it."

Without hemming and hawing, he grabbed her head and had the bridle on before either of us knew what he was doing. She tried to get away, but he tied her up short, threw that great heavy blanket and saddle on her back, and had her cinched up in seconds. Then he yanked the reins loose and was in the saddle in one motion. Poor Creampuff didn't know what hit her. She tried her best to get out of this terrible new situation, but he jerked on the bridle and raked her with his spurs, forcing her to go in jumping circles all around the lot. She made short, deep grunts as she bucked and twisted, and I couldn't stand it. I ran out and tried to catch hold of the reins, screaming, "Stop it, now you stop it. Get off! This is my horse. Stop that, get off! Stoooooop!"

He had to either knock me down or stop and get off, so he got off, saying to my father, "Now, mister, you paid me to do a job and I aim to do it, but you'll have to take your kid in the house and let me get on with it."

I screamed, "I'll kill you if you try to get back on my horse." Creampuff was standing there trembling, blood at the corner of her mouth. I pulled the bridle over her ears and threw it on the ground and began fumbling at the cinch. "Now you get out of here. You're not going to break my horse. Get your old filthy saddle off of her."

The man said, "Mister, you better ... "

My Dad said, "I'm sorry, sir, my little girl is upset and I think we'd better take the saddle off. You can keep the money, but I don't think we should try and break the horse today. It's the girl's horse, you understand, so let's just get this saddle off and you can be on your way."

That was the closest I felt to my father in a year. He felt it, too, for the next day he said, "Baby Jo, you may not know this, but I saddle-broke quite a few horses when I was a young man. I'm going to put a surcingle on Creampuff and train her for you."

Mother came out to watch while Dad tied the rope around Creampuff's withers, cinched it tight, led her to an overturned bucket, and climbed on. A second later he was flat on his back on the ground. She had just given one stiff-legged jump and Dad flew up in the air and came down with a jarring thump. Creampuff looked at him in surprise as we ran over to him to see if he was broken. Dad made light of it and called her a "buckin' bronco," but he was hurt, and from then on his back always bothered him.

After Mother had helped Dad in the house, I led Creampuff over to the bucket again, climbed up on it and just leaned up over her for a while. She waited to see what I was going to do next, but when I did nothing, she simply walked off while I hung over her back. She didn't seem to mind that, and I kept hanging over her holding the halter rope until I could sit astride while she walked around, and that was all there was to it. She was "broken."

I had no idea my father had ridden a horse, much less broken one, but then I never heard him say anything about his early life. Mother had told me that Dad had run away from his home in California and was working on a farm in Ohio when he had to marry the farmer's daughter. She was 23 and he was 18, and by the time he was 25, they had five children. Then his wife got fat, and he left his family and went back to California and worked as an extra in the movies before he went to Texas and struck it rich in Odessa. But Dad never told me anything about himself. He and I could have been born on the same day for all he spoke about the past. He only talked about the future.

Once I could ride bareback, only a centaur could have felt more a part of a horse's body than I. Other than sleeping or performing, my time was spent on her back, gloriously aware of her warm, soft, smooth skin over the hard bones, alive and responsive. Having never been expected to even pick up after myself, much less do chores of any kind, I'd have complained bitterly if asked to exert the physical labor involved in cleaning up around her trailer for any other purpose, but even shoveling manure was a pleasure which I performed diligently. She loved oats and every nickel I got went into buying her a double handful from an obliging feed store.

Holding my hands behind me, "Creampuff, do you want a surprise?"

A fast look toward me, "Huh-huh-huh-huh."

"Well, come on then. You have to guess which hand it's in."

Smelling the oats, she poked her nose against first one elbow and then the other, "Huh-huh-huh-huh."

"OK, you guessed the right hand. Here it is."

It was delightful to feel her bristly lips nibbling the oats out of my hand, then the long tongue making slow, slurpy licks.

But nickels were hard to come by and mostly I brought her surprises of fresh grass from the roadside, or talked the feed store man out of the lovely alfalfa leaves left on the floor under the bales. My mother always said that "invention is nine-tenths of the law."

On my ninth birthday, Dad and Mother woke me and told me to go outside to see something. There was Creampuff all dolled up in a new bridle, saddle, and blanket. Dad had gotten up early to get her saddled, and Mother had washed and combed her mane and tail. She was a thing of beauty. She thought so, too, and preened every which way. I knew that saddle meant beans on the table for a long time; it must have taken every cent Dad had to pay for it when it came c.o.d. out of a Sears Roebuck catalog, but now I was airborne, the saddle gave us both wings. Creampuff loved to run flat out as much as I did. I had never played games. "Hide and Seek" doesn't work out too well by yourself, and though I'd heard kids yelling "Ollie, Ollie, Oxenfree," I never knew what it meant. Now Creampuff and I made up our own games. One of our favorites was to get set at an imaginary gate, start forward at full speed, and then I'd try to get to the ground before she could come to a full stop, like cowboys in rodeos. As soon as she felt me start to swing my weight off, she would brace her feet and begin a dirt-spraying stop. If my feet hit the ground before she could completely stop, I won; if not, she did.

Since I spent my whole day with her, it wasn't long before I had taught Creampuff to count, nod and shake her head, bow so low her nose touched her outstretched knee, and rear straight up in the air. Dad built a slatted ramp to the stage and put blocks under it, and she and I became the star attraction of the show. After she'd climbed up the ramp and assumed an elegant stance center stage, I'd say, "Which number shall I sing for the folks, Creampuff? Number one or two?"

With a little nudging, she loudly pawed the stage three times.

"Three?"

Vigorous nod of her head.

"You don't want to hear number one?"

Rattling shake of her head.

"Well, all right then. Number three is pretty long, but here it is. 'Strawberry Roan'."

"Was hangin' around town, just spendin' my time, out of a job, and not makin' a dime."

The verses to "Strawberry Roan" were short, but there were lots of them. Creampuff looked with lofty interest at the audience throughout.

During the applause, she bowed and held it as long as possible. After the encore, she performed her talented straight-up rear and we went down the ramp to big applause.

On horseback, I began to overcome my prejudice against the Texas plains. The vantage point of the saddle lifted me high enough to begin to see and know the mysterious charm of its boundless horizon. The fascination of the world of tall trees and running streams is best experienced close to the ground where its music sounds intimate and soft and sweet. You need height to experience the essence of that vast expanse of land and sky that stretched flat on forever — its music awesome and splendid and muted as though coming from a far distant organ as big as a mountain. Learning to be in harmony with that music steadily increased the joyful sense of self and contentment that came only when I was alone with nature.

A pivotal experience came for me one day when something went wrong with the trailer we were using to tow Creampuff to a new town. It couldn't carry her until it was repaired, so Dad put me on her and I rode the rest of the way, 15 or 20 miles through big West Texas country. It took all day. At age eight, I remember clearly thinking "I can do this, all by myself. I am doing it!" That knowledge I required in that moment put me in good stead for the rest of my life. I had courage.

But while my private world was better than ever, my public world had changed beyond repair. My father and I were no longer a team. Of course, we worked together as before but as two separate performers, not as two halves of a whole. My father always told me there was nothing I couldn't do, but he was wrong. I couldn't forgive him. No matter how loving and tender he was to me, or how deep and desperate my yearning to be held close and safe in his arms, fear and pride kept me rigidly unbending. Dad was now an "other" like Mother, and I could not share myself with others.

When five years later Creampuff died from getting into some green wheat at my Uncle Lowe's ranch, it was a blow I could not absorb, and I immediately shut down all feelings. After that, I had a dog named Fritz. I learned a lot from him about gaiety, loyalty, and most importantly, love. His death was also painful, yet a minor thing compared to the joy he had given me. I had cut myself off from love, but the whole-hearted love of that little dog permeated my soul, and I finally let myself love again. I was better equipped for life after having loved him. The extraordinary thing is that because I cried for him, I never lost him. That dog, the real essence of him, stayed with me forever. Because I wouldn't cry for Creampuff, wouldn't let myself think of her or remember what she was to me for fear of the pain it would bring. I lost her. Not the memory of her, but the special essence of the horse I had loved for five years was buried with the pain. I know now it is better to cry and remember.

My father always pulled the strings.

Grandpa

Grandpa (with pegleg) and Grandma, Hale Center,
Texas. 1924.

To pacify my restlessness as we drove between towns, Mother had told me stories about her childhood. Some of them I wanted to hear over and over. Particularly about my grandfather. He was a cowboy.

In answer to urgent requests, Mother would say "Did I ever tell you about how your Grandpa met Grandma? Well, when he was a young man, he was riding herd for a fellow down around San Antonio. One day, a man rode up to him and asked him if he'd like to help drive a big herd up to Abilene."

Pa said, "Abilene, Texas?"

"No, Abilene, Kansas," says the man.

"And that's how Pa happened to go on the first trail ride on the Chisholm Trail, as they came to call it. In those days, they couldn't get nothing for beef in Texas and so they had to drive them all that way to where the railroad was to ship 'em back east."

"One night, when they had bedded down the herd, the cook asked Pa to ride up to a nearby farmhouse to buy some eggs. When Pa got there and hollered out, Mama came to see what he wanted. She looked mighty pretty to him, Pa said, and he asked her name and they got to talkin'."

"The next morning early, Pa came riding back on his horse and called Mama outside. 'Mattie,' Pa said, 'How old are you?'"

"Ma said, 'Fourteen.'"

"'Well, before you're 15 I'm going to be coming back this way and I'm going to marry you,' Pa told her. And sure enough, he came back from Abilene with his wage and they got married."

They settled down and Grandpa became a cotton farmer. One night, while driving a load of cotton on a horse-drawn wagon, Grandpa had a bad accident and ended up with a pegleg that he'd made himself. His 14 kids did the farming work from then on, but the children were "allowed" to go to school up to the 4th grade as long as they could skip class during picking time.

I was immensely curious when we took a break from the road one winter and went to stay with my grandparents at a wide spot in the road called Hale, Texas.

There in a high-backed wooden chair by the window sat a saint dressed like a cowboy on his way to church in a black, shiny broad-cloth suit and white shirt buttoned to the throat with no tie. I stared at him in confusion. Was this my grandfather? Was this the dreaded Simon Legree with the cottonwood stick of wrath? I'd expected he'd have a heavy, cruel, mean face, but this face was lean, benign, and beautiful.

A snow-white, silky beard, clean and combed, hung to the center of his chest with a pretty cream-colored spot on his moustache where he kept his large, curved pipe; hair the same color and texture of his beard hung just below his collar. High forehead and cheekbones over an eagle-nose enhanced his black sparkling eyes. I realized it had to be my grandfather because a light yellow, shining-smooth pegleg with a nail-studded leather pad and tip leaned against his chair. After the introduction, he took the pipe out of his mouth. "Well, I'll declare. So this is Baby Jo-Carroll. I don't believe I'd have known you from those fancy pictures your mama sent us," and he put his pipe back in his mouth.

I immediately fell under Grandpa's spell. Because he didn't care one way or the other, I shed the chips on my shoulder without a clatter and whenever possible sat by him on the little wooden footstool he'd carved. I couldn't figure him out. He was completely open, yet completely hidden. He was detached from everything, yet interested in everything. At 88, I never saw him angry or irritable, nor heard him utter a sound of complaint or boredom. He sat in his chair all day except for three trips into the kitchen for meals and his morning and evening stroll to the outhouse. But there were no grunts or groans when he hoisted himself up from his chair with one hand, while holding the board attached to the pegleg with the other and fitting it smoothly into the belt around his waist. He got the pegleg around in front, his stump in the leather pad, the belt pulled tight, and himself in locomotion with practiced ease. He took no chances on falling, but he never allowed anyone to help him. His hands were unwrinkled, translucent, and elegant; it was impossible to imagine them gripping a hoe or plow, but easy to visualize his long agile, slightly knotted fingers manipulating the reins of a horse and a roping loop at the same time.

One day I asked him: "Grandpa, did you love being a cowboy?"

"Well, I can't say I loved it. It was a job."

"Didn't you love going on the Chisholm Trail?"

"It wasn't called the Chisholm Trail then. It was a mighty long ride."

"What was your horse's name?"

"I didn't have any special horse. Just whichever one I could catch."

I couldn't understand what he ever saw in Grandma. She looked like her butter-churn, grey and squat, and her long dresses covered her legs. She had no neck, a small, round head with sparse white hair, and a shapeless, fat face. When I had to kiss her, I was repelled by a strange bitter odor from some brownish stuff running down the creases of her chin. I asked Mother, "What is that on Grandma's face?"

"Snuff."

"Snuff? What's that?"

"You put it under your lip with a little stick and keep it there sort of like gum. It's tobacco powder."

"Tobacco!" Yuchhh!

That finished off Grandma for me. She wasn't interesting to talk to anyway. Not like Grandpa.

My grandma and grandpa and their 14 children. My mother is in the middle row at the far right.

It was when relatives came that Grandpa really made contact, and that was with music. When his kids got together with him, the music was how they spoke to one another. Grandpa liked the fiddle best, and in square dance tunes like "Turkey in the Straw" and "Fiddler's Rag," he really made that little instrument talk. Most of his kids inherited his musical abilities, and when they had two fiddles and three guitars going, their improvisational variations were personal communications. Three of his children lived in Hale Center and more came to visit for Christmas so, since most of them had seven or eight children in their families, often more people were crowded into those two rooms or playing games outside than attended our medicine show. When the last strains of the fiddle made a little tag finish to a number, everyone broke into laughter and loud "wahoo's." I wouldn't have thought anyone could have as much fun together as that family did. Between numbers, they repeated funny stories about each other, and the victim of the joke laughed as wholeheartedly at the punch line as everyone else.

Another day I asked: "Grandpa, what was your favorite time? I mean, when you were the happiest. Which part of your life would you like to relive?"

I thought he would say something about the Chisholm Trail, or some other cowboy thing, but after much thought he said.

"Waaall, Jo-Carroll, I haf-ta say, this here right now is the best part. I've noticed that every year seems to be better than the last."

"Really Grandpa?" I was astounded. "Really, Grandpa?"

His approach to life made a huge impression on me. Thanks to him, I was never afraid of growing old.

Men!

The way he dressed and spoke, Dad stood out among these farm people like a fox in a pack of coyotes. They called him Mr. Ennis, and listened respectfully to what he had to say.

He decided to stay for awhile at Grandpa's and put on a Home Talent play in the local movie theater. He got a cast together, and sure enough managed to find a young blonde visiting her folks whom he felt he could make into a star in show business. After he changed her name, that is. I told him I didn't want to be in this production.

Mother became a different person when her relatives were around. I couldn't understand why she let them call her an ugly name like Lizzie, nor why she laughed and cut-up so much with them. Sometimes when she and her sisters sang four-part harmony, she'd give a little back kick with one foot and twitch up the side of her skirt during the fast parts. Sort of like Creampuff kicked up when she was feeling good after a rain. When Creampuff did it, I laughed even if she threw me off, but when Mother flipped up her skirt, I thought she looked silly. Dad thought so too and often afterwards when we were alone in the housecar, he lit into her. He never struck her with his fists, but he seemed to want to smash her into nothing with words. Just the look on Dad's face before one of his tirades twisted my insides, so when I saw it corning, I lit out on Creampuff.

One evening, when I came home from such a ride he was gone, had packed his clothes and moved into the back of the movie theater. And Mother had the same look on her face she'd had in Wayside. I heard Aunt Ruth tell her, "Lizzie, you shouldn't give two toots about him. Any man that'd leave his family for a blonde hussy like that isn't worth crying over." I totally agreed with her, but for days Mother's mouth kept getting more and more twisted.

About a week later, while walking back to our housecar in the dark, she fell over an old bedstead. She started to cry from the pain of her scraped shins and I had to help her inside. She lay on the bed and cried harder and harder. Once she got started, it didn't seem to be about the hurt leg anymore. Again I heard those terrible "Ah-hah-hah-hah's." I stood there gritting my teeth, wanting to get away, not wanting to light the lantern so I'd have to see her.

Out of the darkness, I heard her draw a ragged breath, try to get hold of herself, and then in a desperate pleading tone, "Josie, go ask him to come home. He's too proud to do it when I ask him, but he'll do anything for you. Go ask him, honey, please get him to come home."

There was nothing I could think of I'd rather not do than go beg my father to come back, but when she cried like that I had to. Getting a halter on Creampuff, I swung on and rode down to the theater. "Boy, I'm telling you, Creampuff, I don't see how she can be so pukey as to want him back. I'd rather stay here with Grandpa and let him go off with that girl if he wants to. See how long she stays with him. I hope he doesn't think it's me who wants him to come back. Oh, this is so dumb!"

When I got to the theater it was dark, but the front door was un-locked. I could barely see by the light coming from behind the screen as I walked down the dusty aisle which smelled of Cracker Jacks and kids. Coming up the steps to the stage, through the wings I could see the back of his head lying on a cot. He didn't hear me as I came up behind him, just lay there with his hands behind his head staring up at the bare bulb hanging from the ceiling. There was no scenery backstage, just caterpillars of dust and an empty dank smell. He'd fixed it up back there with a broom handle stuck across one corner to hang his clothes on, a folding chair and a table with a one-burner hotplate, and the cot with one of our blankets on it. Looking at the greyish stubble on his chin and taking a deep breath, I said, "Daddy."

Jumping up quickly, he began automatically to smooth his hair and button up his shirt. "Baby Jo! I didn't hear you. You startled me, I wasn't expecting company." Looking around with a little laugh, "Now, let me see. Where can I find you a comfortable place to sit."

Using all my years of theatrical training, I said pitifully, "Daddy, I want you to come home. I miss you — and I need you. Please come home."

Starting to cry, he grabbed me and held on so tightly I almost smothered against his chest. "Of course, I'll come home, Baby Jo. You know anytime you need me, I'll be there."

I got my face turned so I could breathe as he held me tighter. "Your daddy loves you, my darling, you know your daddy loves you."

As his shoulders shook, I was aware of the perspiration under his arms. I tried to breathe through my mouth and thought, "OK,

Mother, I've done it. The good little daughter has gotten the erring father to come home. I ought to be able to, I've played this scene often enough:

"Father, dear Father, come home with me now.

The clock in the steeple strikes one ... "

So my father came home, the Home Talent play got on, and the blonde hussy left town. Winter over, Dad had enough money to buy some more Tate-Lax stock, wrote his son Joe to join him, and we were back on the road. I was sorry to leave Grandpa.

One day when Dad was away looking for locations, as I started up the steps to our housecar, I heard Joe's quiet, angry voice inside, and when I came in saw Mother with her head in her hands crying. Joe left instantly, and I said, "What's the matter?"

Mother started drying her eyes on her apron. "Nothing." Trying to catch her breath, "Nothing's the matter. Just some silly thing."

Before I understood what I was doing, I shot out looking for Joe. I found him squatting by his housecar starting to change a tire. Rage was making my heart pound violently as I said, "Joe, what were you saying to my mother?"

He didn't answer or look up. My kneecaps and hands began to shake while I struggled mightily to keep my voice steady. "Well, you just better not talk to her like that any more. I mean it. I'll tell Daddy if you ever do it again."

He ignored me completely, and I walked away feeling victorious, but lightheaded and weepy. Both of us had behaved unexpectedly. Explosions of anger were menacing to me and I had never let the anger I felt flow out like that. And if I had thought about it beforehand, I'd have expected Joe to hit me with the wrench if I did.

I never found out what Joe was saying to Mother, but after that she was quieter than usual and went around with a white set expression I had never seen before.

A few weeks later, she said, "Josie, how would you feel about going to Oklahoma City to live with your Aunt Bertie? She's had a stroke and needs me to take care of her."

"Oklahoma City? For how long?"

"Well, for a while."

"What about Creampuff?"

"We'd have to leave her with Dad. Anyway, for now. We can take Fuzzy, though."

I was dumbfounded. I knew Aunt Bertie had her stroke years ago so I realized Mother was leaving Dad for good and I hadn't expected her to ever do that, but I thought it served him right. I figured I would find a way to get Creampuff to Oklahoma City somehow, so I said, "All right. Sure, let's go."

I never knew what the final straw was. Maybe it had hurt her more than I had known for him to take up with that girl right there in front of her relatives, to have to send me after him. Or maybe it was just Joe. Anyway, she packed our clothes and we left. Saying goodbye to Creampuff was so hard, I had to do it quickly in order to do it at all.

When we said goodbye to Dad at the bus stop, he looked down at his pocket to hide his tears and brought out some change. He picked over a quarter, two nickels and some pennies in his hand, then gave me the quarter.

"Here, Baby Jo. Buy yourself something nice to eat on the bus." Then he walked away from me as fast as I'd had to walk away from Creampuff.

Oklahoma City is mighty pretty, as the song says. It was my first experience with a big city, a house with a large porch and lots of rooms, a paralyzed person, and a man like Uncle Binyon. He had just retired after having been Chief of Police for many years. He was a big man with heavy features, thick, white hair and moustache, and a deep, gruff voice. Two cousins, Bertie Mae, 12, and Shirley, 10, lived with them since their parents couldn't take care of them. They adored him and were jealous of his attention. They told me when Uncle Binyon was younger, he'd been a member of those fierce mounted state police, the Texas Rangers. I was very impressed with that, but he and I never hit it off together. Maybe it was that he didn't seem much impressed with me. Or maybe it was because he treated Mother like a servant.

Aunt Bertie was kind of faded-looking. She was much older than Mother, and more "well-off" than any of the other sisters. She couldn't move or speak, but I got to know and like her and felt she liked me. Mother had to bathe, dress, feed, and lift her into her chair and onto the toilet. The cousins were coldly polite to me, but took me with them places like the Saturday afternoon movies. I was in that half-way spot of being partly the servant's daughter and partly a relative. But I didn't care that much what they or Uncle Binyon thought, except I was in a bad fix since I couldn't see any way to get Creampuff. Even when we rode the bus for 30 minutes downtown to the movies, I never saw any corrals or a place to keep her. I didn't think Uncle Binyon would let me anyway. And I didn't want to ask Mother to go back to Dad.

However, on my tenth birthday everything changed. After school, some of the neighbor kids were playing with me and my cousins on the front lawn, when I decided to go in and see how Mother was coming with my cake. As I pushed open the swinging door between the dining room and the kitchen, I saw my cake on the counter, and standing at the sink with their backs to me were my mother and Uncle Binyon. He had his arms around her from behind, his hands holding her breasts. Pulling at them like they were bread dough. In the mirror over the sink I could see Mother's tight face, her eyes fixed on her hands, with Uncle Binyon's flushed face, grotesquely smiling, pressed close to hers.

I let go of the door like it was aflame and ran to our room, pole-axed by the blow of what I had seen. The housekeeper's room Mother and I shared was a small L-shaped room at the back of the house. A bed filled the recessed crook of the "L" and was always dark from the shade of a huge elm which covered it. Uncle Binyon didn't allow Fuzzy in any other part of the house, so it was here I held my conversations with her when I needed to talk things out. Fuzzy was the only one I could talk to about what I had just witnessed. I knew women's breasts were mixed up somehow with their private parts, and one didn't touch them. It was dirty to do so. I remembered the little boy's whitish thumb-looking thing, and the sickening shock I'd had from Mother's reaction to finding me with him. And here was Mother doing something even worse. I huddled as far away from that image as I could in the corner of the bed and held Fuzzy tightly.

"Oh, Fuzzy; how does he dare do that to her? He's married. His wife's an invalid right here in this house. I wonder if Aunt Bertie knows he does that to Mother?" Fuzzy cocked her little, intelligent face from side to side trying to understand what I was saying, eagerly wanting to help. "Does he do that to her all the time, do you think? Oh, how can she let him? She's as dirty as he is and I hate them both!"

Mother, without noticing me, came in and closed the door softly, leaning her forehead against it, making quiet moaning sounds. She rocked her head against the door saying almost under her breath, "Oh, God. What am I going to do? What am I going to do?"

I had no pity for her. I thought, "She's a grown woman, she ought to know what to do." She turned away from the door and discovered me staring at her; with a gasping cry, she threw her apron up over her face and turned her back. Stiff with anger, I pushed past her and went out.

The neighbor boys were showing off for my cousins on the lawn, playing a game called "Uncle." The object was to pin another's shoulders to the ground until he gave up and said, "Uncle." They giggled when I said I wanted to play, but I knocked the biggest boy down and fought him with all my strength. I had begun to grow during the past year and was as big as he. Also, tap dancing gives you strong leg muscles, trick riding gives you strong arms, and hatred gives you a strong will. The boy's will not to be overpowered by a girl was no match for the manic strength fury had aroused in me. He was Uncle Binyon to me in this physical contest for a few moments while we grappled together, and then straining every muscle, slowly I forced him down and managed to get astride. Panting, but fiercely determined, I summoned the strength for a final extra-hard push and got both his shoulders flat and held them there. I was aware of the sharp, scratchy lawn under my bare knees and a new thrill of power. Uncle!" "Go on, say it." A savage added push, "Say it. Say Uncle!"

He said it, but after I let him up he pretended he had let me win because I was a girl. After they left, I climbed up in the big elm in the backyard. My heart was thudding with a new sense of power so intense that I wanted to climb to the top of the tree, pound my chest, and hurl Tarzan's triumphant battle cry at the world. I had beaten him. And I could beat Uncle Binyon, too! But first I decided I had to go see my horse.

"Mother, I want to go see Daddy for Christmas."

"Oh, honey, you know I can't leave Aunt Bertie."

"You don't have to go with me. I'm 10 now, I can go by myself."

"Dad writes he's playing way down near Greenville and you'd have to change buses several times. I can't let you do that by yourself."

"Nothing can happen to me, I don't think Daddy should be alone for Christmas."

Of course, Joe was with Dad so he wasn't alone, and I didn't want to see him anyway, it was Creampuff I had to go to. But I knew Mother couldn't resist this sentimental logic.

I wasn't worried about changing buses, and I wasn't lonely on the 2-day trip. When you are on your way to someone you love, you aren't alone. I kept picturing how it would be when I saw her. I used a particular whistle to call Creampuff, it was part of one of the games we played. I would try to creep near wherever she was without her seeing me, hide, then whistle. She'd throw up her head, give a "huh-huh-huh-huh" whicker, and come to look for me. If she didn't find me immediately, when she finally did, she'd sling her head from side to side in mock anger and run right up as if to step on me. Then she'd look out over my shoulder to convince me she was keenly interested in something she saw far away. It tickled me so, and I'd say, "I fooled you, didn't I? You didn't know where I was, did you? Come on, now. You know I fooled you, look at me and admit it." That was how I got to play hide-and-seek after all, and was what I kept imagining on the bus.

The Daunting Art of Writing

Out of the past and back in the present, now here I was once more back at the event I felt was the primary cause of my sexual fears. Having arrived at the monster's lair again, I stomped on its lava-crusted entrance through several drafts without making a crack. Frustrated, and strangely agitated, one day I left the typewriter to lie on the couch and search the ceiling for what my father's leaving me for another woman, as I looked at it, really meant to me. Mentally, I began to laboriously lift off layers of shock absorbers and pain protectors. Suddenly, like Gregory Peck in the movie *Spellbound*, desperately buried images from the past and the emotions that went with them flashed clear in my mind. That little 7-year-old girl the psychiatrist had glimpsed crying out for help was me — 7 years old again — lost and alone and terrified. In a way I would not have thought possible, I could actually again feel the galvanic shock of my father's abandonment like a chain saw that ripped through all the layers of my sense of self and safety, leaving me in cut-up bleeding pieces. The annihilating emotion I had made every effort to avoid for all these intervening years was instantly back in full, wracking my whole adult body with the tears and pain of being rejected by the most important figure in my life. And now, without my blinders on, I could understand that it had been vital at that time to find the reason my father had gone off and left me. Egocentric as I was, I was sure that it must have certainly been my fault. It had seemed to me he could not have rejected me if he had not somehow found me bad – inadequate — worthless. Why else would he leave me?

Finally coming face to face with the monster, I saw that its name was fear. Fear of future pain and loss of self. I could see that for that child at that time the only antidote to that pain and loss, the only way to survive, was anger. I'd had to hate my father in order not to hate myself as a bad person. I'd had to bury the pain of abandonment and horror of being without value under layers of angry scar tissue and sew my pieces back together with the thread of hatred. Lying there on the couch in San Miguel de Allende, I clearly remembered for the first time in almost 50 years what had been the crux of the matter.

Certainly, I needn't be afraid of the commonplace in writing about my past. And even though it was hard trying to learn to write clearly like E.B. White demanded, I found I liked trying to put memories into words. Remembering my bravery and determination as a very little girl strengthened my present resolve to persevere, and helped me feel that the mantra"Go on, Baby Jo, you can do it!" would eventually come true again. Just because you know how to read and write doesn't necessarily mean that you know how to skillfully put your thoughts into the written word, however, and my beginning writer's skill was about on a par with *"Mary Had a Little Lamb."* I soon arranged to take writing lessons from a teacher Liz had told me about. As had many Americans, these two gay guys had come to San Miguel on a vacation and had fallen in love with it, and bought a lovely old house close to the center of town to set up shop as writing teachers. They were themselves writers of some note and well qualified to help the many other American and foreign would-be writers who came to live in the warm sunshine and charm of San Miguel, where the peso was currently twenty-five to the dollar.

Liz studied with Keith, the older of the two, and he turned out to be an amusing, plump, cuddly man in his 50s who put me at ease and gently got me started on the rudiments of writing. Coming into their house from the bright, hot sunshine outside was like walking into a maharajah's palace with its thick-walled, shady inner court cooled by a burbling fountain and potted trees and flowering plants. The many-arched living room was filled with beautiful rugs, low billowy couches and ottomans, and the many museum-quality artifacts they had collected from all over Mexico. Keith's partner, Ronnie, was slender, tall, and reserved, just the opposite of Keith, but it was easy to see the ease and affection between them. The loves of their lives were two absolutely gorgeous German Shepherds named Lucy and Luther. I was very taken with these beautiful animals, but they made me miss my own dog terribly.

With Keith's encouragement, I soon settled into a satisfying routine. Up with the rooster at 6:30 a.m., take a moment to enjoy the beauty of the sun-drenched yard through the bedroom sliding glass door, 30 minutes of yoga stretches, breakfast of toast, two soft-boiled eggs and milk, at the typewriter by 7:30 a.m. The den was highly conducive to writing. One wall was covered with built-in bookshelves, a desk and drawers, with everything arranged neat and tidy close at hand so Liz could just sit down and type. One set of windows faced the street below and the arroyo with its lovely trees stretching off into the distance. Just outside the windows was a patio retaining wall covered with morning glory flowering vines and the top of a pepper tree's lovely drooping branches and shiny pink berries. The house itself was on a hill so that the windows on the opposite wall overlooked the rooftops of the village all the way down to the high towers of La Parroquia. A big comfortable chair in the corner overlooking this view, and a day bed with a night stand on the fourth wall were the only furniture in this good-sized room. It perfectly suited Liz's evident desire for a place to write that was light, airy, and uncluttered, with beauty available when she wanted to look at it. It was perfect for me, too.

At 11:30 a.m., I would break for lunch, usually a ham sandwich with a salad from the garden while sitting on a stool at the kitchen counter looking at the goings on of the small birds in the trees, who seemed to love the flowered patio as much as I did. After a half-hour nap in the den, it was back at the typewriter until 5 p.m., when I would either take a walk up the arroyo until I was tired, or just sit at the patio table and watch the sunset while I had dinner. I was usually in bed by 8 p.m. correcting my day's pages. Then I luxuriously took my reward for a day's work done and read a book from San Miguel's excellent English language library until a 9:30 p.m. lights-out, when I slept the sleep of the just all night long. Often, I would have spent the entire day without speaking to or seeing another living soul, except in the distance.

Luciano stayed out of sight unless I called him. I never found where he went for his many siestas, but he would always quickly appear when called, rubbing his sleepy eyes. He went into the village for anything I needed, but our communication skills were minimal so I rarely asked him to do anything for me. It was comforting to know he was within call, however, and I was exceedingly grateful that Liz had obviously trained him not to be around where she was working.

On Saturday afternoons I went down to have my lesson with Keith (I *loved* it when he praised my work, and tried very hard to master his suggestions or not to be too discouraged when he pointed out my amateurish mistakes), and then to the *banco* to cash some travelers checks before going to the big out-door *mercado* for my week's supplies. It was a huge barn of a building several blocks off the plaza, open on all sides, where the vendors set up their daily supplies of fruits, vegetables, meats, and other perishable foods. I always thought when in foreign countries it was important to try to speak their language, no matter how meager my vocabulary, so I ventured forth in French, Italian or Spanish in foreign countries with a big smile on my face and an eagerness to be friendly in my heart. It usually worked extremely well, except in one case that I recall. There was one woman selling onions and potatoes who caught my attention by the stony, angry, defeated look on her face, and I always went to her stall and tried to make friends with her. She was very Indian in physical appearance, wore only black, and sat stolidly on her stool without smiling back or offering to help me in any way, just taking my money and handing me change without saying a word. I was determined to establish a relationship with her, make her feel good in some way, but no matter how hard I tried to be friendly during the coming months, she never altered her demeanor or spoke directly to me. Consequently, she has always stayed in my mind, a challenge unmet.

There was a *super mercado* on the plaza, infinitesimal by California standards, but recognizable in structure and merchandise. I was astonished to find I could read most of the labels: rows of *Campbell's Legumbre Sopa, Kellogg's Grano, Del Monte Peras* and almost every kind of American canned or packaged foods was available on the shelves. I tried the Campbell's soup once just to see what it was like and it tasted much the same only spicier. I much preferred the exotic, colorful atmosphere of the open-air market, except for the meats and cheeses. Non-refrigerated, fly-visited meat and cheese turned my stomach, so I bought these items out of the refrigerated cases of the super mercado. I soon found my favorite *panaderia* for the brown bread I liked best, and was delighted when the clerks in the various stores remembered me and said hello. I was quick to learn their names and tell them mine. Like every one else who lives in a foreign country, I guess, I wanted to be thought of as a member of the community rather than an alien.

A few times on Saturday afternoons I stopped by to chat with one or another of the several friends Liz had introduced me to and they were each interesting women, but my thoughts were always too much on what I was working on to really enjoy their company. One auspicious day, Leonardo and his wife stopped by to see me. His wife, Julia, was short, with a curvaceous figure, reddish, curly hair, amber eyes, and fair skin with a lot of freckles. She also came from a Spanish land grant family, she soon told me. I judged her to be around the same age as Leonardo, which was 43, but she was clearly a dynamo running at full speed. They had come by to take me to lunch, Leonardo said, and to see how I was making out. It pleased me greatly to tell him that I was making out just fine.

At lunch, I felt I was being bounced around in the shock wave of a tempestuous power struggle that had become a way of life for Leonardo and Julia. She constantly challenged him in one way or another with a fierce, excited gleam in her eye and seemed as frustrated and determined as a mongoose baiting a coiled rattlesnake that wouldn't strike. When she loudly ordered another drink and he quietly said he thought she'd had enough; she ordered a double. Leonardo spoke only English, as I was his guest, but although she could speak a little English, she fired off her opinions of him in Spanish like machine gun bursts. I was glad when lunch was over and I was back in my quiet house.

On late Sunday afternoons, I gave myself a treat. The *Sierra Nevada* had the best restaurant in town, and I went there for cocktails and dinner. The hotel was in a large, old remodeled house with a walled-in patio for diners who preferred the outdoors to its very elegant indoor dining room. The owner-chef was a Scot who had been trained in nouvelle cuisine at the Cordon Bleu in Paris, and served excellent French food. Her delicious entrees with small portions beautifully arranged on lovely china made an elegant change from my own cooking. I had fallen in love with French cuisine at first bite on my first day in France. In my quest to become a good housewife I had taken several French cooking classes over the years, but I could never get my own cooking to taste *French* enough. To sit there under the trees alone in this flower-filled patio having the food I loved best was somehow completely fulfilling. I enjoyed watching other diners and making up stories about who they were and what their relationship was, or checking in on a nearby conversation and imagining what their lives were like at home. In a way, I was making up my own story about myself. Once, a very attractive man who was dining alone, approached and asked if he could buy me a drink, and I mournfully replied, "Oh, I'm sorry. That's very kind of you, but I have just had a devastating loss and I need to be by myself." He fell all over himself making apologies and scrambling back to his table. I enjoyed our little interchange immensely.

I didn't want or need company. Sitting there drinking my margarita, I mused over the fact that ever since I had been around 28 I had at least two large martinis every single night. My proven formula was Grey Goose vodka in chilled glasses with just a few drops vermouth and a lemon twist. In earlier years, milk or Dr. Pepper had been my beverage of choice; even when I was scoffed at I always prided myself on not giving in to social pressure. Anyway, bourbon or Scotch had seemed to me a lot like the medicine we sold on the show until I tasted my first very cold, very dry martini. Henceforth, the evening's martini or two became one of the most important parts of my day. But during the months I had been here in San Miguel, I hadn't wanted a drink at all during the week. I sat on my patio every evening and thought about new things to put in what I had been writing, or better ways to phrase something, and never thought about making myself a drink. An act that had seemed absolutely vital to my well being in relieving tension or achieving exhilaration at the end of the day was no longer important at all. The only reason I could imagine for that was that I was happy. For the first time in too long I was really completely *happy*. Relieved of all responsibility for the well being of anyone other than myself, proving each day that I could persevere for eight hours a day at a job that was very hard, and feeling that I was back on the track of what was right for me, had put the shimmer back in my soul, the confidence back in my walk.

In 1963, when my mother was dying and in and out of a coma, one day I was sitting beside her bed reading when she suddenly said, "You walk like a boy," and I looked up to find her watching me with tender love and admiration. I knew she meant that as the highest compliment, that she saw me as walking, not masculine, but tall and free and strong. Laurence Olivier said, "When I've got the walk, I've got the character." I couldn't remember how I was walking before I came to San Miguel, but I was aware now that sometime during these last months I had begun striding up and down those cobble-stoned streets with that old feeling of being tall and free and strong. I felt that I was walking in San Miguel the way I had walked on the stage and down the runway in Atlantic City in 1942 when I won the Miss America Pageant and the newspapers called me *The Texas Tornado*. I never thought I had won that contest because of the way I *looked*, but rather because of the way I *felt* about myself. It was a kind of "Stand well back, I'm coming through!" feeling. I had lost that sense of self somewhere along the way, but now I had it back again. I felt like saying to myself, "Well, hello there! I'm so glad to see you again." And giving myself a big hug. I knew that feeling came from achieving what I had set out to achieve, and having had the courage to get out there and begin again to be who I was meant to be. I tipped my little red hat to myself.

When I first started to write, I knew that in order to overcome my accumulated inertia and fear of the future, and to make a sense of order out of the chaos of my memories, I must make a stringent set of rules by which to proceed. First of all, it had to be the truth. I had really set myself the challenge of writing a book, not for publication (though that would be nice if it came later), but to uncover the true feelings of childhood by putting on paper the experiences that had caused them. That was the challenge: to recover the accurate past and the actual emotions it engendered. I wasn't interested in learning to write fiction. I knew only too well how to pretend and to live in the realm of the superficial. What I was determined to achieve now was what was real, actually, positively real. I had brought Mother's old box of photographs, so I could put together a lot of the pieces of the jigsaw of my life based on them. When I was little, as we were traveling from town to town in the Model T, Mother would tell me stories about the people in the photographs, about her childhood and her life with Dad, and about what had happened to me as a child. She was a wonderful storyteller. Therefore, much of what I was writing was from the memory of her stories rather than from total recall of my own experiences. Although, the more I got into the writing, the more actual experiences began to come back to me in vivid detail. I tried to make all the memories come alive in that way, but I found I needed imagined dialogue to do so.

Secondly, I determined that in order to honor the written word which had brought me so much pleasure all my life, I must make what I wrote grammatically correct. From having read so much, my mind had absorbed correct spelling fairly well, but while reading E.B. White's book I was horrified at my lack of knowledge of grammatical structure. Perseverance was clearly my only way to master this forbidding labyrinth of the English language. I tried sleeping with E.B. White's *The Elements of Style* under my pillow in hope that the rules of grammar would enter my subconscious, but it didn't help. Dedicated study was the only hope.

Thirdly, in order to have some structure, I needed a beginning, a middle, and an end, so I had determined to take my book from birth through the Miss America Pageant, ending when I had just turned 19 and was on my way to Hollywood to fulfill my contract at 20th Century Fox. It seemed to me everything important that had happened to shape me and my fears had already happened by that time. When I arrived in Hollywood, I was firmly set in concrete by previous experiences into the person I would be for the foreseeable future. But unlike my husband, I was now determined to break through that cement with this hammer of remembering.

Most importantly, I made a rule for myself that I must write, or at least sit in front of the typewriter, eight hours a day, four in the morning and four in the afternoon. There could be no reading or daydreaming during those hours, nothing but focus and self-discipline — two qualities of which I had always been in short supply. But I felt I must persevere relentlessly at my chosen goal, in part to appease the gods of miracles who had showered me with this marvelous opportunity. Strictly following these rules, after four months I had literally fought my way through to a draft of the book that I was satisfied with for the time being. Although I had been able to recover an astonishing amount of past experiences, I was no closer to uncovering the basic causes of my sexual inhibitions. The draft was 460 pages, at least a third of which needed cutting, but I had gotten all the way from the Arizona State Men's Prison where I was born to the train to Hollywood and could write "The End" with an enormous feeling of accomplishment. I knew I needed to make more drafts before I could feel it was really as good as I could get it and returned to San Miguel several more times to work on it. But for now, I had achieved my original purpose and could go home and see my kids. *I had written a book!*

Home Again

FROM OUR HOME TO YOURS!

Peter, John, Jo, Russ Stoneham

Family holiday card, taken in our backyard in Brentwood, California, c. 1969.

When my Russ picked me up at the airport that June, he behaved as though I had just been away on a two-week vacation in the mountains and kept up a friendly chatter about friends of ours and what was happening at the studio. Because of the lack of a phone, I had only been in touch with him and the boys by mail, and I felt I had changed so much in these past months that I wouldn't have been surprised if he hadn't recognized me. It doesn't make sense, when you think of it, that a person with whom I had shared more than a third of my life — love, birth, ups, downs — could become merely someone I used to know who was being kind enough to give me a ride home. But so it was.

During our early marriage, I used to fantasize that my commitment to Russ was so strong that if we were on the sinking Titanic, I would choose to sink with him, and now — well — I felt a kind of painless pity for us both. We had each covered ourselves in rolls of defensive cement against our differing childish fears until we resembled the Michelin Tire man, and had bumped softly and fruitlessly against one another for years in the pathetic hope of getting close. At 30, when I had said "I do" to the minister as I married Russ, I was making a pledge of fidelity to him and a commitment to my belief that marriage would bring fulfillment to me of a new and different kind. A totally different kind of relationship than I had in my first marriage to my first husband, Phil.

When I was 21, I had said "I do" to marrying someone who was not sexually threatening because his real passion was gambling, and because he made me laugh, to not living with my mother anymore, and to rolling the new experience dice to see what they came up with. The roll of the dice turned up snake eyes after five years, so I got a divorce (1950) and embarked on a hopeful journey of sexual discovery. I fell wildly, wonderfully, and woefully in love with one of my partners at a major stopover on that odyssey, and learned a lot about good sex during a couple of short stays, but the other bedded relationships were meaningless, really, and finally began to be degrading. So by the time I was 30, I was ready to say "I do" to: waking up and going to sleep with the same person for the rest of my life, always having that same person to say "Oh, look at that!" with, and the comfort of a loving hand to hold through the glory and gory of life. I was eager to have children and I was ready to make a permanent commitment to the man I chose to be the father of my children — and I had chosen Russ. And I *believed*. Oh, how I believed in the Kahlil Gibran marriage concepts of two young trees standing shoulder to shoulder, branches intertwined, looking out in the same direction. I grasped wholeheartedly at the vision of two souls blending, supporting, and sharing, mating for life, while remaining separate individuals. I even asked the minister to read these passages at our wedding ceremony:

> *"Love one another, but make not a bond of love;*
> *Let it rather be a moving sea between the shores of your souls.*
> *Sing and dance together and be joyous, but let each one of you be alone,*
> *Even as the strings of a lute are alone though they quiver with the same music."*

I feel now a tender pity for my youthful naivete, and amusement at what Russ' family must have thought of these esoteric wedding sentiments. Oddly enough, I was convinced that I could make those fanciful concepts come true for me. Like my father before me, I thought I could catch the golden ring on the marry-go-round. After 25 years of marriage, however, this man who met me at the airport was a stranger to me and our relationship a mystery. Oh, well.

I found, also, as I walked in the door of my home, that it was now only a house where I used to live. I knew where things were, but

I was no longer connected to my beautiful house in my heart. I felt deeply nostalgic for how much I had loved it.

I had planned my return around the coinciding of John's eighteenth birthday and his graduation from high school. I could hardly wait to tell him of the grand present I had for him. Some time ago I

A moment in LIFE *magazine, at home in Pacific Palisades, with son Peter, 1959.*
Allan GrantAllan Grant/The LIFE Picture Collection/Shutterstock

had set aside for some special occasion $3,000 earned from the work I did with a little theater company.

This seemed the most special occasion possible, so I told John that I would give the money to him for a graduation/birthday present IF he would use it to go to Europe — two weeks, charter flight, hostel lodging, public transportation – ALONE. I had learned so many vital things about myself and life while traveling alone in Europe, and I told John that if he would accept, what I was offering him wasn't just a present, it was the gift of *Freedom from Fear*! Otherwise, I would give him a watch.

He agreed, so I bought him a bunch of books, like *Europe on 5 Dollars a Day* to give him encouragement. One day, I was in the kitchen looking out the window at John stretched out by the pool reading the books. After a bit, he got up and leaned on the glass fence looking out over the ocean deep in thought. I thought to myself, "Oh, lordy, he is not going to do it. It's too much to expect from him to go to Europe all alone," but later he came in and said, "Mom, I've been thinking that if I really watch my money, I could stay three weeks instead of two. But rather than England and France, I would like to go to Greece. We've been studying Greece my senior year in history, and I would really like to see it." My heart swelled with pride.

Peter was also home for the summer, but at first he made no comment about my sleeping in the playroom rather than in the master bedroom with his father. (It hadn't occurred to me to ask *Russ* to sleep in the playroom!) Peter was now consumed with music. He had been playing guitar and singing with a rock group he had assembled during his years at the University of California at Santa Barbara, and he loved it. His stated major was Political Science, but I could see he had really majored in music and having a good time. He had inherited my mother's musical talent, my father's charm, his father's wit, and my eyes and temperament. I had hated study when I was in school, too. My hope was that he would fall in love with learning later in life as I had. Peter was extraordinarily articulate, and wrote wonderful, creative essays. His vocabulary and unique graphic images were often so accurate and outrageously funny that he made everyone laugh whether they wanted to or not. And he was extraordinarily handsome. I had always been in awe that this handsome being had come out of my body, even more so now at 23 when he had grown into this slim-hipped, wide-shouldered, wonderful-looking young man. My mother and my father would have been so proud of who he was and that he was a good musician.

John looked exactly like the photographs of Russ when he was his age (which is to say, he took your breath away he was so beautiful), but he didn't seem to have inherited anything besides his looks from anyone on either side of our family. Even as a newborn, he was smiling all the time, and very soon, I could see him beginning to understand all sorts of things long before babies were supposed to. Before John was two, he developed the extraordinary ability to understand other people's feelings, and empathize with them. He almost made me believe in reincarnation as he seemed such an old soul who must have been around many times before in order to have learned all the things he already knew when he was born. Without prompting, John had looked in the want ads when he was 15 and gotten a job dishing up 31 Flavors to save money to buy a car. To pay for gas and stuff, he had gotten a job at Datsun Motors as a clerk when he was 16. John always had it together I thought, and I was enormously proud of him.

At home in Brentwood, California, age 43 (1966).

Only my close friends knew that my husband and I were really separated. I was confident that Russ had revealed nothing to his friends as we continued to be invited out together, and we maintained a friendly attitude toward one another at home and abroad. Indeed, now that I felt unencumbered by wifedom, I wished him well. And all *seemed* well until one night at a party a friend said, "Jo, I hear you are writing a book. How exciting!"

I had tried not to care that Russ and the boys never asked about the book that I had been writing, or seemed curious about my time in San Miguel de Allende at all. But now I could see that they were feeling threatened and angry with me for bouncing precariously on the limb of their nest.

The next day, I said, "Russ, I see you don't think much of my writing, you despise my politics, and think I am emotionally excessive, so just for the fun of it, what *do* you like about me?"

After an unflatteringly long pause, he said judiciously, "You're a good cook."

It makes you think, doesn't it? After 25 years, from a multitude of possibilities,

"You're a good cook?"

It amazed, rather than hurt me.

Of course, I have to admit that if Russ had asked me the same question, "What do you like about me," it would have given me pause. Upon consideration, I would have to say, "I love the way you look. The way you look still fits my vision of a high class gent."

Shortly after this event, when Peter and I were alone in the car, he took a deep breath and said angrily, "Mom, I don't understand why you went off and left Dad all alone for months. You have been together for all this time, and now that you are old I don't see why you can't just stick it out. You know the saying, 'If you want fidelity, marry a swan!'"

I wanted to shout, "But, Peter, don't you see, I *wanted* to marry a swan. I *yearned* to have a mate to care about me and be faithful forever as we swam side by side around the beautiful lake of life, with little cygnets paddling along behind every now and then. I thought I *was* marrying a swan. That's the pity of it all."

I don't know, maybe the firstborn always has a special porthole into one's heart, for when he said cruel things to me, I knew that he was only venting his frustration and fear. I knew that he felt closest to me, and was sure enough of my love and understanding to take out his feelings of anxiety on me. But while his anger didn't hurt me, his lack of understanding did. He seemed to feel that because his father paid the bills, I *owed* it to Russ to stay and maintain a home for him as long as he wanted. Be there to darn his socks and keep his supper warm, so to speak. (Where do kids *get* these ideas?) He was full of gratitude to his father for buying him things and putting him through good private schools, but he seemed to have none for me. Also, where had the swan analogy come from? I had never discussed Russ' infidelity with the boys, not in any way, shape, or form. How did Peter know that was what was at the bottom of it all? And, anyway, infidelity is no joke. It hurts. It hurts the unsuspecting partner in ways that can never be healed completely. The sense of being diminished, of being somehow to blame, of being betrayed, sears a hurting place in the soul that can be covered over with scar tissue, but it always continues to hurt. Proud flesh, my mother called it.

Struggling for equanimity, I pointed out to Peter that I was making more money than his father when we got married, and if I hadn't chosen to stay at home when he was born, I might still be! I told him that when I was working, I enjoyed it greatly because it was *fun and I was good at it*, and I got lots of positive strokes from all sides, which I hadn't gotten a whole lot of as a wife and mother. I had given that up gladly to try to make the best possible home for him and our family, but I didn't feel I *owed* his father anything for paying the bills! I was *entitled* to whatever financial support I had gotten from this marriage, and to community property, too, by George!

Actually, I thought I was entitled to a lot more than that, but I didn't want to go into that with Peter. In a way I hadn't expected, it seemed to me his siding with his father was a gender kind of thing, two aggrieved males against the untrustworthy female. As *was* to be expected, however, the thought of his parents going their separate ways was scary and he needed someone to blame. He couldn't be grateful for what he'd had while being afraid of losing it. I didn't *expect* gratitude, really, but I went on muttering to myself, "Oh, how sharper than a serpent's tooth is an ungrateful child," until it all struck me funny and familiar. I had been just the same with my own mother.

John, to a lesser degree, seemed to have the same lack of understanding. Of course, I had struggled mightily to make sure that both Peter and John didn't know what I was really feeling during my marriage, but John had always been especially sensitive to nuance. I remembered one time when Russ I were going down to Santa Barbara to hear Peter with his band. For reasons I never really understood, Russ was somehow threatened by trips of a longer duration than to the drugstore, so he always planned to leave much before time, and could tolerate no side trips or sightseeing along the way. It was vitally important to get there in the fastest and most direct route. Mostly, he was irritably anxious for me to be ready to go as soon as he was. The fact that since I had to fix breakfast while he was showering and dressing, clean up the kitchen and shower and dress in my turn, it was *impossible* for me to be ready as fast as he was never seemed to penetrate. He was often in the car honking for me to hurry up, and I rushed around breathlessly to keep the peace. (*Of course, now I think we should have taken turns making breakfast and cleaning up! But never mind.*) When I had zoomed out to the car, I found that I had forgotten the directions to where Peter was playing, which brought a disgusted grunt from Russ when I had to go back to get them. As I dashed past John on the way out again, he said sympathetically, "Good luck."

I always thought from that time on, that he understood.

Yet, when I told John that I was going back to San Miguel soon, he said, in a condemning tone, "Mom, Dad really needs you to be here when he gets home from work."

I said, "John, Flora is here to fix his dinner, the *LA Times* and *Newsweek* are delivered and the television set is in good working order, so if you don't tell him I'm not here, he won't know." That was the last I heard from John on the subject.

Three days before John was ready to leave on his trip to Greece, Russ almost spoiled the whole thing. He had been totally opposed to his beloved younger son going off to strange places with strange people having strange experiences *all by himself!* "God knows *what* might happen to him, my parents would never think of letting me do a thing like that when I was his age," he kept saying. But I persevered because I knew in my soul that John was ready for it, and John in his quiet, perceptive way, kept right on making plans for the trip. Then his father happily presented him with a *Visa credit card* ready to use whenever he might need it! I was shattered because the whole point was that John should manage his finances and his experiences on this relatively small amount of money *without a safety net!* I knew he needed to learn that he could do it on his own.

When I was much younger than John, I had learned that when the spot was tight, and the chips were down — when there was nobody there to take care of me — *I could take care of myself!* That knowledge had strengthened and encouraged me for the rest of my life. I had always been concerned that our sons had lived such an affluent and sheltered life that they never had an opportunity to learn the hard way that they had the right stuff. I knew that we have to learn from personal *experience* if we are brave and capable or not. I knew that *fear* was one of the greatest human evils. I was always concerned that Peter and John had little opportunity to really test themselves and overcome their fears. Many people spend their whole lives being afraid. Being afraid of the school bully, social failure, of taking a chance, of what other people think, of being alone — whatever. They live their whole lives without ever being faced with the survival challenge. I believe most people can find their own reservoir of strength when faced with extreme circumstances, and can dip into it when they need courage. I think that the Maasai had it right. Many cultures have a coming of age rite of passage for their youth, but the Maasai prepare their boys from the time they can walk for the time when they are old enough to kill a lion all by themselves. Then they are men. And can walk proud and unafraid forever after. Of course, the Maasai didn't prepare their girls for anything, but working in the field!

Before he left, I told John that since I had never been to Greece and had always wanted to go, all I asked of him was to sneak over the fence around the Acropolis in the early morning to watch the sun come up, as my cousin had told me it was an experience not to be missed. And, I had often read how purple the Aegean got at sunset, so to be sure to take a look at that for me. I was literally choked with good wishes and pride when we saw him off at the airport in his safari hat, multi-pocketed shorts, drip-dry shirt, heavy walking shoes and backpack. He didn't look back.

I think John's return from Greece three weeks later was my most exciting time in an airport. To see him striding down the ramp in the same clothes he wore as he left was more fun than I'd had in a long time. We were all talking at once on the way home, but gradually the adventures of his trip emerged and it was everything I had hoped for and more. As well as a multitude of marvelous experiences, while he was touring the Greek Islands, he had formed a brief friendship with a Mexican student in his 20s who was on a break from Oxford.

He had toured three islands with him and had gotten into his first fist fight, which was a big surprise from peaceable John. One day on Mykonos, he and his new friend had met and made a date with a couple of English girls for dinner. But when they arrived at the restaurant, they found that two French boys had moved in on the girls and an altercation ensued between Mexico and France. The U.S. got involved when one of the Frenchman swung and broke John's glasses, which resulted in a broken French nose. Imagine! Then in a hostel in Athens on the way home, his unknown roommate overdosed and died in the night. When John awoke, he found that he could successfully deal with this extremely traumatic and possibly dangerous situation in time to catch his charter flight home.

He never used the credit card. He had killed his lion.

Days later, I received a postcard from Greece of a photograph of a boy sitting high on a cliff looking out over the Aegean at sunset, and the message read: "Dear Mom, 'Sometimes as I drift idly on Walden Pond, I cease to live and begin to be.' Thoreau, as if you didn't know. Love, John."

I cried.

Liz's husband received an offer he couldn't refuse for their Malibu ranch, and had bought another ranch in Montana to which they would be in the process of moving for the foreseeable future, and she hoped I would go back and keep the house in San Miguel company. John was back at work at Datsun Motors and planning to start college in the fall. Peter had gone up north to work with his band, so I was overjoyed to once again pack up to go back to my sunshine place to start work on a second draft of my remembrances of things past.

My son Peter.

Russ and my son John with his F-14.

Aftermath of My Father's Death - 1934

When my father died and half-brother Joe ran off with our house car, Mother and I were left with no money and no place to live and, other than our clothes and stuff, no possessions except my horse, her trailer and the Model T, which was out of gas. I was 11 years old. Mother made a collect call to our favorite relative, my Uncle Lowe, to come and help us, and he was with us by the next day. He'd had to drive all night, as it was quite a distance from his ranch near Amarillo to Greenville, but he was there with a big smile on his sweet, freckled face to give us a reassuring hug.

Uncle Lowe was short and stocky, had light red hair and a heart as big as Texas. I loved him very much. He loaned Mother enough gas money to get to my grandmother's house in Hale Center, which was a relief, but I panicked when he started to hitch Creampuff's trailer to his pickup. It had not occurred to me that this disaster which had befallen us would include my losing Creampuff, but Uncle Lowe said, "You be sure I'll take special care of her, Jo-Carroll, until you and your mother get settled, then I'll bring her back to you. She'll be happy with all the other horses on my ranch and have lots of oats to eat." Creampuff was already down to the last wisps in her hay bin, and she surely did love oats, so I had to let her go. But more than anything else that had happened, it made me want to put my head down and just bawl like a baby.

When we got to Grandma's house, she met us at the kitchen door like the big, bad wolf. Grandpa had died some years before. Before I could get her snuff off my face from where I'd kissed her, she said, "Lizzie (my mother's name was Elizabeth, but her family all called her Lizzie, which she hated), I'm awful sorry about poor Mr. Ennis and your trouble, but I'm in my 80s now and I have to be real careful about how I spend my money. Lowe tells me Mr. Ennis died and left you with nothin', so I guess it's up to me to take you in. But as long as yore gonna be livin' offen me, I let you know right now I don't aim to have that chile's horse at my house drawin' flies. Nor that worthless dog ah hers in my house neither. I never had a dog in the house and I never will. Dogs is dirty and should stay outside and protect the house."

I couldn't believe what I was hearing. My little toy poodle could not come in the house! I said to myself, "*Fuzzy* is dirty! With that snuff running down her mouth and all those stains on her clothes, Grandma is the dirtiest thing I ever saw. And Fuzzy would be the first one under the bed at the sight of a burglar or a rat. Some watchdog she'll make." But the stunning blow was about Creampuff, that I couldn't have her here took my breath away. Later I said to Mother, "Can't you talk to her about Creampuff? I'm sure Uncle Lowe would loan us enough hay."

"Honey-baby, times are so hard now Uncle Lowe doesn't have enough money to buy hay. Creampuff is running loose in a pasture and eats grass with the other horses."

"Well, couldn't she eat grass around here?"

"There isn't any pasture land around here that's free, Josie. She'd starve to death trying to find enough grass in the ditches. We'll go see her sometime soon. I'm so sorry, honey."

For the first time I became a real victim of the Depression. There is no poor like a poor relation. When you have no rights in the house where you live and are made to feel every cover that warms you or bite that feeds you is begrudged charity, boy, that is *poor!* And I knew Uncle Lowe had lied about the oats.

Mother said, "We have a roof over our heads and we must be grateful for that."

I found it hard to be grateful. Fuzzy wasn't grateful to have to stay outside in the cold either. Toy poodles don't have any undercoat and it was winter, but I fixed her up a box with my old sweater in it right outside our door, and told her we had to make the best of it. Unlike my instant adoration of Grandpa, Grandma and I had never hit it off. That became readily apparent now that I was at her mercy. She was quickly outraged if Mother tried to slip me something extra to eat. While Mother combed sparse white hair over her scaly scalp, she said, "Now, Lizzie, there's no call for you to go on at me, I aim to have that grub in the smokehouse stay put. You never know when I'm gonna need it. We can get by on corn bread and molasses just fine. It was good enough for your pa and me and it's good enough for you and that puffed-up kid ah yourn."

Mother didn't mind eating corn bread and molasses three times a day for herself, but what thinned her mouth and galled her terribly was when the boxes of outgrown clothes arrived for me from one aunt or another. I hated being dictated to and forced to eat icky molasses and corn bread; she hated my having to wear hand-me-downs.

Hale Center was small, even for the small towns I was used to. It consisted of a block's worth of dirt-colored buildings, bisected by a thin line of macadam stretching straight in either direction until it seemed to fall off both ends of the earth. The only outstanding inter-ruption to the vast empty skyline was the jutting cotton gin, which seemed to float in the shimmery heat-haze several feet in the air.

During the week, you wouldn't see more than a dozen people on the street until school let out. On Saturday mornings the farmers did their shopping at the one grocery, hardware, or farm implement store. While their parents gassed up at the one filling station, the kids dug for bottles of pop in the Nehi box next to the faded and cracked "Ice Cold Watermelon" sign. Some Saturdays, there was a Hoot Gibson movie at the auditorium where they had community meetings. On Sunday mornings, *everyone* came into town to attend one of the five churches, and then went home for the big Sunday dinner. Not a lot happened in Hale Center.

Apparently, I was supposed to think of Hale Center as my home town; the place where I was going to live permanently. I couldn't do it. All my life I had been a transient. Even at Wayside I knew I was only passing through. That was my life and I liked it that way. Es-pecially when it came to Hale Center; I couldn't pass through it fast enough. There was no place to be alone that wasn't bare, flat, and ugly. It was like living in a giant sandbox. I missed Creampuff sorely. However, I had to make a life for myself among these hicks, so I went at it. I didn't wear my little red hat to school because I didn't need it. All the girls fought to sit next to me at recess because I had seen the Pacific Ocean, could sing and dance, and (I always thought) had an unusual personality. I chose the fifth grade to be in as my Aunt Pat taught it, and I managed to con her out of learning anything. Having learned to read and write at my father's knee, so to speak, and being naturally good at English, I had always escaped anything to do with arithmetic or any other subject I didn't like at the little schools I had intermittently attended by telling the teacher, "They hadn't gotten to that part yet in the schools where I've been" in a pitiful voice. The teachers had to either take their time to start me from the beginning or let it pass. They always let it pass.

The big weekly recreational events in Hale Center were Sunday Church and Wednesday Night Prayer Meetings. I was surprised to find that Mother was an ardent hard-shelled Baptist like the rest of her family, but I would go anywhere to get out of Grandma's house, so I willingly went with her to the First Baptist Church. Right away ,I could see that the preacher, Mr. Fairchild, was as phony as a circus barker for a freak show. Obviously, he was just trying to warm up the audience when he shouted about Jehovah's fearful wrath and an eminent Hell of Fire and Brimstone just waiting to crisp up all us sinners. He used the same tone of voice and arm gestures the barkers used to excite *his* crowd to pay *their* admission to Heaven when the collection plate was passed around. But he didn't fool me, what he was talking about had nothing to do with the God *I* knew. I believed that God was *loving*, a little strict about certain things surely, but never *wrathful*, and I certainly didn't hear any *love* coming from that preacher. And when he talked about God giving people *dominion* over the birds and animals and making a woman out of a man's *rib* and little babies being created in *sin* and going to some awful place called Limbo if they weren't baptized, I knew he was as phony as a two-dollar bill. He was just pushing his product.

Mrs. Fairchild taught Sunday School, and she went on and on about the sin of dancing. Everything seemed to be sinful. Not one thing she talked about that was fun wasn't sinful. I asked her if "Jesus forgave the third thief on the cross at the last minute, why should any of us be good until the last minute?" And she said, "Well! What if you were in an automobile accident and didn't have time and didn't have clean underwear on?" That did it for me.

Living with Grandma in Hale Center was like being compressed in a pressure cooker, and after a year something happened that blew the lid off. One day the electrifying sound of an animal in extreme pain propelled me out of the house to see my little Fuzzy being attacked by a much larger dog. He had her held between his front legs and was pumping furiously into her while she emitted a steady shriek like a stuck pig. Mother rushed after me and tried to pull me back in the house, saying there was nothing we could do to stop it. I shook her off and ran to them, kicking the big dog and trying to pull him away from little Fuzzy. Mother yelled to me that I would only make him hurt her worse and went back in the house.

I kept kicking him until an incredible thing happened. He released Fuzzy and turned around, but somehow her rear end and his rear end were connected. Fuzzy was *hanging* from him, back to back, making desperate little gasps of pain as he faced away from her, panting. It was a nightmare, like watching someone you love being drawn and quartered. I could make no sense of what I was seeing, and was afraid to touch them. After an unbelievably long time, she dropped from him and he ran off. I gathered her up, all bloody, and carried her behind the smokehouse where the two of us lay down together and cried.

I'd had animals that were in pain from a broken leg or wounds from sticks, but I never heard them utter more than a whimper. I could only imagine that Fuzzy's pain had been almost unbearable for her to have screamed like that. And it took so long. And she had been so helpless. The image of that weird position of them joined end to end — her hanging — I was never able to erase that image from my mind.

But the worst was yet to come. My grandmother was relentless and still refused to let Fuzzy come in her stinky house. Fuzzy had been sleeping in a little box outside our door, but now Mother fixed her a place in a filthy old shed by the smokehouse which hadn't been used in years. It was full of moldy sacks and rusty, junky stuff, but it seemed to be a safe place to keep her. Poor little dog. How bewildered she must have been by what was happening to her.

When I came home from school the next day, I found the same dog digging frantically at the door of the shed; he had almost broken it down. This time I found a stick and for the first time in my life really beat an animal. I tried to kill him. Finally he slunk off. I comforted a whimpering Fuzzy but I was forced to leave her there. As I came out of the shed, I saw Grandma sitting in her rocker on the porch in clear view of the shed door. She had her hand over her mouth, and as I approached her I could tell that she was snickering! Breathing hard, I said, "You could see what that dog was doing. Why didn't you drive him off? He almost got in with her again."

She gave herself a complacent push in the rocker, "I didn't think I should spoil his fun. Anyways, a body shouldn't try to go agin' nature." She snickered again. She had *enjoyed* watching that dog trying to break the door down to get in with my little dog and hurt her again. Having had 14 children, one would think she would have had enough of that "nature!" I wanted to beat her as hard as I had beaten that dog. The intensity of the hatred between us was as fierce as his lust for Fuzzy.

My grandmother knew about nature all right. The next morning when I went out to feed Fuzzy, I found the dog had dug his way under the shed and was inside there with her. I was shaking with fury as I looked for the stick, but he ran off before I could find it. Fuzzy was huddled up in a corner, all bloody again. My imagination went wild at the thought of what she had gone through during the night: listening to the terrifying sound of his digging his way through the hard-packed earth, then being locked inside all night with him. My insides exploded with horror for her, and again we cried together. I was too stricken with grief to even rage against my grandmother for having put us in this situation. There seemed no escape for either of us.

But there was an escape for Fuzzy. Nine weeks later, when I went out to feed her, I found her dead. She had tried to give birth to puppies that were too big to pass through her pelvis, and she had died in the effort. She lay there like a dirty, little, broken toy, all bloody and twisted with dried vomit all around her, her eyes and mouth wide open. The pups, one out and one half out, were dead, too. There she was, my little companion, her sweet-smelling pink skin, tiny black nose and intelligent black eyes all dirty and slimy with the smell of violent death. Her white curly hair, that I loved to clean and brush and tie up with ribbons, was all matted and brown and yellow and red. It was too important to cry about.

That night as I lay in bed I reached out to God. I prayed, "Help me, God. I can't stand it any longer. I have to get away from here and I can't think how to do it. Please, God, just point out a way. I promise that I will stop hating Grandma if you will just help me get away from her. Help me, God, please help me." By sunup, I knew what to do: I wrote a letter to Dr. N. F. Tate in Waco, Texas, at the address on a bottle of Tate-Lax medicine we had left over from the show. I didn't tell Mother what I had done in case it didn't work out, and anyway I kind of blamed her for getting us into this fix. I was strung up with suspense and went to the post office every day with a pounding heart. Two weeks later, my heart seemed to stop altogether when the post mistress gave me a letter. I tore part of it as I tried to get the envelope open quickly. It read:

> *Dear Jo-Carroll,*
>
> *Of course, I know who you are. I was very sorry to hear of your father's death, and offer you and your mother my sincere condolences.*
>
> *I would be glad to have you become a member of my troupe, along with your horse, and can offer you a salary of $20 dollars a week. I am sorry that I have no opening for your mother, but as I am in need of a housekeeper/cook at the present time it might be she would like to fill that position. There are separate living quarters in my house car and you and your mother could have free room and board in return for her services.*
>
> *If this is agreeable to you, we will be playing Amarillo for the next three weeks and you can join us there.*
>
> *Cordially yours,*
> *Dr. N. F. Tate*

I didn't know whether to dissolve on the post office floor in a puddle of joyous tears because now I could have Creampuff back, or do a triumphant running forward flip because I had beaten Grandma. Instead, I ran all the way home and gave Mother the letter, breathlessly trying to get the words out, "Mother, he wants me ... and Creampuff ... and I'll make $20 a week ... Oh, Mother, he wants me!"

Any apprehension she might have had about this enormous move were washed away in the flood of my enthusiasm. We started at daybreak that Sunday, as it would be a full day's drive to pick up Creampuff at Uncle Lowe's ranch and get on to Amarillo. Grandma was up to see us off to give Mother dire warnings of fast-approaching disaster. "Lizzie, you must have been chewin' loco weed. You don't know this man Tate from Adam's off-ox, yet here you are high-tailin' it out ah here fastern you can say Jack Rabbit. You fixin' to git yourself in a peck ah trouble an I'm tellin' you right now, if you let this chile lead you around by the nose thisaway, you needn't come runnin' back to me to take you in agin."

Mother said, "Well, Mama ... I know, but ... "

I broke in, "Goodbye, Grandma. We're leaving now." We glared grimly at one another as she took another chew on her snuff stick. I was the winner of our pugilistic contest and we both knew it.

Doctor Tate's elixir.

The Big Medicine Show - 1935

When I wrote Dr. N. F. Tate asking for a job, I was writing to a giant in the medicine show business. His was an imposing figure guaranteed to cause awe and respect in the beholder. Over 6-feet tall and barrel-chested, his face with its large nose and small, close-set gray eyes looked like it could have been carved from the granite of Mount Rushmore. In his 60s, his rare smile showed slightly yellowed teeth which seemed larger than ordinary teeth, and his slow, heavy, walk strove for a kind of majesty. He wore well-tailored three-piece suits, the kind of white Stetson hat wealthy ranchers wore, and a sure-fire eye-grabber of a watch fob made up of 100-, 50-, 25- and 10-dollar gold pieces on a gold chain which hung down the front of his vest and shone with all the allure of pirate's treasure. Needless to say, he never buttoned his coat as these beautifully polished gold pieces were a perfect showman's come-on; they gave him an aura of stability like the Bank of England and the attraction of a jewelry store window. A gold watch and a gold ring with a large diamond on his little finger enhanced his overall image of glamour and money in the bank. He got your attention.

His wife, a dried up prune of a woman who rarely visited the show, managed his laboratory in Waco where they manufactured Tate-Lax, his famous tonic, Tate-O-Rub, an ointment, and Blistol, Jr., a liniment. The medicines were shipped to other medicine shows like my father's, and sold on Dr. Tate's own show all over Texas. They must have worked fairly well because he returned to the same large towns year after year and did a brisk business. I personally never used them.

I was dazzled and not a little daunted when Mother and I first drove up to the lot where his show covered the end of a whole city block. The setup was four huge, bright orange trailers, called "show cars," lined up half a length apart from one another. From one of the middle ones was hung a stage that covered its entire length; an orange canvas hung at the back covered the stage entrance as "wings," and two more pieces of masking canvas stretched out on either side of the stage to cover the space between the show cars. In front of the stage were about 100 reserved seat benches in two sections, with picket fencing surrounding them and a ticket stand at the front. Everything was painted a blaring orange with huge, black block lettering spelling out Dr. N. F. Tate, M.D. and the names of his wares. Fanning out on either side of the stage were the concession stands. There was a charge for the reserved seating, but the people in the cars parked all over the lot watched the show for free.

First in line was Dr. Tate's own show car, with built-in glass enclosed exhibits of artifacts like arrowheads, odd rock formations, enormous mounted Texas longhorns and a huge *brain* and a giant *tapeworm* floating in alcohol in glass jars all along its side that faced the audience. Little signs beside the jars said they were diseased human organs, but probably they came from the stockyard. During the day, thankfully, the exhibits were hidden by a flap that was only raised at night.

The center "stock car" stored boxes of medicine at either end and was backstage for the performers. There were mirrors and make-up tables, costume closets, and benches for us to sit on. We performers entered the stage from behind either side of the hanging canvas wings. Strings of lights outlined both show cars and seats, with double rows around the stage, and ran from the stage out to the concessions, which fanned out on either side of the seats and were themselves spotlighted in lights of various colors.

Most amazing was the show car next to the stage which was a 20-by-30-foot Sequoia tree log hollowed out to make a museum filled with Western artifacts. It seemed incredible to be able to walk right *inside* a tree! Then came the "bally-hoo wagon," a show car with removable sides which, as on the tent show, was used to parade around town with entertainers in costume, instruments in hand, singing loudly and calling to passers-by to come see the show. It was also used as sleeping quarters for the roustabouts and to carry the equipment on the move. The concession stands were for a fortune teller, a hypnotist, games of chance, novelties (balloons, toys, whirligigs, etc), and popcorn and snow cones. At night, when all the lights were lit around the show cars, stage, and concessions, the outfit was a dazzling spectacle indeed. Garish, but dazzling.

Hidden behind the show wagons was a whole little community of house cars. Each was set a bit apart from the other with something a little distinctive like a moveable picket fence, an umbrella with table and chairs, a dog or even a monkey on a chain by its door. It was important that each house car give an indication of its owner's individuality.

I was so grateful to be rescued from the dreaded grandmother that I worked harder than I ever had in my life to improve my act. I had always been billed as "Baby Jo-Carroll" and wore little fluffy white or pink costumes, but I asked the Master of Ceremonies, the wonderful Todd Fields who was top comic, to introduce me as "Miss Jo-Carroll Dennison," and set out to be a grown-up performer.

Mother scurried to make me new costumes befitting the change, and I scurried to find new songs and dance routines. I still sang "Strawberry Roan" on Creampuff, but instead of "Tie Me to Your Apron Strings Again," I worked up "Blue Skies" done in two rhythms, and "Yes Sir, That's My Baby" for my dance number.

I was not what you would call an accomplished tap dancer, but the steps I did were long on "flash." It looked hard, but it wasn't. For my song numbers, Mother made a simple cowgirl costume for my song on Creampuff, a backless, red satin evening gown for my other number, and for my dance costume, a black satin halter top with rhinestones on the collar and short shorts. With a black top hat and cane and my old tap shoes covered in shoe black, I was all set for my Opening Night in the Big Time.

Now, I don't care who you are or where you are, if you are a true performer, the moment just before you enter a stage is a magic one. No matter how often you do it. There is as much tense excitement among the players backstage on a medicine show as there is among famous actors backstage in a Broadway theater in New York just before the curtain goes up.

Our curtain didn't go up; we stepped out from behind it, but the feeling was the same. Of course, technique and polish count for a great deal, but the vibrations that begin to hum in actors before they go on is the creativity that determines how good they are. If they don't have any vibrations, they should be working in a department store!

Medicine shows start with a loud bang. The performers are their own overture, and the object of the Opening is to quiet the audience and warm them up fast. While fiddle, piano, banjo, and guitars were going at top speed, all the performers sang with fiery enthusiasm:

"Hello, everybody, how do you do?
We're going to entertain you for an hour or two,
We'll sing and dance for you and when we're done,
We know that you are going to have a lot of fun," … *and so on.*

Todd, the blackface comic MC, then stepped forward and gave his "hello, folks," a funny, folksy rundown of the evening's entertainment. He introduced us each with proud exaggeration as we stepped forward to take a bow to a resounding chord on the piano. Together we sang an upbeat number like "Dark Town Strutter's Ball," with Todd and Banjo Bob taking a solo chorus on their instruments; then we all sang a final chorus and exited, leaving Todd and Banjo Bob to do the first comedy sketch.

Todd worked in typical "black face" costume: a cloth cap turned sideways, tieless, collarless shirt, overlarge, shapeless pants held up with suspenders, and "slapstick" shoes. Slapstick shoes are specially made extra-long with a thin board in the soles that could be "slapped" on the floor for emphasis — and to stumble over for laughs. Todd's face and body were in constant motion, half zany, half sly little boy; his fluid movements were an energetic accent to his words. (Later in my life I was to know some of the best comedians and comics in the world, but I never thought any of them were as funny as Todd.) Also, now I cringe at the disrespect shown to Blacks by blackface comedy, but at the time, no one I knew thought anything about it. Minstrel shows went back hundreds of years and were the first kind of vaudeville show. Many of the first ones were done by Blacks themselves. But in retrospect, it is clear.

Banjo Bob was a good foil for Todd as they were complete opposites. Banjo Bob, an excellent banjo and accordion musician, worked in a "Toby" makeup and costume: a carrot-top wig under a torn straw hat, loud plaid shirt, oversized pants, and "white face" with big red dots for freckles, heavy eyebrows and large over-painted red mouth. He kept his face and body as completely still and emotionless as possible. Unlike Buster Keaton, who gave the impression of grief or bewilderment behind his blank face, Banjo Bob gave the impression of *nothing* behind his white makeup. His economy of movement and straight face were very funny opposite Todd's mobility.

Other than the specialty acts — contortionist, juggler, magic or dog act — the performers "doubled in brass" in individual musical or song and dance numbers as well as in the comedy sketches and the "Last Act," a short one-act play. The sketches and plays were passed down from generation to generation, and were the same ones that were done from time immemorial in the medicine shows, tent shows, vaudeville and burlesque houses all over the country. Except on a medicine show, the lines and jokes were cleaned up for the family trade.

The member of our troupe who filled me with unaccustomed awe was Lena Rhinehart. She had a voluptuous figure and her hair was such a deep red that it almost looked purple above a face ruined by alcoholism. When she slowly walked out on the stage in her gorgeous beaded gown, she radiated an inner hum that instantly stilled the audience. Abruptly, she'd begin to play "Bugle Call Rag" on her violin with a consuming, passionate violence that should have made the little instrument go up in smoke. It didn't seem possible that the power she poured into her violin could be withstood by a frail material like wood and catgut. Lena was a headliner who had made the big fall from the stage of the Palace Theatre in New York to the stage of Dr. Tate's medicine show because she drank too much. But she made me proud to be in the same profession with her.

Of course, the basic reason for our show was the medicine we sold, and when Dr. Tate walked out center stage for his three lectures in his majestic way, he *sold* the audience. He could have been playing the lead in a melodrama as he walked back and forth on the stage making constant references to the Bible in his sales pitches; he was the epitome of piety and rectitude. For his last lecture, he began in his deep resonant voice, "Good evening, my friends. And you *are* my friends. I stand before you tonight because I want to be *your* friend. I have a beautiful home in Waco where my wife and children are active in their church and schools. But I am a doctor of medicine and I have seen so much suffering around me, so much illness and despair. So as a young doctor, I began to search for a way to *heal* this illness. *Help* those in despair. After many years of diligent scientific experiment in my own laboratory in Waco, I met with success." A pause while he fingered his gold pieces. "I *found* those combinations of ingredients that will help our bodies heal themselves. We are here tonight to give you an opportunity to benefit from the discovery I made of these secret healing ingredients."

He would pick up a big brown bottle and hold it reverently aloft, saying "Tate-Lax is the medicine that will *kill* those poisons. Clean out your system. Allow you to be the healthy individual our God in Heaven wants you to be. If your system is poisoned, your *brain* is poisoned, did you ever think of that? All the blood and corpuscles in your body *circulate* through the brain! Tate-Lax, if used regularly, will tone up your system and leave your brain clean as a whistle."

And so on until he had the whole audience mesmerized. Tate-Lax was his biggest seller. Maybe it was the part about the brain poisoning, or maybe it was because it tasted so terrible, people thought it must be good for them.

At the end of each of Dr. Tate's dramatic pitches to the audience, all the entertainers except Lena worked the audience for sales, running back to the stage for refills yelling, "Sooooold out, Doctor!" We kept up a running patter of encouragement to the audience between us, pretending to compete for the most sales, so that there was no letup of sound until Dr. Tate judged the sales were about over and called us back in saying there was no more time as the show must go on.

Happy the Clown followed Dr. Tate's pitch. He wore dead-white makeup with black inverted "v"s for eyebrows, black outlined eyes and mouth, and a wardrobe of a white pointed cap and loose white shirt and pants. His job as a clown was to get the crowd's mind off pestilence and poisons. He came originally from a circus and made everyone laugh with his inept juggling act or by getting hit over the head with a popper, a loud noise-making stick, when he worked with Todd in a comedy sketch. Happy was an expert at letting air out of a pig's bladder, jumping guiltily at the bleating noise, and looking frantically behind him to see what had made the sound. Bathroom humor. But this is the kind of thing most clowns do to make the audience laugh. Only the great ones can make them cry, too.

Just before the Last Act came the candy pitch. Hung around the performers' necks were large trays of boxes the size of Cracker-Jacks containing five small pieces of taffy and a tiny prize or a numbered slip of paper. They sold for fifty cents and in every twenty-fifth box was a slip to win one of the prizes that now covered the stage. The prizes, called "flash," were a few colorful bedspreads, dolls, shawls, lamps, clocks and many small, colorful cheap items. As if the prizes were also numbered, when presented with a winning number, Dr.

Tate would ostensibly search for a prize to match the number. He gave out a few big prizes early on and then spaced them out to keep sales going.

Since in those days a haircut cost a quarter and a hamburger a dime, the 50-cent boxes of candy were expensive. They cost Dr. Tate about ten cents; and the wholesale prizes not much more, so the candy pitch was highly profitable. I never felt right about it and kept expecting that some customer would catch on and make a fuss, but they never did. Growing up alone, getting most of my information about life from the books I read and the heroes I chose to emulate, my rigid sense of right and wrong was offended by this subterfuge. The code of honor I had gleaned from my reading, which made me feel safe and right with God, also made me an opinionated, intolerant, and judgmental prude.

But officious or no, I didn't have any trouble fitting in with the other entertainers. The slogan, "It takes one to know one" works with show folk. People whose sense of well-being and livelihood depend on applause and laughter are "kin" in a very real way. Everyone else is an outsider to whom they feel slightly superior. They have their own customs, standards, and even language, which makes them part of a specific family whose members connect with one another all over the world. Outsiders were known by such derogatory names as townies, boobs, hicks, yokels or rubes. There are strict divisions between the "star" and the "chorus girl," but it is acknowledged that they are part of the same family. Of course, there is never *enough* applause or laughter for an entertainer, and when eventually it stops, something important dies in his soul. But that kinship among show folk is always with them. There is a comfort level between people in the entertainment business that is never present with anyone else.

Yet, most performers are basically loners. Their intimate relationships are with an audience, not other people. As long as I worked on Dr. Tate's Medicine Show, I was helped and supported by everyone on the show, but I rarely, if ever, visited in their house cars or they in mine. Only if danger from a townie threatened any member of the show did their solidarity show up. You could be sure of an instant, sometimes armed, response of all show folk within earshot to the alarm call of, "Hey, Rube!" That call was an imperative for immediate support on a circus, carnival or any type of show.

It is interesting to think that from the mists of time, daring or restless souls who wanted to make a living without having to work hard for it had learned that if they could make someone laugh or enthrall them with music or magic tricks, they could get something for nothing. By the 12th century, that conniving soul had also found that he could *sell* almost anything to an audience if he was entertaining and fleet of mind. Thus, was born the medicine show. It was that "something for nothing" that caused them to be called charlatans and mountebanks, even to this day. The ancestry of show business has a very long line.

Dr. Tate's large house car, where Mother and I lived, was neatly divided into sections. When first showing us through it, Dr. Tate had said about the first section, "This is my office and bedroom. I always keep my outside door and the hall door locked. I expect you will want to do the same. I need privacy to prepare my lectures, and I keep valuables in my desk so I must be wary of intruders."

Taking us through the hall, he opened a door into a side compartment to reveal a wash basin and a real toilet and some kind of tin contraption. He said, "This is the bathroom and shower which we will share. I trust you don't take too many showers as we only carry 40 gallons of water." We had then followed him into a room that was twice as big as our old house car, with built-ins made of stained wood, long high windows on both sides and pretty upholstered chairs and couch. A fully equipped kitchen with a pull-down table for four was at the end.

Dr. Tate said, "You see the couch there makes into a double bed. I had this built for my two sons when they come to visit, but I don't expect them for some time and then we will make other arrangements. There is a gas stove and water heater, which I'm sure you will use caution in lighting. When you need ice for the icebox, tell one of the roustabouts and he will get it for you. I prefer simple meals, but I like to have them served punctually. I hope you will be comfortable here." Bending his head down to go through the door, he went down the hall and we could hear him locking the door at his end.

This big man with his even bigger personality left me limp. He seemed so much bigger inside the house car. But his business-like attitude and rules and regulations were a relief as we could follow them without trouble. Since I had never had a shower anyway, it was no great deprivation for me not to take one often. Mother knew how to light a gas stove and a water heater shouldn't be too much different. I wasn't too sure what "simple fare" meant, but once he tasted Mother's pies, I knew he would think she was a good cook. I was intensely grateful for this nice place to live.

It was a very satisfying sensation to be handed a weekly paycheck for the first time in my life, and all was right with my world for about a year; my act was a success with the audience, and when I did my number with Creampuff, we were a smash. As I turned 12, I started to walk differently. Taller, with a "Hey, look me over," swagger. As I walked out through the audience, murmuring "Excuse me. Excuse me, please," I distinctly felt I was better than the crowd. I was confident that I was more *special* than the average person. My boyish figure began to develop and Todd, always clowning, said, "Why look there, Baby Jo, a bee has stung you right on the chest. Why, it stung you twice," as he tapped me lightly on each side of my chest. I pretended to be insulted, but actually I was kind of proud of the change. I began to sing more sophisticated songs like "I've Got a Feeling You're Foolin'" and "I Can't Give You Anything But Love, Baby."

I was growing up.

The Loss of Innocence

But then one night everything changed drastically. The show was "dark" on Sundays, and one Sunday Mother went to a nearby town to visit some relatives. Since my mother was one of 14 children, and most of her brothers and sisters quite prolific in the progeny department, we had lots of relatives. Being an only child, I didn't have the family feeling that Mother did, and it never bothered me that none of her relatives ever visited us in Dr. Tate's house car, but Mother always kept in touch and went to see any relative we might be working close to. Although Mother was quite musical, she was more comfortable on a farm than on a stage and was like a different species altogether from the other people on the show. She didn't have anything to do except cook for Dr. Tate. Perhaps she was lonely.

It was very disturbing to me when she had not returned by nightfall, and even more so when it got to be midnight and still no Mother. When I was getting ready for bed, Dr. Tate opened his door and called to me from down the hall, "I know you are worried about your mother, but she has probably just been delayed for some reason, had a flat tire or something. I'll leave the doors open between our rooms until your mother gets back so you'll know I'm right here."

Lying there in the dark, waiting to hear the sound of her car pulling up, I was all tense with anxiety. At 12, I liked to think that I was very independent and didn't ever pay much attention to what my mother said about anything; still, having something bad happen to her was intolerable. I remembered a time when my half-brother Joe had said something to her that made her cry, and I flew at him in a rage and told him if he ever hurt my mother again I would tell my father on him! I replayed that scene over in my mind and told him off again in even worse terms to try to make myself feel better because I'd defended her, but it didn't help. I still kept thinking of times I had hurt her myself and my anxiety kept getting worse.

It was well after midnight when Dr. Tate called to me, "Jo-Carroll, are you awake?'

"Yes."

"Come in here to my room for a moment."

It was a very unusual request from Dr. Tate; he rarely allowed people in his office, but I was used to obeying him, so I got up in my pajamas and went down the long hall to his bedroom.

I could see from the light he kept burning outside his front door as a safeguard that he was in bed holding up the covers. He said, "Come get in bed with me or you'll get cold standing out there. I want to talk to you."

I hesitated because I had never been in bed next to a man; even with my father; my mother was always in the bed between us and it seemed so strange to me that he would even suggest it. But I couldn't think of a good excuse to refuse, so I crawled into his bed and turned my back to him, keeping so far over to the side that I was almost falling out.

He said, "Now, Jo-Carroll, you mustn't worry about your mother. She might have gotten away late and decided to spend the night with your relatives and has no way to let you know. But you don't have to be afraid of being alone because I'm here with you." He put his arm around me and I realized with a stunning shock that he wasn't wearing pajamas; he was in his *underwear*! "You have become like a daughter to me this year you've been on my show. I feel like I was meant to take your dead father's place. I want you to love me just like your father." He slid his other arm under me and I could smell his body odor. It wasn't a bad odor, but a kind of sweetish, musky smell that began to make me feel a little sick.

Close to my ear, he said, "You are very dear to me, did you know that? I wouldn't let anything hurt you. I'm going to take care of you from now on." He held me tighter against him and his voice became hoarse as he was saying these things and I could feel his hot breath on my neck as it got faster and hotter, until his mouth was touching my cheek.

Suddenly I was terrified and tried to jerk away, but he grasped me harder and said, "No! No, don't be afraid of Dr. Tate. He loves you. See, he loves you." He put one arm around my breasts and the other between my legs, rubbing his arm over my breasts until it hurt and jerked me between the legs hard up against him – making harsh, gasping sounds as he grabbed and fumbled at me in short, rhythmic jerks.

Panic crashed over me and I felt as though I was drowning, unable to get my head up or breathe underwater, I said, "Let me go! I want to go back to my room now." With all my strength I struggled to get away from him, yelling, "Let me go!" The more I fought him the tighter he held me, and his breath was coming in groans like he was in pain as he locked his legs around me in a scissor hold.

Hysterically I screamed at him, "*Don't! Stop!* Leave me *alone!* Suddenly I felt against my buttocks a convulsive movement from between his legs. I was paralyzed with shock at this inexplicable *movement* as it became a hard pushing object against my bottom. A horrible image flashed before my eyes and I thought, "Oh, the Lord help me, it's his long black *thing!*" I could see little Fuzzy being impaled by that big dog's thing, hear her shrieking, and my whole insides convulsed at the thought of Dr. Tate's long black thing pumping violently up inside me like a red-hot poker.

He clasped me even tighter and began to rhythmically jerk me into his thing with his hand between my legs. He continued to make his deep terrifying sounds, "Ahhh — ahhh — ughhh — ughhh" into my ear as though he was about to have a fit right there and then. As his grunts rose to a rapid crescendo, he started to claw at my pajama bottoms and try to turn me around to him at the same time. He blurted hoarsely, "Turn around to me. Don't be afraid. Don't be afraid. I won't hurt you." As he released his scissor hold on my legs to turn me to him, I screamed, "No. *Nooooh!*" and yanked myself away from him and up onto my feet in one movement. I ran down the hall, sliding the bolt on both doors behind me with fingers that seemed made of boiled noodles, and sat gasping on my bed.

I couldn't stop shaking or think what to do as I listened desperately for the sound of him coming down the hall. I knew that those flimsy locks would not hold if he was determined to get in after me. I was in a frenzy of indecision: Should I quick get dressed and get out of the house car? Should I run over to one of the other house cars and ask for help? What would I tell them? Would they believe me? He was their *boss!*

In the back of my mind was my mother's reaction a few years ago to my going under the building with that little boy who showed me his thing and asked to see mine. In a fury, she had blamed *me*. She had behaved as though *I* had done something terrible. In a way I couldn't understand, I felt I was somehow to blame for what had happened — then and now — and *dirty* and *sinful* because of it. I kept replaying the whole thing over in my mind: dark, grotesque images chased themselves around in ugly circles like a merry-go-round from hell.

Shame, blame, and horror were one with astonishment as I tried to sort out my emotions. Astonishment was the overall emotion as I tried to understand that *Dr. Tate* — a married man with two sons, a deacon of his church, the authority figure in my life and someone in whom I'd had total trust — would do such a thing. How could he tell me that he loved me like a daughter at the same time he was trying to do that terrible thing to me? It made no sense at all that this upright, self-proclaimed honorable man could turn into a rapacious grizzly bear in an instant. And yet it had happened.

Sitting there on the bed, suffocating with fear and indecision, too afraid to cry, my relief was truly like a reprieve from heaven when I heard Mother's car drive up behind the house car. I wanted to rush out and ask her to hold me and take care of me. Protect me. But then my pride turned relief into anger. Quickly, I was able to shift all blame to her. I thought, "If she hadn't been late none of this would have happened. It's all her fault!" Then the anger turned to exhaustion and I felt like I didn't have the energy to even tell her about it right now, so I got in bed and pulled the covers way up and pretended to be asleep when she came tiptoeing in.

But when I awoke the next morning and thought about what had happened, I couldn't wait to tell her so she could take over and decide what to do about it. I hurried over to her at the sink and whispered, "Mother, last night when you didn't come home, Dr. Tate called me in his room and made me get in bed with him. And then he started trying to push his thing in me and I had to fight him to get away."

I knew Mother had never stood up to my father, but this was different. I thought that when she knew what Dr. Tate had tried to do to me, she would pour the righteous wrath of God upon him. I waited breathlessly for her reaction, I waited for her to take *charge* and rectify this horrible wrong. But without turning to me she kind of hunched up and held a dishcloth up between her eyes as she said softly, "I'm so sorry I was delayed, Josie. My car broke down and I had a dickens of a time finding a garage. I'm so sorry ... but ... well, you're all right now. Just don't think about it anymore."

Scalded with anger and bewilderment, I whirled away from her, hurriedly got dressed and without saying another word went out to Creampuff. I got a bridle on her and put her into a run. Nothing made me feel more in control than a wild bareback ride. When we were both run down, I found a big live oak on a vacant lot and got off to sit under it. While Creampuff cropped what little grass there was around it, I sat with my back pressed into the rough old trunk and took stock of my situation.

I had wanted Mother to make things right — make *life* right – I wanted her to do a grown-up thing and create justice out of evil. Create clarity out of confusion. But she couldn't do that. She knew how to kiss a skinned knee and make it better, but she didn't know how to make this better. "Mothers are supposed to *protect* their children," I thought angrily. But it was clear that in this case Mother was not going to protect me and I was on my own. There was no one to guard my back. I would have to take care of myself and make my own decisions.

The choices all looked bad. Should I just quit, leave Creampuff on Uncle Lowe's ranch, and go back to the hateful Grandma's, if she would take us? Or stay on the show with the threat of Dr. Tate?

"Don't think about it," Mother said. "How am I going to *not* think about it, tell me that if you please? How can I think about anything else?" I told myself.

As the effects of the ride began to wear off, I fell victim to that same sense of little-girl-lost feeling I'd had when my father ran off. Sitting there, thinking about what Dr. Tate had done made the earth seem unsteady underneath me. I kept feeling that *movement* from between his legs. I had a blinding, desperate need for someone *else* to take over the responsibility for my future action. I wanted someone who was trustworthy and capable to magically materialize and take care of me. But soon I doused that lovely thought with the icy cold water of reality. That wasn't going to happen. The only one here to help me was me. I had to figure out my own way for myself. My stomach gave a sickening lurch as I peered into the abyss of self-doubt and fear that was always just beneath me.

So, prayerfully, I called out to God and all my fictional heroes, King Arthur, Lassie, Zorro, Tarzan, those that I had identified with over the years to come help me be brave and strong. What would *they* do? They had all fought successfully for justice, for right against wrong. In my imagination, all my life I had prevailed over peril right alongside the powerful and fearless characters I'd read about in books. Now I had to take courage from those heroes and follow their example of self-reliance, but this time for real. Of course, most of my fictional heroes were men, but I knew I could learn to be as tough as a man any day. I was tougher than the boys I knew! But the voice that rang the loudest in my ears was my father's saying, "Let her go, Carroll. She knows how to take care of herself." I could — and I would.

When you get right down to basics, they become very few. Mother would do whatever I said so it was up to me to make a choice: go back to Grandma's and endure that humiliation and have to leave Creampuff with Uncle Lowe — or stay on the show and somehow fend off Dr. Tate. The most important basic was that I needed my $20 a week in order to live. And keep Creampuff. The next most important basic was that Dr. Tate was no more the honorable man I'd thought he was than my father had been.

Anger was my Excalibur sword in my fight for justice and against pain and fear. It wasn't *fair* that my father had abandoned me for that blonde 18-year-old girl. It wasn't *fair* that Grandma made little Fuzzy stay out in that awful shed and die alone. It wasn't *fair* that Dr. Tate would try to rape a 12-year-old girl who was in his care. It wasn't *fair* that I had no one to protect me. But fair or not fair, I was going to have to defend myself, and the only defensive weapon I had against injustice, and the paralyzing fear of the hurt I experienced with my father, Grandma, and Dr. Tate, was anger. Thinking of how unfair it all was recreated the anger and resolve with which I had sustained myself when I was seven, and I thought, "I was stronger than my father then, and I can be stronger than Dr. Tate now. I will just hold him off with hate like I did my father." And I felt better.

Watching Creampuff snuffling at the dry grass around the tree, I loved her every hair, every muscle in her body; the miraculous wonder of her made me swell with pride and determination, and I said to her, "You are the most important thing in the world to me and I can take anything to keep you with me. That's all. I can handle that rotten old man if I have to. But I will *never* let a man do that horrible thing to me again. And I'm not going to *cry* about it either!"

I pressed myself hard against the tree trunk until I could literally *feel* its strength and the strength of my heroes flooding into me. I knew that God helps those who help themselves, so I reached out for my faith in God's protection, as I said aloud to Creampuff, "I can take care of myself and I will just *do* it! I'm not going to be afraid." Resolution overcame fear and I began to feel powerful and capable. I pulled on Creampuff's reins until she ambled over to me, and I said, "Listen, you are *my* horse and don't you forget it. Give me a kiss."

She raised her head and looked far away as though she was seeing something vitally interesting in the distance.

I grabbed her bridle and forced her head close to my face, "Come on now, give me a kiss. Come on!"

With a snort of resignation, she leaned down and flipped her soft lip a few times against my cheek, then looked quickly away as though she didn't really mean it. But I laughed and felt somehow victorious and capable.

I couldn't understand at the time that Mother had been trained by experts from birth not to *fight* but to *accept*. She'd read the Bible instead of Zane Grey. In her 50s, she was a physically strong, beautiful woman, and I know she would have fought a tiger with her bare hands to protect me from physical harm; however I had not been attacked by a tiger, I had been attacked by a man, and she had never had the nerve to fight a *man*. Her father had early taught her the value of submission to men with his ever-ready belt. She had taken my father back without a word when he returned because she was dependent on him and had nowhere else to go. Now, she thought we were dependent on Dr. Tate, so we must just accept his behavior. She couldn't teach me by example how to fight, only to endure. She never had a red hat of her own. Her father had never told her she was special and that there was nothing she couldn't do.

As for me, the loss of innocence and trust was a greater loss than I understood at the time, but I used it as a spine-stiffener. I began to put my mother's example of endurance to good use. For the next five years my relationship with Dr. Tate became one of unwilling compromise: I didn't leave the show and he didn't try to rape me. In my own mind, I maintained my independence by an attitude toward him of never giving an inch. Incredibly, after that horrendous night he behaved as though nothing at all had happened, but from then on it became a constant battle of wills between us: his will to embrace me and my will to push him away. We played a game of hide and seek. He was always *touching* me. Not in ways that I could take exception to, as I managed never to be alone with him, but his hands seemed to be constantly touching my head or shoulder or arm in a public show of paternal affection. He began to pull me down on his lap when he came in for meals and say to Mother, "Carroll, what are we going to do with our girl? She is getting so big she will soon be taller than you are. I think you are feeding her too much," and he would chuckle.

Mother kind of disappeared when he talked to her like that, while I sat totally rigid and deliberately sent out hatred to him from every pore. But to be held close to him, to *smell* him, was a heavy price to pay for financial freedom. Having to endure his touch defiled my sense of self. The need to be constantly taut and vigilant against the touch of a human hand was destructive not only of innocence, but of the ability to give and receive love and warmth as well. Dr. Tate's penis had not penetrated my body – but it had penetrated my mind irrevocably. The lasting residue of his sexual assault remained a loathsome burden that I learned to be strong enough to bear – but not strong enough to eliminate.

When the show was closing for its winter hiatus, Dr. Tate said, "Carroll, I'm letting the Abbotts go, and next year you can have the popcorn and snow cone concession. Also, I've decided to give my girl here the candy concession which will enable her to make good money. She deserves it." I knew it was a bribe, but I could use the extra money for some future need, and Mother was delighted to have something to do.

Dr. Tate asked us to stay in his house car and winter in Waco, but I had decided to go back to Grandma's and go to high school for awhile. I had saved enough money to buy a lot of new clothes and a brand new, navy blue Chevy coupe, so I thought I would really make the Hale Center kids' eyes pop out. I hated to leave Creampuff at Uncle Lowe's again, but I needed a break from the high-wire tension of Dr. Tate and thought it was time I went to school a little.

It galled Mother to have to ask Grandma if we could come back for a few months, but she was between a rock and a hard place, as they say. I guess blood was thicker than water for Grandma, because she agreed. Maybe she just wanted to have me to torment again. She and the house looked and smelled the same, but while not glad to see *me*, Grandma was glad to see the food my money put on the table. For someone who was so cantankerous about the virtues of corn bread and molasses, she dug in amazingly fast to the chicken and chicken-fried steak Mother put on the table. We fashioned a kind of armed truce and got along fairly well by just ignoring each other.

Mother and I both loved bright colors like red and yellow and purple, and the new clothes I had bought were all in those colors, and styled for the flashy type of young woman I considered myself. I thought I looked terrific in them and very grown up. I certainly did look *different* in my crepe and satin from the other girls in their cotton and wool.

I found, though, that high school wasn't all that much fun. As always, the principal and the teachers didn't know what to do with me. By age, I was a freshman in high school and could read and write as well as the teachers, but apart from making change for a dollar, division and long division could have been Arabic for all the sense I could make of them. Forget about algebra! They decided to let me take two classes of home economics (a joke in itself as I could not boil water) instead of math and science, and let me hang out in band a lot. I learned how to play the clarinet and was chosen Drum Major, and became great friends with the music teacher. I enjoyed history classes, and having read so much I had absorbed grammar and spelling by osmosis so English was a snap, but the rest of the curriculum held no interest for me at all and I just couldn't put my mind to it. The teachers gave up trying. In other words, they did what teachers do now: they passed me on.

First Love

Blackie Sherrod: 1942.

By the end of the school year, my money had run out so Mother and I were ready to go back on the show. I thought that maybe the separation would have brought about a change in Dr. Tate's behavior, and soon found out that it had. He had become like a man obsessed and literally insanely jealous and possessive. If he saw a boy speak to me when I was out in the audience selling medicine, he would come down off the stage and go at that boy with a rage that was sickening. After the show, I could hear Dr. Tate pacing in his room and the atmosphere became charged with a familiar tension. I would sit at the table while both Mother and I waited for the explosion that was sure to come. Soon he would burst in without knocking and yell, "What did you think you were doing with that boy? You can't wait until it gets dark so you can go out front and get next to some boy, can you?

You just have to do it, don't you? Don't you!" He towered over me, his massive fists clenched white. "*Look* at me when I'm talking to you."

When I looked up at him I saw his insane desire to destroy my independence, to control me completely with the fear of him. I would stare venomously back at him, but I knew his eyes weren't seeing me. They were seeing some explicit sex act between me and somebody who wasn't him. His breath whistled through his nose as his chest swelled up and down with his thoughts. "What did you want him to do to you? Put his hand up your dress? Hummm? Is that what you want? You want him to rub up against you and put his hand up your dress? Well, I won't stand for anything like that on my show. Do you understand? I won't have it!"

When he had reached his climax of rage, he would go to bed. Mother and I silently did the same. But each of his hugs or his tirades strengthened the wall of resistance and hatred I felt for him. The wall my father had started between me and love and trust grew taller and stronger every day.

For a reason I've forgotten, many years later, my mother said to me wistfully, "You were such a sweet little girl." I don't remember much about ever being sweet, but if sweetness there had been — then Dr. Tate surely killed it. Each time he raged at me, I closed myself off to intimacy and caring a little bit more.

And that was my situation at 17 when the show played in Texas. I was delighted to see my friend Janelle Temple who was attending college there. We met at the local drugstore and caught up on the girl talk that I had been missing since leaving Hale Center. While talking, a man came by and, apropos of nothing, asked my friend to introduce us.

He had expressive, dark brown eyes, smooth olive skin, a clearly defined mouth, and a square chin with a deep dimple. He wore a snappy chocolate-brown pinstripe suit and vest, and a brown snap-brim hat, which he suddenly remembered and took off. He searched my face as though it was terribly important to remember where he'd seen it.

We met every afternoon for the next 10 days. I had never known anyone remotely like him. The boys I had known before were, well — boys. He was a young man. There was no period of adjustment; from the moment I sat down opposite him in the booth, words poured out of the two of us as though we had a lifetime to catch up on. He seemed to know me better than I knew myself; he took my inarticulate feelings about nature and things of the spirit and put them into words which expressed what I felt, but hadn't known how to say. And he laughed at my conceit and arrogance like Todd did. Blackie had a deep, spontaneous laugh that made me tingle every time I heard it. Even when it was at some self-important dumb thing I said. I felt like Fritz, I wanted to do tricks to make him laugh some more. It was so marvelous to me that he thought I was funny.

And he made *me* laugh. He had a naturally funny way of looking at things, unexpected descriptive phrases. His black, curly hair was combed smooth when first we'd meet, but as he shook his head with excitement or laughter, little black curls popped down over his forehead. His name was Forrest, but everyone called him Blackie. I loved his husky voice which was like his laugh, and the way he thought about things. He was going to be a newspaperman, and then a famous writer. And he was very, very romantic; he held my hands right up on the table where anyone could see. He was so relaxed and self-confident, not full of nervous tension the way I was; he looked directly at my face as though he wanted to memorize it. I rationed direct contact with his eyes, looking more often at his hands holding mine. They were a smooth olive like his face with long tapering fingers ending in square well-kept nails. His hands felt warm and strong.

After we'd talked for what seemed days, he pulled my hand closer to him and said, "Jo-Carroll, I'm beginning to fall in love with you." I looked at him in amazement at such grown-up words. "Do you know you have brown speckles in your eyes like a trout?"

I did know it, but no one else ever seemed to, and the way he said it made me feel like my bones were dissolving. "Jo-Carroll, I am fascinated by your face, it never stays the same for more than a minute at a time. First it's suspicious, then gay, enthusiastic, then sad. I want to see your face every day for the rest of my life, but I want to make it always gay and loving."

And then he sang the words to "All My Life," an Artie Shaw record that was playing on the jukebox. In that deep voice.

I don't know what I said to him, my heart was acting so crazy I couldn't hear what I was saying. I blathered on about the story of my life, too excited to try to put what I felt about the present into words. This had happened so fast that I never had time to gather my forces and challenge him the way I always had with other boys. Before I could get my defenses up — they were down. We were in love; we vowed to marry. But any potential intimacy was vexed by earlier traumas.

Shortly after we had moved on from that town, and from Blackie, I decided to express my independence by making a date to go to the movies one Sunday night when the show was dark with a pleasant townie I had met in a drugstore. I wanted to test the water, so to speak. Mother got seriously faint when I told her I was going out on a date, but she couldn't stop me.

Admittedly, I was nervous about it inside, but outwardly I was supremely defiant about the whole thing, until after the movies as the boy and I were approaching the house car in the dark — the blast of a gunshot split the night.

I said to the boy, "Go home," and he vanished. I knew that Dr. Tate had a loaded revolver in his desk drawer, and I knew that he was furious that I would go on a date, but I never imagined that he would take a shot at me. I didn't think he had been trying to kill us, but rather to scare me to prove his point. Nonetheless, an all-consuming rage filled my whole body at the enormity of what he had done.

Mother came flying out of the house car screaming, "Oh, my baby, my baby! Are you hurt? Oh, I knew something like this would happen! Are you all right?"

I pushed her away as I said, "I'm all right. I'm not hurt. Stop crying," and walked on up to the house car.

Dr. Tate was leaning against the wall sobbing, the gun hanging limp in his hand. Coming quite close to him, my heart pounding so hard it shook my chest, I raged at him, "You filthy, dirty old man. You are a sick old man and I hate you. I have *always* hated you, did you know that? I am 17 and you don't *own* me, and I'm not going to let you tell me what to do anymore. *How dare you take a shot at me!* You are *crazy!*"

Still sobbing, he said, "Oh, my own little girl. Don't say things like that to Dr. Tate who loves you. I'm sorry, I'm so sorry. I don't know what came over me. I'll never do it again. It's just because I love you so much that I did such a terrible thing. Please forgive your silly old Dr. Tate. I promise you, I'll never do it again," and he tried to embrace me.

I jumped back and screamed, *"Get away from me. Don't you dare touch me ever again,"* and I went on into the house car.

As always, when I was in deep trouble I reached out to God for help and guidance. Lying in bed after Mother was asleep I said, "Help me, God. Please tell me what to do. I have to get away from this show and Dr. Tate. Blackie is just getting started in the Navy and I don't want to be in show business anymore. What else can I do? I know I ask a lot of you, but I'll never ask for anything else, if you will just please help me know how to get away."

By morning, I knew what to do. Before anyone else was awake, I got up and went down to the railway station to use the public phone to call one of Mother's sisters who lived in Tyler, Texas, and asked her if I could come and live with her while I went to business school. I knew that her daughter had just married and moved away and I couldn't wait for Blackie to come on his white horse; I had to jump out of the ivory tower by myself. But knowing him had given me the power, and the gunshot had given me the impetus to get away from Dr. Tate. In answer to my desperate plea, my Aunt Lou really had no choice but to agree to my coming to stay with her so I could learn to be a secretary (whatever *that* was).

When I got back to the house car, Dr. Tate was slumped over a cup of coffee at the kitchen table. As soon as he saw me he jumped up and stretched out both hands, "Josie, my little girl. Forgive me. Forgive your crazy old Dr. Tate."

I said to Mother, "I called Aunt Minnie Lou and she says I can come live with her and go to business school. Help me to get packed, I'm leaving on the 10-o'clock train."

Dr. Tate dropped to his knees and began to hit himself on the forehead with his clenched fists. "Don't leave me. Don't leave me, Josie. I'll do anything for you if you, just don't leave me."

I started emptying drawers, and said to Mother, "I'm going to pack everything I want to keep. I'm never coming back."

Dr. Tate inched toward me on his knees, saying, "I'll kill myself if you leave me. I swear to God I'll kill myself."

With relish I threw all my costumes, evening gowns, and tap shoes in a big pile. I told Mother, "Give all this stuff away; I'm never going to wear them again." I handed a small collection of my plainest clothes to Mother, and said, "Just pack these." While Mother went to get a cardboard box to put them in, I went through my top drawer. It was full of keepsakes, stage jewelry, makeup, and odds and ends for the stage. With a silent vow to never wear anything like it again, I took out only Blackie's picture and a box containing photos of Creampuff and my other animals and slammed the drawer shut.

Dr. Tate had gotten up and begun to pace. He said in a calm voice, "Josie, if you don't want to work on the show anymore, I'll close it down. We'll go to Waco and you can go to business school there, if that's what you want. His voice got higher, nervous little giggles every now and then as Mother and I packed the box and tied it up. He said, "And another thing. You are almost old enough to get married. You should marry some nice, clean boy. My son, Norman, would be just the right one. You like Norman. If you will marry Norman I will give you $20,000 in your own name." He tried to get in front of me. "Josie? Do you understand me? You and your mother would never have to work again if you didn't want to."

Pushing past him, I said to Mother, "Come on, I'm ready," and without a word she followed me out the door. As we walked across the lot, I said, "Norman. Marry Norman! Dr. Tate really is crazy. I knew he was, but I never thought he would be so crazy as to think I would marry *Norman!* Not for all the money in the world."

The only one I wanted to say goodbye to was Todd and I knocked on his door and waited until he poked his sleepy head out after a bit. Of course, everyone on the lot had heard the shot last night, but being show folk, they hadn't come to investigate. I was sure, however, Todd knew exactly what had happened as I said, "Todd, I'm leaving. I'm going to go live with an aunt and go to business school to be a secretary."

He came out, buttoning his pants over his underwear, and took my face in his hands. "What am I going to do without my favorite talking woman? We'll have to hire five new girls to replace you."

Todd's wife, Dorothy, came out in her rumpled robe, and I told her, "I'm leaving for good. Tell everyone goodbye for me, I don't want to wake them up."

Surprisingly, she teared up and wiped her eyes after she gave me a kiss on the forehead, and said, "Take care of yourself, Jo-Carroll. We'll miss you."

Todd gave me a long, hard hug and whispered in my ear, "Go get 'em, Baby Jo."

I looked for a long time into his grinning face, every line and wrinkle dear to me. I said, "I will, Todd. I will."

Mother and I had a long wait at the station and not much to say to each other. What was there to say? I was thinking, "How could I have been afraid of Dr. Tate all these years? He's nothing but a weak, pitiful bully who can only frighten those who are afraid of him. If he had to resort to shooting a gun over someone to make them do what he wanted and then cry and carry on like that, then clearly he was all bluff. He lived in a world of make-believe just like everyone else on the show and I had not been clever enough to see the real man beneath the costume." I had to laugh when I remembered that recently I had accidentally found out that his medical degree he bragged about so much really only granted him a D.V.M. instead of an M.D. after his name. I had run into someone who had gone to veterinary school with him and learned that the medicine he was legally qualified to make and dispense was for *horses!* He was legally a *vet*. No wonder his liniment nearly took your skin off. Boy, what a fraud.

Finally I said to Mother, "You can keep my Chevy coupe. I don't think I'll need it in Tyler. If I do, I'll let you know."

Mother sat there trying not to cry, pleating her skirt into long strips. She said, "Give my love to Min." More long strips, "Don't forget to write to me, Josie. It would mean a lot if you would write to me." Putting her hand tentatively on my thigh, she said, "Do you have enough money, honey?

"Yes."

It was ironic that most of the money buying my ticket to freedom had come to me from the candy concession given me by Dr. Tate to bind me to him. I had more than $500 saved which would pay my way to Aunt Minnie's and see me through business school. Mother was making more money on the popcorn and snow cone stand than she ever had before, too, so she would be all right.

When the train pulled in, Mother hugged me tightly and said, "I love you, Josie. I will pray for you every night. Here's something a little extra." She pressed $25 into my hand. "I'll send you some more when I can," and she was still waving after me as the train pulled out.

In my imagination, my little red hat was firmly in place as the train took me out of the past and into the future. I tried to imagine what that future would be. I didn't know what business school was going to teach me. Surely, it was not going to be anything I wanted to learn. But it was a respite. A place for me to go to rest up and let my guardian angel bring my future to me. I knew one thing, though, I was finished with show business. I had learned my lesson about the glory of being "different' and a "star." I was leaving my past on the stage behind forever. In my future, I didn't want to be different anymore.

My guardian angel must have smiled affectionately at that childish thought. She knew that before the year was out, my future held an adventure for me that was far, far beyond my wildest dreams.

Born Again: Tyler, Texas

Back in Tyler, TX, following Miss America pageant.

Tyler, population 25,000, was known throughout Texas as "The City of Roses." My first impression was that it was like the Emerald City right out of the *Wizard of Oz*. The myriad shades of green everywhere made it a beneficent, welcoming oasis compared to the vast expanses of sandy, monotonous West Texas where I had been living. Everywhere you looked, there were glorious old trees, broad sweeps of lawn, and bushes of every description. The scattered brilliance of the flowers, mainly roses, only deepened the green. The biggest oil men of East Texas built their stately homes here out of sight of those giant praying mantis scaffolds whose tireless arms pumped seemingly endless gallons of oil, and whose eternal flames of unwanted natural gas burned brightly in the night. Some of the largest oil fields in the country surrounded the green oasis of Tyler. I thought it was the most beautiful place I had ever seen.

I can see now that I had lived in a fantasy world for much of my life. My only clear goal was simple — *it was to be really and truly happy as I had been as a child.* One could laugh a little at the immensity of that simple goal, but the joyous happiness I'd felt working with my father on the stage — the secure elation of being alone in a friendly, tall tree somewhere — the wild exultation of riding my horse flat out — these feelings were captured for me in my memory as securely and vividly as a flower in a glass ball. I was confident that I could find that pure happiness again with dedicated effort, and I constantly searched for a situation that would repeat it. Until then, I was caught in a limbo of waiting, and creating fantasies about where that bluebird of happiness might be perched. In that child-like search, I longingly pictured the situations which would make me happy again. Growing up on Dr. Tate's medicine show, I had dreamed of living in a big white house on a hill with a father who worked in a bank and a mother who was president of the PTA. They took care of me, made decisions for me, and I went on dates and to proms. I had Cokes in the drugstore with a best friend while she and I listened to the jukebox. I wore white sweater sets instead of red satin evening gowns and saddle shoes instead of high heels. Living in Tyler after I quit the show, all that became available to me. But I found it didn't make me happy after all.

Living with Aunt Lou was instant middle-class. Hers was a pleasant, red-brick house set amidst carefully manicured lawns. There was a separate dining room where they ate salmon patties on Friday night and roast chicken on Sundays, and there were handmade, starched lace doilies on the overstuffed chairs and sofa, and highly polished tables in the living room. I had a neat, pretty bedroom all to myself. I never felt it was mine, though, for as long as I stayed there it seemed to be holding its breath until its owner, the daughter who had gotten married, came back. The whole house and its inhabitants were quiet like an indrawn breath. Aunt Lou's big, dark eyes were loving, but vaguely apprehensive; her square, soft, pretty face had a constant, placating smile. She knew not what to do with me, she wanted to feel like a mother to me but that wasn't possible. I didn't want a mother, I just wanted a place to stay. Her husband had dropped dead of a heart attack some years previously, and Aunt Lou was doing her best to raise her two sons to be upstanding, good men like he was. Wayne, her 19-year-old, was extraordinarily handsome and reserved, like a French aristocrat who survived the Revolution and had to go to work for a living. He took his position as head of this fatherless household quite seriously, worked at an insurance company, was engaged to a girl from a good family, and intended to make something of himself. Gale, the 14-year-old, was blonde with a cowlick, had a wide freckled grin, a sweet mischievous nature, and was terribly in awe of his older brother. We each made our adjustments to one another, or glossed over those we couldn't make, and it was a peaceful house to live in.

Eager to propitiate the gods of chance, I hurried to enroll at Federal Institute. I paid my tuition and got my schedule of classes with nary a concern about what it was I would have to learn in order to be a "well-qualified executive secretary" as promised in its brochure. It was with a slight feeling of dismay that I glanced through the totally incomprehensible books on typing, shorthand, and bookkeeping with which I was presented on the first day. I was less equipped to master them than I had been at six to be a circus bareback rider. At least then I had *seen* a horse before. These crazily placed letters on the typewriter keyboard didn't even go in alphabetical order, and the ridiculous squiggles somehow supposed to represent shorthand words made no sense at all. However, I had fingers and I could read so it seemed to me that with dedicated practice I could learn to type, and if I could memorize a whole script in a day, there shouldn't be any reason why I couldn't transform those squiggles into beautifully spaced business letters as it showed in the book. Bookkeeping, on the other hand, clearly required more knowledge of arithmetic than making change for a dollar, so I decided I would just skip that part of the course. As it turned out, taking down shorthand was not too hard, but when I tried to transcribe it, I found the words had magically turned into incomprehensible hieroglyphics. After awhile, I achieved speed with typing, not accuracy, just speed. But I kept flailing away, feeling virtuous if not proficient. Destiny stepped in after about four months as a reward for my perseverance.

One day, a man intercepted me as I was passing a bank on my way to school and said, "I am Mr. Johnson, vice president of the Citizen's National Bank. We at the bank have noticed you walking by and we would like to ask you to represent us in the Miss Tyler Contest to be held at our new community center next month."

"In the what?"

"In our Miss Tyler Contest. Haven't you heard about the opening celebration of Tyler's new Municipal Community Center the Junior Chamber of Commerce is putting on?"

"No, sir." (Nice girls in Texas always said "sir" and "ma'am" to anyone the least bit older than they were Aunt Lou had told me.)

"Girls from some of the finest families in Tyler will be participating as representatives of our local business concerns. The judges, like Senator Earle B. Mayfield, are some of our most outstanding citizens. It will be a very big event in Tyler and we would be proud to have you represent us as Miss Citizen's National Bank."

Clearly this was to be an event in front of the public and therefore something I was not about to be involved in ever again, so I said, "Gee, Mr. Johnson, I sure do appreciate your asking me, but I couldn't do that."

"Oh, don't say no. It is going to be quite a family affair, nothing tawdry or cheap about it. And we are asking our representative to pick out any bathing suit at Swartz's Department Store at our expense. Please say you'll reconsider."

Now, I hadn't had a bathing suit since I was a child, I used to love to swim, Swartz's was a very high class store — so — putting scruples aside, I was *sold* for the price of one bathing suit!

The other girls I competed against for Miss Tyler were really pretty and, never mind that I had sworn never to perform in front of the public again, my competitive juices kicked in and I strode out around that swimming pool in my new black and white bathing suit with an attitude to kill. My father had taught me early the power of "stage presence," he taught me to always walk on a stage as if it and the audience *belonged* to you, and it was by now instinctive. Plus, it was my self-pride that had gotten me out of the deep holes into which I'd fallen in the past, and now that self pride was not about to let those other girls beat me, I had to come out tops on the applause meter. So — Miss Tyler.

And had I but known it, the first step on the road to Atlantic City.

Me as Miss Tyler.

A few days after the contest, Mr. Collins, the owner of Federal Institute, called me into his office. He said, "Miss Dennison, Senator Earle B. Mayfield has called me and says that he wants to hire you as his personal secretary in his law office. I told him that your inability to progress with your studies here at the institute make you totally unqualified for the job. I must tell you that I informed the Senator that you had learned less here at the institute than any student we have ever had in all our years." He frowned at me portentously, but then went on, "The Senator has disregarded my advice, however, and asks that you be in his office in the Citizen's National Bank this afternoon where he will explain your duties." (Of course!)

Destiny called and another miracle ensued.

Senator Mayfield was a much respected four-time Texas State Senator and a two-time United States Senator, a major force in Texas politics, and owned some very productive oil wells. I remembered the Senator from when he was a judge at the Miss Tyler contest. He was a short, chubby man in his 60s, who had long hairs plastered over his bald spot, high, white starched collars, and a twinkling eye or two for a pretty girl. He looked like an aging cherub. He took me into his beautiful office, which had autographed photographs of U.S. presidents and famous people on the walls and an enormous carved mahogany desk, quite free of papers. He said, "Sit down, Miss Dennison," and leaned back in his leather chair and twinkled at me with a kind of secret merriment.

I said hurriedly, "Mr. Collins told you that I have not gotten very ..."

He twinkled more joyfully, "Oh, yes. He told me you'd not quite ... ah ... finished your studies at the institute. But we have a legal secretary here in our law firm who has been with us for many years and she does all our legal work, and I don't do much legal work anymore, anyway. Mrs. Mayfield likes to get me out of the house, you see? I come down here to the office to keep her happy. But I like to have my mail right away and it is not delivered until noon, so I need someone to go to the post office and get it for me by 9:30 a.m. every morning, you see? And then ... well ... maybe take a personal letter or two now and then. I like to keep in touch with my friends all over the country. Mostly, I like to have a pretty girl around to listen to an old man's stories, you see?"

I saw. With great relief, I said, "Well, Senator, that sounds like a job I can handle. I am very good at picking up mail and I love listening to stories."

He put his little hands over his little paunch and smiled at me with his buck teeth, "Fine. We'll get along just fine."

And we did. It was not hard to work for the Senator. When he dictated a letter to me, he talked very slowly and stopped all the time to tell a story he was reminded of. I sure learned a lot about politics. It was hard to believe what went on. Naively, I had thought "Majority rule" and "May the best man win" was the way a democracy worked. From the Senator, I learned that "All's fair in love and politics" and "To the victor belongs the spoils" was more to the mark. The Senator was a good storyteller, and, even though I thought most of the tricks of the trade he told me about should be against the law, I was fascinated by his stories.

After a few weeks of getting a regular salary, I figured my darling Aunt Lou would be happy to have her spare room back, so I moved into a boarding house with another girl from Federal. But soon after, one day the Senator said, "Little Miss, I don't like to think of you out on your own this way. Mrs. Mayfield and I just rattle around in that big old house with nobody except the servants, now that the boys are gone. We need someone lively to stir us up and keep us from getting old, you see? Why don't you come live with us and that way you won't have to pay room and board and can save up some money."

Stunned, I said, "Wouldn't Mrs. Mayfield mind?"

She was on the phone within minutes. "Now, darlin', you just pack your things and come right on over here tonight. I'll have your room ready for you."

I knew that their younger son had died the year before from an allergic reaction to a bee sting and that their elder son lived in New York, so I could imagine that they were a little lonely, and, anyway, this was obviously another one of my miracles: the Mayfields lived in a big white house on a hill.

The reality of living in their big, white house was much better than anything I had ever been able to imagine. Nothing I had ever read adequately described this stately house with its wide verandas, thick white columns, and more rooms than I could count. Walking into its cool, quiet rooms with their high ceilings and brass revolving fans, and the elegant, comfortable furniture in muted, gorgeous colors, exquisite old rugs and polished wood and silver you could see yourself in, was like entering into an altogether different life. The house itself had an atmosphere that made me want to whisper.

My room was at the top of a beautiful, curving staircase and it overlooked the deep back yard. It was cheerful and cozy, with a slanted ceiling between large dormer windows, which framed a tall, black oak tree that kept the light skipping and dancing on the ceiling. I felt as though no one else had ever lived there before, that everything in it was private and personal to me. I made an instant adjustment to the house and to being waited on by their "colored" staff.

The best part was that Mrs. Mayfield grew fond of me. She became the role model I had always looked for. Tall, beautifully groomed, gracious, soft-spoken, this lovely lady was able to make everyone feel at ease and that she was especially interested in them. She flowed between taking care of the Senator, directing the staff, and her many interests without apparent strain or self-interest. I *ached* to be just like her. With her I was never a show-off. I knew we were exact opposites, but I thought if I tried extremely hard, maybe I could pick up her manner.

Just to make everything perfect, another wonderful little miracle happened: I made a best friend! Her name was Bette Pace, and she was 18, as was I. She had large hazel eyes, a wide high-cornered smile, and a warm, vivid personality. She was as tall as I, but the rest of her was so slender that I felt she ought to be in a box labeled: "Fragile – Handle with Care," like fine, delicate china. With her calm, tightly-knit family of banker father, school teacher mother, and adoring older brother, our backgrounds were as alien to one another as an Eskimo to a Hottentot, but from the moment we met we were akin. Although I had more relatives than you could shake a stick at, as my mother would say, and had girl friends in Hale Center, I never felt "kin" in this way to anyone before. It was such a marvel to me that Bette and I were the closest of friends and spent all our free time together. Our friendship was so precious to me. There didn't seem to be any limit to the number of things we had to say to one another, or the length of time it took to say it. It was like drinking joy juice, I couldn't get enough of it.

Bette was a sophomore at Tyler Junior College and she magically opened the door into the fun of the teen years I'd never had: juke box afternoons at the drugstore, double dates, and dancing to the big bands which played at the Mayfair Ballroom on Saturday nights. The joy that permeated my whole body was like the joy I'd felt performing with my father and being connected to nature and riding my horse bareback all coalesced into one big ball of bliss. As the song goes, "There's a bluebird on my shoulder," and *everything* was right with my world. Living in a big white house on a hill, having a best friend, dancing to the sound of Glenn Miller and Jimmy Lunceford in white socks and saddle shoes — well, it just didn't get any better than this. Probably the bliss of being a teenager was unadulterated because I had never had a chance to really be one before.

Of course, I told Bette all about Blackie and how we were going to be married someday. She thought it was all so romantic, and I was feeling carefree and smug about my marvelous future. And in the meantime, I was having more fun than I had ever had in my life. I quite literally felt like skipping everywhere I went. But then — it was December 7, 1941 — and there was Pearl Harbor. I never read the newspapers or listened to the news on the radio so Hitler, Nazi, Poland, concentration camps, all those names and words were totally abstract to me, and I had never known anyone in the military. I had no idea where Pearl Harbor was or what our fleet was doing there. All I knew about Japan was that "Made in Japan" stamped on something meant that it was cheap. The magnitude of what that single incident would mean to me, those I knew and loved, my country and its future, escaped me entirely. It stupidly didn't occur to me that Bette's brother, Johnny, who had joined the Army Air Force on December 8th would be in harm's way. Like a great many people, Bette and I thought President Roosevelt would take care of everything, and that our boys would lick those "Japs" and be back home in no time flat, and we went blindly on with our lives.

After I had lived with the Mayfields a few months, an amazing thing happened. One night after dinner the Senator asked me to sit with them in the library, and said, "Little Miss, we want to ask you something. You have become like the daughter we never had to Mrs. Mayfield and me, and we worry about your future. Not that you aren't a jim-dandy secretary," his sly, pixie smile at this absurdity, "but we don't feel you will always want to be one and we want you to be protected, you see? With our sons gone, you fill an empty spot. We have talked it over and we would like to legally adopt you. Mayfield is not a poorly-known name and you might find it useful as you go along."

I was dumbfounded! Adopt? I didn't think one adopted a full-grown person, only children. And those came from an *orphanage*. I wasn't Little Orphan Annie, for heaven's sake. And while Mayfield was a terrific name for them, I already had a name that was specific to *me*, and unlike my father with his name changes, I most certainly didn't want to change mine. Without a moment's hesitation, I said, "My goodness, Senator. That is really nice of you and Mrs. Mayfield, and I surely do appreciate it, but I don't think I'd better. I mean, I would really love it but I'm afraid it would hurt my mother, you see?"

Mrs. Mayfield said, "Darlin', the last thing we would want to do is to hurt your sweet mother, but she is certainly welcome in our home anytime she'd like to come, and you would naturally visit her as often as you want. It's only that we are in a better position to help you just now."

The Senator, his lower lip tucked under his front teeth, studied me as he tried to figure out what was really in my mind. He knew that I had only been to see my mother once at Christmas time, and I rarely spoke of her. He said in his most persuasive tone, "Little Miss, I don't think you understand. You know that I have a few little oil wells that I expect will keep producing for some time to come, and you, as my adopted daughter, would share equally in my estate in my will. You see? You'd be a wealthy woman someday, and you would have a pretty nice allowance in the meantime. Of course, Mrs. Mayfield is right, we certainly wouldn't want to hurt your mother in any way. But I have the feeling that she would understand the advantages for you."

The advantages were clear. Why I didn't want them was not. I had used my mother's feelings as an excuse, she might be grieved but she wouldn't make a fuss about something that would benefit me. To be legally adopted by the Mayfields would make my dream of living in — *belonging* in — a white house on a hill come true in an absolute, concrete way. But I didn't want to do it. I loved and admired Mrs. Mayfield more than anyone I'd ever known, and I had come to love the Senator in many ways. But I didn't want to belong to them. Deep inside, I'd always had a wistful desire for the sweetness in life that I thought came with truly belonging to a family, a person, a place. I was always struggling to make myself in tune with a cosmic harmony that I could sense but not hear. But even deeper inside was the fear that *if someone really knew me they wouldn't love me.* Would abandon me. I couldn't take that risk. I was like a starfish, when the part of me that was my father had been ripped away, I had grown the missing arms again but they came back stunted and covered with sharp protective stickers. The memory of the lost parts remained in the pores of my skin, and whenever someone approached too near, those stickers sprang up like bayonets to defend me from further harm. I had conditioned myself to be constantly on guard against being caught, exposed, or vulnerable.

Oddly, the thought of being a wealthy woman held no lure for me. I had learned a powerful lesson about money on Dr. Tate's show that I never forgot. After Dr. Tate gave me the candy concession, I was making between $50 and $75 a week, and my life wasn't worth living. At the Senator's, I was making $25 a week, and my life was totally fulfilled. Experience had taught me that, depending on the circumstances, a *little* money was all I needed to be happy. The lessons I had learned from Dr. Tate made me a fanatic about not ever being *beholden* to anyone for money or anything else. I'd had to let him pull me down on his lap because I was dependent on him for money. I would never do that, or anything like it, again. The horror of seeing my mother sobbing her heart out when my dad left was always with me. I thought she cried because she was not in control of her life. I was in control of mine now and I intended to keep it that way. And it wasn't as if I was a *waif* looking for charity, I was *me*. Most importantly, somewhere down the line there would be dues to be paid. If I didn't want to pay the piper, I had better not dance to his music.

The Mayfields reluctantly seemed to understand my feelings, and my life continued on its ecstatic path with the minor distractions of the Tyler Junior Chamber of Commerce, who seemed to think that just because I had won their Miss Tyler Contest I owed them something. That "something" being to participate in the Miss East Texas Contest in Dallas as their representative. When I told them I didn't want to go, they got the Senator to inform me that it was my obligation to my community to do so. OK, fine, but then they wanted me to go to Austin to compete in the *Miss Texas* contest as their Miss East Texas representative! There was just no satisfying them.

No one but Bette could understand why I didn't want to compete in those contests. I had an instinctive feeling that somehow they were going to rock this perfect boat I had landed in. Living with Grandma or Dr. Tate had been like being imprisoned in a stifling grey cell where the colors and sounds were all muted and flat. I thought because I had been brave enough to jump out into the unknown, my reward had been to have all the glorious colors and sounds of the universe turned on full for me. I was *free* and *alive* for the first time in too many years. Nothing in my life had filled me with as much joyous electricity as dancing to the music of the Big Bands. The beauty contests were held on the weekend — and the Big Bands came to the Mayfair on the weekend! My priority was clear.

Winning those contests meant nothing to me at all, and I didn't want their prizes. The prizes for winning Miss Tyler were a scholarship to Federal Institute (of all things) and flying lessons. I didn't need the flying lessons, I was already flying. The main prize for winning Miss East Texas was a meeting with Bill Mayberry, the talent scout for Metro-Goldwyn-Mayer who was one of the judges. I went to see Mr. Mayberry for the fun of finding out what he would say. He offered me a stock contract for one year with options at $75 a week at Metro-Goldwyn-Mayer (MGM). I told him thank you but my mother didn't want me to be in the movies without a second thought. I turned down what I thought to be fame and fortune to preserve what I wanted most, which was to stay in Tyler.

The really fun thing that happened, though, was when I was coming out of the Baker Hotel there in Dallas after seeing Mr. Mayberry. I was feeling pretty cocky as I started across the street and noticed an army private on the other side staring at me. I wasn't surprised when he spoke to me as I walked past him. He said, "Excuse me, Miss. My name is Ayres, and I want to speak to you about something. I assure you I have never done a thing like this before, but as I was looking at you just now I felt I should ask if you ever thought of being an actress?" He was a slight, slender man, not much taller than I in his neat GI uniform, with a delicate, quizzical face. It was his voice that I recognized first, and an electrical charge almost paralyzed me as I realized that instead of the nondescript soldier he appeared, the man standing before me was actually one of my two favorite movie stars. He was *Lew Ayres!*

Clark Gable or Errol Flynn, with their lady-killer image, had never done anything for me in the movies, it was Franchot Tone and Lew Ayres who were my ideals because they were high-class, sensitive, and non-aggressive. Of course, it was for being non-aggressive that Ayres was a private and not an officer in the army. When he was called up at the beginning of World War II, he had declared himself a conscientious objector and there had been a big hoo-raw about it. He had volunteered for the Army Medical Corps, providing he didn't have to carry a gun. So here he was in some god-awful army camp in Texas as a private, and probably persecuted, member of our Armed Forces.

Having trouble speaking with a tongue that suddenly seemed as big as a watermelon, I said, "Ah … gee … no, Mr. … ah … Ayres. I never have thought of being an actress." In his familiar voice, he said, "Well, I think you should. I believe you have something special. Don't misunderstand, it has nothing to do with me, but I thought you should have a chance in Hollywood. I'm here on a weekend pass to see a friend of mine who is head talent-scout for 20th Century Fox. I've just come from him at the Baker Hotel, and if you have time I'd like to take you there to meet him."

Dizzy with a sense of unreality, I would have agreed to try and walk on water if he'd suggested it, so we went back to the Baker to meet Ivan Kahn. After he introduced us, Ayres left abruptly, murmuring excuses. Mr. Kahn was a big, Germanic-looking man with a bluff manner. Still in a delightful daze from having been noticed by my favorite movie star, I didn't concentrate on our conversation until I became aware that he was saying, "Miss Dennison, many girls want to go to Hollywood to become movie stars. Most of them don't make it and their hearts are broken. They wind up having to go home without ever being successful, or even working as an actress in pictures. You need a unique quality to make good in Hollywood, and I am doing you a favor when I tell you that I think you should forget about being an actress."

With a serious face, I said, "Mr. Kahn, I understand what you're saying, and I believe you're right. I think I had better give up my dream of going to Hollywood. But I sure do thank you for talking so nice with me." We gravely shook hands and I departed. I giggled to myself all the way out of the Baker. Of course, fate giggles at moments like these, too, and a year later when I had twice as good a contract at 20th Century Fox as I'd been offered at Metro-Goldwyn-Mayer, Ivan Kahn and I became good friends.

But even though I had already refused to go to the Miss Texas Contest, I was snookered because the Senator got Mrs. Mayfield to weigh in. She said, "Darlin,' you *are* Miss East Texas. It wouldn't look right for them to send another girl. Why don't you want to go?"

I said, "Oh, Mrs. Mayfield, *Benny Goodman* is going to be playing at the Mayfair that weekend. I don't know how much you know about him, but they call him "The King of Swing" and he has such a Big Band that he's never played here before and probably won't again. I just *couldn't* miss it."

Mrs. Mayfield's face was a study, as she softly said, "I don't believe I ever heard Benny Goodman, but I'm sure it would be lovely. But, darlin,' this contest represents the whole state of Texas. I can't believe any orchestra could be more important than that." A loving smile as she took one of my hands in hers, "I'll tell you what I'll do. The new Governor, Coke Stevens, and his wife are old friends of the Senator, and I know they would just be glad to have us come and spend that weekend with them. I'll go with you, and we can stay at the Governor's mansion in Austin and see the Capitol and make it a special little trip for the two of us. Would you like that?"

Of course, I had to go.

I thought the Mayfield's house looked more like a "mansion" than the Governor's, but Mrs. Coke Stevens was an enchanting, dumpy little woman with tiny feet who welcomed Mrs. Mayfield and me like long lost friends. The contest the next night was held in a huge football stadium and, as Camp Swift in Austin was one of the biggest army camps in the country, the stands were overflowing with soldiers. As soon as "Jo-Carroll Dennison – Miss East Texas" blared out over the loud speakers, the stadium erupted in loud applause, and as I walked up and down the platform before the judges, it rose into a roar of rebel yells and whistles. I couldn't understand why everyone in the stands seemed to be rooting for me before they even saw me, but I reckoned without my two middle-aged politician's wives who knew the value of warming up the crowd before your candidate arrives. Tall, elegantly groomed Mrs. Mayfield and plump, dressed fit-to-kill Mrs. Stevens had trotted all over the stands hustling votes, urging, "Vote for Miss East Texas" and "Be sure to clap for Miss East Texas," and the soldiers responded enthusiastically.

Later that night, I heard for the first time about a Miss America Pageant in Atlantic City, New Jersey, and that as Miss Texas, I was obligated to go there for a week the third week in September. My scream of outrage could have been heard all the way back to Tyler. I didn't want to hear about a new wardrobe or the train tickets and expenses for me and a chaperone the Texas JCs would finance, I wanted this whole bathing beauty thing to *end*!

But then my mother called. She had heard about my winning Miss Texas on the radio, and ran out to get newspapers and there was my picture on the front page of all of them. She didn't know where I was, so she had called the Senator and he had told her I was going to Atlantic City, taking her with me as chaperone, and gave her the Governor's phone number.

Laughing and crying at the same time, she said, "Oh, Josie, I'm so happy for you, honey. I knew my baby would do something like this someday, but I had no idea what my little dickens was up to. I just couldn't believe my ears when I heard your name right there on the radio. I didn't even know there *was* a Miss Texas contest. And when Senator Mayfield told me I was going to get to go with you as chaperone, well, I just broke down and cried like a baby. Dr. Tate has come with me to the telephone and he wants to talk to you. I told him he would have to get someone else to run the snow cone stand because I had to go with my baby to Atlantic City. Oh, honey, I'm just so proud of you."

I broke in, "Yes, well, you see ..."

Mother broke in, "I've just been laughing and crying all day. This is the best thing that has ever happened to me. Everyone on the show is so proud and sends love to you. It says here in the paper, we'll go to Atlantic City on the third week in September. Do you want me to come to Tyler right now to help you get ready to go?"

"Ah, no, not right now. Oh ... well ... I'll be home tomorrow and you can call me then when I'll know more about it. Say hello to Todd for me but I don't want to talk to Dr. Tate." I wanted to jump up and down and scream with frustration like Rumpelstiltskin, but what could I do? I couldn't fight the whole state of Texas single-handedly — and my mother, too.

My fate was sealed.

On Winning Miss America - 1942

*Singing "Deep in the Heart of Texas" Miss America Competition, 1942,
as other finalists look on.*

Mother was trainsick every mile of the way during the three days it took us to get to Atlantic City, but once we arrived, she was bright-eyed and bushy tailed, and thrilled to pieces about everything and everybody. Shepherded firmly by our individual local chaperones, we contestants were whisked onto an assembly line as rapid as Henry Ford's. We attended receptions, luncheons, interminable photo sessions in our bathing suits for photographers from all over the world, as well as rehearsals for the elaborate four-performance show the Pageant put on. I had been affronted by the news that we were not to leave our rooms unless accompanied by our local individual chaperone, and there would be no smoking, drinking or talking to strange men in public. Evidently, there had been a little misbehaving by previous contestants. However, I had to admit it would have been nigh impossible to be on time and at the right place for our jam-packed schedule, get in and out of our rapid wardrobe changes, and on and off the stage properly without the aid of these conscientious, Atlantic City society women chaperones.

The previous beauty contests I had been in were pleasant community events that took a few hours, but the Miss America Pageant was a very big deal nationally in those days, especially during that first year of World War II, and it lasted five days. In Atlantic City, it was the most important thing that ever happened. The entire town, its police force and its citizens, was geared toward making the Pageant a splendid event, and "our girls" protected and appreciated. The big resort hotels and other businesses had started the Pageant in 1920 as a way to entice tourists to stay past Labor Day, and by now it had achieved national prominence.

It was a good show put on by professionals: MC, dancers, conductor and orchestra, but the crowd was there to see the girls. For the first three nights, the contestants were separated into three groups, each to compete in swim suit, evening gown and talent on alternating nights. The fourth night, the top 10 were announced, who then repeated their various competitions until the winner was chosen. The girls came in all shapes and sizes and varying degrees of feminine pulchritude and talent, but each eagerly behaved as though the enabling crown of Miss America was a cherished possibility.

Senator Mayfield had spared no expense for this trip. He had paid a local dance and music teacher, Alfred Gilliam, a tall, limber, curly-haired man whose smile looked a mile wide, to arrange a terrific song and dance number of "Deep In the Heart of Texas" for me. He also paid for him to come with me to work with the orchestra on his intricate arrangement and play piano while I performed. It is a short, upbeat song, each couplet ending with four hand claps and the title:

> *"The stars at night,*
> *Are big and bright,*
> *(clap, clap, clap, clap)*
> *Deep in the heart of Texas," and so on.*

Alfred had made an arrangement which started off with a blasting, up-beat rhythm, a repeat in a fancy conga rhythm, an exaggerated slow minor key addition of "Oh, Bury Me Out on the Lone Prairie" at the bridge, then back to the rhythm for the last eight bars and into a swinging tap dance done to the same changing rhythms.

One day at morning rehearsal, another contestant, Patricia Hill, sat down beside me and said, "Isn't this fun? You're so pretty, I don't doubt you will be in the top ten." I was in awe of Patricia. Most of the girls were around 18, but she was 21 and so much more mature than the rest of us. Always relaxed and gracious. I couldn't understand why a "wealthy-popular-debutante" would want to be in a bathing beauty contest, it seemed so much beneath her. Emboldened by her friendliness, I asked bluntly, "How come you entered this contest, Patricia?"She gave her trilling laugh which started low and ran all the way up the scale, "Call me Patty. Oh, just for a lark. On a dare from some of my friends, I entered the Miss Michigan contest, never thinking for a minute I would win it. But here I am. Mother was furious at first, but she's having the time of her life in Atlantic City."

I was relieved to know she had entered just for a lark. I decided that's what I'd say if someone asked me.

Not all the contestants were so nice. My talent group was on the first night, and, as I watched, the other girls performed their numbers. One of the contestants standing next to me said, "Are you nervous?" — in a seemingly nice way.

"No, I'm not nervous."

She held out a tiny packet. "I thought this might help clear your throat if you were nervous. It's salt, and good for your voice." I was touched by her concern. I took it and swallowed it. "Thanks. Thanks a lot."

The excitement transmitted from the 5,000 people in the theater to the stage rose to such a pitch that by the time I heard, "… to do a song about her native state — Jo-Carroll Dennison, Miss Texaaaas," I was out of the wings and down to the microphone like it was something I had been waiting for all my life. With my darling Todd Fields whispering in my ear, "Go get 'em, Baby Jo," I swung into my song with the zeal of Ethel Merman. And one of my miracles happened: the audience, particularly the hundreds of servicemen in the balcony, responded to my invitation to join me in the hand claps with astonishing force. Then it was as though a lever controlling an electrical current between me and the audience was pushed all the way up until there was *fusion* between us and we became one body, one soul. For the first time in my life, I was *in the zone* with my song and dance and I experienced an exaltation I would remember for the rest of my days.

Then a really strange thing happened, when I got to the slow minor key change — I couldn't swallow.

Now, if you can't swallow, you can't sing. The only sound I could get out was a rather agonized mangled cawing. For a second, I was completely paralyzed. I couldn't imagine what had happened. Alfred was staring up at me with a terrified white face as the music ground to a halt. Then I realized what was the matter. The salt had dried up my saliva. "That bitch!" I was so electrified with fury at my stupidity in taking the darn stuff that my adrenaline started pumping — and so did my salivary glands — and I swallowed.

You don't work all your life in front of an audience for nothing. I could hear Todd saying, "If you fall down on stage, make a joke of it and the audience will love you." So I smiled my warmest smile and said, "I don't know what is the matter with me. I guess this is a pretty important night and I'm a little nervous, let's try it one more time." Dramatic pause. Arms flung wide, "Alfred, take it from the top!"

Well, the house went wild. When I came again to the slow minor key, I paused and then really let 'em have it with "Oh, bury me out — on the lo-oon-ne praireee." Alfred stayed with me and by the time I finished that number, there was little doubt I was over the top. The will to prevail over my adversary gave me new powers and, if I had not had the contest won before — I did now.

When I finished the number, the house came down. I got a lump in my throat at the storm of applause, whistles and rebel yells that just wouldn't stop. It was truly overwhelming. The look on Alfred's face down in the orchestra pit made the lump get bigger. He had created this number, taught it to me, worked with the orchestra and played his heart out on the piano. Now he was beaming up at me, his whole face illuminated by the enormous success we shared.

Years later, I heard great actors and performers speak about those rare moments when they held an audience enthralled. When the union between sender and receiver is joined in such a way that another dimension is reached for both and they are — as performers — inspired and inspiring. This was like that. It was a soaring, larger than life experience on that stage in Atlantic City. I was a much better entertainer than I ever thought I could be.

As I lay in bed that night, remembering the extraordinary experience it had been on that stage on this extraordinary night, I heard the echo of a long-ago voice saying, "Ladies and Gentlemen, this is my little girl's second birthday. If we give her a big hand maybe she will recite something for us." A lot had happened since then.

With her black eyes glittering like diamonds from excitement, the next morning Mother laid a bunch of newspapers on my bed. She had been up early to get the papers from the lobby, part of the job she had assigned herself for the duration. (The chaperones who accompanied the contestants had been politely but firmly replaced by the local chaperones; they were given tickets to the show, but they didn't have much to do otherwise.) Mother said breathlessly, "They say your picture is on all the front pages of newspapers as far away as Paris, France! The New York papers are calling you 'The Texas Tornado' and in the Atlantic City papers they are saying you are the odds-on favorite to win. Oh, Josie, just imagine!"

In the papers, it didn't seem to be me they were talking about.

That night I was again caught up in the spirit of competition. I smiled triumphantly at the giver of salt as we changed into our bathing suits for the Swim Suit Competition, and was rarin' to go as we 10, we band of sisters, answered to our rollcall. Now, there were no kneecaps jumping up and down. No butterflies. And no little, hard cold ball. Just a calm, soaring feeling that lasted all through the walks out the runway and the turns before the judges, both in my bathing suit and in my new evening gown. (I have to admit the velvet felt good as it swirled around my legs.)

I won for Swim Suit and the following night, I won the Evening Gown competition. I was inordinately proud of my long, white organza gown with its puffed sleeves and sweetheart neckline. The rest of the contestants wore elaborate, very expensive, off-the-shoulder or halter-neck dresses, but you had to have worn red satin, backless gowns from the time you were 11 to appreciate my dress. I hadn't had a high school graduation prom, and this simple, loose-fitting dress, which had cost $29.95 in Austin, would have been my choice for a prom. Actually, it looked a lot like the white organza dress my mother had made for me when I was five. Both Mrs. Mayfield and Mrs. Stevens had tried to talk me into a more elaborate gown, but I loved this simple white one and thought I looked great in it.

Pinning up my hair that night at the hotel, Mother said, "I have chewed all the fingers off my gloves waiting for the MC to call out your name. I think the judges have made very good choices except for that Miss Chicago. She's got a good figure, but her mouth is hard." A pause. "Josie, do you think you are going to …?"

"Mother, hurry up with those curls. We've got a long day tomorrow and I am just worn out."

"But, honey, what if you should win?"

I wore my white organza gown, despite push-back from the pros.

"Oh, Mother, don't be silly. The crowd just liked 'Deep in the Heart of Texas' and the papers picked up on it. There are several girls prettier than I am, and it is a beauty contest, after all, not a talent contest. Gosh, Miss Michigan is the most beautiful girl I ever saw,and Miss California is not far behind."

Me and the two runner-ups.

"But what if they do pick you? You've won three competitions."

"Good night, will you stop it? If they did, I would just turn it down, that's all."

She said softly, "Why don't you want to win, Josie?"

Why didn't I want to win? That had been the question since I was first approached to be Miss Citizen's National Bank. But nobody understood or even believed my answer. It was no *achievement* for me to win a beauty contest. It didn't *mean* anything. None of the contests I'd won had gotten me one step closer to where I wanted to be, particularly this one. Nobody had told me until we arrived in Atlantic City that each of the contestants had to sign a contract agreeing to go on tour for a year if she won. It honestly had not occurred to me that I would win or I wouldn't have signed the contract. I was conceited all right, thought I was cute and had a good personality, but I certainly never thought I was the most beautiful girl in America, for heaven's sake.

The problem was every time I'd been persuaded to enter a contest, once I got out on the stage I had to try to win. Something in me overrode all mental objections when I got in front of an audience, whether it was on a medicine show stage or around that swimming pool in Tyler. Certainly, there was no subduing that will to win under the skyrocketing stimulus of the wildly enthusiastic Atlantic City crowd. What I could never explain is that it was the *winning* itself that was fun. It had never been the resulting prize I wanted. Or sought. If they would say, "OK — You win — you are Miss America" and let me go home — fine. But it had taken me 18 years to get to my perfect situation in Tyler and no way did I want to leave it to go back on the road for a year.

But the applause never stopped from the audience when I was on the stage — mightier forces than mine prevailed — and I was crowned Miss America of 1942. Miss Chicago was 1st runner up (she cried, I didn't), Miss Detroit was 2nd runner up and Miss Mississippi won Miss Congeniality.

Mother cried all the way through.

Coronation.

Miss America on Tour

Singing for the boys at Camp Swift, TX.

In retrospect, I wish I had let myself enjoy the whole experience more. I mean, how often does an 18-year-old girl get her picture and story known by a majority of the people in the country she lives in, and a bunch in Europe, too? How often does a girl off a medicine show get to walk into The Stork Club in New York, one of the most famous nightclubs in the world, and have the orchestra stop everything and play "her" song? But — mostly — pick a sound. Any sound. There just is none as exhilarating as the sound of winning. Whether it's a national election, a World Series baseball game, or a Miss America Pageant, that vibrating hum of expectation that builds into an exultant roar is a thrill like nothing else. I'll admit I loved the moment. But I had come to Atlantic City determined not to have a good time and — with the notable exception of the audience response to my song and dance number — I didn't. However, that seems a shame to me now; it could have been an extraordinarily marvelous experience, if I had just cancelled my reservations and fully enjoyed it.

Also, it seems incredible that forever after, I would be written about or introduced as a "Former Miss America." No matter how many interesting things happened to me, or how old and decrepit I was to become, as such I am still introduced. As if that was the most important and defining thing I had ever done.

My year's tour as Miss America began with a week in New York for an additional onslaught of interviews and photographers, radio and civic appearances, and appointments with various dignitaries. New York was sure a lot bigger than Dallas; its sheer size and sound left me open-mouthed and a little stunned, but Mother just ate it up. While I was sitting crunched up in a corner of a taxi, she was leaning out the window looking up at the tall buildings and taking in the sights in a zenith of excitement. I had never seen this side of her as she swallowed up the things that were happening to us with great gulps of pleasure. She was in her glory and just loved it all. In her new role of scrapbook collector, she had practically emptied the newsstands, and had sent my news clippings and photographs to everyone she had ever known. She sent a continuing stream of my publicity to relatives. It is interesting to imagine the many scores and humiliating moments in her life for which the clippings were payback.

Revenge was not all that sweet for me. Admittedly, I was glad that she sent my publicity and photos to half-brother Joe. I hope he choked on them. Among the congratulatory telegrams was one from Blackie: "Congratulations and goodbye from your most ardent admirer." Blackie had joined the Navy soon after Pearl Harbor and I laughed at his self-sacrificing tone, but quickly wired him that nothing had changed between us. I didn't laugh at the telegram from Dr. Tate: "Come back to me and I will make you a millionaire." It didn't even make me smile. I found that thoughts of him and his lunacy were now only ironic; the cataclysmic events which had overtaken me made me want to think of him as just a faded and unimportant part of my past. The telegram from the folks in Hale Center: "Congratulations, and please rectify the mistake in the newspapers that your home town is Hale Center, not Tyler," was in the same category: Ironic and no longer important.

There had been a time in my life when it was all-important what the good folks of Hale Center thought of me. In my senior year, an unexpected blow had fallen on me that broke my spirit as well as my heart. Quite literally overnight, my good friends and the other kids in school stopped speaking to me. From one day to the next, I went from being the most popular girl in school to a pariah. The first day this ostracism became apparent to me in school, I thought it must be some kind of cosmic joke. That every kid in school, boy and girl, would turn away and not speak to me was as bewildering as if I had suddenly become invisible to everyone but me. When I tracked my two closest friends down in the girl's bathroom and forced them to tell me why — Janelle, the cute chubby one whose mother was the president of the PTA, said through her tears, "Jo-Carroll, our mothers made us promise not to associate with you any more. The PTA and the Bible Study Group called a special meeting because of Leta Faye getting pregnant without being married, and those kids getting drunk and being killed in that car wreck. They decided that nothing like this had happened in Hale Center before you came, so you must be the bad influence in town. They thought that because of your working on a medicine show and the way you dress and drive around town in your own car all the time without any supervision, you were giving the kids bad ideas. Your grandmother has been saying that you are gone all hours, and you don't go to church, and, well, anyway, that's what they decided. They forbid any of us to speak to you or have anything to do with you at all anymore."

I looked at my other closest friend, Jo Ann. Her mother was handicapped and didn't belong to the PTA or Bible Group, but Jo Ann said, "Last Sunday, the preacher based his whole sermon on medicine shows and the people who work on them. He said your show was the work of the devil and that you all were here to spread evil among the rest of us. He said medicine shows were a contamination and there ought to be a law against them," and she turned away and burst into tears, too.

Ostracism! It is truly medieval in its intent and infliction of pain. The shame and humiliation I endured the rest of that school year seared my soul in a deeply crippling way. The day-to-day piercing of constant little rejections from the same kids who had been shoving to sit next to me for years was nothing compared to the annihilating sense of injustice I felt. I was the biggest prude in town, I didn't smoke, drink, talk dirty or kiss fellas! True: Mother stayed on the show to keep her job while I came back alone to stay at Grandma's — unlike other kids, I had my own car and expensive, flashy clothes — I stayed away from Grandma's house as much as possible — I thought my God was nowhere to be found in their church and was quick to say so — but I was a good girl by my own criteria! Because of some circumstance or other, my father long ago told me that the most important maxim was "To thine own self be true," and as long as I followed that thought in my heart, it didn't really matter what other people thought of me. He explained that the only truly important thing was that I was doing what was right for me. My mother had taught me the Ten Commandments, but "To thine own self be true" resonated in my soul in a way that "Love Thy Neighbor" never did. I devoutly followed the rules of behavior I had set for myself long ago, and was true to myself — so how could this terrible thing have happened to me? It wasn't fair, and I could make no sense of it.

I had always thought everyone envied me for entertaining on a medicine show. I thought show folk were so much more interesting than ordinary people. Now to be called "sinful" and "evil" was a devastating shock to my whole system of thought. The way I saw who I was and the world I lived in was turned upside down. Trying to puzzle it through, finally I could see that the way I was different, turned society against me. No matter how much I told myself that I didn't care what these hicks, these yokels, these boobs, thought about me, it was a crushing blow to my sense of self. I did care. But, determined not to let them know how much I cared, I stuck it out until the end of term, and though I wasn't going to go to the school prom, I decided to go on the school trip to some distant canyon on the bus. No one saved me a seat, so I had to sit on the back bench by myself until one of the farm boys I would never give the time of day came back and tried to kiss me! He never would have dared do that before and it was the final degradation. I got my high school diploma, and left Hale Center forever.

The shame and turnabout in my thinking, however, went with me. Once back on the show, I sank into a thick, opaque shell of depression. Fuzzy and Creampuff had died horribly. People whom I thought had loved me had turned from me as though I was nasty. The courage and determination engendered in me by my reading, and, most importantly, the feeling of being special bred in me by my father had been brutally erased, and there was no foreseeable escape from this dead-end trap I was in. My enthusiasm for life, and faith in miracles and my God were just gone. I wasn't aware of being depressed, I just felt as if I was in a decompression chamber where no thought or color or feeling could penetrate. There was a bed in an enclosed compartment above the cab in the bally wagon and I spent the day there for months. Mother said, "Josie honey, you have to eat something besides milk and crackers or you're going to starve to death."

I thought sullenly, "Good. That's the best plan I can think of." I didn't have the energy to contemplate suicide, but my hopelessness made extinction seem possibly preferable to my murky future.

This shell of apathetic inertia was burst asunder by the miracle of Blackie. His overriding enthusiasm and certainty about our future together was irresistible and I was lifted up out of my quagmire in one fell swoop. He loved me, understood me, and was my shining future. Because of him, I got myself back — my enthusiasm, my security, and my faith in God. But I never wanted to wear red satin again.

Now, it seemed that Hale Center was all too proud of their "hometown girl," and revenge was mine, but it had come too late to do any good. Like with childbirth, the pain had faded away. But in any kind of interview I gave, I talked about the sailor I was going to marry when the war was over and Tyler and the Mayfields. I never, ever, mentioned Hale Center, the medicine show — or my father.

One appointment that had been made for me by Miss Slaughter in New York was with a William Morris agent named Marty Jurow. He said, "I saw that 'Deep in the Heart of Texas' number that you did, kid, and you were a knockout. I told Lew Schreiber about you and he has agreed to meet with you. You are in luck because Lew Schreiber is the head man next to Darryl Zanuck at 20th Century Fox and he just happens to be in New York at this time."

Marty was shorter than I, a dark-haired young man with a sweet smile and fast-flowing speech. Mr. Schreiber was a middle-aged, grey-haired man with no smile at all and very little speech. He studied me and asked a few questions, then he said, "I'll give you a 5-year contract starting at $150 a week going up to $750."

I said, "I sure do appreciate that, Mr. Schreiber, but I don't want to be an actress."

We stared at one another, Marty's mouth agape, Mr. Schreiber's and mine firmly closed. Finally, Mr. Schreiber opened his mouth to say, "Let me know if you change your mind," and he was on the phone already as Marty hurried me out.

Once outside the office, Marty whirled on me, "Kid! What did you do that for? You made me look bad. If you don't want to be an actress, why did you come on the interview? Mr. Schreiber offered you a Player's contract! That's big money and more than most kids get. Are you crazy?"

"Nobody asked me if I wanted to come on this interview or if I wanted to be an actress. This was your idea and they just told me to come. If you'd asked me if I would like to go to Hollywood, I'd have told you I didn't want to be an actress."

Marty clapped his hand to his forehead, "Nobody asked you!" Then he laughed and grabbed my arm to lead me to the elevator. "Listen, kid, you're right. This is a killer business and the only thing that makes it worthwhile is if you love it. I love it, but if you don't then you are absolutely right not to get into it. No hard feelings, OK?"

I liked Marty, and it hadn't occurred to me that I would make him "look bad" by going on the interview. I had gone because it was a no-risk challenge. As with Mr. Mayberry of Metro-Goldwyn-Mayer, I was just told to meet with him and if he didn't want me, I hadn't lost anything. If he did, it made me feel good and I didn't have to do it."

Fulfilling my $500 a week touring contract as Miss America, my first booking was the Fay Theatre in Philadelphia. My shock was cataclysmic when I learned that the act I was following was Margy Hart, the most famous stripper next to Gypsy Rose Lee. I said to the manager, "Is this a burlesque house?"

A small man with sharp bones and face, he said, "Only when we can get a headliner like Margy, which isn't too often anymore. The chorus line won't strip during the number you're in; it's a patriotic number about the Armed Forces and you come in and just stand there in your bathing suit while you do your act."

I felt seriously dizzy. "I'm not going to work in my bathing suit!"

"Oh, yes, you are, Miss. It says in your contract that you will appear on our stage as you did in the Miss America Pageant and that's what you're going to do. Get into your suit right now as we're ready to rehearse that number."

He wasn't angry, just adamant, but his authoritative, contemptuous tone clamped my stomach muscles and straightened my spine in a fury of rebellion. I said, "Now, you better listen to me. I entertained on the stage of the Miss America Pageant in a cowgirl costume, and that's how I am going to appear on this stage. If I appear on it at all! I'm going back to my hotel and if you want me to do my number in my cowgirl outfit, then you call me."

Riding back to the Adelphia Hotel in a taxi, the thought struck me – how did a Miss America get booked into a "sometime" burlesque house anyway? From the moment we got off the train in Atlantic City, everyone talked about their healthy, intelligent, clean-living beautiful ideal of American womanhood. They made such a big fuss about not smoking, drinking or talking to men during the Pageant. Was good, clean pornography OK as long as they didn't see it? I shouldn't have been surprised. I had learned from Dr. Tate that behind the mighty morality of a hard-shelled Southern Baptist can hide a rapist of little girls, and really, when you come right down to it, what is the difference between the chorus line of strippers at the Fay Theatre and the chorus line of Miss America contestants, except a few yards of cloth? Or the difference between Margy Hart and Greta Garbo or Hedy Lamarr? In Garbo's movies, although with a unique high-class style, she was selling sex just as much as Margy Hart; and Lamarr got her start appearing nude in a movie. Behind the righteous, dignified façade of the Pageant Board, they were selling sex just like the manager of the Fay Theatre. The contestants just didn't grind and bump.

When I got to the hotel there was a message to call the manager. He calmly said to come back and rehearse my cowgirl number. By the time I got back there wasn't much time to go over "Deep in the Heart of Texas" with the orchestra, but they weren't enthusiastic about learning that difficult arrangement anyway. With no Alfred there to lead them during the five shows a day, they didn't bother much with the changing tempos, just kind of faked it and threw in a lot of cymbal crashes. I counted myself lucky, however, that the audience didn't yell "Take it off" when I asked them to clap.

But something wonderful happened to me in Philadelphia — I joined the war effort. The war itself was still not personally threatening to me. The outcome of what Blackie was doing in training camp was not real to me; his letters sounded as cheerful as the servicemen in the theater balcony who seemed to be having such a good time. It was exciting to see the country in full gear now to produce enough war material to enable our Armed Forces to prevail. Service camps and defense plants were everywhere in the east and I began to visit them each day. It touched my heart in a strange, new way to see the almost reverent enthusiasm the servicemen had toward me as their national symbol. Their respectful interest didn't seem to be about sex; it was more like the awe and admiration they felt for their President in a war year. It had to do with their country and what they were so willing and proud to fight for. I felt so humbled by their attitude. I didn't take it personally because I honestly never thought I had done anything to deserve it, and I could tell they were greeting me as a symbol like the Statue of Liberty, but I promised myself right there and then that someday I would do something to deserve the honor they bestowed upon me.

The brass wanted me to eat with them, but I insisted on eating with the troops at Camp Hood, TX.

Many of the workers at the defense plants were women, the majority of whom had never been out of the kitchen before. As I moved among them, signing autographs and shaking hands, I was caught up in the exuberance they had about what they were doing; it was evident that they took such pride in their work and their individual ability to turn it out faster and better than anyone else in the world. Those workers I couldn't meet personally hung out of windows to wave and yell words of encouragement and appreciation.

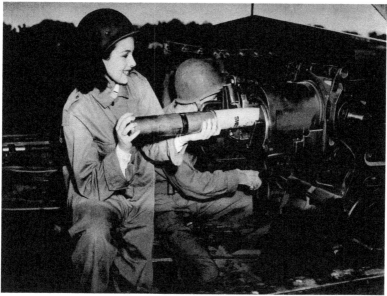

Shooting live ammunition at Camp Hood, TX.
No one warned me about the tank gun's recoil.

All my life, I had faced groups of people of various sizes, but they had been faceless, without individual personality. I neither knew nor cared to know about their traditions, background or moral fiber. The meaning of the words "democracy" or "forefathers" or "American know-how" was outside my knowledge or interest. But I sensed in the people I was meeting now a sureness about themselves as a people that was based on their heritage. Our heritage. The show business society I grew up in was insular. The meaning of holidays like Thanksgiving, the Fourth of July or Labor Day had no value for me other than how it affected the number of people in the audience. I had never felt a part of a greater whole. Now I was seeing at first hand the living results of the American dream of freedom and democracy, and the early Americans' ability to tame a continent and make it the foremost country in the world. The servicemen and defense workers showed such pure and untarnished pride in themselves and their country that I sincerely felt like coming to attention and giving them a snappy salute.

I was meeting and being embraced by "We, the People," in enormous numbers, and they were marvelous.

With the soldiers at Camp Hood, TX. The men had just been forced to run a brutal obstacle course, including barbed wire and life ammunition, on my behalf. Their commander was cruel.

Arriving at my next stop, the Hippodrome Theater in Baltimore, I was ready to do battle about wearing a bathing suit on the stage, but was totally disarmed to see that Bea Wain, my favorite singer, was on the bill with me instead of a stripper. It turned out to be a classy theater with all class acts and a class orchestra, and all was well until, on my last day, the bookkeeper's daughter drew me aside as she was handing me my check. She asked me not to tell her father as she pointed out the odd figures on my withholding slip. I hadn't even looked at the previous slip as I was so impressed with how much my check was for, but now she pointed out that the amount of social security being withheld represented a salary of one thousand dollars for the week. She explained obliquely that the Miss America act was being paid $1,000 minus $500 to me and $500 to someone else she would not name, and she hustled off.

On the medicine show I had squirmed with embarrassment because people paid 50 cents for a 5-cent box of candy hoping to win a big prize, not knowing they were playing with a marked deck. That was small potatoes compared to a 50-percent kickback, plus the 10 percent I was contracted to give the Miss America Pageant. The Miss America tour had been arranged by the owner of the Steel Pier in Atlantic City, which was part of the theater circuit I was playing, and presumably the kickback was going to him. I didn't think the Pageant Board of hoteliers and bankers knew anything about it. But I thought they should have made it their business to do so.

After the Hippodrome I had hopes for The Hot Spot in Toledo, but I should have known from the name. It was a nightclub, not a theater, and out front were pictures of nearly nude girls in cutesy poses. It had a "fifty – count 'em, fifty" type show and the girls didn't strip because they didn't wear enough to take off. Right away I told the manager I wouldn't appear in a bathing suit, but he didn't seem to care if I appeared in the rear end of a horse costume as long as

Armed and dangerous at Camp Hood, TX.

they could announce, "And here she is, Miss America of 1942!" The band was even worse than the one at the Fay, so it was back to the cymbal crashes and vainly trying to slow the band down during the bridge by stamping my foot as though trying to put out a fire.

But worse than the band was the audience. Nothing in show business had prepared me for working on a stage nearly surrounded by loud, vulgar patrons drinking and eating while I was on. The only clapping they did during my song was in trying to get the waiter for another drink. But the thing that ground my stomach up like hamburger was how the men in the audience responded to the grinding and bumping chorus girls. The big room was dark except for small table lamps with red shades which accentuated the makeup on the women's faces and cast a brutal glow on the faces of the men as they yelled, "Give me a piece of it, baby" reaching for the girl's crotch undulating in front of them. A man shouting "Come with me, Tootsie," as the dancers shook their bouncing breasts under his nose, brought forth encouraging yells and laughter from the other men in the audience, whose avid concentration was a collective visceral excitement like a pack of hyenas waiting to grab a piece of meat and run off with it.

I felt such a deep hostility for those men that it made one side of me feel separate from and angry at men and all they represented, while the other side of me felt lovingly toward Blackie and all he represented. With an affirmation from neither side, I was cut adrift by the knife of my own fears to free-float — disconnected and disenchanted. I wrote Blackie about my confusion, not about sex, of course, but about things in general. He included in his reply part of a poem he liked:

> *"When I and the universe disagree,*
> *I go and sit under the raspberry tree,*
> *And think thoughts that are silly and kind,*
> *And lie on my back and wiggle my mind."*

It was because of what he wrote me that I continued to plan to marry Blackie some day; his letters were my security blanket. I riffled through any mail looking for his familiar illegible signature on the upper left hand of the envelope. Already, he had developed a famous man's way of writing his name: the capital letters big and bold and the rest of the letters running almost flat. He was unfailingly funny, romantic and positive about our future. He was my future held safe in my own layaway plan, his picture a constant protective amulet against the evil eye. But he was far away from the reality I was living.

I did a lot of mind wiggling in Toledo, and in the following week of the Detroit nightclub, which was much the same as The Hot Spot. But I and the universe couldn't come to a real agreement — so I wrote to the Miss America Pageant Board stating that I was canceling the rest of the tour and going home to Texas. They threatened to sue me for breach of contract until I sent them copies of the "odd" withholding slips and reminded them of how happy the press would be to know about them. They agreed to let me go.

When I got to Detroit from Toledo, I took Patty Hill — 2nd runner-up in the Miss America competition — up on her invitation to stay with her. It was like waking up to a bright sunny day after a night of bad dreams. Grosse Pointe was incredibly beautiful, essentially a wooded park with mansions set among glorious gardens. I had only seen houses like these in the movies; even the big oil men in Tyler had nothing like this. Set atop a knoll at the end of a winding driveway, Patty's graceful two-storied white house with four columns on the porch at the top of the steps looked just right for a wealthy popular debutante.

Inside, the rooms were magnificent: cool and spacious, deep, white carpets, fresh flowers everywhere. They had more rooms to eat in than you could shake a stick at. An almost round room with lots of windows overlooking the park for breakfast, one with tall glass doors that opened on the terrace for lunch, and two different rooms, one big and one really big with pictures on the walls for dinner. It was the first time I'd ever seen a staff of white servants. Her parents seemed a little stiff and distant to me. Her father was a famous surgeon. At dinner one night he mentioned a patient that had come to him asking to be changed from a boy to a girl. He was astonished, but said he was going to try. This was new to everyone in that day.

Patty was lovely and gracious as always and asked if I was having a good time on tour. I said "Well, yes and no. I just love the people in the defense plants, and the boys in the camps have been darling. But I'm bored to death with all the press and radio interviews; they always ask the same questions and I feel so dumb giving the same answers over and over." I didn't want to tell her what the Fay Theater and the Hot Spot were like.

White teeth flashing, low laugh trilling, "Oh, you make it sound terrible. However, now that you're here I want you to relax and have a wonderful time. You deserve a little rest. I'll take over the interviews for you and you won't have to bother. I've planned a small tea party for you tomorrow afternoon to meet a few of my friends. We'll see to it that you have some fun for a change."

What Patty called a tea party was in the most luxurious hotel dining room: red wallpaper and red plush chairs, gorgeous chandeliers and a big orchestra. Her two girlfriends were as gay and charming as she, and the four boys were as nice as they could be. Patty's striking dark beauty made her a standout, but the other two girls were quite pretty, too, and most elegantly dressed. Two of the boys were brothers named Fisher. Both had pale blonde hair and skin, it was impossible to tell which was the older, and Patty said their father was very important in the automotive industry. Though the orchestra was larger, it played the same kind of music as · the Stork Club, without a good solid beat, but the dance floor was big enough so you could really dance on it. I was amazed the boys didn't know how to Lindy and volunteered to teach them. There weren't many dancers on the floor so I had plenty of room to demonstrate, and pretty soon they were flinging themselves around with abandon.

When I was finally breathless and came back to the table, one of Patty's girlfriends said, "You are such a wonderful dancer, do you do anything else as well as you dance?"

"My biggest talent is picking good watermelons without cutting a plug." They looked at me blankly; I could see they didn't know I was joking. "No, actually, what I do best is ride horses. I can do anything on a horse."

Patty said, "Really? That's marvelous. We'll take you riding tomorrow. Do you ride English?"

I wasn't sure what "English" meant, but hurriedly said, "I can ride anything."

I hadn't been so happy since I left Tyler. The dancing made me feel good physically and I wanted so much for them to like me, see I was something more than just a beauty queen. Showing them how well I could handle a horse seemed the best possible way to impress them.

The next morning the three girls wore Jodhpurs and short boots to go riding, with sweaters tied round their open shirts by the sleeves. They looked marvelous. I was wearing slacks and loafers and Patty said, "Would you like to borrow some riding clothes of mine? We seem to wear the same size."

"No, no. I can ride in anything."

The three debutantes plotting to send me on a wild ride. Miss America 2nd-place runner-up Patricia "Patty" Hill (left) and me after the wild ride (right).

The stable was right in the Grosse Pointe Park, and bridle paths branched out in all directions through the trees. Patty had telephoned ahead and a groom had their beautiful shining horses ready, but their saddles looked like a good-sized ham split in two. The bridles looked funny, too, with one strap too many. Patty and the groom had some kind of private argument and he seemed reluctant when he went to get the horse I was to ride. Patty explained, "Roger hasn't been ridden for some time. The groom was afraid you wouldn't be able to handle him, but I told him what an accomplished horsewoman you are."

Bliss! To show them what I could do with a horse that was hard to handle made my cup runneth over.

But when the groom came plunging out with Roger, I could see why he had been hesitant to go in and get him. First off, he was the biggest horse I had ever seen. He was huge. And all muscle — an explosion of repressed energy.

"Roger!" If he had been a buckin' bronco, they'd have named him "Dynamite." My jaw dropped and my stomach rose to meet it as he threw the groom around the paddock, and in Roger's wide open mouth I could see a bit that was broken in the middle. I longed for a heavy Western saddle with its big curving tree and a Spanish bit with its tongue depressor. If the groom couldn't hold him hanging on the bridle with all his weight, I didn't see how I was going to do so on that postage stamp of a saddle without even a normal straight bit. The groom stared at me in horror when it became apparent to him I had never ridden English style, and began to babble instructions about the 'bottom strap being the "check rein," but I couldn't see what he meant too well because the foam Roger was slinging about kept getting in my eyes. I had a terrible moment of indecision until the groom stammered, "I ... I don't think a girl can manage Roger."

My dander, along with my courage, rose, and my fight-instead-of-flight glands came to the rescue. With a great show of casual, cool professionalism, I got up on the mounting block and said, "Of course, I can manage him. Bring him over."

The groom dragged those quivering tons of destructive force over and tried to hold them still. The other girls were looking a little pale so I smiled reassuringly at them, grabbed those odd straps, got my foot up in the high tiny stirrup, and swung over. With a look of despair, the groom let go and Roger took off as if someone had fired the starting gun. With frantic screams of the girls growing dimmer in my ears, I began my battle with that brute.

We were not evenly matched.

I had learned to ride under the conditions that if you wanted a horse to stop, you pulled on the reins hard and yelled "Whoa". But, with a fully determined Roger fiercely holding that ineffectual bit between his teeth, I was hurtled with what seemed the speed of light down the bridle path, the other startled riders sedately bobbing up and down on their short stirrups and holding their horses firmly in hand with their check reins; however, nothing short of a mailed fist could have held Roger.

I was no slouch either when it came to determination, particularly as I was quickly convinced it was a fight for survival. With all my strength, I made abrupt, short, downward yanks on his mouth; I hated to do that to a horse, but I would have used thumb screws on Roger if I'd had any handy. He was making me mad.

However, as I jerked backward, he jerked forward. I made "Keystone Kop" lunges backward over the saddle with my feet braced up in the air, shouting epithets, then he jerked me forward onto his neck with my feet extended behind. Desperately, I remembered that the surefire way to stop a runaway horse is to drag its head around to one side so it must go in a circle and either stop or fall down. I stopped the jerking and pulled on the right side of those stupid straps with all the leverage I could manage, and off we went into the woods like a demented locomotive. Bushes, saplings, and branches were rent asunder as we careened through masses of wet leaves. We narrowly missed bunches of massive trees that seemed too thick to walk through, much less circle a runaway horse in. I thought, out of sheer self preservation, Roger would have to at least slow up, but he was as committed to winning our war as I was and we slammed through those woods flat out.

Suddenly we burst out of the trees — and right onto a highway. The woods ended and there was open meadow — a fence — a highway — a fence — and another open meadow before the woods began again. I had never jumped anything more than a deep ditch, but we sailed over the first fence, out onto the highway, a clatter of hooves, squealing of brakes, and over the other fence before I had time to wonder how to do it. When the shock wore off and I realized we were in the open, I took a manic grip on the right side of the reins and pulled that fool horse's head into his stomach. He turned, his knees buckled and he staggered then stopped.

I didn't have the strength to get off. I hadn't felt the strain while we were making that mad dash, but now I couldn't stop my hands and knees from trembling violently. Roger was blowing hard and content to stand until the girls arrived on the other side of the highway. They had been able to track us by the clear swath Roger made on his rampage, and now showed me an underpass nearby and we went wearily back to the stable.

Aside from the harrowing horseback adventure, I was having such a good time that I had decided to stay over a few days. But when I mentioned this to Mrs. Hill, she said "Guests are like fish; they stink after three days." I didn't know what to make of that, but decided to move on.

Patricia arranged a farewell party. Upon finding that my mother didn't have an evening gown, Mrs. Hill asked that she eat off a tray in her room. I accepted that. During the party, the Fischer brothers took me outside for some fresh air. On the terrace, they gave me some startling news. They said, "We want you to know, Jo-Carroll, that we think you're swell. You mustn't mind what Patty does. She's desperate to get her name in the paper, which is why she asked you to stay home while she did all your interviews for you. And she and her friends were just making fun of you when they arranged for you to ride that crazy horse." I was stunned. Riding out of Detroit with mother the next day, I felt guilty that I had allowed her to be banished from my farewell party, and foolish that I had let Patricia make a fool of me. I should have said that if my mother's not invited. I won't attend either. A regret I've carried with me ever since.

With Detroit behind me, I had to admit it was thrilling to get off the train in Tyler to the sound of bands playing and crowds cheering their "Hometown Miss America." Suddenly, it was all worthwhile. Everyone made a big fuss over me; the Junior Chamber of Commerce gave me a really lovely diamond ring, and it was a lot of fun to be the toast of the town. When the Senator learned I was coming home, he had arranged for me to visit the surrounding service camps and make appearances to sell war bonds. The newly opened Camp Hood, one of the biggest armored divisions in the country was nearby, and Mrs. Mayfield went with me for a full day's appearance there. My own defensive armor was pierced repeatedly by the sweetness and vulnerability of the enlisted men. I kept a "hands off" attitude with the officers, particularly the generals, but I loved dancing the Lindy with the enlisted men and was deeply touched by their awe and shy enthusiasm. Boy, could they Lindy, particularly those boys from the east.

I was giddy with happiness to be back with Bette, sharing Cokes in the drugstore. We couldn't stop laughing and talking, but one thing she said gave me a jolt. With a joyous smile, she said, "Oh, Jo-Carroll, isn't it just too perfect for words that after the sad life you've had, everything should turn out so wonderful for you!"

Greatly affronted, I said, "How do you mean a 'sad life?' I haven't had a sad life, I've had a terrific life! Where did you ever get such an idea?"

That was the only time Bette failed to understand me, and I deeply resented her implications. Of course, things had been pretty bad with Dr. Tate and the PTA ladies in Hale Center, and a few other things here and there, but all in all, I'd had an extraordinarily interesting life before I ever heard of a Miss America Pageant, for heaven's sake. I certainly wouldn't trade my life for an ordinary one like Bette's. Or anyone else's. Not in a million years. I loved my miracle-filled life. I loved who I was, always had, really. I was proud that I had never been ordinary like most people! Perhaps Bette would much rather have lived my life than her own. I never gave a thought to my earlier wish to live in a white house on a hill. I guess I always knew it was not right for me. I finally understood that people thought I was different because I was different. And proud of it!

One day, Mrs. Mayfield drew me beside her on the couch, and said in her serene voice, "Darlin,' what are your plans for the future?"

I had been keeping my plans a secret from everyone, but now it was a relief to share them with her. I said solemnly, "Mrs. Mayfield, I want to go to Texas University in Austin like you did."

After a pause, she said, "What do you want to study, Jo-Carroll?"

"Oh, anything. I just think it would do me a lot of good to learn a lot of things, and I want to be a Kappa Kappa Gamma sorority girl just like you. I haven't been spending much money and I have saved $5,000 from endorsements and appearances, so I think I'll have enough for the four years."

Mrs. Mayfield took both my hands in hers, and said, "Darlin,' do you really want to have to study that hard after all this time? It isn't easy, you know. And what would you want to do when you got out?" Putting her hand softly on my cheek, she said, "Why don't you want to accept Mr. Schrieber's offer to go to Hollywood and be in the movies?"

Desperate to make her understand, I said, "I just don't. Would you, Mrs. Mayfield, if you were in my place?"

Her high cheekbones stretched with her soft laugh. "Mercy me. No one in Hollywood would ever want me in the movies. But you are young and beautiful and talented. We had no idea how talented you were until we read all those things they said about you in the papers. You should take this opportunity to do something important with your life when it's offered to you, darlin.' Really, I think you should. Why, I don't think there is a girl in the country who wouldn't jump at the chance you've been offered."

It was bewildering that my role model, elegant Mrs. Mayfield, seemed to envy me. All of a sudden everything was bewildering. On the Miss America Tour I had kept myself going by thinking that when it was over I would go back to Tyler and everything would be the same. Bette and I, the Mayfair with the Big Bands, my life as I had lived and loved it would all be the same. It was a serious shock to my system to realize that everything had irrevocably changed. The dichotomies everywhere I looked were a continuing puzzle: I didn't want to go to Atlantic City, but I had to try to win. I hated the way men were, but I longed to be with Blackie. I wanted to be a "hometown" sort of girl, but I knew in my heart that I just wasn't and never could be. I didn't want to be a movie star, but I didn't want to be ordinary either. Upon due consideration, I knew I hadn't the grades in high school or, truly, the inclination to be a student in a university; I hadn't considered that I would have to study hard and take math and all that. It was just another of my unrealizable fantasy dreams of being high class, of being different than I was. Now Bette was going away to finish college at Southern Methodist University. The Mayfair was closed as the Big Bands were dispersing because of the draft and gas rationing; Glenn Miller and his band were already overseas. Blackie had made rear gunner on a fighter plane and was assigned to a carrier in the Pacific. And then, worst of all, Aunt Min said when we met, "Jo-Carroll, we are all just as pleased as punch about you winning that big contest. And it is wonderful that you have made all that money so that your mama can stop working on that medicine show. That was such a hard job shaving all that ice, and she has had to work like a slave all her life and really deserves to get to take it easy now."

Shielded by my blinders, I had been thinking that what Mother would do now was up to her. She had changed trains in Dallas for Hale Center while I blithely went on to Tyler. I had wanted to think that she'd had a marvelous adventure for two months and could pick up her life where she left it. But, with a sinking feeling, I realized that

I couldn't do it. If she'd ever asked me for anything, I could have gotten mad about it, but she never did. Not for anything ever except to write to her and I'd not done much of that. All things considered, it was clear what I had to do.

At first, I had a hard time getting Mr. Lew Schreiber on the phone. It was a scramble, first to get put through to his secretary, and then to get her to let me speak to him. Finally I said, "Just tell Mr. Schreiber Miss America wants to speak to him." He picked up right away and I said quickly, "Listen, Mr. Schreiber, I've been thinking. If you still want me, I will come on out to Hollywood."

Very well."

"I mean, I'll come if I don't have to be there until after Christmas. I can't start until January."

"That will be all right."

"Well, ah, then I'll be there."

"Fine. I'll turn you back to my secretary and she can take your address and send you a contract.

And that was it. World War II had ended, the Big Band Era — and my life in Tyler was ended as well. To keep my mother from shoveling ice for snow cones, I had to go to Hollywood and become a movie star. But I decided that the first thing I did when I got there would be to buy myself a yellow convertible with the money I was no longer going to use to go to college, and ride around all day with the top down.

Hollywood

Starlet in the making. 20th Century Fox, age 19 (1943).

To me, the train that carried Mother and me from Tyler to Los Angeles seemed a magic conveyance that could turn gold into dross. The gold of cool, shady, green Tyler, with its widely-spaced, stately white houses and lavish flower gardens, was turned into apparently endless rows of tacky buildings, with garish neon signs in hideous colors, all jammed together under what appeared to be endless rows of extremely tall, artificial-looking palm trees in glaring, hot sunshine. The gold of my being a real, special individual was turned into the dross of being just another *commodity* — 120 pounds of youthful girlish flesh in the land of a surplus of such commodities.

The knowledge that I had become a commodity was made clear to me as soon as I stepped off the train in Pasadena, California. Mr. Schreiber had mailed me a contract to be signed, and (without asking) a contract with the William Morris Agency. In the accompanying letter, he explained that henceforth a Mr. Murray Feil would be my agent, meet me at the train in Pasadena, arrange for an apartment, and bring me to the studio after arrival. Murray was a small, dark man like Marty Jurow, the William Morris Agent I'd met in New York, but where Marty was direct and enthusiastic, Murray was impersonal and all business. He had a thin, sharp-nosed face and a down-turned mouth, and he soon made me understand my duties and obligations according to contract, and what behavior was expected of me. He explained that I had been told to get off the train at the dreary, miniscule Pasadena station instead of the next stop in Los Angeles (thereby depriving us of arriving in the glorious, cathedral-like Union Station) because it was more convenient for *him*. He said that his secretary had arranged an apartment for Mother and me near the studio in Beverly Hills. No consideration had been given to our picking out our *own* apartment. In hundreds of subtle little ways, he made it plain that I was not a human being with feelings and likes and dislikes, I was a possibly lucrative business venture. The William Morris Agency, through the medium of 20th Century Fox, was taking a gamble that their merchandise would someday prove to be a big seller, given the right packaging and marketing. Nothing personal in it, you understand. If the merchandise didn't catch on with the public, well, they dropped your option and hadn't lost anything but a little time and money, but if you hit it big, their gamble paid off and they made a lot of money.

Whereas arriving in New York gave one the shock of incredibly high, fabulous buildings of infinite variety designed by an architectural genius, arriving in Beverly Hills was like going through block after block of white stucco, one and two-storied buildings that looked like the building blocks constructed by a 6-year-old child. It was a Sunday afternoon that Mother and I were taken to a small, one-bedroom apartment in a building on Crescent Heights between Wiltshire and Santa Monica and released with instructions to be ready at 9:00 a.m. the next morning to be taken to the studio. That afternoon, we gingerly walked around our new neighborhood with all those silly-looking, shadeless, tall palm trees trying to get a fix on what our new life would be like, but all of Beverly Hills seemed blindingly white and hot and empty. So quiet it was kind of spooky. It didn't seem possible to me that this was Hollywood, the movie metropolis of the world; there weren't enough *people* around. It made me feel strange and lonely. It was only later that I learned that Beverly Hills wasn't a Sunday kind of town. Streets that would be jam-packed during the week were practically empty because the folks who lived there were all sitting around their swimming pools having a party!

Of course, this was Beverly Hills, anyway, not Hollywood, but then there really isn't the place I'd imagined called Hollywood. I came to find that there was a Hollywood Boulevard which ran from Beverly Hills to downtown Los Angeles, and the first movie studios were built in an area around Hollywood Boulevard and Vine Street. But now, only Columbia, Paramount, and RKO were in that vicinity; Metro-Goldwyn-Mayer was miles away in Culver City, 20th Century Fox was on the edge of Beverly Hills and West Los Angeles, and Warner Bros., Republic, and Universal were over the hills in the San Fernando Valley, for heaven's sake. The Hollywood people thought they could visit or become famous in was as illusionary as the movies. Still, everyone knew exactly what you meant when you said "Hollywood."

For my first day on the job, I was trying not to look like an awestruck yokel as Murray got us past the guard at the enormous black iron gates of 20th Century Fox, past its high stucco outside walls, and into what looked like a Moroccan fortress. I'd had no preconceived notion of what a major motion picture studio would be like, I had no idea it would look to be larger than all of Hale Center, Texas. Everything seemed to be made of white stucco. Huge administration buildings with different sized arches in the Spanish style were scattered here and there, each with its own parking spaces and flower beds. Across the wide street from them were rows of small bungalows where writers, directors, musicians, and assorted others involved in running this movie factory had their offices. On one side were the big guns and on the other were the little pistols, so to speak. Jutting up behind the bungalows like gigantic children's building blocks were the enormous, windowless, gray-stucco sound stages and projection rooms, with huge block numerals painted on their sides. I had never seen anything remotely like it. It was all a bewildering blur on that first day, anyway. Murray had been as sparing of words on the drive over as if each one cost money, and I had the feeling he was transporting an unopened box to its destination with as little inconvenience to himself as possible. After we were parked in front of the largest administration building, however, as he was guiding me through the towering front entrance, he said, "You are going to meet Ivan Kahn. He is the casting director and will tell you what is expected of you."

I said, "I thought I was going to see Lew Schreiber."

"No, Ivan Kahn is the one you have an appointment with."

Thinking he didn't understand my personal connection with Lew Schreiber, I said, "But I think Mr. Schreiber would want to see me. I met him in New York and he signed me personally, you know."

Without slowing down or looking at me, he said, "Mr. Schreiber knows you're here. His secretary will let me know if he wants to see you. However, I doubt that he will. As production head under Mr. Zanuck, he is a very busy man."

"But he wrote me personally and everything. He is the one who got you for my agent."

Stopping, he turned to me and said firmly, "Look, Jo-Carroll, you will have to learn to trust what I tell you. I know how the studios work and you don't, so please, just leave everything to me. Now, we have to go in for we mustn't keep Mr. Kahn waiting."

I had looked forward to seeing Mr. Schreiber. True, he hadn't been overly warm when I met him in New York or spoke to him on the phone from Tyler, but it was he who had wanted me at his studio, and I thought he would want to help me get started. Anyway, I felt I *knew* him and trusted him; I didn't feel I knew Murray and I certainly didn't trust him. From the moment I had met him, he made me feel like a "thing," not a person. I thought between Mr. Schreiber and me it would be *personal. And anyway, I had already met Ivan Kahn in Dallas! He was the man Lew Ayres had taken me to see when I had won the Miss East Texas contest.* He was the one who had told me I would never make it in Hollywood, and besides my Texas accent was terrible. I felt apprehensive about seeing him. Would he remember me at all, or would we have a jolly laugh about how strange life is?

The big lobby of the administration building was as well guarded as a bank vault, but evidently our names were on the admittance list and quickly we were ushered into Mr. Kahn's elegant office. Without taking the cigar out of his mouth or getting up from his chair, the rotund head of casting rested his hands on his belly and looked me over judgmentally. Whether he remembered me or not was well concealed behind his stony face. I had to muster up all the courage my imaginary little red hat could give me not to be overpowered by his appraising look and stared back at him with chin-up composure. Murray sat quietly and behaved as though he was just a casual observer, no help from him. After our get-acquainted staring contest, and after I had answered a few innocuous questions, Mr. Kahn said without interest, "Come back tomorrow morning and my secretary will give you a list of your appointments and the necessary directions. She will issue you a parking pass so that you will be able to drive on the lot."

And that was that. Certainly nothing personal there. I hadn't expected a welcome banner or a brass band when I arrived, but all my life I had been treated as someone special and since winning Miss America, the banners had really been flying and the bands playing loudly for me everywhere, so my lackluster arrival in Hollywood to become a movie star was something of a letdown. I felt so minimized by my initial reception at Fox (as I came to call it) that I went right out that afternoon and bought myself a yellow Dodge convertible with red leather seats. Even so, I was quite apprehensive about my status when I drove it up to the massive gates the next morning. I had put the top down on my car to give me courage. I wasn't at all sure the guard would let me in without Murray, but when I leaned my head out and gave my name to the elderly man in uniform, he consulted a list on his desk and said, "Yes, Miss Dennison, drive right in. Do you know where to park?"

My yellow Dodge convertible, just after arriving in Hollywood.

Greatly relieved, I said, "Well ... ah, I guess not."

Beaming at me, he raised the gate and said, "Just go around in front of the administration building and park in any of the spaces without a name on it." I got to know that guard well over the four years I was at Fox, but there was no way he could know what a restorative his friendly attitude was to me on that first day. He was one of the few out of a multitude who treated me like a real person.

To begin with, one of Ivan Kahn's secretaries took me in tow. There was nothing friendly or personal about her attitude as she told me that the first order of business was that I must have some publicity photographs made, and get prepared for an introductory screen test. She forthwith launched me into the machinery of movie making. I felt like Charlie Chaplin in *Modern Times* in the scenes where the factory worker is whisked around like a cog on enormous revolving wheels, while he desperately tries not to fall off the rapidly moving assembly line.

The first big wheel was the drama coach, Helena Sorrel, a tiny woman with fiery red hair all done up in small, tight curls that looked so hard they would hurt you if you touched them. She wore more makeup than any woman I had ever seen on or off the stage. Her enormous brown eyes were outlined with several shades of violet, and her huge false eyelashes were heavily mascaraed. Her large mouth was made even larger with bright red lipstick, and with her dead white pancake makeup, she looked like she was wearing a mask that would crack if she moved a muscle. Her voice was deep and vibrant, and her beautiful, bejeweled hands were in constant motion. I put her down for a phony.

She said in her deep voice, "Miss Dennison, our first order of business is to prepare you for a screen test."

Somewhat offended, I said, "A screen test? I already have a contract, why do I have to have a screen test?"

Arched eyebrows raised even higher. "My dear, all newcomers to the lot (all the acreage within the high walls of a studio is called "the lot") must make a screen test so that Mr. Zanuck and the other producers can see what their type is and assess their potential. We have junior writers who write the test scenes and junior directors who direct them. We have many people on the lot who are learning their craft, and I am here to teach you yours." She gave me a scene to work on and made an appointment for me to come back the next day to learn how to act. I, who had been *acting* all my life!

Next was for me to get ready for a publicity photo shoot. The secretary took me to the makeup department, which looked much like a barber shop. Its white walls were brightly lit and a line of about six or seven barber chairs faced a solid wall of mirrors, with hand mirrors, magnifying mirrors, and pots of makeup and brushes set on the counter before each one, all very clean and tidy. As movie making started promptly at 7 a.m. on the set, this room would be a torrent of activity at 6 a.m., with every chair filled and makeup artists putting finishing touches on each famous supine face. Only the contract players, which included the stars, were made up here; the stock bit players, dancers, and singers were made up on the stage, and the extras did their own makeup and wardrobe at home before they came to work. But this was in the middle of the morning and the room was empty except for three or four makeup men, two of whom clustered around me with appraising, critical eyes. After one of the men (I was never introduced to them by name) had applied *three* different coats of pancake makeup to my face, the other one said while peering at my face in the wall mirror, "Where are her cheek bones? You haven't given her any cheek bones." Prodding my round face here and there, the chastised one replied, "I can't find them." It was no wonder to me that he couldn't find them under all that pancake, and I was astonished to find that there was only one acceptable way to put on makeup. Eyebrows and mouth had to conform to a preconceived pattern, no account whatsoever being taken of natural contours. The enormous false eyelashes were itchy and I thought I looked ridiculous in them. Hairdressing looked much like the makeup department, with the addition of sinks and hair dryers. The hairdresser was contemptuous of the hairstyle I held dear and had taken years to perfect and she piled my hair high on my head in tiny flat curls like Betty Grable's. I thought the style didn't look like *me* at all. The wheels of the studios ground very fine in order to bring conformity to its product.

Then on to wardrobe, where it became finally clear that I was fighting a losing battle if I thought I was going to have any say in creating my own image. The head of the department and her assistant turned me this way and that as I stood on a raised circle before a large mirror while surveying my face and figure, and speaking about me as though I was an inanimate object. Determined to fight on against insurmountable odds, I kept trying to interrupt their discussion to tell them that I looked best in tailored, simple lines, but it was quite literally as though my voice was completely inaudible. The assistant kept bringing out one frilly, ruffled dress after another, all Southern Belle where I wanted Eastern Sophisticate. But I did my dead level best to be a good sport; after all it was *their* studio and it was the studio who was going to pay my salary, so I posed endlessly in those fluffy costumes for the photographer and blinked my false eyelashes with as much grace as possible.

The photographer thought he made me look sexy, but I think I looked nauseous.

They did let me wear my own bathing suit and loose hair for what the photographer called the "sexy" shots, however, but right away I ran into trouble. With as much alacrity as I could, I responded to the photographer's demands to, "Turn this way and stick out your chest — hold this ball high over your head — bend over with your hands on your knees — until he said with a hint of exasperation, "Now, stick out your chest and sit with your legs outstretched and look *sexy*." Look sexy? I didn't know *how* to look sexy! Jane Russell had just made a big splash in *The Outlaw* for Howard Hughes, and huge billboards lined the streets of Hollywood with a giant picture of her lying propped on one elbow in some straw, wearing an off-the-shoulder white angora sweater with her large breasts partially exposed, while sucking on a piece of straw.

JO CARROL DENNISON — 20th Century-Fox Player

Sexy?

That was what the photographer wanted me to look like he said, and the wardrobe woman scurried to get me a white angora sweater. Well, I could wear a white angora sweater off one shoulder, lie propped on one elbow, stick out my chest and lower lip and try my darndest to look sultry and sexy like Jane Russell did — but I only succeeded in looking like I was trying not to throw up.

This photo shoot was right after Jane Russell in "The Outlaw."

Faced with the shattering realization that I didn't feel a cataclysmic sexual response when Blackie kissed me two years ago, ashamed and alarmed when the earth didn't move like Hemingway said it should if one was a real woman. Like a cat I had quickly covered over the shame and scraped it smooth with denial. I told myself that when I was older everything would be all right. Well, I was older — but the fact that I still wasn't all right with sex suddenly became painfully clear. Lying there on the floor in front of the pitiless photographer and camera, I had to face the vastly humiliating fact that I couldn't *look* sexy because I couldn't *feel* sexy.

The publicity department made much of the fact that the GI magazine, *Stars and Stripes,* had voted my photograph in a bathing suit in *LIFE* magazine the number-two pin up girl among the servicemen. Betty Grable in a bathing suit and standing with her back to the camera looking over her shoulder was named number one.

Within a week after my arrival, Louella Parsons, the Queen of Hollywood reporters, referred to me in her *Los Angeles Times* column as "The Body." Hedda Hopper, the rival queen, referred to me in her column as the sultry sex symbol 20th Century Fox was putting up against Metro-Goldwyn-Mayer's reigning sex goddess, Lana Turner. It was the period when the studios described their chosen sex symbols as "The Sweater Girl," "The Oomph Girl," "The It Girl," and the like. I was "The Body." It terrified me. What would they do when they found out I really wasn't sexy? Arrest me for fraud? Or just drop my option?

When I was in front of the judges in Atlantic City in a bathing suit, I had thought it was *me*, the real person I was, that the judges were applauding. I'd thought the judges and the audience were responding to my talent and my personality. My looks, of course, but not my sexuality. I didn't *want* to be a sex symbol. I wanted to be *some body* all right, but that was not the "body" I wanted to be.

Obviously, the purpose of the half-exposed breast, the seductive photograph, was to arouse the male viewer's desire for sexual intercourse. The image of that insertion into the vagina and the face and smell of Dr. Tate instantly commingled in my mind. The memory of his powerful gripping arms, his hot breath against my ear, the sound of his hoarse grunts, his *smell*, and the feel of the urgent thrust of his organ against my buttocks made my stomach muscles clench. It was like a giant, gray octopus floating just beneath the surface of my consciousness, whose suckered arms could reach up and snatch me down if disturbed.

Me in LIFE *magazine, 1942.*
Myron Davis (cover) and Eliot Elisofon (photos of the author)/
The LIFE Picture Collection/Shutterstock

That vivid memory conjured up a revulsion that colored and directed my every reaction. It wasn't only that one near-rape experience that motivated me, it was the ongoing horror of the five years of being forced to allow Dr. Tate to fondle and pull me down on his lap in order to keep my job that had destroyed something vital in me. To be the sex symbol *inviting* that copulating desire in the opposite sex by wearing provocative clothes, sticking out my breasts, and leering seductively at the camera made my stomach turn. As opposed to the pleasure presumably some women took in looking "sexy," I resented being categorized in that way. Was I *just* a sex symbol? Is that all I was worth?

I don't surf.

Did I want the men looking at my photograph to think I looked nice? Yes. Pretty? Absolutely. Did I want them to think I was saying in essence, "Sock it to me, Big Boy?" Never!

It seemed like fate had played a game of tic-tac-toe with Blackie and me. Every time we were about to get our Os in a row, fate threw in an X. By the time he had gotten enough money saved from his job on his hometown paper for us to get married — it was December 7, 1941 and our whole world changed. Blackie had joined the Navy, and I had to go to Hollywood to become a movie star. But I never fantasized about being a movie star like Jane Russell; rather my dreams were about being safely married to Blackie after the war and learning to cook and have babies and living happily ever after. What was entailed with having babies I left to my guardian angel to put right sometime in the distant future. My future was lovely, all storybook and rhyme. And in the meantime, I felt the life raft that Blackie was for me would keep me safely afloat in the perilous waters of Hollywood.

In order for my mother not to have to shovel ice for snow cones, I'd had to sign a contract at Fox, and in those days when a hamburger was 25 cents and a gallon of gas 23 cents, a hundred and $50 a week was a lot of money, so I made up my mind that while I was waiting for Blackie, I would amiably do whatever the studio asked of me as well as I could: take acting and elocution lessons, endure publicity photos and junkets, make screen tests, and go to the parties I was supposed to go to as a starlet to get my name in the columns. When cast in a movie, I would do the best I could, but I didn't look forward to playing a part in a movie; I was already playing the part of the brave, forthright, untouchable girl I had cast myself as long ago. I had been able to get off the stage when I went to Tyler, be myself without playing a part at all for that short time. But I was back on the stage now and I had the feeling that I was standing outside of myself watching a command performance of Baby Jo-Carroll driving on the Fox lot, going to coaches, being photographed, and my real self not being there at all. For my own stubborn reasons, I would do everything I was asked to do — but I was determined never to make the slightest effort to be in a movie. And in all the four years I was under contract to Fox, I never did.

There were, however, three things I was asked to do in Hollywood that were a distinct pleasure. One, I worked at the Hollywood Canteen. Bette Davis and John Garfield started the Hollywood Canteen as a place where the military could come free of charge to eat and socialize with movie stars. John Garfield came to the movies from the New York stage, and it was his idea to start something in Hollywood like the *Stage Door Canteen* in New York. He and Bette Davis were both at Warner Brothers Studios, so he went to her about it, she went to her MCA agent, Jules Stein, about it — and together they made it happen. Bette Davis was designated president and John Garfield vice president of the Hollywood Canteen Board of Directors and Jules Stein got to raise the money. They took over an old building, which had formerly been a livery stable and then a nightclub called "The Old Barn" at 145 Cahuenga, just off Sunset Boulevard in Hollywood. Members of the 14 guilds and unions of the motion picture industry pitched in to install lighting, a stage, and a large dance floor, with a bar along one side of the room for soft drinks and food. Famous artists and cartoonists painted murals on the walls. The then famous Chef Milani volunteered to be in charge of procuring the food and drink. Although a great deal of supplies were donated, the average weekly food bill was over $3,000, but in a wonderfully heartwarming way, Hollywood went to war. I don't think there was anyone employed by or connected to the industry who did not contribute money, time, and talent toward making the Hollywood Canteen a huge success.

Members of the Armed Forces lined up by the hundreds to spend a few hours being supplied with sandwiches and root beer by stars and starlets like me, watch some of the best entertainers in the world, like Dick Haymes, the Andrews Sisters, and Donald O'Connor perform, dance with glamorous top stars to the best bands of the Swing Era like Benny Goodman and Artie Shaw, and get autographs and chat with their favorite movie celebrities. And the celebrities all came. Every star in Hollywood came night after night to serve, dance, perform, or just talk with the servicemen. You can only imagine what it must have been like for those boys from all over the country to look around the Canteen and find that almost every person who wasn't in uniform had a breathtakingly familiar face. For some, it was the most wondrous thing that would ever happen to them. I could just hear one of them saying to his grandchildren, "You won't believe this, but one night back in 1943 I actually danced with that great movie star, Claudette Colbert!" It really made me proud to be a part of it.

I was asked to be a part of it because I was the current Miss America, and the servicemen were sweet and glowing and eager to make contact with *their* Miss America. Again, I didn't feel it was personal or sexual; I was a symbol representing their country, the country for which they had put on a uniform, and they treated me accordingly. I loved them. I greatly enjoyed standing behind the bar to serve food and drink, sign autographs, and just talk with the excited servicemen, but it was bliss indeed to dance with them; particularly with the boys from New York who could do a fantastic jitterbug. I could have done it all night, every night. The Hollywood Canteen was a terrific morale builder for the men, and a second Stage Door Canteen was opened in Paris right after D-Day, with stars like Maurice Chevalier and Noel Coward entertaining. (*It only occurs to me now that I don't remember seeing any female military there.*)

The second thing I loved was touring the military camps, and as soon as I had gotten organized at Fox, I was assigned to the "Victory Committee." In 1942, an organization of top studio executives, called the Motion Picture Production Defense Committee or the Victory Committee, was formed to provide entertainment for the troops at home and abroad.

The first tour they sent out was comprised of Kay Kyser and his orchestra, Lucy (as she was then known) Ball, Kay Francis (actress), Judy Carnova (comedian), Larry Adler (fabulous harmonica player), Desi Arnez (singer), Pat O'Brien (actor), and Ann Miller (dancer). Not a bad group, and obviously they wowed the troops. Similar groups were sent on tour all over the country and wherever American troops were located around the world for the duration of the war. Bob Hope, of course, organized his own troupe and never stopped touring, as did Marlene Dietrich.

The first tour I was assigned to entertain Army and Army Air Force camps in the surrounding California desert. In all the tours I went on the audience reaction was the same: big, respectful applause for the star, laughter for the comic, hoots and whistles for the scantily clad dancer, and enthusiastic applause for the singer. But for their Miss America, they all stood up and yelled their appreciation. For the first time in my life, I felt humble. I sang, "Deep in the Heart of Texas" and talked with the boys a lot from the stage, I had a gimmick that I would point to a boy in the audience (everyone called these men "boys" no matter their age, but most of them were indeed just boys) would ask him what state he was from, and then I would sing a chorus about that state. Indiana? "Back Home Again in Indiana." Georgia?

"Georgia on my Mind." New York? East Side, West Side," and so on.
The accompaniment, piano or band, always knew the songs, too, or
they could fake it. When I thought I had been on long enough, I said
to the audience, "Well, listen. When this war is over I'm inviting you
all to my house for dinner. Now y'all come. Y'hear?" They all yelled
acceptance. I loved those boys and they knew it.

But the bad thing I remember about that first tour I was on is
that while Jane Wyman was nice to me, Margaret Whiting (my favorite vocalist next to Bea Wain) was mean to me. I found that top actors
and entertainers didn't take bathing beauties very seriously as being
a real part of show business. I didn't blame them, I didn't either. It
might have been different if I had told them that I had been a part
of show business on a medicine show my whole life, but I didn't. I
had a stubborn pride thing that made me want people to like me for
who I was not who I had been — Miss America or medicine show
girl. Anyway, somehow Margaret took an instant dislike to me and
snubbed me deliberately and often as though I didn't belong in their
company. (I remember her scorn even now.)

The third good thing was the Victory Committee also sent stars
from all the studios on War Bond Tours all over the country. The first
one to which I was assigned brought about one of the most inflating
and deflating experiences of my life. This was the first countrywide
tour that was formed and, with the exception of me, it was made up
of dozens of the very top stars in Hollywood. Lana Turner, Greer
Garson, Spencer Tracy, Ronald Colman, Ginger Rogers, Jimmy Cag-
ney, the list went on and on. I mean, you could name your favorite
star and they were on that train. I had gotten used to being treated
as though I was invisible by the major entertainers I travelled with,
but it did make it kind of lonely on tour. At the camps, I had lots of
company from the servicemen, but when it was just us movie stars
— I was odd man out. With one exciting exception.

For this War Bond Tour, a special Super Chief train was designated to take the stars from L.A. to Chicago, where we would split
up in smaller groups to travel to different parts of the country. In the
club car that first night, Franchot Tone came and sat down beside me
and began to question me about myself. Now, Lew Ayres and Franchot Tone were my favorite movie stars. They were the two I would
have chosen to have with me on a desert island ever since I first saw

Early days at Fox.

them. They were high-class gentlemen in my book, and suave and sophisticated, and I admired them greatly. I had been so excited after I had won Miss East Texas to have *Lew Ayres* himself stop me on the street that time in Dallas and introduce me to Ivan Kahn, and now to have *Franchot Tone* single me out was a thrill of the highest order. I was dazzled and delighted to tell him all about myself at great length. I couldn't seem to stop talking. He was fascinated. In the two days it took the train to get to Chicago, he spent a lot of time with me and I felt we really got to know one another. When we were coming into Chicago, I was feeling let down as the tours were breaking up there to go in different directions, and I would probably not see Franchot Tone again. In those days, all trains from west to east went to Chicago, where you then had to change trains for the rest of the country.

But, the gods be praised, before we changed trains, Franchot Tone suggested that in the layover we have lunch together at the Pump Room of the Ambassador East Hotel (a restaurant so famous even I had heard of it). I sat in a red velvet booth in this fabulous room watching waiters waltzing around with flaming food of some kind on a sword and listening to soft marvelous music while Franchot Tone quoted *poetry* to me! In my naivete, I quoted back to him the only poem I knew by heart, "Ah my beloved" from the Rubaiyat of Omar Khayyam, not realizing how provocative it would sound. It was truly an out-of-this-world experience, and I was wistfully sad when we said goodbye, as his train would be taking him to St. Louis and mine taking me to New York that afternoon.

That night, in my blue and red butcher-boy pajamas as I was putting my hair up in curlers and cold cream on my face, I was still glowing because Franchot Tone had taken me to lunch in the Pump Room. His wife, Jean Wallace, was a starlet at Fox, also, and I liked her. She was blonde and beautiful and about 20 years his junior, as I was, and I was kind of trying to imagine what it would be like to be married to him, when there was a soft knock on my compartment door. I was blank with astonishment when Franchot Tone quickly came in and shut the door behind him. Startled that he was *here* and not on the train to St. Louis, and shamed at my unattractive appearance, I jumped in the pull-down bed and jerked the covers up over my silly butcher-boy pajamas, but there was nothing I could do to hide the curlers in my hair and the cold cream on my face.

Sitting gently on the side of my bed, he said in his charmingly familiar voice, "Don't be disturbed. I found that I just didn't want to leave you so I made arrangements to continue on with you to New York. I can make connections for St. Louis from there, but I wanted to have one more night with you." He leaned down toward me and said softly, "You are a new experience for me, so fresh and lovely, I can't get enough of you," and he smiled that kind of one-sided famous smile of his.

His familiar face and the things he was saying were so right out of a romantic movie that I was mesmerized and breathlessly waiting to see how the scene turned out. As in a dream, I watched him put his hand out to caress my face, only to change his mind when he encountered the cold cream and instead slipped his hand under my covers and try to find the buttons on my button-less pajama top. As his fingers touched the skin of my chest, the dream sequence shattered against the hard rock of the here and now. I instantly took his hand and put it back on top of the covers and pulled them tightly up around my neck, as I stammered, "Oh, gosh, it is so nice of you to have changed your plans and everything, but you'll have to go now. My mother would just have a conniption fit if she knew I was alone in a bedroom with a man. And you're married and everything. I mean, I really appreciate what you said and I'll never forget it, but – well, I sure do hope that you understand that my mother just wouldn't like it at all for you to stay here with me in bed and everything."

There was a long silence, and then he said, "I am sure your mother is a very wise woman. I have never been said 'no' to so nicely," and got up, knocking his head slightly against the upper bunk, and left, closing my door firmly behind him.

I lay there in awe that Franchot Tone had fallen in love with me. I wondered if when he got back from the tour, he would want to divorce Jean Wallace and marry me. Not that I would do it, of course, I was not about to *marry* him, but it was fun to think about. I savored imagining the romantic scene of how he would greet me the next morning as we were all getting off the train at the station in New York. When I finally found him, however, he was frantically trying to get his travel tickets rearranged with the conductor and he didn't even seem to know who I was.

When everyone on the tour had assembled that first day on the Super Chief, we had all been given the itinerary and personnel of our individual tours. Mine was to be through New England with Charles Bickford and two servicemen we would pick up in New York. Bickford was a dour, silent man who combed his thinning reddish hair in heavily lacquered waves over his bald spot, and had brought his "secretary" along. Many of the female stars were accompanied by makeup/hairdressers, but Bickford was the only one who had brought a secretary. She was a timid, bulging-blue-eyed blonde who was assigned to share a compartment with me, but I never saw her again until we got off the train in New York. After we started the tour, I never saw them either except during the times Bickford and I were making our sales pitch for war bonds at our various stops. Neither of them ever said more than six words to me all told and I was fascinated to know what they talked about all the time they were alone.

Our two servicemen turned out to be a captain and a first lieutenant in the Army Air Force. They both flew on B-26s, the captain a pilot and the lieutenant a navigator, although they were from different crews. They were sent home because they had been injured when their planes had crashed and instead of being sent back overseas when they were released from the hospital, they had been ordered to go on this bond tour as a public relations thing. The captain was a big man, quiet and reserved, who wore his dress uniform all the time and looked a lot like Dana Andrews. The lieutenant looked like the fresh-faced, happy-go-lucky kid next door, who wore a leather bomber jacket and pinks (casual beige gabardine), with his cap on the back of his head, and he handled his crutches as though they were just for fun. They were totally different and totally adorable. We hung out together and had a great time the three weeks of our tour of all the major cities of New England. This was in the winter, and I had never been to New England or tried to get around in three and four feet of snow before, and I loved it. It was the first time since I left Tyler that I could really immerse myself in nature and I went slogging through the woods every chance I got. What a glorious part of the world it is. I determined I would live in this kind of country someday. And I had a memorable time with the two servicemen. I remember one night as the two guys and I were leaving a restaurant, we found it was snowing and the captain picked me up and ran with me all the way back to our hotel. Nobody ever picked me up and ran with me again and I never forgot it.

I say we had a great time; actually on the airmen's part the great time was superficial because underneath the fun stuff was the horror of what they had just been through, and mostly I think they had a feeling of unease and almost guilt because they were here being wined and dined in the States and safe on a stage trying to sell war bonds, while their buddies were still being shot at or dead in Europe. These men had flown more missions than the human spirit had been wired to do. Although the rule was that crews would be rotated home after a certain number of combat missions, because of the shortage of bomber crews, they had flown more than twice as many missions as the rule allowed in those unstable, often dangerous B-26s. But they took their best shot at being good sports and good representatives of their country. Bickford was a good actor and did his sincere best, and between us all we sold a lot of war bonds.

I have never forgotten those wonderful brave men.

The other units around the country selling war bonds did equally well. Hollywood used many ways to sell war bonds, Bing Crosby, *the number-one star in Hollywood at that time)* made a short which played in all movie theaters, singing to a marching tune:

"Buy, buy, buy, buy a bond,

And the bonds you buy will lead to victory … "

Every theater had that request to buy war bonds on a placard before and after every movie. J. Edgar Hoover made a short film warning that "Loose lips sink ships"; there were posters everywhere warning that the enemy was listening, and someone thought they saw an enemy submarine off the coast of Santa Barbara, California. The whole country was at red alert, and during that first year of the war, $12 *billion* worth of war bonds were sold. That helped a lot to make planes, tanks, ships, guns and ammunition faster and better than had ever been done before.

Going home again on the Super Chief from Chicago, I found that I was to share a compartment with Joan Blondel. On the screen she played the brassy, blonde with a heart of gold, and that's what she was in person. She was warm and seemed genuinely interested in helping me spot the pitfalls I faced in Hollywood. As a longtime participant in the ways and wars of the movie business, she was well equipped to give me a lot of inside advice. After the snobbery I had

taken from most of the female movie stars I had met, I was patheti-
cally grateful to her. But, partly because I liked her so much, sharing
a compartment with her put me in an agony of indecision about
using our communal toilet. In our small compartment, there was no
way I could use the tiny bathroom without her hearing the splash.
Even though I was almost 20 and had been exposed to many kinds of
society and situations, I was still a virgin and I had never said "penis"
or "vagina" aloud, or used any kind of curse words or "smut," never
put my hand on my private parts except through a wash rag, or peed
in a toilet where anyone could hear me. I even ran the water in the
sink when I was with my best friend Bette back in Tyler, for heaven's
sake. I don't know where that vital prohibition came from, but I would
go to any length to avoid someone else overhearing my pee, or even
knowing that I was *going* to go pee. I couldn't bring myself to even
say the words "pee" or "toilet." Euphemisms like "have to go" and
"bathroom" were hard enough to articulate. I couldn't even *think* of
or imagine or look at a picture of a penis or vagina.

   I solved this problem with Joan Blondel by using the toilet in
the club car when she was in the compartment, but the night before
we got in to L.A. we sat up talking in our pajamas after I had already
gone to the club car — and before I went to sleep, I had to either use
the toilet again where she could hear, or go to bed without. Well, I
climbed into my upper bunk without and during the night, the gentle
rocking of the train was my undoing. The next morning my agony
of embarrassment was annihilating when I awoke to find myself in
a foul-smelling puddle of urine. Joan Blondel was already up and
finishing her packing, and I agonized over the horrifying decision
of whether to take off my soaked pajama bottoms and leave them
in the bunk while I climbed down the ladder bare-assed, or sliding
down the ladder with a pillow to cover myself while I yanked the offending bottoms off and hid them in my suitcase at high speed. The
thought that Joan Blondel could smell what I smelled made it almost
impossible for me to breathe. She, to her everlasting credit, busied
herself with finishing her dressing and left the compartment to go get
her breakfast as quickly as possible. I didn't feel like I would ever eat
breakfast again, and I was miserable at the thought of the steward
finding all those wet bed linens later.

   Why, against all common sense, would such stupid inhibitions
control a grown-up person? Where did they come from? Obviously,

for me they came mostly from my mother in a hundred subtle and unsubtle warnings and examples, but how did *she* get them? And *why*? Why would natural functions and body parts become socially identified as unmentionable, dirty, *un*natural, and revolting? Why had something that should be thought of as natural, clean, healthy, and openly discussable, become such a strict and embarrassing social taboo? Was it originally a man thing to keep women and their sexuality shamed, confined, and restricted? Like clitoral castration? Was it that pee was connected to the vagina and the vagina was connected to original sin, so that society deemed it shameful? Who said that for "nice" girls, words like penis, vagina, and anything connected to either were to be so painfully avoided? Whatever the causes, at this time in my life, normal feelings below the waist and any form of reference to "private parts" or their functions were as restricted as if a huge boa constrictor named "shame" had squeezed the vital life out of me. Natural instincts and hormonal urges never had a chance. The why of this silly phobia is still a mystery to me. I know these unnatural restrictive morals and manners of women's appropriate language and conduct goes much further back than the Victorian age, but why has it lasted so long? I often wonder how new brides of the 1700s and 1800s, who had been trained to be just as silly as I was about these kinds of things, had managed on their wedding night with sex and chamber pots. What horrors of fear and embarrassment they must have suffered. I sympathize totally with them. None of the classic books about those periods I read ever referred to it. Of course, in the coming decades, those particular inhibitions were to become obsolete, but it still interests me that they occurred in the first place. And I wonder if new ones have taken their place?

After I got back home, it was a while before I let myself understand that Franchot Tone had mistaken my childish excitement at being with my favorite movie star for sexual excitement toward him as a man. How he must have gritted his teeth at my misleading behavior and naiveté. It sure had been fun for me at the time, though. When I got home, I said to Mother, "Oh, you should have met Franchot Tone. He just *eludes* charm!" (I often got my newfound dictionary words mixed up in those days. In retrospect, though, I guess I had it right the first time.)

Before Mother and I had been in our new apartment on Crescent Drive a month, I had found us another one in the newspaper ads. For one thing, I wanted a two-bedroom apartment, and for another, I didn't like living in the middle of a lot of shops, cafes, and hotels in the business district of Beverly Hills. Our first apartment was only a few blocks from Rodeo Drive, which was famous all over the world for its expensive shops, but I hardly ever walked along it. I didn't yearn for clothes or jewelry or furs, never had, and I wasn't about to spend my money on them. I loved my new yellow convertible, with its green and red lights on the dashboard, but, aside from that, what I was willing to spend money on was rent. I had always lived in cramped, tacky places until I moved in with the Mayfields in their big, white house on a hill. Oh, my Aunt Lou's house in Tyler was nice, but it had little crocheted things on the arms of all the chairs and another house right on either side of it and I always felt in transit there. But from the moment I walked into the Mayfield's spacious, gracious, glory of a house, I knew I had found my kind of place. I luxuriated in the height and width of the rooms and the exquisite elegance of their furnishings, and drew deep nourishing breaths from the view of their extensive yard and gardens available from every window. It made me feel nourished and peaceful, and for the rest of my life, I sought to find a place to live that duplicated that feeling. Not the size or the luxury, necessarily, but the *feeling* of that house. The square little one-bedroom apartment in a square little apartment building on Crescent Drive didn't do it for me, so I quickly found a larger two-bedroom furnished apartment on Smithwood Drive just off Olympic right behind Fox on the edge of Beverly Hills. The apartment complex was built on the incline of a hill in a residential area filled with trees, *real* trees, not those shadeless palm things, where each apartment was on a different level and had its own lawn and flower garden area. The rent was twice as much, but I felt I could breathe there, and, what the heck, I could afford it!

I was never especially fond of the furniture in the apartment because it was all dark and heavy, but Mother loved it, furniture and all, because the rooms were larger than any she had ever lived in and for the first time in her life, she had a separate dining room. Mostly she was happy because the absentee landlady let her plant a vegetable garden in the area behind our apartment complex and more flowers in the yard all around. Mother loved flowers and they loved her.

She had the greenest thumb of anyone I ever knew; she could grow peonies as big as dinner plates and roses as big as saucers, but she had never lived in a situation where she could indulge her passion for growing beautiful things before. Mother gave constant thanks to God for the miracle that her daughter had such a good job in this town of wonders and was going to be a movie star. She spent all her spare time writing letters and sending clippings and photographs to a multitude of relatives and friends to keep them informed about our wonderful goings-on.

My new life of becoming a movie star had its upsides and its downsides. Dancing with the servicemen at the Hollywood Canteen and touring for the Victory Committee to the military camps and on war bond junkets was definitely up and I enjoyed it greatly — working with acting and voice coaches and photographers was a job I had to do and I tried hard not to let it get me down. Fox had three acting coaches: Helena Sorrel, who worked with actors on parts and screen tests, Ludmilla Piteof, a classical drama coach, and Lee Strasberg, who was teaching the then-new Method Acting. Ludmilla Piteof was a famous Russian actress from the French stage who had gotten too old to play her usual young heroines, and when her actor/director husband died, had come to America to teach. A tiny person who looked like a French doll herself, she was quick to see that the ability to play Shakespeare was far in my future (if ever), but I loved to listen to her stories of the life she and her husband had lived on the stage both in Russia and in France. She was kind of lost and vulnerable here, and, as she had never learned to drive, I enjoyed driving her places and helping her in little ways. Lee Strasberg, on the other hand, was a big turnoff for me. He was a small, gray man who sat hunched up behind his desk like a disgruntled turtle, as he explained the Stanislavsky Method of Acting and Sensory Memory to me. He said, "An actor's body can consume and respond to all kinds of purely psychophysical values. Therefore, for an actor's development, special psychophysical exercises must be found and applied to the actor's art. Try to experience or assume the psychology of different persons, historical periods, or objects. All such vicarious experiences will sink gradually into your body and make it more sensitive, noble, and flexible. And your ability to penetrate the inner life of the characters you are studying professionally will become sharper. Now to begin, please try to assume and experience the psychology of a fire hydrant."

I stared at him blankly. With a slight frown, he said, "Just stand up and try to *become* a fire hydrant."

I thought, "A *fire* hydrant? He's got to be kidding!" But he wasn't, and I stood up for awhile, desperately trying to *become* my watch so that I would know how much longer I would have to stand there.

Finally, with resignation, Strasberg said, "All right, that's enough. Come back tomorrow and we'll work on it some more."

But I never went back. I had the feeling that his paycheck was more important to him than my learning to become a fire hydrant, and that he wouldn't turn me in as a truant. And he didn't.

It always astonished me later that Marlon Brando, Paul Newman, Robert De Niro, Meryl Streep and others said that they learned their craft at the feet of Lee Strasberg at the Actor's Studio in New York. I could never imagine how they learned to be such fine actors by pretending to be a fire hydrant. Marilyn Monroe studied with Strasberg for years. I'd like to have seen *her* as a fire hydrant.

Helena Sorrel, on the other hand, brooked no dillydally about getting ready for my introductory screen test. After two weeks of "lessons," she evidently thought she had passed on as much of her dramatic knowhow to me as I was able to receive at the time, so she brought in a male starlet who was to be my partner in the scene. William Hudson was in his early 20s, a slender, sensitive, dark-haired man with serious brilliant-blue eyes who had just recently been signed to a contract. He had been in Hollywood for several years trying to get into pictures and was delighted to have finally made it this far and determined to make a good impression in the test. I was just kind of going with the flow, but I got caught up in his earnestness and tried hard to do the fairly simple scene as well as I could.

On the morning of the test, I again felt like a cog in a very large wheel, as I was carried along the assembly line through makeup and hairdressing, where, even though I was to wear a turban in the scene, my hair was shampooed, set, dried, combed out, and then put up in little curls to fit under the turban. That made no sense to me at all, but mine was not to reason why. The wardrobe lady got me into an elegant beige suit with the enormous shoulder pads of Adrian design, which made me look like a line backer, and from there onto the sound stage. The mood I had been trying to maintain for the scene went up in smoke the moment I walked through the huge, padded doors of the sound stage. The thing I had not considered about a sound stage is that there is no "sound" from outside. At first it was as though I had been struck suddenly deaf as the abrupt cessation of the ordinary sounds one takes for granted and doesn't really hear — cars passing, people walking and talking, birds, wind — all were instantly silenced. From the outside, the sound stage had appeared to be a 3-or-4-story building with no windows, and I had unconsciously expected to see an ordinary lobby with different floors and stairs or elevators, but once I stepped inside its padded walls, with only a shaded red light over the door to see by, the dark, cavernous immensity of the single-floored sound stage was overwhelming. At first, the walls seemed to go on up into the gloom of infinity and the whole building appeared empty as it spread out into the dim distance. But then my eyes adjusted and I could see a network of wooden walkways with pipe railings high overhead, and here and there, I began to see the stacked backs of wood-framed canvas sets. The wooden floors seemed to be embedded with the dust of centuries and the distinct smell of the sound stage itself evoked the unique sensory memory of every backstage I'd ever been in. The "smell of the grease paint" is a show business cliché, but anyone who has ever worked in a theater or on a movie set, will instantly recognize that olfactory mixture of makeup, hot lights, dust, and the indefinable remnants of performances long gone.

Then I became aware that one small corner of this gigantic building was brightly lit, and there was literally a beehive of activity around and above that corner. Almost obscured, men were soundlessly adjusting lights that hung from the towering catwalks onto that semi-circle of a "dressed" set, around which dozens of figures were quietly talking as they stepped over the web of electrical cables on the floor and around the cameras and sound equipment that were focused on the set. Watching them for a moment, I was struck dumb by the realization that some 25 people were involved in the transfer of our little scene onto film, which a bunch of other people would look at and judge. It was a paralyzing thought. Somehow, I had imagined a director, a cameraman, and a sound man would be all that was necessary for a screen test, but I knew nothing at the time about the mighty might of the multiple unions involved in the single turn of a camera in Hollywood. Of course, the set, the furniture, the props, the numerous kinds of lights and equipment, and the vast array of minutiae involved in making motion pictures doesn't just magically appear before the camera; it takes an incredible number of people in a multitude of departments to "set the stage," so to speak. But, no matter how talented and creative they are, it's the art or the beauty of the performers that brings the indefinable magic into what all these dozens, if not hundreds, of people have put together for a motion picture — when the actor has what it takes, that is. Helena Sorrel told me that the actor's magic is to make the camera fall in love with you.

Well, there was no magic coming from me that day on the set. I was instantly weighted down with the feeling of total responsibility for justifying the effort that all these people were putting forth to put me and Bill "in the can." Bill was already on the set when I arrived, looking preoccupied and nervous. Helena Sorrel was standing behind the camera listening to what the director was saying to the cameraman, and she just nodded to me as if to say, "I've done my part, now it's up to you." Swell! The nervousness of the young director as he discussed camera angles with the cameraman in a language made of strange words like "broads" and "key light" and "dolly" and "gobo" and "best boy" added to the weight of the burden on my shoulders, and I felt the first flutter of panic. It was as though a large cone of professionals in all the departments of the studio — coach, writer, makeup, hairdressing, wardrobe, set decorator, props, lighting, camera, director and all their assistants — were finished with their business and had now narrowed their pinpoint focus in on me. Well, on Bill, too, of course.

The director didn't give us any "direction" as far as mood or feelings, he just showed us where to stand and move and which lines to sit on and where to hit our marks for the camera, while I concentrated fiercely on remembering each move. Everyone on the set got very quiet and watched the director as they leaned on a light stand or squatted on their heels and smoked a cigarette. Except on the set, there were no chairs anywhere other than the one canvas chair with "Director" painted on its back, which no one ever sat in. No one paid any attention to the actors, except the director; each member of the crew was focused solely on their individual job. But while the crew all appeared casual and detached, the moment the director asked a question, the sound man, cameraman or assistant director was right there to answer it for him. They all seemed to want to help him. When he wanted to move an ashtray from one spot to another on the coffee table though, the assistant director quickly stopped him and we had to wait while the prop man was called to move the ashtray a few inches. (The motion picture business had developed very strong unions!) We went through the scene following the director's blocking as best we could a couple of times, and I learned that I could find my key light when I was so blinded that I couldn't see anything else, and be sure I had hit my "mark" only by instinct. After a few stops because of technical difficulties, the director said tightly, "OK, let's try one," and in a blur of concentration, terror, and a feeling of unreality, I heard the words, "Camera, lights, ACTION!" Then after what seemed a very long time, during which Bill and I were reciting our lines in our own enclosed vacuum, the director yelled, "Cut, let's do one more," and we did the scene again. As far as I could tell, we did it no better or no worse, but we did hit our marks and key lights and the director yelled, "Cut, and print the second one," and we broke for lunch. Instead of applause, there was the immediate snap and clank sound of lights being shut off and a hum of conversation from among the crew.

It was staggering to think that all these people had been doing their job from six o'clock this morning until noon in order to get possibly 20 minutes of film in the can. I was worn out. I looked to Helena Sorrel for some feedback as to how the scene had gone, but she got busy talking to the director and neither of them gave us a yea or nay of approval. That scared me a little. I did not look forward to coming back from lunch to do close-ups.

I had never been in the commissary on the lot, always preferring to go home for lunch, but now having only an hour, that is where Bill and I headed. He said, "I hope we can get a table in the commissary, there are two big companies shooting on the lot today, so it will be crowded. I call the woman at the desk "the witch" because she is uncanny about knowing who is important and who isn't. Even though I have a player's contract, she has always treated me like a peon who is lucky to get a table next to the kitchen."

Now, one of the first things I learned at my father's knee was how to walk on a stage with *presence*. There is a fine line between self-confidence and arrogance, or a positive outreach and obsequiousness, which you have to find to win the audience over. However, you can talk about self-confidence all you want, but to really *feel* it you have to *believe* in yourself, and to believe in yourself, you have to jump out

there with blind faith to learn from experience. Once you have found
it, it works like a charm. It's an inner thing, a learned way of keeping the instinctive fear of rejection hidden under an assured, calm
attitude of body language and facial expression, with a tone of voice
which is a forceful, attention-getting projection of: "I am here!" You
need to have that presence when you walk on a stage — or to get a
good table in a restaurant.

Feeling a bit peevish about the lack of feedback from director or
coach, and to get my self-confidence back, I strode up to the woman
at the front desk with all the presence of my father's early training,
and said, "I am Jo-Carroll Dennison and I'd like a table for two." The
tall, well-groomed woman looked at me for a moment, and then said
to the hovering waitress, "Take them to table 12," and the waitress
led us to a table in the right side of the commissary by the windows.

The commissary was a big rectangular room, of which the right
side had well-spaced tables by lots of windows showing the outside
plants and trees, the middle had the tables too close together, and the
left end was dark and close to the kitchen. Clearly impressed, Bill said,
"I've never sat over here before, it's usually reserved for the stars."
Sure enough as I glanced around, the whole place took on a surreal
quality as I saw faces that were familiar from the silver screen all over
the world sitting at tables near us in colorful, abbreviated costumes for
the musicals and gorgeous exact replicas of 18th century clothes for
the dramas gave evidence of the type of movies that were being shot
on the lot that day. I was not a big movie fan, except for Lew Ayres
and Franchot Tone, partly because I had not gone to the movies very
much. I worked at night on the medicine show and had only gone to
the movies in Tyler, but also, I thought of movie stars as professionals just like I was who had made it big. I didn't think Jack Oakie or
Jack Benny were nearly as funny as the blackface comic, Todd, on
the medicine show, and I have never seen a movie star as talented as
Lena Rhinehart, so it was not a big deal to me to be sitting close to
these famous faces.

Bill said, "Zanuck and the big producers have their own dining
room upstairs, and the star system is very much in order in the seating
in the commissary. Usually, the stars and their entourage and important directors and writers get to sit over here, those with a player's or
stock contract sit in the middle, while the junior writers, extras, and
others working on the lot sit over at the other end. When there are

really big productions shooting, extras and a lot of crafts people have to eat across the street in the coffee shop. Usually the crews bring their lunch and eat on the set or just sit outside the stage."

Never having really understood the terms, I said, "What's the difference between a player's contract and a stock contract?"

Happy to teach me the ropes, Bill said, "Those with a player's contract can only be used in parts that are big enough to be listed in the credits. A stock contract means you can be used in any way the studio sees fit, as background, a small bit, or as a dancer." Fox probably has 20 to 30 contract players, not counting the stars, and 40 or so stock players, counting the dancers. Normally, stock players make a steady $75 a week for a given period, while the contract players start at $125 to $150 a week going up to $500 in five years, with yearly options. Of course, the studio can raise your salary each year if they pick up your option or keep you at the same salary if they so choose."

Confused, I said, "But I already have a 5-year-contract."

"But you have yearly options, don't you?"

"Gee, I'm not sure. I guess so. Are you saying that the studio can drop my option after a year if they don't like me?"

"Of course. They drop options all the time. Didn't you know that?"

I wondered what I would do about my 1-year-lease on our apartment if they didn't pick up my option. "Can I drop their option?"

"No, no. If they want to keep you, you have to stay and take whatever parts they assign you for five years. Sometimes actors are able to renegotiate their contracts after they become famous, but mostly the studios make them stick to what it says in their contract. Sometimes stars like Bette Davis or Olivia de Haviland get mad and refuse a part they are assigned to by the studio, and they get suspended without pay until they agree. Nobody has ever been able to beat the system, though some have tried. But the stars that have just stayed mad and sat out their contract, found that when their time was up, no other studio would give them a job."

That didn't seem fair to me. The studios had you every whichway from Sunday, as my mother would say. What I would do to support my mother and myself if Fox should drop my option was something I left to my guardian angel to worry about.

The measurement of personal success is of constant concern to those in the movie business, and the tangible ways in which it is measured are not always apparent to others. Two major yardsticks that are visible to everyone are where you can park your car and where you are seated in the studio commissary. Next to having a parking pass to get on the lot, the fact that I always got a table in the best section of the commissary was about the most satisfying thing that happened to me the whole time I was at Fox. A parking pass and a privileged table in the commissary may not seem like a lot of accomplishment for four years at a studio, but the movies I was in never gave me that same sense of satisfaction. It gave me a feeling of being special when both Betty Grable and I got to park on the lot and eat in the pretty, quiet part of the room. Those privileges that I enjoyed went a long way toward making me feel I wasn't just a commodity.

I never saw my screen test. The only feedback I got was from Rufus LaMaire, the casting director. I was called into his office and he said, "Zanuck saw your screen test. He said you looked OK but he couldn't understand a word you said. From now on you will show up at your speech teacher five days a week until you lose that heavy Texas accent. That's all. My secretary will make your appointments as you go out."

I didn't want to lose my Texas accent. I went to the lovely, white-haired Miss Folger because I had to, and she did her sweet, gentle utmost to teach me to speak those from the front of the mouth in pear-shaped tones, while I struggled not to sound like her. The problem for me was that I had a good ear for accents. I never had a Texas accent until I went to Tyler. Medicine show folk don't have any regional accent, unless it's for comedic effect; it's not good for their business. But because I loved Bette and the Mayfields, I picked up *their* accent and now I didn't want to lose it. I thought it made me sound individual and special in Hollywood. But before long, almost by osmosis I began to sound like every other starlet on the lot. When I called the Mayfields or Bette on the phone I got the accent right back — but I lost it again as soon as I hung up.

There was another repercussion from the screen test. Bill Winters, a tall, good looking, blonde publicity man, whose attractiveness was diminished by a constantly stressed face and a harassed attitude, had arranged interviews (during which I could tell by his expression that I always said the wrong things) and publicity junkets like the War

Bond Tour for me. He called the day after the test to say that I was to have dinner the next night with Billy Wilkerson.

Astonished, I said, "Who's Billy Wilkerson?"

Bill said patiently, "Don't you read *The Hollywood Reporter*? He is the owner and is a very influential man in town."

"But I don't know him. Why should I have dinner with him?"

Not so patiently, Bill said, "Because Mr. Zanuck wants you to. Billy Wilkerson saw you in the commissary and asked Mr. Zanuck about you and so you are to have dinner with him tomorrow night."

"I don't want to go out with someone I don't know."

"Mr. Zanuck is your boss and you are under contract to do as he asks. Now, be a good girl and be ready for Billy Wilkerson to pick you up at seven."

There were two daily show business newspaper/magazines that were avidly read by most people in the movie business first thing in the morning: *The Hollywood Reporter* and *Daily Variety*. *The Reporter* was local and *Variety* was national, but they both covered the who — what — where — and when — of the doings of Hollywood, and their gossip columns furnished the primary focus of morning conversations all over town. Even I could see that Billy Wilkerson must be an important man if he could tell Zanuck what to do, but being *required* to go out on a personal date with someone, bigwig or no, didn't set well with me at all. Billy Wilkerson must have noticed me on the day of my test in the commissary; consequently, he had seen me in full makeup, a sophisticated suit and turban, and very high heels. So I dressed carefully for my date with him that night in a dirndl, cotton daytime dress, saddle shoes and socks, my hair in pigtails tied with a bow, and a shiny face completely devoid of any kind of makeup, except lipstick. When I opened the door for him, I saw he was a middle-aged, little dried-up fellow with a pencil-thin mustache wearing a beautifully tailored suit. He said imperiously, "Is your sister here?"

I said, smiling sweetly, "I don't have a sister."

A tad confused, he said, "Well, is Miss Jo-Carroll Dennison here?"

With a bigger smile and almost a curtsy, I simpered, "I'm Jo-Carroll Dennison."

He stared at me. It took him awhile to get the picture that standing before him was his date for the evening, then turning abruptly and starting down the steps, he said, "Well, come along then."

We went to the Mocambo, the best dinner/dance nightclub on the Sunset Strip, where we were joined by Ray Milland and his wife. (Ray Milland was famous for playing the leading man in sophisticated comedies, but two years later, he won an Academy Award for playing an alcoholic in *Lost Weekend.*) During dinner Billy, as I liked to mischievously call him, devoted himself exclusively to the Milland's and said nary a word to me. The trouble with a practical joke is that the joker needs someone else to be in on the joke. I thought this was a pretty funny prank to have played on Billy Wilkerson, but after a while it didn't seem so funny. In later years, I could have explained the joke to the Milland's and made it even funnier, but at the time, it was beyond my self-assurance to do more than sit quietly and try to finish my dinner. Finally, Ray Milland sympathetically asked me to dance and the horror of the evening was exacerbated as we sat back down when I saw that I had unknowingly emblazoned the front of his white dinner jacket with the perfect outline of my bright red lipstick.

That evening with Billy Wilkerson was my one and only practical joke, and I never really got a good laugh out of it. I later learned that it was common practice for the big producers, or even little producers, to furnish starlets or want-to-be starlets as escorts for visiting out-of-towners or anyone else they wanted to impress or do a favor. The girls were expected to dress up, look pretty, and be nice. How nice depended on the individual girl, but when they were as a rule desperate to become a movie star by getting in good with the boss, they were faced with a difficult decision. I was lucky, I didn't want to be a movie star.

News in Hollywood traveled faster than by tribal drum, so I have always thought that in ways I never knew my joke paid off because I was not asked by anyone to go out with someone I didn't know or be an "escort" ever again.

Oh, I take that back. Once I and another starlet, Nancy Guild, were sent to Las Vegas with Bill Winters to model some sportswear for a movie magazine layout. Nancy was also recently under contract to Fox, and though she was a year younger than I, she somewhat intimidated me with her style and poise. We shared a room in the hotel, and I was fascinated to watch her comb her long, straight light brown hair for 10 or 15 minutes at a time in order to get the part down the exact center of her head, to the last hair. I had never before witnessed such exactitude and I thought it was a very high-class attention to detail. Nancy and I were modeling bathing suits and shorts with halter tops around the pool at the New Frontier Hotel in Las Vegas, instead of around the pool in the back lot of Fox, because there was some kind of a not-verbalized connection between the major studios and organized crime. Word was that the New Frontier was mob owned. Fox had almost been taken over by the "mob" a few years before I arrived on the lot, and it had taken some vigorous federal lawsuits to dislodge them, but there was still some kind of subterranean relationship between Hollywood and Las Vegas, where the mob was busy building up a West Coast base. My *Hollywood Reporter* friend, Billy Wilkerson, and famous Mafia figure, Bugsy Siegel, were soon to build the Flamingo Hotel in Las Vegas together. Anyway, for whatever purpose, here were Nancy and I being requested to stick our chests out as we lounged around the New Frontier pool in various poses for the photographer.

After the photo shoot, Bill took me aside to tell me portentously that *Howard Hughes* had asked me to have dinner with him that night. I would have thought Bill had learned his lesson with me and Billy, but presumably Hughes was too big to be denied. And he was big, no doubt about that. First American billionaire, highly successful inventor and businessman, lover of numerous Hollywood stars, and obsessively secretive, rumor had it that Hughes was intimately involved with both organized crime and the CIA in his quest to dominate government policy to forward his business concerns. And indeed, it was said he was part of the CIA's "dirty tricks" efforts to assassinate Fidel Castro, and was at least part owner of the New Frontier Hotel. Now in his 40s, Hughes not only had made Hughes Aircraft Company one of the largest manufacturers of aircraft and its related parts in the world, but in 1935 he had built, tested, and flown his own plane, the H-1, to set a new speed record of 352 mph. In 1937, he set two new records for transcontinental flight; and in 1938, he cut Lindberg's record from New York to Paris in half by making the flight in three days, 19 hours, and 17 minutes. Even as a young man he was incredibly successful in many fields. Closer to home, in 1928, he had produced an Academy Award winning movie, *Two Arabian Nights;* in 1930, he wrote and directed the classic *Hell's Angels* starring Jean Harlow. At $3.8 million, it was the most expensive movie ever produced at that time; and in 1932, he produced the highly successful *Scarface* starring Paul Muni, which was censored as against public morality until Hughes fought a successful lawsuit to allow it to be released. In 1941 he produced and was deeply involved in the writing and directing of the controversial, *The Outlaw,* starring Jane Russell. It was hotly denounced by various morality leagues because of its "lewd and sexually explicit" contents and publicity, primarily the before-its-time emphasis of Jane Russell's breasts. One of Hughes' longer-lasting inventions was the half-bra, which he designed for his *Outlaw* star to give her what he thought was the proper, ah, exposure.

So Hughes was a figure to be reckoned with in the motion picture industry, and Bill, looking more harassed than usual, said, "Now, Jo-Carroll, I don't want to have any trouble with you over this. Mr. Hughes is our host for this publicity junket and it would be very impolite not to have dinner with him as he suggests. Anyway, you'll find that he is a much nicer man than Billy Wilkerson and his feelings would be hurt if you refused. Now, be a good girl and remember that he is a little hard of hearing, so don't forget to speak up when you address him."

(It was interesting that Bill was always telling me to be a good girl when he was setting me up to possibly be a bad girl!)

I said, "Well, I'm not going to have dinner with him alone. If you want me to go, you'll have to come with me."

And so it was that I was sitting across the table from the mysterious, enigmatic, very strange Howard Hughes in this elegant hotel dining room, while Bill kept up a desperately eager monologue of current events. Hughes was a tall, thin, dark man with a mustache who said hardly a word until he softly asked me if I would care to dance. On the dance floor, we seemed to be having a contest to see who would speak first; consequently, neither of us spoke. At the end of the dance number, he returned me to the table and quietly ate his dessert. Bill was very tense. But I had nothing to say to Hughes. Actually, I felt kind of sorry for him as he seemed to be ill at ease somehow, and was a really bad dancer. No sense of rhythm at all.

Bill was very quiet, too, on the trip back to L.A. in the limo.

I had a built-in protection from the predatory bigshots in Hollywood, or anyone else for that matter. Even in a white angora off-the shoulder sweater, my long-established code was like a neon "No Trespassing" sign across my chest, and I think there must be some kind of scent or signal that tells a man when a girl is just not available or vulnerable to attack. I didn't want the big shots to do anything for me so they had no leverage over me. That was the trick, you see. Consequently, in all the years I lived and worked in Hollywood, I never had to fight for my honor or even politely refuse an improper advance. Except once.

A photographer on another publicity shoot up in the Hollywood Hills, who seemed like a pleasant enough guy, asked me to have dinner with him. We had a good time, but when he stopped in front of my apartment, he suddenly grabbed me to him with one arm like in a horror movie while he forced my face up to him with his other hand — and *he stuck his tongue deep into my mouth!* In a swift reflex action, I jerked away from him and slammed my elbow into his throat. I must have hit his Adam's apple because he grabbed his throat and choked. When he could speak, he snarled, "You frigid bitch, what are you playing at? What did you expect? Get on in the house where you belong, you frigid bitch!" and he started his engine.

I was overwhelmed by the inexplicable *contempt* in his voice, and bewildered by what he had done. In Texas, to spit in someone's face was the utmost insult possible, yet he seemed to feel he was totally justified to push his spit in my *mouth* with his tongue. Uggh! But, mostly, his contemptuous description of me as "frigid" somehow filled me with shame. I thought the word had something to do with a refrigerator, but when I looked it up, the dictionary said, "sexually unfeeling, cold." That inner sexual feeling thing that presumably sex symbols like Lana Turner, Jane Russell, and Rita Hayworth had was a complete *mystery* to me. I hadn't a clue how to achieve that inner thing, even if I wanted to. But I was humiliated by the thought that I was *lacking* something of vital importance that other women had. Should a Miss America be frigid? I felt like a three-legged stool with that missing leg being the part that would have made me a complete woman. And without that missing link I was beginning to feel inadequate.

Blackie

Blackie and me between friends at the Bar of Music in Hollywood listening to Nat King Cole in 1943.

Blackie was at a naval training base, and I eagerly looked in the mailbox daily for one of his funny, loving letters, but cringed when he addressed me as "Dear Ann" after Ann Sheridan, saying I was his very own "oomph" girl. First of all, I always wanted people to think I was unique, not like anyone else. But secondly, it literally burned me that he thought I was like sultry-eyed, sex symbol Ann Sheridan. What would he think when he found out that I wasn't? "Frigid" was one of the most repulsive words to me now, and "pretense" wasn't far behind, but I had to pretend my darndest to cover up how insecure I felt about myself sexually when I thought about Blackie. The cover-up became imperative when Blackie wrote that he had made tail gunner on a torpedo bomber crew assigned to a carrier, the SS Saratoga. He was euphoric that he would be joining his ship at San Diego where he would have a two-day pass, and asked that Mother and I drive down to be with him. I was instantly sick to my stomach.

Blackie had sent me some photographs of himself in a bathing suit sitting on some grass at boot camp. The pictures made me feel very strange indeed — there was no hair on his chest! Other men I'd seen at a swimming pool were all hairy and scrawny or hairy and paunchy, but Blackie's Comanche background showed in his smooth, muscled, great-looking body and it gave me a peculiar catch in the dent in my throat. I could imagine touching his crisp, curly black hair and dimpled chin, even sliding my hand down his sleek, sculptured chest — but my stomach shriveled and my imagination failed at the thought of sliding my hand anywhere else. On the back of the photos was written, "This guy loves you" and "Me, too."

I hadn't actually seen Blackie in almost two years, and a lot of extraordinary things had happened to us both during that time. I knew that being face-to-face with him, so to speak, after all the loving letters that had passed between us, was going to be a real challenge and a moment of truth about myself. Blackie had made hotel reservations for us, and Mother and I were both on edge when Blackie knocked at our hotel room door. Upon opening the door, however, it was as though the photograph I had kept on my dresser and looked at daily for comfort and support had suddenly become animated. His navy blue sailor suit looked quite different from the business suit in the photo but he himself, *Blackie*, was exactly the same as he had been in "our" drugstore right there in front of me. I had a hit of an instant adrenalin high and rattled on shrilly with my greetings, but Blackie was all at ease and steady. As soon as I heard his familiar husky voice, our relationship became real to me and my nerves went every-which-away, as my mother would say. Blackie greeted my mother in his courtly, easy way, and then he turned and studied me with a tender, direct, intimate, long look. Then he smiled at me in his familiar one-sided way. His smile clearly said, "Darling Jo, don't be nervous. I'm nervous, too. But everything is going to be all right." He was so authentic and sweet and funny and smart and so much more mature and interesting than any other man I knew. A little shiver of delight skittled up and down my spine at the thought that he was *mine*. I was so *proud* of him. My pulse rate settled down and it became wonderful to have him right there beside me, magically materialized as the humorous, fascinating Blackie I had fallen in love with.

Later that night, when he parked my yellow convertible down by the ocean, I was literally praying that I would meet this coming challenge satisfactorily, that I would *not* be "frigid" or inadequate when he kissed me. I prayed that my guardian angel would rescue me once more and supply that fourth leg of the stool that would make me a complete, sexually responsive woman. But oh, so sad to say, fear was stronger than prayer, and, although he was tender and gentle in his love making, the reality of Blackie's strong masculinity and passionate, possessive ardor terrified me. In no way did he try to force me beyond just kissing, or attempt to push his tongue between my tightly closed lips, but my worst fears about my inadequacies were confirmed anyway. Whatever or wherever those mysterious glands or nerve cells or womanly impulses I'd heard about were, they tightened up their tiny toes and refused to come out and play.

Later, I could see that Mother was as pleased as punch that I was going to marry Blackie and so was he. I was, and I wasn't. I was tossed precariously from one horn of a dilemma to another — on one horn, my future would be safely and happily-ever-after settled, but on the other horn, I would be faced with the dreaded consummation demanded by marriage, and consequent exposure as a womanly fraud. One of the reasons I loved Blackie was that I could tell him what I was thinking and feeling about my life in Hollywood or anything else in my letters and he understood and was comforting, but the thought of revealing my humiliating sexual failure to him burned my soul to a crisp. Would he blame me or himself? I was not sure what Blackie thought about our courting session that night. He was certainly not stupid and must have been aware of my lack of sexual passion; I just hoped Blackie thought that nice girls shouldn't be overtly sexually responsive until after they were married, like my mother said. Whatever, when we said goodbye, he was firm and excited about plans for our future when the war was over, and I gave him one of a pair of bird earrings I was wearing to bring back to me.

But on the drive back to L.A., I was limp with relief that this face-to-face stuff was behind me and we could get back to our comfortable loving letter writing, and hastily put my shroud of denial back in its place. But a nagging uneasy thought crossed my mind that if Blackie was "mine," then by the same token I was also "his." Now that I was alone, my old fear of *belonging* to someone else, of being *beholden* to someone else, raised its unappealing little toad face. The ugly horror of my memory of sexual molestation was stronger than the beauty of Blackie's love.

Social Ineptitude

Getting back to my life in Hollywood was not smooth sailing. Bill Winters called and told me I was to go with my testing partner, William Hudson, to a party at Jack Benny's house, as the publicity department was trying to get our names in the gossip columns as an "item." Benny had just finished *The Horn Blows at Midnight* at Fox and publicity was needed for the movie. It was already clear to William that there would be no romantic attachment between us, so as soon as we arrived at the party he went off on his own to mingle advantageously with the important people. It was my first experience with a big Hollywood party. The valet parking, dozens of white-jacketed waiters, all the big name familiar faces from Fox, and a noise level just below that of a football team's winning goal was a little daunting. We were not really greeted at the door by anyone ,except a uniformed maid who took my coat and a waiter with a tray of pink champagne. I had never drunk champagne, but I hastily took a glass, as I was embarrassed to ask him for my preferred Coke (in those days I thought alcohol tasted a lot like Tate-Lax), but I was relieved to find that champagne was like a sweet punch and drank it right down. It helped me to feel a part of the party to have a drink in my hand, so the next time the waiter offered me another glass, I took it intending to just sip it, but my mouth was so dry that without noticing I again drank it right down. Nobody spoke to me, nobody introduced me to anyone, I didn't dare sit down for fear that I would look like a wallflower, so I just stood and watched the show. I could see from the paintings on the wall and the giant flower arrangements here and there that it must be a beautiful and much loved house, but the furnishings were obscured by the talking, laughing, gesticulating mob of beautifully gowned women and men in black tie. To me, it looked more like a movie in progress than a private party, but I was astonished to see the exquisite Linda Darnell was wearing a huge set of false eyelashes and full makeup! In my experience, show folk didn't wear stage makeup in private, and nature had given her an almost perfect face with lovely big eyes so I couldn't understand why she would want to cover her face up with so much makeup.

As I puzzled over the inner workings of the minds of beautiful women, I kept absently drinking the proffered champagne glasses until suddenly the paintings on the wall began to slowly revolve and the noise of the room was turned down to a low hum. Suddenly I knew that I was in desperate immediate need of a bathroom. Trying with grim determination to walk straight, and afraid to open my mouth to ask directions for fear of what might pass through it if I relaxed my concentration for a moment, I staggered down a nearby hall and into a large bedroom. Obviously, it was the master bedroom: pink satin comforter on king-size bed, white walls, pink carpet, white furniture with soft, pink-shaded lamps, and gratefully, I could see an open doorway into what was surely a bathroom. Alas, the relief of seeing opportune rescue was too much for my much-abused stomach and right beside Jack Benny's pink satin bed, I spilled its entire contents all over his luxurious pink carpet.

Everything except the memory of the horrendous nausea, which had forced me to my hands and knees to continue trying to throw up the lining of my stomach, remains a blur to me. Evidently, someone found me, found William, found my coat, and got me into William's car for the ride home. I have always felt blessed that I don't remember the details. All I know is that I didn't get to meet Jack Benny, and I know I never, ever, in my whole life drank pink champagne again.

I don't know. Somehow I never could get it together in Hollywood. My social life was almost nil; if I did venture out something terrible often happened. I met a nice man, whose name I can't remember, who was well known as a supporting actor and played sophisticated villains or the "other" man in movies. He was tall, dark, and broad shouldered, and wore his black hair parted in the middle and slicked down like a proper villain. He asked me to go to dinner and we went to Ciro's, the larger of the two most famous nightclubs on the Sunset Strip. He was a kind man who was nothing like the characters he played, and a perfectly marvelous dancer. I was blissfully happy to be really dancing again and able to show this older man what a great dancer I was, until he swung me out in a fast turn and somehow I lost my grip on his hand and went crashing into the ringside tables, drinks, chairs, and curses flying everywhere. He never called me again.

Anyway, Blackie made the men I met seem immature and uninteresting. All they wanted to talk about was themselves or the movie business, and Blackie's letters were all the romance I needed or wanted. He mostly talked about *me* and I always found that interesting. He was *safe*.

As a kind of college-level grooming for its starlets, Fox had its own little theater where male and female starlets were asked to sing, dance, or perform in a skit on variety nights. I sang "I Can't Give You Anything But Love, Baby," but I couldn't say it went over big. More fun was when we were schooled by junior directors to perform in various famous plays. The object was to gain experience as well as to be seen and judged by directors and producers for future reference. Friends and relatives were invited to the performances and Mother always came early to get a front row seat and applauded mightily at every opportunity. I remember being so disappointed to be cast in *The Dough Girls* as the sweet little girl next door instead of the much more interesting tough girl Ann Sheridan had played. But what I remember most about rehearsing and appearing in various plays was the education I got from my fellow starlets about the ways of the world and the vagaries of individual men of renown. One of the starlets who had been around for awhile was Kay Aldrich, a famous model and society debutante from New York. She was my idol and role model, not only because she was so elegant and put together, but because of the story she told about her first meeting with Zanuck. It seemed that every female starlet was obliged to have a private meeting with him in his office, and many were the stories about what went on there on his big white "casting" couch. In her case, when Zanuck made his move on her, she remained calm until he went into his bathroom to "freshen up" and then she took out her bright red lipstick, wrote "Fuck You" in huge letters on the back of his white couch, and left. I greatly admired her for that. The interesting part was that Zanuck did nothing about it and her contract was picked up as usual, but the funny part was imagining the trouble and embarrassment he must have had in getting the lipstick off his big white couch.

Anyway, when I had been told by his secretary that Mr. Zanuck would see me at 11 o'clock one morning, I was expecting him to be a lot like Mr. Schreiber, only more important, so I was not ill at ease when I sat down in the big chair opposite his desk. Actually, I was pretty disappointed in him as he was a little scrunched-up man who almost disappeared behind his huge, ornate desk. He had a small, sharp face with receding sandy hair and a kind of sparse, wide mustache, and he asked me questions about myself in a high, tiny voice.

After a bit, peering at me over the top of his desk, he said, "Well, I have many phone calls stacking up on me so it would be best if you left now and returned about eight this evening when things will be more quiet. My secretary will have left, by then but I have to work late so just come on in to my office. The door will be open."

With images of the red-lipsticked couch in my mind, I said in a pitiful voice, "Oh, Mr. Zanuck, my mother would never let me be alone in his office with a man after dark. She would just have a fit."

After a pause, he said briskly, "Very well. That will be all then." And, clearly dismissed, I giggled to myself all the way to my car. It still makes my blood boil though, to imagine what my meeting with Zanuck would have been like, if I had been desperate to be a movie star, like most girls in that position.

Discovering Intellectualism

The grooming part that I really enjoyed was when certain starlets were sent to the Actors' Lab for study. It was something else entirely from the little theater plays I had been in. The Actors' Lab was made up of writers, directors and actors from the elite Group Theatre in New York, which had produced many successful plays on Broadway. The roots of the Group Theatre grew out of the Yiddish Theatre in New York and the WPA theater projects during the Depression. Young directors, producers, writers, and actors, who were soon to be famous like Elia Kazan, Harold Clurman, Clifford Odetts, Budd Schulberg, Paul Muni, John Garfield, Stella and Larry Adler, and others came together to form an ensemble company that they hoped would become a national theater. Financially, it had become tough going so they had formed this splinter group in Hollywood to put on plays, as well as act in the movies, in order to make extra production money. To further that goal, some of their directors, like Michael Chekhov and George Shdanoff, gave acting classes to students provided to them by the major studios. Their theater and workshop was just off Sunset Boulevard and Laurel Canyon right behind Schawb's Drugstore where Lana Turner was discovered sitting at the counter, and I fell in love with everyone I met there. Chekhov and Shdanoff not only were interesting to study acting with, but they were fascinating to know. They had been leading actors and directors in the Moscow Art Theatre before the war and worked directly with Stanislavsky during the originating of Method Acting, which Lee Strasberg was disseminating at Fox, but they asked me to imagine I was Anna Karenina instead of a fire hydrant. The people I met at the Actors' Lab were not only professionals from the New York Theatre, but they were also the first radical liberals, as the current term was, and real intellectuals I had ever met. They were intensely vocal about the arts and all kinds of cultural things, but their passion reached its highest pitch about RIGHTS: civil rights, racial rights, women's rights, animal rights, organized labor's rights, and the Bill of Rights; they were volubly committed to them all. While I was instinctively dedicated to my idea of justice, and had acted on those instincts all my life, I had never been around other people who felt as strongly as I did about the unjust ways I had experienced. But while my intermittent passion for righting wrongs had been focused mostly on little boys hurting animals, these exciting people were consumed with a burning passion for righting all the wrongs in the whole world. I just ate it up.

Even though I was professionally related to the show business folk on the medicine show, I never wanted to be *like* them individually. Possibly because my father had instilled the belief that I was "unique" and "special" from birth, or possibly because of my father's example of abstinence from drinking, smoking, swearing, or carousing, I thought that not only was I different from the drinking-smoking-swearing-carousing people on the medicine show, I thought that my life was going to be *better* than theirs. It was not something I could have put into words, or even concrete thought; it was just that according to my own scale of measurement — I was going to have a quite different life from theirs someday. Of course, even more so, I knew I was *not* related to the folks in the farming community of Hale Center when I was going to school there, and I knew that my life's experience would be totally different and *better* than theirs. That unwarranted arrogance was not based on anything real, you understand, it was just something I had chosen to feel. I had a powerful *need* to be what I thought of as high-class, and I felt the people on the show or in Hale Center were either low-class or middle class at best. It took me many years to understand what the important qualities of a "high-class" person really were, and to define for myself what high-class truly was. When I had wanted to be like the upper-class Mayfields in Tyler — I found that I could not. I was not. And, in so many ways, I was not like the other starlets at Fox. Not *better* I didn't think, it was just that we didn't have anything in common, didn't want the same things, and I didn't want to be like them either.

Now, as though I was discovering an unexpected oasis in the desert, I found some people I wanted to be like. The important part of my past cultural experience had been learning about nature and animals, the code of the west from Zane Gray, and the vital fact that I could protect and take care of myself. I had never been to a museum or a concert or an art show or read the classics; the only art I had been exposed to came from the *Saturday Evening Post*, concerts were limited to groups like *The Sons of the Pioneers*, and *Lassie* was at the top of my classic literature list. My acquired knowledge could not have been more different from these mostly Jewish New Yorkers whose whole background of philosophic thought, the arts, and literature was diametrically opposite of mine, and I drank down their way of thinking like it was a life-giving potion. I had never known any Jewish people before, and I felt these multifaceted, complex, knowledgeable people *knew* what I wanted to know. And I wanted to be like them.

And then something happened that put my entire life in perspective. I had gotten to know Ivan Kahn, the head talent scout at Fox, quite well, and because of the irony involved in his rejecting me as starlet material over a year ago in Dallas when Lew Ayres had first introduced us, we had become sort of friends. One day, Ivan called me and said that Lew Ayres was home from overseas on furlough and asked me to come to dinner at his house as a surprise guest for him. That *Lew Ayres* had seen something special in me and thought I should be in the movies was still the most flattering and treasured thing that had ever happened to me, but it had seemed like a magical happening. Now that I was to see him on a social occasion, I was deeply apprehensive that he would be disappointed in me and not think I was special after all. When threatened by man or beast, my immediate "fight" response kicked in, but when someone was especially kind to me, I got tongue-tied and fumbled around and said dumb things. Therefore, that night I resolved for once in my life to keep my big mouth shut and just listen!

As it turned out, that was no problem as the conversation that night left me speechless anyway. Ivan Kahn's wife looked a lot like my grandmother: short, dumpy figure and round pudding face, but when the four of us were seated around the dinner table, her commanding attitude and stunning intellect made her seem like my image of the Queen of England. The conversation between the three of them during and after dinner opened up a vista into a brilliant, engrossing new world for me. Their casual exercise of mind and interests moved from philosophic concepts, to a new recording of Mozart, to an archeological discovery in China, to the influence of Nietzsche and Wagner on Hitler, and far horizons beyond. They weren't showing off or preachy or pedantic; they were just having a relaxed, wonderful time talking about things that interested them. By the end of the evening, I had become convinced about my fervent goal in life: *I wanted to be like them.* I wanted to know what they knew, hear what they heard in music, see what they saw in art, and *think* like they did about everything. I had found one of my life's greatest passions: I wanted to be like the people at the Actors' Lab and the people in the Kahn's living room.

I had found the answer to the question that had puzzled me most of my life: "If I don't want to be a performer, what do I want to be?" Like finding the last piece in a jigsaw puzzle where each piece was vitally important, my picture of myself was finally complete — *I wanted to be an intellectual!* The problem was, just at the moment it seemed like a vast undertaking, and I was not too sure how to go about it.

It was just another part of the fairy tale magic of Lew Ayres that he asked me to have dinner with him the next night. He took me to a charming, dark restaurant with soft leather booths and candles on the table, and I so badly wanted to impress him that I lost my head entirely. At Ivan Kahn's house, I had been so overwhelmed with him and the whole evening that I hardly said a word. Now that I had gotten my breath, so to speak, I desperately wanted to prove to him that he should feel justified in picking me out of the crowd on the street there in Dallas. Then, too, I wanted him to think I was worthy in my new-found quest of becoming an intellectual — so I never for one moment stopped talking. Beginning with my birth in the Florence Arizona Men's Prison infirmary, the medicine show, God, my love of nature, and how I loved Tyler and hated Hollywood. I don't remember that I ate anything as I needed my mouth free for talking, but by the time he took me home, I was sure that I had so astonished him with my extraordinary past and exceptional mind for the future that he was sure to call me the next day and want to spend the rest of his leave with me.

It was my turn to be astonished when I didn't hear from him for a couple of days, but then he did call — and it was one of the worst experiences of my life. This sweet, gentle, quiet man had turned into a raving maniac. For a long time, I couldn't make out what he was talking about as he poured out vituperation about my manners and morals and mischief-making. Finally, I made out that Louella Parsons had done an article in the Sunday edition of the *Los Angeles Examiner* about a supposed romance between the two of us and our marriage plans! Desperately, I tried to explain to him that the publicity department called the starlets every Monday to find out if anyone had an interesting date over the weekend, and I never had anything to tell them, so when they called me, I had told them, rather proudly, that I'd had dinner with Lew Ayres. That's all. Not another word had I told them. Only somewhat mollified, Lew Ayres said what an unfortunate thing it had been and hung up, leaving me with the sure impression that I would never hear from him again.

I went right out and got a paper and was horrified to my very soul to see that Louella Parsons had written a whole page of lies about us. There was a huge photo of me in a bathing suit with the Miss America banner, waving gaily to the multitude, surrounded by glamour photographs of Lew Ayres and his former wives, Lola Lane and Ginger Rogers, one of him looking handsome and dear in an early publicity shot, and a drab, awful-looking picture of him being inducted into the Army. The text raved on about his unhappy marriages and his shame in being a conscientious objector. It reported that the theaters vowed never to show his films again, and asked if the American public would ever forgive him. The ridiculous, deliberately demeaning article ended with the pious hope that he would finally find love and happiness in his upcoming marriage to this 19-year-old beauty queen, who was 25 years his junior. She never said a word about his having served as a medic in the Medical Corps under fire in the South Pacific and as a chaplain's aide in New Guinea and the Philippines.

It was all the worst possible lies at this difficult time in his life. The fact that he knew Louella Parsons and her ilk were despicable liars who would destroy people's lives and careers without a moment's remorse for the sake of a titillating story didn't make me feel any better. Thinking about how extraordinary Lew had been to me, I would have pulled my tongue out by its roots before I would have misrepresented our relationship and said that we were engaged, or deliberately caused this extraordinary and ethical man such pain and humiliation. If there is indeed a just God, dishonest, self-serving reporters like Louella Parsons will be forced to forever pierce their tongue with every callous and cruel word they ever wrote when they get to Hell. Though I didn't feel I had done anything wrong exactly, still I had been in Hollywood long enough to have foreseen what might happen and should not have been so stupid. The shame of that experience scalded me for the rest of my life.

Lew was one of the most honorable, intelligent, courageous, men of integrity I have ever met, a completely high-class man for sure. I could only imagine the humiliations he suffered in the Army but he bore them with grace. Ivan Kahn told me that Lew had formed his strong feelings about killing when he played the lead in the best anti-war film ever made, *All Quiet on the Western Front* in 1934, and no matter the cost, he had stuck by his beliefs. After the war, he was asked to return to his best-known movie character, Dr. Kildare, in a TV series, but he turned it down because it had a cigarette company sponsor. Richard Chamberlain got the part instead and it made him a star.

Les Girls

At that time at Fox, some of the starlets under contract were Jeanne Crain, Coleen Gray, Judy Holliday, Cara Williams, Jean Wallace, Kay Aldrich, Jane Nigh, Nancy Guild, and Martha Montgomery. As we often did things together as a group, Judy nicknamed us "Les Girls." One had to be a member of the Screen Actor's Guild and each year the Guild put out a large reference catalogue with the photographs, short bios, and agents for all its members. It was divided into sections for both male and female such as Leading Ladies, Ingenues, Character Actors, Children, Specialty Acts, etc., and copies of these catalogues were in every office. I was disappointed to see my own picture listed under "Ingenues" instead of "Leading Ladies," but Mother was thrilled. There was a different book from the Screen Extras Guild. Stand-ins and stunt men and women were hired individually, often at the request of the star.

There was a great deal of "loan outs" between studios where actors from one studio would be loaned to another for a certain part, but actually it should have been called a "sell out." Clearly, the studio made a profit which was not disclosed to the actor, whose salary remained the same. Small studios like David O. Selznick's sometimes kept afloat by the money they made from loaning out their contract stars. Selznick, who made few movies himself, was particularly adept at signing European soon-to-be stars like David Niven, Ingrid Bergman, Laurance Olivier, and Vivian Leigh to long-term, small-salaried contracts — once his actors became known, he asked and got astronomical figures from other studios for their "loan."

I had been at Fox well over a year, doing USO and War Bond tours, and being endlessly groomed, before I appeared in a movie. That 1944 movie was *Something for the Boys,* directed by Lewis Seiler and starring Vivian Blaine, Michael O'Shea, Perry Como, Phil Silvers, and Carmen Miranda, with a score by Cole Porter. The minimal plot was set in heiress Blaine's southern plantation, which had been recruited as a home for soldier's wives during the war. Several of Les Girls took our first step on the ladder to fame in small parts as the wives. To my disgust, Cara got the part with the most lines. Compared to the set of my screen test, coming on to the set of *Something for the Boys* was like the difference between Hale Center and New York;

it had about the same ratio of people involved, too. The screen test set had been about 10-by-20 feet while this set took up almost half of the entire sound stage. The several sets of the interior and exterior plantation formed a kind of outward-looking circle, around which the camera could move and the lights be set from the scaffolds above. The brilliance of the lights and the elaborate colors and glitter of the musical costumes enveloped the senses like a loud blast of music. The number of crew around and above the sets seemed uncountable, like worker bees swirling around the queen bee director. In the cavernous space of the sound stage, all noise seemed muted and distant, until the Assistant Director screamed, "Quiet, please," and then all noise ceased entirely.

Extras on a set were endlessly fascinating to me. They were a closed circle of professionals who had their own standards, hierarchy, and values. "Dress" extras, those who had extensive wardrobes for occasions such as ballrooms, theater lobbies, and front row seats, were much in demand by producers, and prided themselves on knowing how to chatter and laugh in a crowd that was both noiseless and unintrusive, and move or mingle in a way that was in keeping with the action without having to be told by the director. Most extras were satisfied with their profession as it was; it was rare that someone like Clark Gable or David Niven started as extras and worked their way up to be stars. It seemed to me that extras made enough money to live on, took pride in their work, and were a happy bunch, which is more than I could say for a lot of stars.

The waits between shots while the actor's marks, camera angles, and lighting were set seemed endless, particularly on the big dance numbers of a musical. However, the waits were made less tedious by the informative conversations among Les Girls as we sat in our allotted "director's" chairs. Only the stars and the director got their names on the back canvas of the chairs, but several nameless chairs were placed on the stage back from the set for those with speaking parts. Stock players (unbilled parts, dancers, chorus), and extras sat anywhere they could find, but not in those chairs. I never saw members of the crew sit on anything. The stars had their own canvas dressing rooms on the set, and they either rested in them or sat in their own reserved chairs and talked to one another or the director. Besides a drive-on pass and a special seat in the commissary, the only other thing I coveted at Fox was a chair with my name on it.

While my intellectual pursuit was not much advanced, I got a liberal education in Sexual Relations 101 from my fellow starlets. Judy Holliday, a Brooklyn girl, had been one of a nightclub comedy act named *The Revuers* in New York, and was, to my mind, very sophisticated, cynical, and experienced. Jeanne Crain was reticent and had a smile that suggested she secretly knew much more than any of us. Martha Montgomery was a perfectly lovely blonde who was the epitome of soft Southern charm. Jane Nigh was a typical California Valley girl, pretty, sharp, and knowing. Cara Williams was small and dimpled with pale carrot-colored curls and a mean streak.

It is hard for me to judge now what I was like, except that I was all ears as we sat around together talking, mainly about movie gossip and men — what men were like and how to attract them. Since I didn't read the "trades" or newspapers or listen to the radio much, the gossip about who was doing it with whom and the like, both in the past and present, was all news to me and took my breath away at the magnitude of chicanery and monkey business that went on. When it came to man/woman monkey business, after the renewed shame of being called "frigid," and not able to be sexually responsive with Blackie, I was determined to learn (verbally) all I could about sex and its workings, so I had many unanswered questions. Best friend Bette back in Tyler hadn't known any more about it than I did, and I had learned absolutely nothing from Mother or anyone else, so my lack of knowledge about the real workings of sex was almost total. What I learned from Les Girls, however, was mind-boggling. The graphic images conjured up by such expressions as "hand job," "get in your muff" "going down on him," and "tonguing" left me mystified and horrified. When my imagination tried to make graphic sense of the sexual exercises they were describing, I almost went into shock. I said to myself, "I never heard of such a thing. My mother would certainly never do such a nasty thing as "going down" and neither would I. Never in a million years! Surely Blackie would not expect me to do that, would he?" Also, and just as bad, much emphasis was put on a whole new challenge for me as I learned for the first time about a seemingly imperative female physical action called an *orgasm*. Its merits, longevity, numerical repetitions, and the differences between a vaginal orgasm and a clitoral orgasm were completely beyond my comprehension. And it scared the bejesus out of me. They all agreed that a woman was not a real woman until she could have multiple orgasms. One of them even said she had been having orgasms since she was 13. *Thirteen!* I was stunned. And now I had an *orgasm* to worry about.

Phil

Phil and me at the Academy Awards (c. 1945).

One day on the set of *Something for the Boys* with Betty Grable, something seemingly innocuous happened on the set that was to change my life completely. Martha Montgomery, a dazzling blonde, and I were chatting between takes, when Phil Silvers, the comedy lead in the movie, came swinging over in that loose-jointed way he had of walking, and said to me winsomely, "Hello, Miss Montgomery."

Puzzled, I said haughtily, "I'm not Miss Montgomery."

Phil turned and yelled at the assistant director "Get over here," in that mock angry voice he used, and then said to him, "What did you just tell me when I asked you who that beautiful girl is over there?"

The assistant director said, "I told you that was Martha Montgomery."

Phil in his rapid-fire delivery, "But I meant *this* beautiful girl." Ducking his head apologetically to Martha, "No offense, dear," then pretending outrage at the assistant director, "I wanted to know the name of *this* beautiful girl. What is *her* name? Quick. Be quick!"

Amused, the assistant director said, "This is Jo-Carroll Dennison."

Phil quickly pulled a chair over to me and coming close to my ear said confidingly, "Obviously the man is an idiot. How could he think I didn't mean you? Now, listen, I have something very important to ask you. Will you marry me?"

Astonished, I said, "No."

Phil put on his most enticing little boy face, "Well, then, will you have dinner with me?"

There was something about Phil that reminded me strongly of Todd, the blackface comic on the medicine show whom I loved so much. They didn't look alike: where Todd was tall and thin, with a lean, sculptured face and full head of hair, Phil was medium height and weight, with a full, Semitic face and a receding hairline, but they both had the same zany, sly little boy, harmless kind of humor that appealed to me. Todd had made me laugh all the time, and I had missed laughing a lot since I had gotten to Hollywood. I had never been amused by most comics or comedians, I thought so many were vulgar and I was still prudish about "smut," or else their humor was mean-spirited and I never liked "put down" stuff. A well-known saying was "What is humor but the misfortune of others?", and for most comedy that was true. But Phil's humor was never about the misfortune of others; it was about the human comedy and a witty way of looking at things. His stage persona was of the cheery con man who never really hurt anyone. His personal persona was much the same, and his outrageous humor was so original that, like Todd, he made me laugh all the time.

Comedy is hard to do. As the old joke goes about the dying actor who, when asked for his final words, said, "Dying is easy, *comedy* is hard," only a few can really make comedy pay off. Actors who can play so-called "light comedy," like Carole Lombard and Robert Montgomery, were just good actors who had learned to play comedy straight with a slight twinkle, but with people who are naturally funny like Phil, it is a heightened inner rhythm, an individual skewed perception, that they are born with.

That perception is honed by their environment and circumstances, surely, but it is also a part of their nature. Of my grandmother's 14 children, only my Uncle Jack was born with the ability
to make the whole family laugh, all the time. Of course, he was my
grandmother's favorite. I believe comedy is the gift to a certain few of
a slanted way of looking at things that provides an instant funny reaction to almost anything. As those with a mathematical mind will think
of the right numbers, the comic thinks of the humor in anything he
hears or sees. With most natural comics that reaction comes without
forethought. Often, when they *try* to be funny it falls flat. Milton Berle
and the guy at the Rotary Club could learn jokes and wear drag and
make fools of themselves before an audience and get laughs, but to
my mind they were not really funny. Robin Williams and Jonathan
Winters were. Phil was.

The thing to remember about comedy is that it is the other side
of tragedy, which is why they are represented as two sides of the same
coin. I have never yet met someone who was naturally funny who had
not polished that humor early in life to protect themselves from some
kind of emotional pain and fear. It is making other people laugh that
protects them from tears. (It is sad that there can never be enough
applause or laughter to ease their early fears.)

Like Blackie, Phil was amused rather than critical of my clumsy
efforts to sound like my idea of an intellectual. All my life I had
wanted to be classy, now more than ever since I wanted so badly
to shed my "beauty queen" image, and Phil seemed to understand
that. Our upbringing was similar in many ways — doted on by our
parents, performing on the stage by the time we could walk and talk,
growing up living out of trunks in constantly changing places with
constantly changing companions, learning to read our billing rather
than Dick and Jane, and playing parts rather than hide-and-seek.
But Phil's experiences in vaudeville, burlesque, and on Broadway
had made the social scene in Hollywood his natural habitat, stimulated all his creative juices, while I could never keep track of who I
really was at parties and became stiff, uncomfortable, and prone to
defensive hostility. After the men I had been meeting in Hollywood,
Phil was a tremendous relief. He made me laugh and he was not
sexually threatening. He went out of his way to charm Mother and
she adored him. The sweet thing was that he adored her, too. This
show-biz veteran and Texas farm girl somehow hit it off and under-

stood each other perfectly. On our first date, Phil and I went to the Coconut Grove for dinner and dancing to Freddie Martin's orchestra. Phil was extremely light on his feet and an excellent dancer — which went a long way with me. But we only went dancing that first night, after that we went to parties.

Everybody loved Phil. His was a creative improvisational humor, always character driven, and he was so much funnier in a living room than he was with the written word in a scene in a movie. His pure inventive sense of what was humanly funny in an impromptu situation and his seemingly constant good humor made him eagerly welcomed everywhere he went. Even in this town where the social groups were as rigidly stratified as the walls of the Grand Canyon, Phil moved fluidly from one strata to another. He was "in" everywhere — and he took me with him. At that time the social life in Hollywood mostly consisted of dinner at Chasen's or Romanoff's, dancing at the Coconut Grove, Mocambo or Ciro's — or going to people's houses for dinner or parties, which Phil preferred.

At that time in Hollywood, motion picture people habitually got together at someone's house on Saturday nights because working actors had to be up at 5:00 or 5:30 a.m. on week days looking like a million dollars later on the set, so they needed their sleep. Those who weren't working needed to pretend that they were. Phil's comic genius made him a major attraction for any gathering, but the parties he chose most often to attend were at the homes of Frank Sinatra, Bing Crosby, Danny Kaye, or Harry Cohn, head muckymuck and ogre of Columbia Pictures. Their groups were cliquish and male dominated. At Crosby's and Sinatra's, the guests were mostly songwriters, comedy writers, actors and hangers-on who entertained one another with show biz stories or played cards; at Danny Kaye's, there were intellectuals like Groucho and Harpo Marx, Ira Gershwin, and George Burns, who talked of weighty philosophical things and prided themselves on knowing all the lyrics to Gilbert and Sullivan; and at Harry Cohn's, people from his studio sat around and told Harry how great he was.

My problem was that I was treated as a Woolworth's pretty-girl in this Cartier's of talent, wit, intellect, and power. The Miss America was more a stigma than an accolade, and I couldn't seem to shake it. I was as much Phil's appendage as the Talking Woman is to the Straight Man in the sketches we had both done in vaudeville. Except that I didn't talk much anymore. Trying to pretend that I was an intellectual like they were, one night I ventured to join the conversation at Danny Kaye's, for example, and Groucho Marx shut me up by saying dryly, "You're almost articulate for a bathing beauty." If he had cut me across the face with a rawhide quirt, he couldn't have hurt me more. I couldn't find a place for myself that I was proud of in Hollywood.

And then one night, Phil said "Open Sesame" and the door at 725 North Rodeo Drive opened for me into the most completely joyous time of my life. That door was the one leading into Gene Kelly's living room and almost immediately all my feelings of being a stranger in a strange land vanished. The Kelly group, like the other Hollywood groups Phil had introduced me to, was a cohesive bunch of regulars, but in their case there were a lot more drop-ins. Gene's front door was always left unlocked on Saturday nights and some of the most creative, intelligent, amusing people in the whole world came through it and were made welcome at all hours. The Kelly group was everything I had recently come to admire: *They were radical-liberal-intellectuals!* Their knowledge and pleasure in the arts, and their passion for political and actual equality, was total and intense. Plus — they loved to dance and sing and laugh. And they often wore jeans and sweatshirts before it became popular to do so. I was enchanted. It was my well of joy. My soul blossomed.

The regulars were John and Robbie Garfield, Richard and Ruth Conte, Betty Comden and Adolph Green (who later wrote *On the Town* and *Singin' in the Rain*), Stanley Donen (Gene's overall assistant who later became famous in his own right as a director), Carol Haney (brilliant choreographer and dancer), Jeanne Coyne (dance assistant), Eliot (Ted) Reid (a promising young actor who had a hilarious comedic sense), and Artie Julian and Howard ("Howie") Leeds (young comedy writers). More people would always show up unexpectedly, but those were the nucleus one could count on every Saturday night.

Saul Chaplin or Andre Previn were usually at the piano. But seemingly all the important members of all the forms of show business passed through Gene's open door on any given Saturday night. If they came after dinner time the regulars ate at the large lazy-Susan in the dining room, if they came before dinner the regulars were asked to "FFB"(family fall back,) spaghetti and meatballs etc., were added to the pot and we all ate in the living room on the floor. The Kelly's cook didn't stay for dinner on Saturday nights so we women cooked.

A typical Saturday night at the Kelly's usually began with lots of drinks at their sunken playroom/bar. (I quickly overcame my aversion to alcohol in order to fit in.) The phonograph played swing music and the esoteric talk was carried on by the regulars and drop-ins like Judy Garland, Donald O'Connor, and Noel Coward. The talk was all way over my head, but I listened with rapt attention. After dinner, someone invariably would get up and perform a song or a comedy sketch, either improvisational or by request, and usually the evening would end up with everyone singing around the baby grand piano or ballroom dancing to the phonograph. Those playing the piano ranged from teenaged Andre (no one ever called him anything but "Andre") Previn, to Saul "Solly" Chaplin (later produced *West Side Story* and *The Sound of Music*), to Leonard "Lenny" Bernstein, when he was in town. The group sang 8-part harmony with the zest of a barber shop quartet, or vied with one another to see who knew the most lyrics to little-known verses, or songs that were dropped from shows before they opened on Broadway. God be praised, they liked the songs I had sung on the medicine show, and I my ability to hold my own on this early Americana compensated for their superior command of the Broadway material. For the first time since I had left the show, I felt disposed to talk about it and perform some of my old numbers. They applauded me and asked for more.

The Kelly group didn't go to Mocambo or Ciro's; the living room furniture was arranged against the walls, so that there was a large space in the middle for free-wheeling dance. And very often after dinner they chose up sides and played parlor games. Naturally, the group revolved around Gene and Betsy. In his early 30s, Gene was one of the oldest, but surely the youngest in spirit of the group, and he set the tone for everyone else. That tone was unpretentious, cerebral, hard-driving *play*. Gene worked harder at his craft and played harder than anyone I ever knew. From volleyball games on the tennis court in their backyard to intellectual games in the living room, Gene's insatiable desire to *know* everything, *feel* everything, and *do* everything better than it had ever been done before, served to gather young, creative, intelligent people of a like-mind around him in a vital kaleidoscopic whole. Betsy, a 19-year-old, fairly new bride, with her intensely curious, brilliantly wide-ranging mind, had a magnetic attraction all her own. She was already achieving recognition as a fine actress and had been nominated for an Academy Award as support-ing actress in *Snake Pit*. She and Gene were the leaders in the ferocious games of *Charades, Twenty Questions* and *Who Am I?*, which were played with a lightening speed and encyclopedic breadth of knowledge that terrified me as much as it stimulated them. Being a good mimic, I didn't make such a fool of myself playing *Charades*, but my ignorance was abysmal when it came to their other two favorite games. I mean, how would I even guess in *Who Am I?* when one player said, "I am a dead male whose name begins with A," — another player might say, "Are you a Greek god of medicine?" And the first player must say, "No, I am not Asclepius," or lose his turn. The right answer might be Asoka, Indian emperor largely responsible for transforming Bud-dhism into a world religion! How would I know that? Anyway, the only games I ever played as a child were with my horse. I never, ever, got it right in those games, but, oh, how I wanted to, and thus began an all-out dedication to *learning* that I had never before experienced. I could see that they all *enjoyed* the arts — classical music, ballet, paint-ing, literature, and the like — and I wanted to enjoy what they did. I didn't want to miss anything.

I think the intensity of my burning desire to know what they knew encouraged the Kelly group to take pity on me and decide that I had a right to be well-educated, and that it would be interesting to see what they could write on the blank pages of my mind. Adolph took me to art galleries and museums and gave me art books, demanding that I learn to tell the artistic differences between Bernini and Braque. Solly Chaplin and Lenny Bernstein told me which recordings to buy and took me to concerts, and asked me to find the similarities between Bach and Mozart, and Haywood "Woody" Broun opened the doors of learning by loaning me Veblen's *Theory of the Leisure Class* and *Point Counter Point* by Aldous Huxley and asking questions afterwards. Betsy encouraged me to dive into the great playwrights by memorizing Shakespeare, and Gene told me to buy books by Eugene V. Debs, John Reed, and Will Durant, plus the Columbia Encyclopedia. The books I quickly accumulated were a giant step above *Call of the Wild* and *The Riders of the Purple Sage*, by Zane Grey but I thrived on every-thing they exposed me to. I fervently embraced it all as the way to succeed in my quest to become an intellectual.

That these particular people took me into their inner circle, made me one of the regulars, and thought I was worth their encouragement defined me for myself as a grown-up person. Not because I was with Phil or a former Miss America, but I felt they enfolded me into their hearts because they *knew* me as I really was and they *liked* me. Passing through that magic marker of acceptance and belonging made me finally sure of who I was as a person, and all right with myself. Not just all right, but bursting with joy and freedom, so free from my binding inhibitions and restrictions and fears that I could joyously perform in front of an audience for the first time since that extraordinary night I sang "Deep in the Heart of Texas" at the Pageant. With a surging zest, I tore into performing the songs I had done as a child on my father's medicine show like "Tie me to Your Apron Strings" and "Father, Dear Father, Come Home with Me Now" and even a few verses of "Strawberry Roan," and exulted in their applause. And sometimes after a few martinis, I did a solo imitation of the way Gene danced, leaping over couches and swinging from door jams in a paroxysm of gleeful parody. They all laughed at me and they affectionately called me Josie. No one had ever called me "Josie" before, but now the Kelly group did, even Phil, and I reveled in this new name as though it had been bestowed upon me by a monarch or a divine source.

Some of those Saturday nights are as vivid to me now as they were then. I remember one night when Judy Garland (her freshly bandaged wrists pitiful evidence of her inability to deal with the studio's demands on her) perched on the piano singing songs she made famous more meaningfully than I had ever heard her. By the time she ended with "Somewhere Over the Rainbow," her girlish face a forecast of the ruined woman she would become, many among this hardened bunch of professionals were teary-eyed. Another memorable night was when Paul Robeson dropped in and was persuaded to sing "Old Man River," the song he made famous in Show Boat. He had just been blacklisted as a "pinko," so it was especially poignant to hear him sing that song about racial injustice. It was also surreal as Phil's funniest improvisational number was based on Robeson and "Old Man River." One previous Saturday night, with Solly Chaplin at the piano who could improvise right along with him, Phil took off on the concept that Paul Robeson originally refused to sing the song in rehearsal because of its racist lyrics and preferred "Captain Andy," a nothing song in the show. Phil, as Robeson reading the lyrics from sheet music, takes offence at some of the lyrics, stops singing to say emphatically, "What's "ribber?" I went to Rutgers, you know, and majored in *English* when you have the time! The word is *RIVEEER!*" then further on in the song, stopping to say, "What does this mean 'taters' and 'darky?' What *is* that?" With sheer outrage, "The words are pronounced PO-TA-TOES and NE-GRO-ES!" Throwing down the sheet music, "I refuse to sing this song as written," and then he bursts into *Captain Andy* with gusto, "Captain Andy, you're a dandy …" Quickly, Solly gets him back to "Old Man River" and Phil finally gets caught up in the grandeur of that marvelous song and begins to sing it with joyous abandon, really almost as powerfully as Robeson himself. That was the funniest number I have ever seen in my life. People actually rolled around on the floor with laughter during it.

Such creative talent all these people had. Given any excuse like a birthday or a new arrival, Phil and Johnny Mercer, for example, could sit down at the piano and compose marvelously funny songs within a few minutes, which they would then perform for the assembled. One time Lenny Bernstein, who had just written the music for that huge hit, *On the Town*, directed by George Abbott, brought his intended bride, Felicia Amontenegro, to the Kelly's, and Phil and Johnny composed a song for them that ended something like this:

"… *whose name I can't even pronounce on the phone.*
She'll change it to Bernstein, but she'll be fooled,
She thought she was marrying Morton Gould.
Break the habit, of George Abbott.
If you're offered a picture deal,
Grab it.
If New York will release ya,
Come West with Felicia,
To stay.
Happy Bernstein to you, Happy Bernstein to you …"

I was continually amazed at how fast their minds worked, these creative people, and marveled at their facility in so many different ways. It is interesting that some creative people, whether it is in music, math or performing arts, can do all areas of their expertise almost equally well. It seems as though the talent they were given covers all the arts as part of the gift. Charlie Chaplin, for example, could write, direct, produce, act in, and compose the music for his films, ordinarily a five-man job. Phil was just born with the extraordinary ability to act and sing and dance and extemporaneously compose lyrics and comedy sketches. It was a gift.

Speaking of Chaplin, one night he and his wife, Oona, dropped in to the Kelly's. While I was getting dressed that night I had heard the horrible southern bigot, Senator Bilbo, raving on about civil rights in his overblown, rabid way on the radio, and after a few martinis, I did a spontaneous take off on him. As the laughter died down, Chaplin said to me, "You're one of the best comedians in Hollywood."

Imagine! I had never been a big fan of Chaplin's, but everyone said he was a comic genius so I was properly flattered. But I knew very well that I was not that talented as a comedian. My humor was only a momentary gift from the gods of comedy that came on me suddenly when I was with certain people who thought I was funny, as though it was channeled from somewhere else. I couldn't repeat it afterwards; it was a one-time thing. But I knew comedy was not my forte anyway, dancing was. Because I had danced alone on a stage until I was 17, learning to ballroom dance at the Mayfair in Tyler was a whole new technique for me entirely. I found that the trick to dancing with a male partner was to let go of all personal control and follow every physical move of his by fitting my body close and trying to *intuit* his next move by blocking out all thought. It was like a game to see if I could anticipate and merge with my partner's every move, and when I started dancing with Gene, it was the most exciting thing I had ever done to find that I could follow him, even when he was improvising wildly. The highest accolade I ever received was when Gene said I was his favorite ballroom dance partner and asked me to pose with him for a *"Gene Kelly's Illustrated Dance Lessons"* mail order project, like Arthur Murray who was making so much money from his mail order lessons at the time. I got all dressed up and they took photographs of Gene and me performing the steps the illustrated footprints were outlining. I still have that brochure and look at it nostalgically now and then.

(I didn't realize until many years later that dancing close to a man and learning to follow his every physical movement took the place of sex for me. It was the safe way to lose control.)

Gene asked me to pose with him for this huge brochure and fold-out instructions for the Fox Trot.

The Kelly living room was not without its melodrama. Yves Montand and his wife, Simone Signoret, came often when one of them was working in Hollywood, but, even though he was everyone's favorite romantic singer, Yves could never be persuaded to perform for us. He and Simone were more interested in the political talk that abounded until one night Marilyn Monroe, with whom Yves was making a movie, dropped in and he performed a magic disappearing act with her. As Simone sat on alone at the bar, her face and manner stoic, only her heavy-lidded eyes betrayed the pain she was feeling. It was a scene right out of her movie, *Room at the Top* with Laurence Harvey: the aging woman of the world fighting silently to hold the fascinating younger man, who wanders off now and then with the pretty young thing.

(It is sad to remember that while Simone may have been melodrama, Marilyn was surely tragedy.)

The only person I ever saw play the Kelly group for suckers was Noel Coward. Lilli Palmer brought him one night and, as we were all sitting around eating spaghetti, he began to espouse fanatic right-wing blasphemes. In this ultra-liberal bunch it was red-flag-waving of the direst sort, and only his rapier wit protected him from mayhem as he was hotly attacked from all sides until — it finally became obvious that he was putting us on. It was a perfect practical joke, and to show that his triumph was negligible and he bore us no ill-will, the tall, debonair Coward then leaned casually on the piano and pulled us all into a small intimate circle as he talked rather than sang the sometimes witty, sometimes poignant songs he had written. I had never heard a man sing a love song obviously written for another man before, nor a song sung so sadly as when he finished with the last lyrics of his signature song:

> *"I believe that since my life began,*
> *The most I've had is just*
> *A talent to amuse.*
> *Heigh-ho, if love were all."*

The emotion he left us with was so powerful that it took a moment of silent thought before we began to applaud. But the night that stands out in my memory above all others is the one when Betsy was giving a Tupperware party on behalf of a struggling young actress who was having a hard time paying the rent. None of us had any great fascination with plastic containers, but actors have to stick together and we all gathered in the kitchen to quickly buy something and get it over with. The actress had gotten the multitude of Tupperware products spread out on the large table — when George Cukor walked into the kitchen with *Greta Garbo*.

Garbo! No other living human could have stunned this sophisticated group into such instantaneous silence. In this town where beauty, charm, talent, and fame, paled by profusion, Garbo stood alone. Why? I don't know. Surely she was beautiful, but so was Elizabeth Taylor or Hedy Lamarr and they did not cause a slight ripple in this room. She was not famed for her intellect, couldn't sing or dance or tell a joke, she hadn't made a movie in years, hadn't won an Academy Award, yet everyone felt as tongue-tied and gawky as the most ardent autograph hunter unexpectedly confronted with his favorite movie star. There was a mysterious aura about Garbo that was literally both enchanting and unforgettable. Betsy nervously explained about the Tupperware party, while the rest of us slipped into the living room and tried to think of what wonderfully entertaining thing we could do for Garbo to justify the faith Cukor had exhibited in us by bringing her here. Alas, it was to no avail. Garbo hoisted herself up on the edge of the kitchen table and intently asked the girl questions about the merits, differences, and uses of Tupperware for the next hour. Then, as we all sat in the living room still waiting expectantly, she stalked gracefully in laden with almost all the samples the girl had brought, and, thanking Gene and Betsy for a most enjoyable evening, Garbo collected Cukor and left. Nothing could ever top that.

An added bonus in becoming a regular at the Kelly's was that, with or without Phil, I also became a regular at Solly and Ethel Chaplin's. They were typical of the New York Jews I so admired in that, although they came from very poor immigrant families, music, literature, the arts, and humor were a major part of their birthright. Saul Chaplin and Sammy Cahn had been a mildly successful song writing team in New York, who had come to Hollywood like everyone else to seek their fortune. Sammy had left Solly to partner with Jules Styne, with whom he had a great success, and Sammy and Julie had become regulars at Frank Sinatra's. Solly found a job at Columbia Pictures in the music department under the direction of Morris

Stoloff, who was often at Bing Crosby's house. One can see that the
Hollywood artistic society was very convoluted.

At the Chaplin's on Saturday night, you might find Arthur Laurents (later to write *Gypsy*, *West Side Story*, *The Way We Were*), Farley
Granger, Gary Merrill (with or without wife Bette Davis), Sid Caesar,
and always a large group of people who enjoyed singing around their
two pianos and talking politics. Solly didn't make much money yet
at Columbia so they lived in a small rented house on Orange Grove
just off Hollywood Boulevard, and people brought their own liquor
to their weekly get-togethers, and ate dinner before they got there.
What the Chaplin's furnished their drop-in guests was water and
mallomars and marvelous music (they both played piano) and the
very best company. Solly was blonde and extremely tall and thin,
with thick glasses and very prominent teeth. Ethel was dark and vivid
and intensely passionate about music and politics and injustice and
life. She became my mentor, so to speak, and was the first person I
tried to individually emulate (other than my foredoomed attempt to
become a lady like Mrs. Mayfield) in the way she spoke and thought.
In its own way, the Chaplin group welcomed me and enriched me
and made me happy in the same way the Kelly group did.

One of the most fun projects I was ever involved in was when
Solly got a raise and they decided to take a chance on the future and
risk everything to fulfill a lifelong dream to live in their own house.
They put all their money on a down payment for a house on Doheny
Drive on the edge of Beverly Hills, which had only a built-in stove
and refrigerator as furnishings. Since they had come west with only
their daughter Julie and the clothes on their backs, they were going to
sleep on the floor in sleeping bags, and furnish their new house piece-
by-piece as they could afford it. Betsy came up with the idea that all
their friends should furnish the house for them at a surprise party.
She and I and Ruth Conte made lists of what each friend should
bring, according to what they could afford, so that there would be no
duplications and that all the Chaplin's basic needs would be fulfilled.
For example, Betsy bought a beautiful, old oval dining table at a thrift
shop and cut the legs off and refinished it for a coffee table, and with
the aid of imagination and footwork and love — about 30 people
were involved in completely furnishing that new house. Ted Reid
was designated to take the Chaplins out to dinner and a movie, and
when they walked back through their new door, they found that mov-

ing vans, cars, and willing hands had brought and placed furniture, made up beds, filled cabinets, put down rugs, and placed ashtrays, until they were looking at an empty house that had become a home.

There were lots of tears and joyous laughter and the best of human nature passed around that night, and it remains a high point in my life.

Hollywood at War

A Scene from the 20th Century-Fox Production
"WINGED VICTORY"
MADE IN U.S.A.

Me and Mark Daniels on Winged Victory.

A major way in which Hollywood had gone to war was in the immediate change in the types of movies the studios produced. The government, the military and those Jewish immigrants who were now heads of studios joined forces and the movie makers devoted themselves and their resources to the war effort. Errol Flynn playing Custer in *They Died with their Boots On* was replaced by Robert Montgomery in *They Were Expendable. Andy Hardy Gets Spring Fever* turned into *The Sands of Iwo Jima.* Before 1941 only five percent of the Hollywood movies were about events in Europe, but by 1942, almost 50 percent were about the war. For the first time in the movies, the American people were portrayed to themselves as innocent victims, as underdogs, the object being to encourage everyone to shape up and do his part to fight against the overwhelming odds we all faced. After our first major victory at Guadalcanal in 1943, however, the movies began to show our fighting forces as strong, incredibly brave — and winning! John Wayne epitomized the gallant, stoic warrior with his tender heart covered by a steely determination to "lick those Japs" no matter the cost. The Japanese were played by short Chinese actors with very large teeth, as all our Japanese -Americans had been rounded up and bussed off to concentration camps around the country within weeks of war being declared. At the command of a mentally-challenged army general and the agreement of Director of Security Milton Eisenhower, 11,200 Japanese American citizens were stripped of their possessions, liberty, and civil rights and detained in barracks with very little facilities, until after the war was over. The general declared this move necessary on the basis of no evidence, but lack of evidence. He stated that inasmuch as there had been no sabotage so far, there was bound to be some in the future. It makes you wonder, doesn't it?

The major studios were almost as miraculous as the defense plants in what they were able to turn their sound stages into in such a short time. With the help of military consultants, some of the huge stages were turned into an island in the Pacific with uncanny exactitude, complete down to the accurate kinds of palms, foliage, and bird calls. Or they created a Moroccan village and a desert for totally realistically looking battle scenes. The majors all had enormous water-filled tanks half surrounded by gray-blue canvas representing sky that were used for ocean or lake scenes. Giant machines roiled the water to make a violent storm or any degree of wave movement. With the aid of shipboard sets in the water or miniatures of war ships, a realistic naval battle could be fought right on the back lot.

Some Hollywood stars like Clark Gable, Tyrone Powers, James Stewart, Robert Taylor, Henry Fonda, and Glen Ford, joined the military, usually as captains or majors, and served overseas. David Niven went back to England and fought with his old regiment. Some actors and directors like Gene Kelly and John Ford joined up to go and fight, but were entailed to make documentaries for the services instead. Many actors were sent to a Special Forces unit that trained and remained at the old Hal Roach Studio right there in Hollywood, where the military used the actors in many public relations projects. One of these projects was *This Is the Army*, a touring musical about the army, with a score by Irving Berlin. Berlin was one of the performers himself in the show and was a huge hit singing, *"Oh, How I Hate to Get Up in the Morning."*

Some of the lyrics were:

"Oh, how I hate to get up in the morning,
Oh, how I'd like to remain in bed.
Some day I'm going to murder the bugler,
Some day they're going to find him dead.
And then I'll shoot that other pup,
The guy who wakes the bugler up,
And spend the rest of my life in bed."

That cute little Berlin singing his heart out in his snappy army private's uniform among the tallest recruits they could find for the chorus was just what the military and the country needed to make them feel better about the war we were all involved in. Another public relations project, written and directed by Moss Hart, the then most successful Broadway playwright and songwriter, was *Winged Victory*, which was about boys from all over the country trying to make it in the Army Air Corps as pilots, navigators, and gunners. The very popular song "Off We Go into the Wild Blue Yonder" was one of the songs from that play and the huge cast came mostly from that Hollywood unit at Hal Roach.

Zanuck bought the film rights and agreed to use fifteen or so men from the original cast in the movie, Edmond O'Brien, Lon Mc-Callister, Red Buttons, Lee J. Cobb, Karl Malden and other well-known male actors, but he replaced the four New York stage actresses playing the wives with his own starlets. He hired George Cukor, famous for his ability to get great performances out of women, to direct this manly cast, and Cukor watched the screen tests of every starlet on the lot to choose the lucky four wives. He chose Judy Holliday, Jeanne Crain, Jane Ball and me. This was the first important part in an important film for all of us. Judy had blondish hair and flashing dark eyes, with a square face and a driving personality. Jeanne Crain had a sweet, pretty face that usually wore a contained secret little smile, and she had naturally curly, light-chestnut, luxuriant hair that she wore parted in the center and hanging straight down to her shoulders, where it ended in a bushy bunch of curls. The extraordinary part was that it *bounced* when she walked. My hair was almost her same color and was just as long, but it didn't *bounce* when I walked. I studied her to see how she managed that, did her heels go up and down when she walked or what? It looked terrific, but it was a puzzle. Jane Ball was a small-boned blonde with an exquisite, delicate face and a fragile demeanor, just right for the part she played.

Cukor and I hit it off right from the start, and he seemed to give me special attention. At least, I was the only one he took over to Metro, his home studio, to see Sidney Guilleroff, the famous hair stylist about what to do with my hair and makeup, as well as to the ultra-chic Metro costume designer, Valentine, for my wardrobe. I don't know how Zanuck let him get away with that. However, after an hour or so of trying different hair styles on me, Guilleroff and Cukor decided that the way I usually wore my hair was the better way. And after another hour or so, Valentine and Cukor chose a wardrobe that could have come right out of my own closet, but — that's Hollywood.

This was in the beginning of 1944 and it is interesting to see how many of those 15 or so practically unknown names in the cast went on to outstanding careers — and how many didn't. For both the men and the women actors! The plot followed four young men with differing backgrounds who rushed to answer their country's call to war and yearned to fly airplanes. To my knowledge, it was the first movie to show in detail the many tests and difficulties involved in the intensive training of such a program as the Army Air Corps Flight School. There is, of course, high comedy and high tragedy as the cadets struggle to prove they can qualify as pilots, or have to settle for navigator or bombardier — or disastrously wash out. Most civilians at that time had no idea of what it took mentally, physically, and spiritually (spirit may have counted most of all) to become the officers who flew our planes in combat. The four central characters and the rest of the actor cadets work their way through the whole process and eventually one of them receives the coveted pilot's wings, another a bombardier's wings, one dies in a trainer plane crash, and one fails to qualify and leaves, heartbroken and in tears.

The four wives follow them through this experience, hold them tight when they succeed — or don't — and wave bravely as their husbands fly off into the wild blue yonder of war-torn Europe. The ratio of women's parts to men's parts in Hollywood after 1941 was even more slanted in favor of the men than it had been before. At least pre-1941, what women's parts there were often portrayed strong, vital characters. Now, however, for the most part there was no *pith* in women's parts in the movies. They were either meek stay-at-home moms, kindly volunteers, or shadowy nurses scattered here and there. Very little was made of the courage and determination of the thousands of women serving in the WAVES, WACS, or WASPS (Women's Auxiliary Service Pilots.) Those WASPS took the difficult training course of the Army Air Corps and flew transport and supply planes within the U.S. to release the men for service overseas. What a terrific movie their exploits would have made! But – that was the way it was in war time Hollywood, and you might as well face it.

In *Winged Victory*, Judy Holliday was the wife of Edmond O'Brien, who made bombardier, Jeanne Crain the wife of Barry Nelson, navigator, and Jane Ball the wife of Lon McCallister, who gets killed in a plane crash. The actor playing my husband was Mark Daniels, the lucky pilot. He had the handsome good looks of a young John Barrymore, and was one of those actors who look at a spot right above his fellow actor's eyes while playing a scene, which is very disconcerting. Rosalind Russell always did that, I noticed. Anyway, in the movie we were newlyweds, madly in love with one another, and the anxious wife is always there to support and encourage him, and try not to let him know how lonely and worried she is. The so-called chemistry between Mark and me was water-soaked by our individual personalities and never gave off the least spark. The airplanes were really the love objects in this movie, anyway.

Most of the film was shot on location at the Santa Ana Army Air Base, which was located on the old Irvine Ranch in Orange County near Laguna Beach. We shot on this huge base with real cadets and planes and marching and stuff. The real cadets were volunteered by the Army, who got their pay, and the actors mixed in with them doing calisthenics, quick marches, standing at attention, and going through the various tests. The real cadets looked really spiffy in their crisp khakis, crew cuts, shining shoes, and serious/fun loving faces. They were all as concentrated on becoming pilots as the parts the actors were playing, but you could see that they got a big kick out of being pretend actors, and probably talked about it for the rest of their lives. One of the location scenes that involved the wives showed them in the stands wildly applauding and proudly smiling, while off camera presumably their husbands were receiving their wings on the parade grounds in the graduation ceremony. When shooting outdoors, I had never realized what agony actors went through trying not to squint or tear up when the lighting men kept those large silver reflecting screens shining on their faces for close-ups. At least it was agony for me to try to smile lovingly while it felt like my eyes were being burned out. I'm afraid it kind of showed in the final movie. I just hoped the audience put my screwed-up face down to emotion rather than being unprofessional.

The wives were in those location shots and in four more in the interiors, which were shot on the Fox lot. One of those scenes was the cause of my biggest humiliation, an experience that has bothered me for over 70 years. I had heard from all sides that George Cukor was one of the 3-or-4 best directors overall, and the very best at getting great emotional performances out of women. Actresses like Greta Garbo, Vivien Leigh, Joan Crawford, and particularly Katharine Hepburn, fought to get him on their films, and indeed he had directed some of the best dramatic pictures ever made. Compared to how the crew reacted with casual professionalism to other directors I'd worked with, the crew was positively reverential with Cukor. He was a slight, dark man, with black curly hair and brown eyes that sparkled behind thick glasses and a ready ear-to-ear smile. In pre-production, Cukor seemed predisposed to think highly of me, but small-and-not-so-small disasters between the two of us began soon after production started. In my first scene, where my new husband received the letter that he has been accepted into flight school, I had a close-up reacting apprehensively to the news. While Cukor was involved in something else, the camera man told me to stand a certain way and position my face a certain way in order to get the best lighting. When we did a take, I assumed that position and Cukor yelled, "Cut," and repositioning me, said, "No, no. I told you to stand like this. Don't twist your face around like that."

Eager to extricate myself from blame, I said, "But the camera man told me to do it that way."

Cukor whirled on the camera man and gave him a withering look. The camera man looked away. Turning back to me, Cukor said impatiently, "You listen to *me*. Don't *ever* do something I didn't tell you to do. Now, let's try it again."

Afterwards, I sidled up to the camera man, and said, "I'm sorry."

He turned from me indifferently, and said, "I was just trying to help you, but I can see you're just an amateur."

"Amateur!" I was crushed. But, I learned the valuable lesson than an actor must never get in between the camera man and the director.

Jeanne Crain spent most of the time between our scenes standing close behind the camera man watching intently everything that went on. She told me that Marlene Dietrich always did that and knew more about lighting than most camera men. Personally I thought Marlene and Jeanne were wasting their time, and preferred to sit in my chair and talk to Judy Holliday or Edmund O'Brien. One late afternoon when the waits had been interminable, I asked the passing Cukor if I could go home soon. Turning one of his withering glances on me, he continued on his way, saying contemptuously, "Stock girls!"

"Stock girl!" That was worse than "amateur." I felt like the lowest insect. So much condemnation was within those two words indicating: Unprofessional. Insensitive. Self-centered. I felt pinned to the wall by those epithets, and suffered shamefully. As in all forms of show business, to be called a "professional" is the highest praise. To *be* a professional in Hollywood, I was to learn, the actor was on time, knew his lines, stayed behind the camera to feed lines to his partner for his/her close-up, stayed on the set or nearby until the shoot closed down for the day, and endured without complaint the possible desert heat, arctic cold, water submergence, or any extreme physical ordeal the script might call for. Even the stars obeyed those rules if they wanted to be respected within the industry. I was stung to the quick to realize I had acted unprofessionally.

But the worst was yet to come. Each of the wives had a big scene. Jane Ball's character left after her husband died, but the three remaining wives were back in their hotel room after their husbands have departed for overseas. Jeanne and Judy's parts called for them to be depressed and frightened, while my part called for me to be the strong one who supported and comforted them, until she goes in another room to cry privately and noiselessly in a big close-up. As it turned out, that was the last scene of the movie except for a long shot of the planes flying in formation off into the wild blue. I had been trying my hardest to please Cukor in my preceding scenes to get back in his good graces, so to speak, but I went numb when I thought about having to cry for the camera. For most of my life I had trained myself not to cry even when I was alone, so the thought of weeping away in front of a stage full of people and a pitiless camera put me in a state of suspended animation. The night before I practiced for awhile in front of a mirror, but the results brought about the panic of failure, so I had to put my faith in Cukor's skills as a director and hope for the best.

Since it was a silent close-up, Cukor cleared the set and, once the lights and camera were positioned, he called for quiet and began to gently talk me through it.

I couldn't make it happen. I knew what he wanted; I had seen Katharine Hepburn do it many times: the trembling lower lip and chin, the beginning of tears in her eyes, which slowly begin to trickle down her face while she stares bravely straight into the camera — but I just couldn't get the tears to come. In desperation, I thought of how I felt when I got the letter that my horse, Creampuff, had died. Trying to imagine her face, how much I loved her, how catastrophic her death was, I began to bawl at the top of my lungs. "Cut!" Putting his arm around my shaking shoulders, Cukor said, "All right now, stop your crying. You would scare the audience with that kind of face. Calm down and try not to contort your face so much. You've got the emotion now, but just let the tears flow out without breaking down. Now, let's try it again."

It is too painful even now, to try to re-experience what I went through during at least 20 or maybe even 30 takes of that close-up. I don't remember any more now, but I know it sounds unbelievable how many times Cukor said "action" and then "cut." The makeup woman came rushing in between shots trying to conceal my red eyes and nose with makeup and powder. Everyone on the set kept extremely quiet. Cukor continued to be patient and kind, which only made it worse. In the back of my mind was the thought that the makeup woman could squirt something in my eyes to bring tears. I had heard that's what they did sometimes, but when I suggested it to Cukor, he made a face as though that was a degrading thing to do. If I had known that's the way he felt about it, I should have brought my own onion! My humiliation at keeping the crews for what seemed to be hours going over and over what would only be a few seconds of final film, and the agony it was for me not to be able to give Cukor the results he was trying so hard to get, gave me a good idea of what it must feel like to be slowly drawn and quartered. Finally, to my ignominious despair, Cukor turned away and said, "Well, all right.

Just put your hands over your face and bow your head and let's wrap up here." It was the complete shameful cop-out for me as an actress.

When you see actors cover their face with their hands or fall face-down on a bed and shake their shoulders, you know it is because they couldn't make the tears come in a close-up. For the rest of my life, I have rerun that experience in my mind. Sometimes I can make tears come to my eyes, but every time I try to make my lower lip and chin tremble, it breaks my concentration and I have to giggle. I am still envious when I see actors do that successfully on the screen, seemingly without effort. I'm not sure why I couldn't do it. Of course, I had a deep prejudice against crying, and I had never before been called upon as a performer to cry except in a melodramatic phony way, which clearly Cukor would not accept, but I think mostly it was that I just didn't have the innate desire or ability to put myself into the soul of another person. Almost any good actor will tell you that from childhood their happiest times were when they were pretending to be someone else. They loved and had a knack for putting themselves completely inside another person's character. Even in my worst times, I never wanted to be anyone else but me. I still wish I could have cried for Cukor the way he wanted, though.

As tired as I got of sitting around between takes, there was still a kind of lost letdown when the assistant director yelled, "That's a wrap" and the show was over. For one thing, I had bonded with Edmund O'Brien and Judy Holliday from the start, and I knew I would miss seeing them all the time. Eddie was a vibrant, robust, lusty kind of guy, who always had a joke or a song on his lips. We became life-long friends, not hanky-panky friends, but real pals. He liked women in general, and I became his chief listener to the many woes with his many wives and girlfriends, and his reminiscences about his stage experiences. He was a trained Shakespearean actor from New York, and became a brilliant movie actor, although it was only in his last film, *The Man Who Shot Liberty Valance*, that he was nominated for an Academy Award. But he was fun to know and we always kept in touch. Judy had come to Fox with her New York nightclub act, *The Revuers*, which included Betty Comden and Adolph Green, on a one-picture deal. Their act had been cut out of the final film, but Judy herself was offered a player's contract. As in a Fox film, Judy had to make the decision to "Keep the act together" or "Don't worry about us, kid, this will make you a star." Judy followed showbiz tradition and signed the contract, thereby breaking up the act. The ridiculous thing was that within a few weeks after *Winged Victory* wrapped, Fox dropped the option of both Jane Ball and Judy, although Jane gave the best performance of the four of us, and Judy had obvious star quality. As a last gesture, Judy sent her falsies in a package to Zanuck with a note saying, "This is all you really wanted from me so you can keep them," and went back to New York. But within a few months she was cast as the lead in a fantastically successful play called *Born Yesterday* and became a huge star. I never heard of Jane Ball again. It just goes to show that real life is like a movie. By the time the movie was released, it was after June 6, 1944; D-Day was making everyone relieved and happy and *Winged Victory* did very well at the box office. Mrs. Mayfield sent me a photograph of the marquee of the local theater in Tyler with my name above the title. It was not a portent of things to come.

The nice thing was that Cukor continued to be friendly with me; he didn't cast me in another part, but he did invite me now and then to his famous brunches in his extraordinarily beautiful house up in the hills. Usually there were some members of the military present, and I supposed as a former Miss America, he thought I was someone who would interest them, but Cukor made it clear that I was just there as a guest and not a party favor. I was enchanted with his artistically decorated home and the delicious food served on his exquisitely set table and the talk at the table and the whole ambience. I had never seen anything as elegant and impressive as Cukor's home.

After *Winged Victory* shut down, it was back to my social whirl with Phil. A really special time for me was when Edward G. Robinson invited us to his house for a Jewish holiday occasion like Passover Seder, the celebration of the Jews' escape from Egypt. Robinson was especially fond of Phil and loved to speak Yiddish with him, particularly in telling Yiddish jokes. His laughter was full-bodied and contagious. He and his wife had a warm, comfortable, unpretentious home, with the exception of his fabulous collection of Impressionist art displayed nonchalantly on the walls, which was a perfect reflection of Robinson's personality. He was a lovely man. Sweet, curious, openhearted, he was simple and warm, with a brilliant intellect which he displayed nonchalantly now and then. He welcomed me into his home and took pleasure in instructing me in the meanings of the rituals carried out at the Seder table by his family. He was a proud and gentle loving father and husband. All traces of the gangster parts he had become famous for were non-existent. He taught me some meaningful and amusing Yiddish phrases which I never forgot. It was great fun to be in the company of Edward G. Robinson.

But the fun of the Robinson's or the Kelly group was not there for me during my many evenings at Crosby's or Sinatra's. They didn't sing or dance or do sketches, and the games they played were gin rummy or poker. Everyone was pleasant to me, but none of them seemed really interested when I tried to explain my new-found theories of how Schopenhaur's primacy of the will concept influenced Nietzsche, or other things like that. Not being interested in card games, I spent a lot of time at their parties in their extensive libraries reading. They didn't seem to mind.

I didn't really enjoy going to Danny Kaye's anymore after Groucho put me down so hard. The way the comics all sat around in the living room waiting for their chance to tell the next joke or anecdote with the eagerness of a horse in the starting gate, never really listening to the one who had the floor, was a big turn-off for me. Groucho and George Burns were the worst hams of all. Their intense desire to always be "on" destroyed the humor of what they said for me. The only one who didn't do that was Jack Benny, who was a complete patsy for all of them and started laughing wholeheartedly the moment one of them even opened his mouth. He was famous for that. But the thing that burned me up was that the wives never got to say a word. Gracie Allen, who was the real talent of the Burns and Allen act, Sylvia Kaye, who wrote most of Danny's material, and Lee Gershwin, who was a very talented woman, sat around and laughed like a proper audience, except for getting fresh drinks and serving food. You can be sure I never tried to do my medicine show numbers for them!

Harry Cohn's parties were a different story, though even worse where women were concerned. Phil had done his best movies at Columbia; *Thousand and One Nights* and *Cover Girl*, so when Harry summoned him to dinner or a party, he went. The Cohn's lived in a huge mansion up behind the Beverly Hills Hotel. Joan Cohn, a slim, elegant, not-very-successful blonde actress, explained to me the first time I went to their house that they had three swimming pools: one for guests, one for their two children, and one for the servants. None of which they themselves used. When, awestruck, I commented on the palatial black and white tiled, two-story entry hall, with its floor-to-ceiling French windows overlooking the lights of Beverly Hills, she said airily, "Oh, it's just gracious living." I had to use every ounce of my willpower not to burst out laughing in her face. She was the most pretentious person I had ever met and I thought she was hilarious. There was nothing pretentious about Harry, however; he fully lived up to his nickname (behind his back) of "King Kohn," and was truly a sadistic monster. He sat at the head of his dinner table or in his living room like a giant-bodied spider with beady, penetrating eyes pulling people into his web to be devoured. Nothing made him feel more powerful than to viciously intimidate and bully the people who worked for him, particularly the women like Rita Hayworth (even as his wife) and Evelyn Keyes. I despised him.

Oddly enough, or possibly because I never tried very hard to conceal my feelings, he always had me seated on his right at the dinner table. An arch conservative, he seemed to take great delight in haranguing me about my embryonic political views and heaped scorn on "bleeding heart liberals," as I vociferously and passionately leapt to my idols' defense. I never could get my facts quite straight, but I didn't let that stop my arguments. Cohn pretended to think I was amusing and naïve, but clearly it was important to him to ridicule and demolish me. It was amazing to me that this movie mogul who concerned himself with every detail of everything that went on in his studio, had produced some all-time great movies like *It Happened One Night* and *You Can't Take It With You*, took the time to also concern himself with the views of someone he appeared to consider a stupid female pinko. Also, it made him crazy that I didn't wear stockings and high heels.

This was at a time when well-dressed women wore elaborate gowns to dinner parties, and most certainly, they wore stockings and high heels. Movie premiers in those days were a very big deal: klieg lights crisscrossing the sky, bleachers for the fans, limos drawing up with the stars, cameras and interviewers on the red carpet, and the female stars wearing the most glamorous clothes by the most fabulous designers in the world. I had worn what I felt like wearing all my life, regardless of fashion or whether other people liked it or not, and I was determined not to let Hollywood change me in any way. I took pride in that. So, when I was getting dressed to go somewhere, whether it was a premiere, to the movies, or to a dinner party, I wore what I decided I felt like that night. If I didn't feel like getting all gussied up for a big premiere at Grauman's Chinese Theatre, with all that makeup and a fancy hair-do like the studio had taught me, I put on a daytime dress, a snood, thong sandals, and just wore lipstick. I had always loved going barefoot and hated the confinement of bras, girdles, garter belts, stockings, and high heels, so the new flat-heeled thongs were the closest thing to going barefoot and I wore them with everything. For example, if I felt like wearing a lace, ankle-length, very fancy off-the-shoulder dress I was fond of to the Cohn's, with it I wore thong sandals and no stockings. I guess dressing any way I pleased was my way of saying, "Up the Rebels" to phony Hollywood. I was ahead of my time by about 20 years, you might say. I'm sure Cohn knew that and it made him crazy. He complained to Phil that I wasn't wearing shoes and stockings, and pointed out my fashion mistakes to all and sundry. Phil didn't care, he never tried to tell me what to do. Actually, I don't think he noticed. And I didn't care. That was one reason I felt so comfortable at the Kelly's, most of the women there didn't wear stockings either.

I don't know, fashion statements didn't seem all that important to me at this time in our country's history. The Victory Committee and the USO in both Hollywood and New York were indefatigable in assembling and distributing tours to every place American service personnel were located, even on the front lines. Sometimes 40 or 50 groups of performers were entertaining the troops somewhere in the world at the same time. It is impossible to estimate how many uniformed hearts were made momentarily lighter by their efforts and good will. Many stars like John Garfield, Bing Crosby, Marlene Dietrich, and Bette Davis invited some of the servicemen they met on tours to visit at their own homes for a weekend if they could get to Hollywood, and took them to the studios and in general showed them an unforgettable time. A bitter disappointment for me personally was that I was scheduled to go overseas with Jack Benny on a USO tour, but it was cancelled because his wife got ill. By the time she got well, Benny's tour was re-scheduled — and Carole Landis took my place! I was really fond of Jack Benny and have always mourned my planned trip with him, and that I never got overseas to entertain during the war. But I did USO and War Bond Tours all over the U.S., which gave me great satisfaction.

Blackie Comes Home

Blackie.

Love is a funny thing. My first experience with love was what I felt for my father, which came to a bad end, so the only unconditional love I allowed myself after that was for nature, both animal and vegetable. I was so fortunate to have been permitted to explore and become aware of the miracle of the innate spirit of nature when I was a child, but I had never extended that awareness to the spirit of *human* nature until I let myself see it in the servicemen I met while I was entertaining at camps or at the Hollywood Canteen. They were all so outrageously enthusiastic and cheerful while living in the midst of much hardship and imminent peril. The love that I had for them en masse and individually had the force and gaiety of a Sousa Marching Band, and the love I felt for the laughing, proud women I met in defense plants enlarged my heart with a hitherto unknown warmth. It was an entirely new experience for me to love God's creation as a whole.

The love I'd had for Blackie for four years was multi-layered. There was the constant *knowing* that he was the man I most fitted, and he was my comforting lifeline during difficult times — except — there was still that sex thing. Blackie had written that the bird earring I had entrusted him with had gotten very wet when his plane had been shot down over the ocean, but not to worry, after a few hours of wave tossing, they were rescued and were high and dry now. A terrifying thought. Particularly after a recent experience I'd had. In 1943, I had gotten friendly with three Texas boys named Brooks, Carter, and Tom when I entertained at March Army Air Corps Base where they were stationed a few hours from Los Angeles. They were P-38 pilots with the sweetness and buoyancy of a Van Johnson, and my cousin Shirley an I went out with them on a few of their weekend passes before they shipped out for overseas. A few months later I heard from Tom that Brooks and Carter had been shot down and killed soon after they arrived in England. Tom had been shot down over Ireland, his parachute had then been shot up, and he had a free-fall of several hundred feet onto rocky Irish soil. It broke every bone in his body. Unable to move but fully conscious, he heard the anti-British Irish collected around him discussing his demise and how it served the Yanks right, until some MPs arrived to transport him to the hospital. He had been in hospitals abroad and in the States for eight months and, after many operations, was only now able to write, but his letter was full of positive thoughts and the determination to get well and walk back to Texas. A central ingredient of the love I felt for the servicemen and defense plant women was their incredible spirit. But Blackie's spirit and determination to get back home to me filled me with the shame of not being worthy. He, they, all those wonderful boys, deserved a more open and unrestricted loving from the girls they left behind when they returned than I could honestly feel anymore. I hadn't wanted to write him a "Dear John" letter, considering where he was and what he was doing, but I knew someday soon the reckoning would come. I had seen girls in newsreels rushing to meet their returning sweethearts, wide smiles, hair flying, arms outstretched until they wrapped tightly around their loved ones. I didn't feel like that about Blackie anymore. And I hated myself for that lack so much that eventually I began to blame him for it.

Early in 1945, Germany was about to surrender and our forces in the Pacific had retaken the Philippines, Iwo Jima, and Okinawa and were on the verge of invading Japan. There was talk in the air about a super-bomb the scientists were working on in Los Alamos, New Mexico. After more than two years of fighting in the Pacific, Blackie wrote that his carrier was coming into San Francisco and he and two buddies would come to L.A. by train for a 3-day leave. He would then be stationed somewhere back in the States. For him the war was over.

He came to my front door bearing orchids and his love in his hands, and I knew I didn't deserve or want either one. His leave was awkward and uncomfortable for us both, my eyes glazed when I looked at him and I couldn't really see him. I didn't really *want* to see him. I didn't want to see his black, curly hair, or his olive skin, or the dimple in his chin, or really hear his husky voice. I didn't want to make direct contact with his eyes for fear of what I would see in them. I didn't want him to become *real* to me and confuse me with who he was and why I had loved him. I felt like a punching bag from the battering I was giving myself for not being the loving, delighted-to-have-him-back woman he had every reason to expect. I knew what a sickening trauma the deaths and broken body of the three Texas P-38 pilots had been for me, and surely it must be inestimably more horrific for Blackie with what he had seen happening all around him for two years. I didn't even want to try to imagine what his reality must have been as a tail-gunner in a torpedo plane in action, being shot down, waiting and wondering if he would be picked up, and other experiences just as soul-mangling. I had seen the special cama-raderie between buddies in the service, what must Blackie's feelings have been watching his buddies get maimed and killed? What had it done to him? I didn't ask — and he didn't say. We were both struck dumb by our thoughts and uneasy fears.

His first night, my cousin, Shirley, and I took Blackie and his buddies to the *Bar of Music*, my favorite nightclub where *The Nat King Cole Trio* was just making a big hit. We dined and we danced and we made nice. Blackie returned my earring and made light of how it looked a bit bedraggled from sea water. Neither of us had the nerve for a serious talk so we just settled for feeling miserable and laughing a lot. Of course, being the insightful person that he was, Blackie knew without my telling that our plans for a future together were not going to materialize, but he thought it was because of the glamour of Hol-lywood and my wanting to be a movie star. It wasn't quite like that.

Blackie couldn't understand that I thought of myself as fundamentally opposed to the glamour of Hollywood and was proud of my lack of desire to be a movie star. Having given it serious thought, I had never yet met or seen a female movie star who lived the kind of life I wanted. I didn't like to have my picture taken, didn't enjoy working in the movies I'd been in, and the desperate and unending struggle to get famous and stay that way by Hollywood actresses seemed somehow pathetic to me. Other than touring for the war effort, my small celebrity hadn't brought me joy. Though being a "former Miss America" would follow me for the rest of my days, at that point in my life it was not something I was proud of. And already the fickle Louella Parsons had given newcomer Marie McDonald the title she had previously bestowed on me of "The Body." "Good riddance," I said vehemently.

But, mostly, I wasn't the same girl that Blackie had rescued from the medicine show by giving her the courage to pack up and leave. Oh, in some ways I was, but in other important ways, I was not. Blackie had opened the Pandora's box of experiences for me which led directly to my going to Tyler and fatefully meeting Mr. Taylor of the Citizens National Bank — which led directly to the Miss America Pageant and thus to Fox. It was all *his* fault, really, that so much had happened to change me! And now, I was in the process of becoming yet another person. The new focus and purpose I felt in my quest to be an intellectual had taken me to another emotional place entirely from when I first knew Blackie. I didn't want the reality of him to confuse me and deter me from where I was headed. It was as though the viewfinder on my camera of life had zoomed open and revealed this vast panorama of goodies — philosophy, art, music, literature — that were mine for the taking.

In my imagination, I had a vivid image of my life as a just-begun tapestry. It gave me a pleasant feeling of accomplishment to imagine that some part from every good book I read, every glorious concert I heard, every learned thing someone said, even every growing kind of *thought* I had, was imprinted on that tapestry. The rules were that nothing negative, like not being able to cry for Cukor or throwing up on Jack Benny's pink carpet, or even the deep angers from the past, was allowed to be represented in the weave of my tapestry. In my mind's eye, I visualized a colorful abstract wall hanging whose design represented all the exciting new experiences that I was having.

It was filled in like by an elephant with a paintbrush with some blobs of the browny-purple of Puccini arias — a dash of lemon-yellow from Bertrand Russell's quote, "The mark of a happy man is zest." — a wide splash of fire engine-red from dancing with Gene – billowy clouds of silvery-blue and green from a Turner landscape – tidy winding paths from Jane Austin – multicolored sequins of light from Mozart – dark-gray solid strokes from the essays of Montaigne – and tiny spring flowers of all colors of laughter sprinkled here and there. I imagined that every important sight or sound or thought that entered my consciousness was instantly woven into the canvas. I thought the overall colors and shapes of the design of my tapestry would not be clear or make sense until all the directions had been followed and the tapestry was complete. I imagined that on my deathbed, I would see it finally finished and I could say, "Ah ha! *That* is what it was all about." But in the meantime, it was the image of filling in the blank unfinished part that added zest to my quest for learning.

Unquestionably, the force of Blackie's personality and the changes and developments he had brought about in me created a vivid, strong beginning pattern in my tapestry, but envisioning our future together, with me as a housewife in a small town in Texas, was like looking through the wrong end of a telescope — everything looked too small. To be honest, too un-showbiz. Whether I liked it or not, I was born and raised showbiz and that would always be one of my basic qualities. I had been reading omnivorously and some of the books I had read threw up enticing visions. When I turned the telescope right side up, the vista therein revealed magical symbols like Paris and Singapore and Mombassa, and beguiling expanses of unknown exciting adventures. I had inherited a restless spirit and a need for bold adventure from my father. Faced with the immediate decision of marriage to Blackie, I had to realize that I had been living in a fantasy world, and now I needed a new fantasy. The long-held image of myself as a housewife shimmered and dissolved into one of an adventuress in a belted trench coat, collar turned up, suitcase in hand, saying, "One ticket to Cairo, please." The image of a movie star, or a housewife, was all wrong in my imagined tapestry design, but *adventuress*, that was a perfect fit.

I have often wondered what would have happened if Mr. Taylor had not stopped me passing by the Citizens National Bank or the Japanese had not bombed Pearl Harbor. Would I have married

Blackie by the time I was 19? Would we have been happy? Would I have been a pretend wife or could I have learned to be a real wife? We'll never know. Whatever, now was now, and on Blackie's last night when we parked in front of his hotel, filled with miserable and defensive guilt, I told him that I couldn't marry him. He took it silently like a gentleman, of course, and I have never wanted to know if or how much it hurt him. We did stay in each other's lives, through a meaningful exchanges of letters spanning the rest of his life.

After Blackie left, there was a hole in my life where he had been. I had a slightly sinking feeling that I had broken something irreplaceable. But then in March of 1945, I married Phil Silvers.

Marrying for Laughter - 1945

With Phil in our New York apartment.

There were several good reasons why I went out with Phil once or twice a week. One, because he made me laugh. Two, because he was satisfied with a few chaste kisses. Three, because through Phil I got to know almost every successful person connected with show business in America, and a lot from everywhere else. For example, my musical idols were Artie Shaw and Benny Goodman. I got to meet Goodman at Frank Loesser's house (he wrote musicals like *Guys and Dolls*) for dinner, where just the Loessers and Goodman and Phil and I sat around and I listened while they talked for hours. Benny looked and behaved a lot like the local banker, but never mind, he was *Goodman*! Phil was one of Artie Shaw's best friends, and just the two of us were often at his house for an evening where Artie and Phil sat around after dinner playing clarinet duets together. Phil didn't have Artie's superb tone on the clarinet, but he played surprisingly well and used his clarinet in his nightclub act. He and Artie did funny jazz riffs on the clarinet together while Ava Gardner, Artie's wife at the time, and I just sat and laughed and admired.

Then, too, I had been a big fan of Orson Welles ever since *The War of the Worlds*, and loved to go with Phil to Orson's parties, which were sometimes held in his backyard where a permanent stage with wings and a backdrop was set up like a private playhouse. Orson delighted in putting on shows, featuring himself as magician, with various vaudeville and burlesque performers who happened to be in L.A., ranging from dog acts to strip tease artists. Orson's theatrical talents and needs went shooting off in all directions. Now and then, just the two of us were invited to his house, where after dinner Phil and Orson practiced magic tricks together while Rita Hayworth and I just sat and laughed and admired. Orson was fascinated with burlesque and loved to hear Phil's stories about the inner workings of that bawdy kind of show business. As you can see, because of Phil, my life was filled with laughter in a way that I could not have known on my own.

I didn't laugh so much at the frequent dinner parties at Harry Cohn's house, head of Columbia Pictures. This tarantula of a man (and not nearly as nice as the ones Mr. McCandless had taught me to handle in the Texas desert) fed on the blood of those in his power by contemptuously putting them down. The stories of his dominating, mean behavior to all who worked for him at Columbia were legend, as was his paranoia against anyone with liberal thinking, whom he irrespectively called "pinkos" or "commies." I was under no obligation to him so I was free to charge his egomaniacal opinions on my white horse of civil liberties, proudly waving my banner of *Liberté, Egalité, Fraternité!* In that way, I played the fool for Cohn at his dinner parties. One night Cohn had Jacob Javitts, the New York senator, and another congressman for dinner and, presumably for their entertainment, he began to bait me, and like an enraged seal I performed my opinion-spouting tricks on command. Cohn stopped any pretense of politeness and began to brutally attack my shaky positions one after the other until I was on the verge of tears. Suddenly, from his place at the other end of the table, Phil charged to my rescue with his rapier of wit. No one can destroy an opponent as effectively as a comic, for one cannot defend themselves gracefully against humor, and Cohn was vanquished from the field of battle. For Phil to come to the rescue of this fair maiden against the dragon Cohn was as brave a deed as David attacking Goliath with his slingshot, and it was equally effective.

On the way home that night I told Phil that I would marry him. I realized later, that impulse came from the center of the 7-year-old child I had been who wanted to be taken care of by her father. For me to be taken care of, to be protected, was a need that I tried not to know about, but obviously when Phil protected me from Cohn's belittling, it went to the core of that need. His public caring for me opened the floodgates of my heart, and I reached for that caring in the form of agreeing to marry him. Of course, he never did it again. But I always loved him for that one time.

Phil didn't relate to women very well, but he always treated me as though I was refined and somehow precious. During the almost two years I had known Phil, he frequently jokingly asked me to marry him, secure in the knowledge that I would refuse, I imagine. I think it scared him mightily when I accepted his proposal, but he was game and the date was set. Sinatra, Crosby, and Cohn all wanted to give us the wedding and reception at their homes, although Cohn said savagely to the room at large one night, "Phil, I don't know why you want to marry Jo-Carroll. It will never last because she doesn't think you're funny."

He was wrong, of course, I did think Phil was funny, that is why I loved him. He knew that. I just didn't think Harry Cohn was funny. Joan Cohn was funny, though. She took me aside to advise me in her grand manner not to have a "colored" staff of servants after we were married as they were prone to be overly friendly. She said she'd had a staff of seven "colored" for years until one day her personal maid had called her "Honey!" She had fired them all instantly and now had a Swedish staff and advised me to do the same. I had to snicker at that. Joan Cohn was a prime example of what I thought was wrong with rich people!

For a reason I couldn't quite explain, I didn't want a big wedding at anybody's house. It seemed fraudulent somehow. I insisted that we get married before a Justice of the Peace, with only my mother and Phil's brother/manager, Harry, present. Now that our plans were made, however, ice began to gather around Phil's feet and nervously he said, "Josie, you know I am kind of set in my ways. I've been a bachelor and lived alone for a long time and ... ah ... I go to *The Friar's Club* a lot and ... Well, I ..."

I said, "Phil, I don't want to change you or your ways, any more than I want you to try to change me.

We will both stay the same, don't worry."

But his anxiety fueled my own and I began to feel a little light-headed and queasy about the enormity of what I was about to do, so I decided to go back to Tyler to see best friend Bette and the Mayfields before I got married. I hadn't discussed my approaching marriage in detail with Mother, just told her what I was going to do and she seemed pleased; she adored Phil. But the Mayfields were like a real family to me and I trusted their opinion and thought it would make me see things more clearly. Bette was delighted with my news; the Mayfields were not. They were as glad to see me as I was them, and the two years I had been in Hollywood melted away in happy and loving talk until I told them the reason for my visit.

After a shocked pause, Mrs. Mayfield said, "Darlin', you know your happiness is of the utmost importance to us. But I think you should consider this very carefully. Are you sure you love him and are doing the right thing?"

"Yes, I think so."

"Isn't he a lot older than you?"

"Only 11 years."

Delicately, "Darlin', isn't he a Jewish man?"

"Oh, sure."

In her sweet, engaging way, Mrs. Mayfield let me know that, while some Jews were nice enough people, excluding the fact that they killed Christ, still it wouldn't do at all to marry one.

The Senator hadn't said anything, but then he cleared his throat and said, "Little Miss, you've given us something to think about. We'll talk about it again later, but I want you to come down to the office in the morning, I have something I want to show you."

The next morning from behind his familiar desk, the Senator was tapping a legal document in his hand as he said, "You remember my telling you about some property up near Kilgore I own jointly with some British interests? Because of the war, we haven't been able to develop it, but I've had some tests run and there's oil there and plenty of it. Now I want you to look at this," and he handed me the legal document.

I saw that it was his will, and he had marked the place where as his heirs my name was listed with an equal share with his son, after both his and Mrs. Mayfield's death.

Coming around the desk to put his hand on my shoulder, the Senator said in his cunning way, "The war is about over and when those wells come in, if you'll give up this foolishness, I'm going to give you a portion of your inheritance now so you can use it to see the world. What do you think of that?"

I stared at him speechlessly.

Smiling benignly, he continued, "And then when I die you'll be a wealthy woman."

He moved to sit on the edge of the desk so we were face to face. "Little Miss, you don't want to get married to that man. You've got too many things you can do with all that money. And you've got to think of your future children. You see? Once you've had time to think it over, you'll change your mind."

He smiled his cute smile, showing his big front teeth, "I know I'm right."

That did it. The wily politician thought he could prevent me from marrying a Jew by dangling a lot of money in front of my eyes. But he was wrong. If anything was guaranteed to make me marry Phil it was using this kind of tactic to change my mind. I understood that it was not only his prejudice at work here, it was mostly because the Senator loved me and wanted what he thought was best for me. What *he* didn't understand was that my own peculiar sense of honor had always meant a lot more to me than money. I had learned that about myself when I didn't want to let the Mayfields adopt me, and when I turned down that first contract at Metro-Goldwyn-Mayer. Particularly now with my newly-acquired militancy regarding racial equality, my *honor* was at stake, so the Mayfield's prejudice convinced me to go home and marry Phil as soon as possible. Consequently, although I always stayed close to Mrs. Mayfield, I never heard directly from the Senator again. And I never struck oil in Texas.

I never regretted it. The money, that is, but I was deeply regretful to learn the extent of the Mayfield's bigotry. I had loved them deeply and, other than Mother, theirs had been the closest relationship I had to a family, so my loss of respect for them was a serious one. Having lived in Texas, I was not blind to the ingrained prejudice of Texans against Blacks, Mexicans, and even Catholics, but show people as a whole are not prejudiced against any ethnic group, just "townies." I had never known any Jews, that I was aware of, until I met those in Hollywood and it was those Jews that had brought the tragedy of racial injustice into my consciousness. Previously, I had admired the Mayfields without qualification, and now for the first time, I realized that *good* people can have *bad* attitudes.

I didn't want a formal wedding gown, no trailing veil, no fancy cake and reception with lots of people, no photographers or fathers to give me away. I suppose in retrospect, I didn't think of it so much as a celebration as a change of scene. I didn't buy anything new to wear for the big day except a big hat and some very fancy nightgowns. Now that the worrisome wedding night was imminent, I thought I really ought to at least dress sexy for the part. Phil had arranged for Judge Edward Brandt, brother of Harry Brandt, head of Fox publicity, to perform our ceremony. In Judge Brandt's dingy office that morning of March 25, 1945, it took him about 10 minutes to get Mother, Harry, Phil, and me lined up properly in front of him and to say the binding words of "by the powers vested in me," — and — Phil and I were man and wife. Then the judge, without explanation, rushed over, opened a side door, called in a bunch of photographers, grabbed Phil and me and positioned himself between us looking judicial, while for a half-hour the photographers yelled, "One more, please – Hey, Phil and ah – over here, smile – OK, now all five of you together." I was outraged and Phil was apologetic. The judge was the only one of our five to wear an honest smile. Phil and I looked like the judge has just pronounced our jail sentence instead of the beginning of our wedded bliss.

Phil and I were both kind of numb at the enormity of what we had done on our way to my new "home" at his apartment. I had my suitcase of clothes in his car and, once there, I busied myself putting them away to hide my embarrassment. As we sat down together in the living room of this small, dark apartment on Beverly Drive just off Wilshire and looked at each other, neither of us knew what to say. In retrospect, I have great pity for us two babes in the woods. Aged 21 and 32 respectively, a newborn babe in diapers knew as much about what goes into a good marriage as Phil and I did. I don't think either of us had ever sincerely said, "I love you," to anyone, or had any idea of what "love" really meant.

The disparity between what Phil and I expected from being joined together by law became painfully apparent when Phil mentioned that he intended going to the fights that night. Phil and some of his friends had reserved ringside seats for the fights on Friday nights; I had gone with him once and was sickened by the spectacle and vowed never to go again. It had never crossed my mind that since we happened to get married on a Friday, Phil expected to carry on as usual. *On our wedding night!* It was a slap in the face with the cold cloth of reality and I started to cry. While I was sitting there in tears, the doorbell rang and it was darling Danny Kaye delivering a huge silver fruit bowl for our wedding present. Observing that I was in tears, Danny put the bowl down and squatted down beside me, saying gently, "What's the matter with the new bride?"

Phil said plaintively, "I don't know what's the matter. I just said I was going to the fights tonight and she started to cry."

Straightening up, Danny said, "Phil, you insensitive twit. You are married to Miss America and you're going to the *fights* on your wedding night?"

In righteous indignation, Phil said, "But Danny, it's Friday. I *always* go to the fights on Friday night."

Shaking his finger at Phil, his sweet comic's face in a furious scowl, Danny said, "Well, you're not going to the fights *this* Friday night, so just be a gentleman and step up to the plate here."

Phil stayed home, and I got into my glamorous, sheer, black lace nightgown to cover up my inadequacies and waited rigidly in bed with my eyes closed. As it happened, I didn't really need the sexy lingerie because Phil turned the light out before he got in bed and never saw my camouflage allurements while he performed his brief nuptial duties dutifully. My primary thoughts during and after were:

One: "I'm afraid he would rather be at the fights."

Two. "A man's skin is surprisingly smooth."

Three. "It hurt a little, but if that's all there is to it, it isn't too bad."

After all the horror I had built up in myself over the years since Dr. Tate's assaults, rather than frightening, sex was kind of a letdown. While it was kind of "whim-wham, thank you, ma'm," as the saying goes, Phil didn't smell or sound or behave like Dr. Tate, and my relief was enormous.

The next morning, Phil seemed inordinately pleased with the small spots of blood on the sheet, but I put the expensive, lovely lingerie away in the drawer and never wore it again. I was relieved to get back to my cotton butcher boy pajamas. A few days later, I inadvertently went in the bathroom while Phil was having a bath, and stopped to stare at my first view of a man's naked body. He chatted on casually, but I stood transfixed at the amount of hair on his white, flabby body. Without realizing it, I had the image in my mind of Blackie's olive-skinned, hairless-smooth, sculptured-muscle body from photos he'd sent me of him in a bathing suit on the beach in Okinawa as what a man's naked body should look like. Phil didn't look like that at all. It was not a comparison I wanted to make.

Perhaps because of his background, Phil lived in a fantasy world even more than I did. His mother and father were Russian immigrants, and the story went that when his mother was 15 and his father was 18, one day his father was working in the field when he saw Phil's mother being sexually attacked by a passing Cossack. His father killed the Cossack with a scythe, and the two of them were smuggled out of Russia in a manure cart, carrying only a change of clothes, a few drachma, and his mother's precious dowry dishes. When they finally got to New York through the help of relatives, the only job his father could find was working on the high beams of the new skyscrapers – so his father learned to speak English with an Irish accent and his mother never learned to really speak English at all. They always lived in the Brownsville section of Brooklyn and had seven children, of which Phil was the youngest. The other children became accountants and dentists or married accountants and dentists — only Phil was adventurous like his father. In his own way, he walked a high beam all his life.

Phil and I were both working when we first got married, so we had to wait a month to go on a honeymoon to New York. Our first morning on the Super Chief that April of 1945, I was impressed when Phil ordered breakfast served in our compartment; it seemed very grown-up and high-class. But when the Negro waiter brought the tray in, I was shocked to see tears running down his face in a steady stream. I asked, "Are you all right?"

His voice was so broken I could scarcely understand his words: "I'm not ever going to be all right again. Our fathe ... our President ... Mr. Franklin D. Roosevelt is dead."

I was pole-axed at what I understood him to say, "What? What did you say?"

Putting the tray down and burying his face in a napkin, the waiter openly sobbed. Finally he straightened almost to attention, and said in a prayerful tone, "president Franklin Delano Roosevelt died this morning in White Springs, Georgia."

Although I knew President Roosevelt was not a well man, I had never imagined he could *die*. He had been my President and father figure for more than half my life and I *depended* on him to make things right in my world. It didn't seem possible that he could be dead. Besides the incalculable loss it was to me and to the country, as indicated by the reaction of our waiter, it was a bad omen of things to come on our honeymoon.

As the train pulled into the great maelstrom of New York Central, I began to get nervous about meeting Phil's family. Phil's father was dead, but his mother lived in their same attached brownstone in Brooklyn. Phil's brother, Harry, had warned me in dire tones that their mother was Jewish Orthodox and obeyed all the Jewish lore, like breaking dishes by throwing them down the stairs to scare away the devil, if one of her children was really sick. She religiously obeyed the dietary laws by keeping a totally kosher kitchen, and expected her children to marry other Jews. But in truth, Harry didn't understand the goodness of his mother at all. That day when we took a limo out to her house for lunch, she was completely lovely to me and welcomed me into their family in the warmest possible way. Because Phil had told her I drank milk with my meals, she broke all her taboos and served me milk. As a wedding present, she gave me a cup and saucer from her set of the gorgeous embossed dishes she had smuggled out of Russia in a manure cart at such great risk. To this day they have remained one of my most treasured possessions.

That night Phil took me to his favorite restaurant, Toots Shor's, a showbiz/sports figures hangout on 51th Street between 5th and 6th. Toots Shor was a large, sandy-haired man who walked tilted backwards to balance his protruding stomach, and, for reasons I was never clear about, his raucous, put-down humor endeared him to his patrons. Plus, his reputed underworld connections gave him a touch of sinister glamour, I think. His restaurant had warm reddish-brick walls, was brightly lit with a huge circular mahogany bar in front, and comfortable booths and tables filled with more famous people than the Fox commissary, although Broadway and sports figures prevailed. After many bear hugs and much laughter with Toots Shor, Phil proudly introduced his "girl bride" to Toots, who gave me a beneficent welcome and got us settled in a front booth. After we had ordered and been served our drinks, Phil excused himself to go say hello to one of his idols, Joe DiMaggio, at a nearby table. Then he began stopping at other tables, from which much laughter immediately arose, while I sat alone trying to look interested in my surroundings. After awhile, Orson Welles came over and joined me just as our dinners arrived.

Pushing Phil's plate away from in front of him, he said, "How is married life treating you?"

Glad to have someone to talk to, I said, "Great. Just great."

Looking over at Phil, still table hopping, Orson said, "It's not very nice of Phil to leave you alone like this on your honeymoon, though, is it?"

"Well, you know Phil."

Leaning closer to me, Orson said, "But someone might think Phil cared more for his friends than he does for you, mightn't they?"

Beginning to feel humiliated, I replied angrily, "No, they wouldn't. Phil loves me better than anyone!"

With that peculiar intensity that Orson had, he said, "Does he? Do you think he would leave his friends and come if you called him?"

Taking the bait like an idiot, I said, "Of course, he would."

"Well, prove it. Call him and see."

To my unending regret, I made a fool of myself and shouted out, "Phil. Phil!"

Sitting at another nearby table with some men whom I later found out were Meyer Lansky and part of his gangster mob, Phil turned and held up his hand to wave at me as he said, "I'll be there in a minute, honey," and turned back to the men.

After a long pause, Orson gave my hand a little pat and said softly, "Have a nice life, Jo-Carroll," and left.

I sat on alone with my cooling dinner in a sickening blaze of humiliation and realization. I had never let Phil's table-hopping behavior bother me before. I thought of it as just the way he was. Now the sudden full knowledge that I would never come first with Phil, that our repeating the marriage vows together had meant less than social conversation to him, robbed me of appetite for my dinner and my self-respect. I felt like the bricks of Toots Shor's walls had collapsed on my head and seethed with anger at Phil. Also, I was stunned with amazement that a talented, intelligent man like Orson Welles would take time out of a social evening to do such a deliberately cruel and hurtful thing to me. He really knew very little about me. What went on in that brilliant mind that made him want to destroy me? It was somehow sinister and frightening to find that Orson Welles was a mean and petty man. He treated Rita Hayworth like dirt in their private lives. He did seem to have great camaraderie with men.

When Phil and I got back to the Sherry-Netherland, where we were staying in a lovely suite, there was a message for Phil to call Frank Sinatra. That phone call resulted in Phil telling me that he had to leave early the next morning to join Frank on a trip overseas to entertain the troops! It seemed that Frank had a month's trip planned to visit all the American camps and bases in Europe, but the Victory Committee had just told him that the G.I.s were planning various forms of mayhem against this skinny 4-F'er, whom all their girls were

With Phil and my second yellow convertible.

going crazy over. Frank had often done Phil's "The Singing Lesson" number with him at parties, and Frank thought that would be a good way for him to be introduced to the troops.

Pugnacious Sinatra was greatly humiliated to be judged 4-F because of ear canal injuries at birth and was always eager to be involved in the war effort in any way he could. Phil was 4-F because of his chronic asthmatic sinus condition, which was why he never drank or smoked, and Phil was delighted to extend the Victory Committee tours he had done in this country to Europe. Plus the fact *Frank* needed him. He started packing, while I sat and watched with a very lonely feeling.

Later that night, I awoke with an agonizing pain in my stomach. The handsome young hotel doctor told Phil it was acute appendicitis and I must go to the hospital early the next morning to have my appendix removed. Phil went white with anxiety. Since he had already made early morning reservations to leave to join Frank, thence to be immediately transported by the Army Air Force to London later that day, it presented him with a problem. While I writhed on the bed in severe pain, Phil called his hypochondriac friend, famous radio star Goody Ace, for help. Within an hour, Goody's personal, squat, old doctor came to the hotel, pronounced that I had a nervous bellyache, and gave me some Phenobarbital, which immediately put me into an easeful sleep. Early the next morning, a relieved Phil called Louise Schacht, an artist friend of mine in New York whom I had known when she was working on a movie in Hollywood, and told her of our desperate plight. Louise rushed over, and Phil rushed off to entertain the Allied Armies.

"The Singing Lesson" was a number Phil had done with his partner, Rags Ragland in burlesque in which, while teaching Rags to sing, Phil keeps slapping him every time he opens his mouth saying he isn't using the proper breathing technique. The singer gets beat up and never gets to sing a song. It was a natural for the troops as Phil could come out, do his comedy routine, then after Sinatra without introduction unobtrusively slips up to him, Phil starts to slap this famous singer around before the guys realize who he is. With that kind of demeaning introduction, and with Solly Chaplin to play piano for him, once Frank began to sing he was as big a hit with the men as he was with their girlfriends. I understood that. I could see why Frank needed him and why Phil wanted to go. What I also understood was that Orson was right in his assessment that ours was not a marriage made in heaven, and that White Knight Phil was not going to charge to my rescue just because I had a bellyache. Not when Frank needed him, anyway. Thus it was that, a couple of days later, with Pheno-barbital bottle in hand, I returned from my honeymoon in New York alone on the train to California and my mother.

Never having had a sedative of any kind, the Phenobarbital was a blissful experience for me for a few days, but after my "nervous bellyache" had subsided and I could think straight, I did a lot of thinking. I was able to look at my marriage with unclouded eyes, and it made all the skin on my body feel slack and heavy. It usually took me a long time to make a commitment, but once I had made it, I stuck to it. Also, the thought of the suffering my pride would undergo, if I proved the Mayfields and Harry Cohn, and Orson Welles, were right this soon in my marriage made me determined to stick it out.

Still, I had been dealt a body blow by Phil's behavior and I looked around for some kind of payback, not a divorce but revenge. The thought came to me that I would have my teeth capped and charge it to Phil. I had a space between my two front teeth and the studio made me wear plastic veneers fitted over my teeth when I was working. They were a great nuisance; I kept misplacing them, or sit-ting on them, or once lost them overboard on a sickening boat trip to Catalina for a publicity shoot. To have my four front teeth capped by the well-known dentist the studio used was a very expensive under-taking and I thought it a proper price for Phil to pay for abandoning me in New York.

Phil was just a shadowy figure in my imagination as I endured this capital form of dental punishment, and when I received my first letter from him I studied his handwriting as though it could reveal his hidden character to me. It didn't. When Phil got back a month later, however, it was like meeting him afresh all over again and finding out how much fun he was. They had fabulous success wherever they went and Phil had many funny and wonderful tales to relay. I never stopped laughing. It was also funny that until he got the bill, he didn't really notice my new teeth.

Phil didn't want life to be the way it was. He made it up as he went along and I guess that is why he was so good at improvisa-tion. He had an aversion to the truth when a lie sounded better, and could never see anything wrong with that. For example, Johnny Burke and Jimmy Van Huesen wrote songs for Crosby, and one time for Bessie Burke's birthday Phil and Jimmy sat down at the piano and wrote a song entitled, "Bessie with the Laughing Face." Bessie *was* always laughing and everyone loved the song, Bessie particularly. A few months later, at a birthday party at Sinatra's for his little girl, Nancy, Phil sat down at the piano and introduced a new song he said he had just written for the occasion called, "Nancy with the Laughing Face," with only "Nancy" exchanged for "Bessie" in the lyrics. Frank was touched at what Phil had written for Nancy and recorded it to great success. I thought that was a dirty trick on Bessie, but Phil could never understand my attitude at all. His attitude was that both the Burkes and the Sinatras were pleased, and he was pleased that they were pleased, so where was the problem? My attitude had been established by the code of behavior I thought God demanded when I was a child. Strict honesty was a part of my rules that kept me from chaos, and I was rigid in my adherence to that code.

Aside from what seemed to Phil my inexplicable phobia about truth, there were a lot of things about me that bewildered him. I had told Phil I didn't want an engagement ring or an expensive wedding ring; I just wanted a simple, thin, gold band. The day we planned to go and pick it out, Phil had a sudden golf game with Bing Crosby, and I was crushed that I had to go and pick it out by myself. I had not thought of either of us as deeply in love with one another, that was what made our relationship so easy, but still I subconsciously expected some kind of increased intimacy between us, some kind of personal connection through marriage that went beyond just dating. I tried to explain that to Phil, and he did try in his own way to make me happy. Some time later, he took me to the local Buick dealer for a surprise present. New cars were just becoming available and Buick had come out with their new Dynaflow automatic shift transmission, and Phil had ordered a new yellow convertible with red leather seats for me. As soon as I drove it off the lot, I fell in love with the *zooooomm* of the new transmission engine. But, hard as it may be to believe, so help me I would rather that Phil had wanted to go with me to buy my wedding ring than give me a new car.

Mother and I had a joint bank account and my Fox checks went directly to my old address, so when we were married, I told Mother that she could use that bank account for her own needs and that way she would be self-supporting. Mother had made a life for herself that I believe was the best one she had ever had, barring her relationship with my father. She had joined the choir of a Methodist Church, taught in the Sunday School, joined a women's club, *The Rebeccas*, and organized and directed a "Grandma's Kitchen Band," which played at various functions. Mother's friends had a lot of fun playing old-timey songs with thimbles on washboards, spoons on pots and pans, and a wash tub for a drum, and Mother loved organizing and directing the band. They even played on local television once. Phil took great delight in Mother and knew she needed a car so now the fact that she could keep my old car was part of his surprise.

That was one surprise I loved, the one I didn't was on my first birthday after we were married. Phil asked me what I would like for my birthday and I told him that my very best present would be for him to take me dancing at the Coconut Grove as we had done on our first date. As much as we were together, we never went to dinner or dancing alone and I yearned for it. Phil was a very good dancer and the Grove was the most romantic spot in town. That nigh,t I eagerly got all dressed up and was feeling great when Phil suggested we stop by Mother's apartment on the way so she could give me her present. The apartment was dark when we drove up but upon our entering, all the lights went on and there were yells of "Surprise, surprise" from the whole Kelly group, who had been assembled waiting for us. I can't recall ever being so disappointed in my life. I understood that Phil and Mother had planned this surprise party thinking it would be a special treat for me, and I thought it was lovely of these friends to participate on this occasion — *but I wanted to go dancing with Phil alone!* I had been looking forward to it with such anticipation. It was very difficult for me to smile and pretend to be happy opening presents and eating the banquet Mother had prepared, when all I wanted to do was burst into tears.

Unconsciously, I had changed the rules of our marriage. I had told Phil before we were married that I didn't want him to change in any way. But evidently, deep down, I did want him to change. I wanted Phil to *want* to stay home on our wedding night. I wanted him to *want* to go with me to pick out our wedding ring more than he wanted to play golf with Bing. I wanted Phil to *want* to take me dancing alone when he knew how much I cared about it. I had the ugly feeling that I was behaving like a spoiled brat, but going dancing alone was the only specific thing I had ever asked Phil for and it meant a lot of important things to me. I had chosen to marry for laughter rather than for love. But instinctively, marriage meant more to me than some legal interpretation by a Justice of the Peace. Unexpectedly, a yearning I could not explain sought a new tenderness and understanding in an unexplored intimacy with Phil. In some subterranean place, I wanted a *caring* love as well as laughter. Of course, if asked, Phil would have said he *was* showing caring by buying me a car, and by planning a surprise birthday party. I could never explain to Phil the intangible differences in our interpretation of that elastic and mysterious word "love."

How little we know ourselves in our everyday life. If someone had asked me, "What is your most defining trait?" I would have instantly replied, "Courage. I am very brave."

Yet when the chips were down, I had become a turn-tail-and-run coward when it came to facing my sexual fears and the challenge of a real loving life by marrying Blackie. I had sought shelter from my fears in the safety of a *pseudo* marriage with Phil — and now I wanted it to be a *real* marriage. Immature as I was, with totally unrealistic self-deception, I wanted Phil to be *romantic*. Expecting Phil to be romantic was like expecting him to be a physics teacher. Nothing in his nature, experience, or inclination, equipped him to be either one. In retrospect, I think Phil was at a loss for words with an audience of just his wife. He never took me dancing alone again and I never learned not to want it.

The Jolson Story

After Phil and I had been married a few months, I got a call from casting that I had been loaned out to Columbia for a movie starting in two weeks. They sent me a copy of the script and it was *The Jolson Story*, a biography of Al Jolson starring Larry Parks. My part of the next-door-sweetheart of the young Jolson could have been played easily by any one of the many starlets Cohn had under contract to Columbia, so it was clear to me that Cohn had asked for me because he wanted me to be beholden to him. I gritted my teeth, but I was given no choice, by contract I had to do it. Jolson was a huge figure in show business, big star on Broadway in the early 20s, starred in *The Jazz Singer,* the first talking picture in 1927, and would entertain all night at parties if given the chance. He and his new wife, Erle, were often at the Cohn's parties, and I had become friends with her. She was my age, 21, had met the 60-year-old Jolson the year before when she was his nurse in a hospital, and he swept her off her feet with his volcanic personality. She seemed shy and a little lost in Hollywood to me, so I asked her to have lunch some day, and she said very softly, "Oh, that is kind of you, but Al has told me his wife Ruby Keeler divorced him because of what other women told her at lunch, so I must never go out alone with women. He is adamant about that." That selfish, mean old man, he made my blood boil. I have to admit though, he had recorded the songs himself for the movie and even in his 60s, they sounded terrific.

The good part about working on the movie was that Larry and his wife, Betty Garrett, a marvelous actress who had worked opposite Frank Sinatra in *On the Town* at Metro, were good friends of mine from the Solly Chaplin group, and Larry was fun to work with. He was absolutely superb in the part of Jolson; his moves, his mimicry, and his sheer verve and showmanship copied Jolson perfectly. We had several scenes together: I, as his childhood sweetheart, adoringly promising him I will wait for him while he goes off to become famous; shots looking at him adoringly from the audience while he is performing, a scene back in his dressing room; and a final scene after he becomes famous when I look at him adoringly and happily tell him I am going to marry someone else. Since I really was so fond of Larry, as long as I could keep smiling the part made no demand on my acting skills whatever.

My only vivid memory of *The Jolson Story* is when we were about two weeks into shooting and one night I awoke with bad menstrual cramps. I had always had a hard time with my period, perhaps because I resented the inconvenience of it so much. At any rate, this was a particularly painful time and I certainly knew I wasn't going to make my six o'clock call in makeup feeling like this, so I took a couple of Midol and thought I would call in sick later in the morning and went back to sleep. At 6:30 a.m. sharp the phone rang and it was a very angry assistant director shouting, "Where the hell are you?"

I said defensively, "I was going to call you shortly to tell you that I am really feeling terrible and can't come in today." He screamed even louder, "I don't care if you are on your death bed, you are in this first shot and you are not going to hold up this entire production because of a belly ache. You get your ass down here in 30 minutes or I'll come drag you here by the hair on your head." Needless to say, I took some more Midol, got Phil up to drive me, and got my ass down there within 30 minutes. That was something else I learned about being a professional — the show must go on, I think they call it. I was so drugged out I don't remember doing that scene at all, but when I saw the finished product, it humiliated me to see that I didn't look anymore drugged in that scene than I did in the rest of them.

By August of 1945 the war was over, the rent controls were soon lifted, and I couldn't wait to find us another place to live other than this dark little apartment. I found a charming house on a hillside with homey, comfortable furniture and a beautiful garden of flowers, near Metro in the Cheviot Hills section of Culver City. One of the reasons I was so eager to move was that dogs were strictly forbidden in most Beverly Hills apartments and my life was always incomplete without a dog. As soon as we moved into that pretty little house, I got a 6-month-old West Highland Terrier and Phil named him Budget. Phil's zany euphemism for having sex was to "fuss budget around" and somehow he connected a pet and sex together, which tells you something. I had found with Phil that his sexual impulses were seldom, and quickly satisfied, but he always made it seem amusing.

Also, now that we had a big enough place, I hired a cook to come in five days a week. My mother had always done the cooking and, as I could not boil water without burning the pot, except for breakfast out of a carton, Phil and I always ate out after we were married. But once we got the house, although I did not follow Joan Cohn's advice about having a Swedish staff of seven, I did hire one lovely African-American woman named Martha, who was not a very good cook, but was very jolly, and she and I became great friends.

Phil and I were constantly guests in other people's houses, and now that we had a decent place to entertain, I thought it behooved me to reciprocate. It seemed best to start off small, so my first invitation was to the fellows on a baseball night. Just like Friday was fight night for Phil and some of his friends, in season Wednesday was baseball night. Bing Crosby, Sammy Cahn, Julie Styne, and Phil had season's tickets and usually ate out together before the game, so it seemed a good time to try my wings as a hostess. Victim of my present need to show off, and wanting to surprise and impress them with something out of the ordinary, I asked Martha if she knew how to make *Pomme Souffle*, a French specialty dish of puffed-up potatoes I'd had once at Romanoff's; Beef Wellington, which I'd never eaten, but it was the most expensive item on the menu so I figured it must be a treat; and Shoefly Pie, a Southern sweet potato/molasses pie that a currently popular song was based on. Knowing how much this meant to me and not wanting to let me down I suppose, Martha said yes she could do it.

Well, I had flowers on the beautifully set table and when we were seated I ran a little bell for Martha to begin. It is impossible to find words to describe the horror of what befell me. Instead of the steak and baked potatoes my guests would have much preferred, Martha put on the table seasoned cement slices of greasy potatoes and almost blackened cement-covered beef with the consistency of hard tack. They all filled their plates — and then tried not to break their knives attempting to cut into the potatoes and pastry-covered beef. The only thing Phil, Sammy, and Julie managed to eat was the ordinary salad I couldn't think of a way to dress up, but Bing, may his soul rest in ever-lasting peace, hacked his way through most of the cement and ate it down manfully. I, myself, could eat nothing and only sat speechless at the table, absolutely burning up with mortification. For the first and only time, Phil was at a loss for words and also sat speechless, feeling I know not what, as we never talked about it afterwards. When Martha served the runny gooey-gunk that in no way resembled the delicious Shoefly Pie that my mother made back in Texas, I just sat on in my hell-fire, while nobody but Bing ate the pie. If it hadn't been impolite to wear my little red hat to the table as I had done on my first day at school for courage, I might have managed to laugh it off and make a joke of it, but as it was I was as turned to stone as the food and couldn't be graceful about it at all.

When we finally escaped the dinner disaster to go to the game, I tried not to notice when Phil, Sammy, and Julie kept ordering more hot dogs. It was a long time before I invited anyone to dinner again, and when I did we had steak and baked potatoes.

The Menace of McCarthyism

The bad thing about the whole experience of the *Jolson Story* was that disaster struck the lovely Larry Parks, who stood to become a major star after the film was released. Parks was one of the first actors to be interrogated by the House Un-American Activities Committee (HUAC). Because Parks refused to "name names," he was blacklisted and never worked in a major movie again. He was quite literally heartbroken, dying of a heart attack well before his time. He was a beautiful person and a wonderful actor and it makes me sick even today to remember the travesty and the tragedy of that terrible period. The *Jolson Story* has played on television for years, but I never watched it again after that first time. It makes me too sad.

It was not illegal to belong to political parties, even the Communist Party. Nevertheless, the HUAC was originally formed in 1938 to prosecute citizens suspected of having loosely-defined "disloyal" and "subversive" inclinations. A decade later, HUAC launched a campaign to accuse members of the entertainment industry of being communist sympathizers. This paralleled the devastating Joseph McCarthy witch hunts, conducted from the Senate. Ultimately, more than 300 outstanding actors, directors, screenwriters, radio commentators, and musicians were accused of being communist sympathizers and then blacklisted.

Out of craven fear, the heads of the major studios, to a man, fired each employee named by the committee. Even when they had a contract, the studio lawyers argued that they were in breach due to engaging in illegal activity. Some could get jobs as waiters at Hamburger Hamlet, and some lived in more dire straights. In order to eat, they had to forego their sense of honor and self-respect, but consequently, they became unemployable in the industry they loved.

It was all so completely stupid. Charlie Chaplin, for example, was a liberal and self-proclaimed "peacemonger," but was in no way a 'communist sympathizer.' He was arguably the most beloved human being in the world, yet was forced to live in Switzerland with his family rather than be called before the HUAC. To think that Charlie Chaplin, THE Charlie Chaplin, was banished from the industry he helped to create, because some Senators wanted their names in the news, and no other real reason. After 20 years, he was invited back to receive an Academy Award in 1972. He came and cried real tears as he gave his acceptance speech, and received a twelve-minute standing ovation. Thank god that happened.

The other most prominent victims, known as the "Hollywood Ten," were singled out for refusing to answer questions in hearings during 1947 and sentenced to a year in jail. I was among the many who gathered on the tarmac at the airport when they were taken away to serve their sentences.

Gene and Betsy Kelly and Humphrey Bogart and Lauren Bacall were among the 15 or so prominent actors who went as a group to Washington DC to plead their cause, to no avail. I think the only person they really got to talk to at the White House was the doorman, and he only wanted their autographs.

Even with the example of our Founding Fathers, who left their homes and fought for freedom of religion and free speech, under the tutelage of Donald Trump, about 40% of Americans thought it was just fine to sentence people to prison for what they believe.

Without exaggeration, through Phil I met most of the actors and creative people who were working in the movies and on the stage in Hollywood and New York, and I became friends with some of them. On Saturday nights that they got together in small groups and partied or just hung out. I always felt it was my guardian angel presenting me with yet another miracle when, even after Phil and I divorced, I was still regularly invited to these get-togethers. I had an open invitation to the homes of the Gene and Betsy Kelly, Saul and Ethyl Chaplin, Yip Harburg (lyricist for songs such as "Somewhere Over the Rainbow"), and Danny Kaye. I luxuriated in the feeling of being wanted by these people.

I had always been a loner, but now felt so proud to be part of a group of people that I thought were going to make the world a better place. However, after a couple of years, when I began to know them better, I finally realized that my radical friends (not my liberal ones) could be as dogmatic about their beliefs as were the conservatives I knew. I didn't want one of them for president, and the more I learned about communism, the more I understood that while they believed the ends justify the means — absolutely, I believed the ends did not justify the means — absolutely. And, I realized that the only way I could make the world a better place was to make myself a better person.

Life Among the Stars

I couldn't get it straight in my mind about Bing Crosby. He was unfailingly kind and always seemed interested in what I had to say, and he called me "Carroll Jo" in a funny, affectionate way. Also, not only did he prove his "good manners" and sheer guts at my dinner table, but he later showed himself to be one of the most compassionate men I ever knew. Best friend Bette's mother called to say that Bette had been in a terrible automobile accident, almost died, and she promised her that she could come visit me, if she would try to get better. I had often asked her to come, but she always said she couldn't for one reason or another. Now, I found that her Southern Baptist mother wouldn't let her visit Big Bad Hollywood for fear of its contamination, but when she was in the hospital, not responding to treatment because the doctors said she didn't have the will to live, her mother got through to her with the promise that she could come to see me if she would try to get better. I was delighted and asked Phil to find a date for her when we went out to show her the town — and he came up with Bing. When Bette came, thin and on crutches, we her to dinner at Chasen's, where at every other table sat a very famous star or two, and then to Slapsy Maxie's for a great floor show. During the entire evening, Bing devoted himself to being solicitous and amusing to Bette.

(When she came to visit me 50 years later for the last time, it was truly a farewell trip as she had terminal brain cancer. We talked of life and love and the pursuit of happiness, and she said that night with Bing was the high point of her entire life.)

So that was one side of Bing. The other side confused me. His wife, Dixie Dunbar, was a blonde and beautiful pixie who was a big musical comedy star when they married, but by the time I met her about 15 years later, she was a wreck. When Bing entertained at his house, it was usually a Sunday afternoon lawn party. He had a large two-story stucco house in Holmby Hills up high between Beverly Hills and Bel Air. It had a luxurious patio for entertaining, and a beautifully landscaped extensive back yard for just looking. Dixie wore dark glasses in and out of doors and mumbled a bit when she talked and swerved a bit when she walked. She seemed a tragic figure to me. Bing treated her with barely concealed contempt, which didn't seem fair as everyone knew he had been an alcoholic when they married. Now, however, he was an "AA *Recovering* Alcoholic" who had no compassion for his wife and was a stern and removed Father to their three boys. Bing used his home for social parties, but he spent most of his time in an apartment he kept on the Sunset Strip — which made him free to escort Bette when Phil had asked him, and where, I was told, he was free to have friends of the female gender visit from time to time. As he was Catholic, there was no question of a divorce, but seemingly, his faith made allowances for adultery. I never understood that. On the other hand, he was so considerate and caring to me and to Bette. How do you explain that duality? I understood fairly well "Der Bingle," as he was often called, or "Ole Bang," as Phil called him, in his public persona of laid-back, easy-going charm, but his private self was an enigma to me.

(Sad to say, Dixie drank herself to death by the time she was 42.)

While I am on the subject of famous male singers, one time Frank Sinatra demonstrated what a gent he was with Phil the same way Bing did with Bette. Phil had been getting disgruntled with his "friend of the hero" parts in the movies at Fox and Columbia, and hated wearing the toupee the studios demanded, so he jumped at the chance when his agent told him he was offered two weeks as a headliner at the Copacabana, the top nightclub in New York. Phil had done stand up comedy in clubs in Los Angeles, but never in a New York nightclub. He had gone from vaudeville to burlesque to Broadway, in *Yokel Boy*, to Metro to Fox. The Copa was the most prestigious nightclub in the country, so Phil was very nervous about it and asked Rags Ragland, who had worked with him for years in burlesque, to agree to come to New York to do comedy song numbers with Phil in his act. Rags, a tall, big-faced comic, was under contract to Metro at this time. He was a dear, sweet man who, for reasons known only to him, made it a point never to swallow anything he had to chew. Consequently, the day before Phil was to open, Rags was taken to the hospital with acute alcohol poisoning. Phil was in dire straits until Sinatra heard about it, and, even though he was working at the time, he dropped everything and flew in just in time to take Rags' place with Phil for his opening night. It was a bold and daring thing to do for, even though he had often done these numbers with Phil in a living room, the Great Sinatra could have fallen flat on his famous face in doing these numbers without a rehearsal. He didn't though. They were flawless and a huge sensation, and Phil got terrific reviews. If I had to describe Sinatra in one word it would be — passionate. He was passionate about his profession. More than any pop singer I ever knew, he worked constantly to improve his diction, breath control, phrasing, interpretation, and control of his recorded sound. He swam underwater to improve his breath control and was meticulous about distinctly pronouncing all the vowels and consonants in a word, and singing the song the way the composer wrote it. He was even careful to pronounce the "d" sound in "and."

Phil and Frank performing at the Copacabana.

That perfectionism carried over into his acting and dancing. Actually, he was already acting his song numbers in mood and story-line, which is what made his singing so powerful, and parts in movies were just an extension of that natural talent. Frank made three movies with Gene Kelly at Metro and Gene said Frank worked harder and had more natural talent for dance than any non-dancer he ever worked with.

On the The Frank Sinatra Show with Dick Haymes.

Frank was passionate about friendships. Once you were his friend, he would go to any lengths to help you, but he had a very narrow take on loyalty and friendship. It was really *All or Nothing at All* with him. Either you did everything his way and were completely acquiescent to his likes or dislikes, or you were not a true friend and he never forgave you. To me, he seemed a perfect example of the codes and morals of the culture he grew up in. Italians had to be very tough to survive in New Jersey when Frank was growing up. A frail, skinny kid who almost died at birth, he had to prove that he could be tougher than the big guys from his very beginning. He was a product of the "tough-guy" mentality that demanded a constant aggressive attitude, loyalty to male companions, deep respect for mother and wife, and a slightly contemptuous regard for all other dames, chicks, or broads. Feelings and tender emotions were for sissies; Joe DiMaggio and the handsome gangster Bugsy Siegel were their heroes. Phil was much the same, except he dealt with his defensive aggression by making people laugh rather than with his fists. Women, alcohol, and a burning cigarette were a central part of the macho image men like Sinatra cultivated. How that did not affect the quality of his voice, which only continued to get better until almost the end, was something I could never understand.

And Frank was passionate about injustice and the underdog. That he was always ready for a fight with journalists has been well-documented, but they didn't write about his bold courage in the fight for civil rights. Particularly during the time when the Un-American Activities Senate Committee was making cowards of too many big stars. Bing turned down that marvelous song, "The House I Live In," because it was too controversial, but Sinatra took it on and made a hit song and a moving short film of it. He was not afraid to tangle with authority and I always admired him for that. During the years I knew him, he gave generously of his time, talent, and money to the liberal causes that were fighting against the injustices of that period. It was only after he had built a heliport on his Palm Springs estate for President John Kennedy's Christmas visit, and — because of Frank's reputed mafia connections — Kennedy stayed with Bing instead, that Frank became a Republican.

An important part of Frank's charm was his boyish humor. He loved to laugh more than anyone I knew and probably that is what saved him from his extraordinary celebrity. Since it was not possible for Frank to party out in public because of that celebrity, there was a constant round of parties at his home in Tuluca Lake, a lovely area in the San Fernando Valley of estates built around a large lake, or at the hotels he stayed at while on tour. People literally begged to be invited to Sinatra's New Year's Eve parties, which he prepared for all year.

Comedy writers wrote sketches and song writers wrote song numbers about and for the "regulars" of the Sinatra group based on "in" jokes, with props and costumes borrowed from Metro for a small private revue which was better than most Broadway shows. For example, one sketch opened with Sammy Cahn, Phil, and Peter Lawford seated at a restaurant table when Frank comes in dressed as a waiter and carrying a huge tray filled with break-away dishes. Peter says, "Waiter, I'll take that check," Sinatra does a body double-take and both he and the dishes crash to the floor. It got screams of laughter from the audience as everyone was well aware how hard Lawford tried to avoid paying a check. Poor Peter had unknowingly rehearsed a 15-minute scene, only to have the joke be on the very first line — and on him.

Another example of a New Year's Eve entertainment was a song number that Sammy Cahn and Julie Styne wrote for me. It was a long number whose last couplet went like this:

> "I hate that Old Man River more,
> Each time that I sit through it.
> My only hope is next time
> He will throw himself into it.
> I'm the wife of the life of the party,
> And he's boring the life out of me."

No one laughed harder than Phil, and it was only in later years that I wondered if he really thought it was that funny. It didn't bother me at the time that several people seemed to believe that I didn't think Phil was funny. Phil knew that he made me laugh all the time, he knew I loved him for his humor, so I didn't give it much thought. It occurred to me long after, though, that to certain groups of Phil's friends, something in my attitude must have made me a real pain in the ass. And possibly sometimes to Phil, too, although he never let on. I knew how much Phil disappointed me, I never knew if or how much I disappointed him.

Although I admired his politics greatly, Frank never appealed to me sexually, but he had something about him that was intangible, some kind of a possibly-dangerous inner hum of authority and sexuality, that made him irresistible to most women, young and old. What touched me was I sensed a vulnerability and tenderness in him that he tried valiantly to hide. My intuition was that he would only reveal his inner sensitivity in his singing, and it was this which touched off a kind of insanity among young girls over Frank that was a first of its kind. One time when Phil was starring on Broadway and Frank was headlining at the Paramount Theatre, we met him backstage to go out for a late supper. Frank had two frightening-looking bodyguards and they fought our way to the waiting limo through hundreds of screaming, crying, hysterical teenagers, whom dozens of police were vainly trying to control. It was both awesome and frightening to sit in that limo as it inched its way through that swirling chaos of girls flinging their bodies all over the car and beating against the windows as they yelled Frank's name. When we finally escaped, we went to a little Italian restaurant in Greenwich Village whose owner had closed for the night in order for Frank and his friends to have dinner in private. There was no way he could go out in public at that time in his life without this kind of frenzy manifesting itself. It is little wonder that he became even more dictatorial and arrogant in his behavior than possibly he was naturally inclined to be. In later years such fan adulation has become the norm for entertainers in the music business, but in the 40s Sinatra was the first and only one.

The sensational author, Kitty Kelly, wrote a scathing book about Sinatra, called *His Way*. She interviewed me at great length, but jettisoned any positive information I gave her. Making matters, worse she fabricated statements and attributed them to me. I learned the hard way not to cooperate with writers who lacked integrity.

Sex Symbols

Murry Feil, my William Morris agent, whom I almost never heard from, called me early one morning to tell me that Fox had dropped my option. His phone call woke me up and I went right back to sleep, but when I was fully awake again, I felt a small pang of rejection. During the four years I was under contract, I sometimes wondered why they would continue to pay me $150 a week when I rarely paid my way by working in a movie for them; still I felt a little put out that now they agreed with me.

The funny thing was that Cohn personally called me the same day. He said, "Jo-Carroll, I hear they have let you go over there at 20th."

A tad defensive, I said, "That's right, Harry."

In the tone of voice he used when trying to be charming, he said, "Well, that's too bad. I'll tell you what I'll do. I'll give you the same kind of contract here at Columbia, but you'll have to take a pay cut of $25 dollars a week."

I had the exquisite pleasure of saying, "Harry, I wouldn't be under contract to you if I was starving to death!"

He snorted and hung up.

Hollywood sophisticate that I was, I was still amazed at how fast the grapevine worked between the studios, and equally amazed that Cohn himself would offer me a contract after the nothing job I had done in *The Jolson Story.* I could only think it was a power thing with him and if I was under contract to him he thought he could cut me down to size the same way he did Rita Hayworth and Evelyn Keys, and not for anything did I want to be like either of them. Since Phil and the new friends I had now brought me into contact with so many of the famous women in Hollywood, I had made a study of the so-called sex symbols like Rita Hayworth. In so doing, I felt I had discovered an astonishing thing: the sex symbols I knew were insecure and victimized women! Every one of them in one way or another.

I saw Orson Welles treat Rita Hayworth worse than dirt; he wouldn't have gone out of his way to taunt and demean dirt the way he did her. Particularly when Phil and I were alone with them, Orson would put her down with snide remarks about her intellect and aptitude, seemingly as a matter of course. It seemed obvious to me that he married her because of her fame as a sex symbol to improve his own macho reputation, and then it somehow improved his image of himself to have her in his bed, but not in his heart. She was good enough to bear his children but not good enough to respect. I knew that her father and her first husband had used Rita to project themselves, and could only think that she had been programmed to be a victim from childhood, all primed and ready to be victimized by both Cohn and Welles. I wondered if that insecure, vulnerable, eager-to-please little girl she still inhabited was what attracted men to her, both in person and on the screen. Was that vulnerable quality seductive, but not respectable for men? Was there a sadistic pleasure in treating someone beautiful, but fragile with disdain? Rita Hayworth was the top movie star in Hollywood and I was appalled at the way she let Orson treat her. I never tried to hide my disgust with Orson, and most likely that is why he tried to hurt me at Toot's Shor's on my honeymoon. The thing that made me mad was that he *did* hurt me and I didn't do anything about it. I should have poked him in the nose with a fork.

I couldn't understand why so many of the women movie stars thought so little of themselves that they would let men treat them like whores, or worse. When Phil and I visited Artie Shaw and Ava Gardner, Artie was even more sadistic than Orson. Artie prided himself more on being an intellectual than being a musician and loved to talk about esoteric subjects, but if Ava dared to join in, he stripped the skin off her as though his clarinet were a scalpel with scornful remarks like, "Listen to little Miss Intellect over there trying to act smart. Why don't you just keep your stupid mouth shut?"

As opposed to Rita, who took Orson's ridicule as though she thought she deserved it, I could see that Ava was scorched by Artie's remarks. She had been married to short Mickey Rooney while still in her teens and short Mickey's major pleasure was cutting his tall girl friends and wives down to his size, so evidently Ava, this exquisite, intelligent girl, had a problem with low self-esteem already, but Artie was surely doing everything he could to increase it. It is interesting that in later years Ava became a kind of self-protective tough cookie who made men pay in many ways for those scars she sustained early on. But I always thought that she never fully recovered from that previous abuse enough to be truly at peace with herself.

Phil told me that one time when Artie was living with Lana Turner, Phil and Artie were playing clarinet duets late one night when Lana came to the door nude, and with tears in her eyes begged Artie to come to bed — only to be driven back into the bedroom with curses and insults. Phil said Artie treated Lana even worse that he treated Ava. Possibly that is why they were only married four months. I never heard the psychology of this kind of behavior satisfactorily explained. I never understood the mentality of the brutal bully and the accepting victim. As far as I could see, Lana, even being one of the biggest stars at Metro, never gained her self respect as Ava did, and wound up with a two-bit gangster, Johnny Stompanato, who was later murdered by her daughter.

Of course, there are many forms of abuse. Some of the stars I worked with at Fox kind of ran the abuse gamut. Betty Grable was married to band leader Harry James, and sometimes the makeup woman had a hard time covering up a black eye or two for Betty. Alice Faye, on the other hand, was relentlessly put down by her band leader/actor husband, Phil Harris, with humor. He was very funny about it, but it was constantly belittling nonetheless. Linda Darnell, who was so beautiful you just wanted to stand and look at her, was so crushed by her relationships that after her divorces she began to drink too much and was killed in a fire she had accidentally set. Jeanne Crain, with whom I worked on *Winged Victory* and who subsequently became a big star, married Paul Brinkman, a handsome abusive husband who beat her up so often that the police were regular visitors to their home on domestic violence calls. But Jeanne stayed with him through it all and would never press charges. Like Linda Darnell, her escape from abuse came in a bottle, which eventually did her in as well. To me the saddest of these needless and pathetic wastes was Carole Landis. I went on War Bond Tours and publicity junkets for Fox movies with her and you couldn't meet a warmer, nicer woman. She met and fell deeply in love with Rex Harrison when Fox was making *Anna and the King of Siam* with Rex and Irene Dunne. They had a heavy-duty affair until his wife, Lilli Palmer, came to Hollywood from London and he broke it off. Poor resourceless Carole then killed herself and left a note for Rex saying she didn't want to live without him, so the police reports in the newspapers related.

Lilli Palmer, a star in her own right, had worked with my Actors' Lab teachers, George Shdanoff and his wife, Elsa Schrieber, on the movies she had made in this country and had persuaded Rex to work with them on *Anna and the King of Siam*. As this British drawing-room comedian was very nervous about playing a Siamese King, Elsa invented the high, sing-song voice that caught the character for him, and he always said he thought that performance was his best. Anyway, just days after Carole had killed herself, the Shdanoffs gave a party for Rex and Lilli, and I was invited. Phil was not comfortable with the Shdanoff's European salon kind of conversation, and besides the party was on a Friday Fight Night, so I went alone. Elsa didn't allow smoking in her house, and after dinner I was standing on their balcony overlooking the lights of Hollywood smoking a cigarette when Rex joined me for the same purpose. I stood there leaning on the rail beside this tall, elegant man as my mind whirled with all the kinds of angry abuse I wanted to splatter on him for the way he had treated Carole. And his wife. But I could find no words to adequately express what I was feeling and we stood there together silently for a few minutes, until he threw away his cigarette and went back inside. I always kind of thought he knew something of what I was thinking. I, on the other hand, had absolutely no idea what *he* was thinking.

Fearful of sounding like the *National Inquirer*, I hasten to explain that I list all these examples of the abuse I witnessed men giving these beautiful women to make a point that means a lot to me. That point is, I know that girls all over the world thought that if they could just be as beautiful and sexy looking as the movie stars they admired, they would be totally happy. I wanted to take out a full-page ad for all to see saying that "It ain't necessarily so." Girls/women starved themselves, had nose or breast jobs, or hated themselves in the mirror, thinking if only they looked like Rita Hayworth or some other star or magazine model, their lives would be perfect. I was convinced that if they could have magically opened up the mind of Rita, Ava, Betty, or the rest of the "sex symbols" and felt the insecurity and fears, the anxiety about growing old and the self hatred of these world famous beauties, they would not want to change places and be more satisfied with themselves. The stress put upon a beautiful woman to *stay* beautiful, to *feel* complete as a woman, or *interesting* as a person, is enormous and constant. I am also confident that the strain put upon a "sex symbol" to be sexy enough in bed makes faking it the best face-saving way out of it.

The most obvious example of the difficulties of being a "sex symbol" was, of course, Marilyn Monroe. When she came to the Kelly's now and then with someone or other, she said almost nothing at all in her little-girl soft voice. She would sit on the couch in the bar in her low-cut, tight-fitting unbecoming dress with a drink in her hand, and it was clear to me that she desperately wanted to join in the intellectual conversation that was going on around her, but she didn't know what to say, and was afraid of sounding stupid. As I watched her, I felt an odd kinship with her. Obviously, in her public self, she exulted in the adoration she aroused by acting with her body, but in her private self she was eager to prove that she could be a fine dramatic actress, and longed to be admired for her fine mind. I felt she desperately wanted to be a famous movie star, but she desperately wanted the self respect that went with being a grown-up and intelligent person, also. I understood that. And sympathized deeply. I think it was that duality of purpose that finally destroyed her.

One of the least intellectual experiences I had in Hollywood was playing a lead role in the unmemorable film *Prehistoric Women* (1950). It was a truly incongruous movie, and not the least bit believable: Dancing cave ladies. It was made on a skimpy budget, about five women with long wigs wearing also-skimpy animal skins for costumes, and fiercely determined to exterminate all prehistoric men. We tried to shoot them with bows and arrows instead, but it devolved into lots of hugging and kissing. This film was the biggest shame of my acting life. The requirements of the role were so absurd (makeup, costume, story) that I wanted to forget about it. Some of the other primitive actresses were trained dancers. That was the only classy thing about the movie. I was, again, in the position of pretending to be sexy. To my dismay, it is, to this day, one of the films I'm best known for. Fan mail still arrives from around the world, even though I'm now in my late 90s.

One interesting thing about making *Prehistoric Women*, was that American avant-garde dancer Bella Lewitsky was the choreographer. I shared with her that I had trained with Lester Horton, as had Bella. She was exquisitely kind, patient, and supportive. She was as well known for her political activism as for her ground-breaking dance form. Times were hard. I felt for her that she needed to work on a movie like this. It was around the time she was called in front of the House Un-American Activities Committee hearings to be challenged about "communist" activities in the arts community. In her testimony, she bravely said "I'm a dancer, not a singer!"

Me as one of the shameful prehistoric women in a film by the same name: 1950.

The longer I lived in Hollywood the less I could see the benefits of being a movie star, and the more confused I became about life. Foremost, I was lost in a wilderness about the mystery of truly success-ful man/woman relationships — in or out of bed. I was blessed with a group of six close women friends who got together every month for a "girls night," and they helped to furnish me with a road map. The group: Betsy Kelly, Gene's wife; Jeanne Coyne, Gene's dance assistant and later wife number two; Carol Haney, brilliant dancer; Ellen Ray, dancer; Lois McClelland, Gene's personal assistant and me. We were all the same age, give or take a month or two either way, except for Lois who was two years older.

One night, we started going around the circle listing first, best, last, and funniest sexual encounters. I didn't have much other than questions to contribute, but I have never laughed so hard in my life as at some of the revelations that ensued. Although we all knew one another very well, this was the first time such a subject had come up, and in this kind of atmosphere everyone was free to be open and honest without fear of censure or embarrassment and the results were hilarious, as well as informative. To our infinite surprise, Lois, a self-effacing, relatively plain-faced woman, put us all in the shade for quantity, quality, and fascinating sexual adventures. Lois was good at volleyball, sure, but she was not a woman you would look at twice in a crowd, if you noticed her at all. She had been assigned to Gene as his production assistant for the naval documentaries he made in Washington, and when he was discharged from the Navy, he brought Lois with him to Hollywood. I was astonished to learn that she had a very active and passionate sex life, and when she reluctantly described the "whom, where, and under what romantic circumstances" her sexual encounters occurred, plus the delight in her orgasms, it astonished us and curled all my toes with green envy. What bowled me over was that among us all, Lois was the one who most enjoyed sex without inhibition or restriction. I thought, "Lois! Lois a sex goddess? I know she's a lovely person, but she's not big busted or curvaceous or sultry looking. She doesn't look like any sex symbol I ever saw. How did that happen?

After giving it a great deal of consideration, I thought her secret was that she was at peace with *who she was and what she looked like*, and just had *a natural enjoyment of sex without any unnatural sexual hangups!* Imagine that. I'm sure that few celebrated New York models or busty movie stars could say the same. Men responded to her in amazing numbers, but in none of her many relationships had she been the *victim*. Nor was she the aggressor. She was just content to let natural pleasurable things happen between two equally respectful partners. When it came to *sex*, she was not just a symbol! I learned one of the most important lessons of my life from Lois, and was awed and covetous. I am confident that all the sex symbols I knew in Hollywood would have been, too.

New York, New York

In 1947, I fell into a love affair that never grew old or withered. Sammy Cahn and Julie Styne wrote a musical for Phil called *High Button Shoes* from a book by Stephen Longstreet. It was to be produced by Joe Kipness and directed by the great George Abbott on Broadway, and so with high expectations Phil, Budget, my West Highland Terrier, and I moved to New York. I had been in New York three times before but, always as a harassed transient who had been overwhelmed by its gigantic presence. This time, after we settled into a large penthouse apartment with a terrace running around two sides at 81st and Central Park West — I fell in love with New York City. Central Park became my front yard, you might say, as our living and dining rooms overlooked that magical oasis all the way to the tall buildings on its opposite side. I hadn't realized how starved I had been by the lack of real nature in my life in L.A. Oh, there was a plethora of palm trees and gorgeous gardens there, but New York's Central Park was the *nature in the raw* that I had been unconsciously yearning for — which just happened to have handy cement paths here and there. The park became my wilderness, wildlife retreat, and my comfort and joy. Budget and I immersed ourselves in its wonders and wildness on almost a daily basis. In those days, dogs could run free in certain areas, and having been confined to a small backyard for his first year of life, Budget went mad with excitement at this new-found freedom, and his natural terrier hunting instinct blossomed. The first time he saw a squirrel he stared at it in astonishment, looked to me for confirmation, then took off after it with all the savage and delirious joy of his ancient ancestors. He became a different dog ferreting out all the lovely smells available on trees and in the multitude of nooks and crannies. Central Park made both of us whole again.

Phil was constantly in rehearsal, so like an entranced archeologist, most days I explored New York with ever increasing delight and a sense of familiarity. Soon, I didn't feel a stranger in New York as I always had in Los Angeles. Looking backwards, Los Angeles appeared flat, thin, beige, spread out and insubstantial, whereas New York had vividly colorful depths that went all the way to the bottom of the ocean, a width from a river to another river, and there were no apparent limits to the heights of its architecture and intentions. It was an island all compressed and accessible and it roared with multiple colors and sounds. The strength and intensity of New York's constantly changing colors and smells and soul permeated my senses every time I stepped out the door, and inside our apartment the hum of the life of the city streets was always exciting background music. To me, the sound of Los Angeles was like the zzzzzzz of Fred Waring's orchestra, while New York was like a blast of Duke Ellington going full bore. New York presented me with a challenge that I was excited to meet. All those self-protective panels that I kept so firmly in place in Hollywood sprang open in a joyous acceptance of the vivacity and multiplicity of this wondrous city. Sometimes on the street at a stoplight, for example, some stranger beside me would say, "You look happy today," and I felt such vindication as I said, "*I am!*" It wasn't my marriage that made me feel so ebullient, it was that I had been courageous enough to find my way all over the city on the subway, learned which bus to take up to Fort Tryon in the Bronx where the Cloisters Museum was, and had taken fascinating peeps into the lives of real New Yorkers in the subway or out the bus window. I identified completely with them as *fellow* New Yorkers, accents and all. Some- how the special essence of this city and I had meshed as though we were of the same blood, and for the first time in my life I had a "home town." For years afterwards, whenever someone asked me where I was from, I would say proudly, "I'm from New York City," or just to be specific and highfalutin', I'd say, "Manhattan."

Just imagine what living in New York offered to someone who was trying to get well educated and waterlogged with culture over- night. By walking a few blocks in any direction, everything cultural or stimulating to the imagination was all there for the taking. Luckily, there was an east side and a west side to the Kelly group. At least 50 percent of the friends I had made in the Gene Kelly or Solly Chaplin living rooms lived in New York and just worked periodically in Hol- lywood. Among others, Betty Comden and Adolph Green, Leonard Bernstein, and Woody Broun lived in New York, and the friend who was nearest to my heart, the great jazz singer Anita Ellis, so I had a support group ready at hand. As well as exploring on my own, I had one of several friends to stand beside me at the Metropolitan Mu- seum, the Modern Museum of Art (for both of which I immediately signed on as a proud member), and the multitude of art galleries, to help me *see* what I was seeing, and help me carry all those heavy art books home. Other friends took me to the Metropolitan Opera and various concerts, or down to Greenwich Village to hear fantastic jazz. Hoping not to appear so dumb to my friends all the time, I enrolled in classes at Hunter College for Art and Music Appreciation, Comparative Religion, and English Literature. I was giddy with the pleasure all these activities gave me. Best of all, I *knew* that this was such a special time in my life and I was supremely grateful and fully aware of every moment.

From nervous exhaustion, Phil lost his voice in Philadelphia for the out-of-town tryout, but he regained it in full force for opening night in New York — and he and *High Button Shoes* were a huge hit. The show opened in October of 1947 and ran for 727 performances, a very respectable run at the time. The plot was that in circa 1913, a con man, Phil, and his shill partner, Joey Faye, (a former burlesque comic) are running out of suckers in the big cities selling snake oil and go back to Phil's hometown, New Brunswick, N.J. to sell unusable swampland, so they can then abscond with the money. Nancttc Fabray was delightful as the not-so-dumb country housewife. The song and dance numbers were upbeat: "Papa, Won't You Dance with Me," "I Still Get Jealous," and "You're My Girl" the outstanding songs.

The show-stopper was the Jerome Robbins choreography for the opening of the second act "On a Sunday By the Sea" ballet. It was a takeoff on a Mack Sennett comedy with the dancers in old-fashioned bathing suits running in and out of dressing rooms and playing on the Atlantic City Beach, and it remains a classic ballet to this day. The director, George Abbott, and Phil rewrote nearly every line of Stephen Longstreet's book into a snappy mix of nostalgia, vaudeville, burlesque, and contemporary musical comedy, and the show was great fun. Phil was absolutely wonderful, and established his fast-talking, charming, con man character which he used in his succeeding Broadway shows, and with which he was particularly successful on his television series as Sgt. Bilko in the 60s.

The only times I had my old feeling of being uniquely special, though, that "stand well back, I'm comin' through" feeling was when I could walk into Sardi's, the restaurant where the Broadway theater community gathered most, and get a table in the front room all by myself. That the owner, Vincent, was always gracious and gave me a good table in this jammed restaurant was my greatest personal achievement of that special time. As lovely as my friends were to me, clearly I was the least talented of them all and it gave me a much appreciated sense of self to come in alone and get a booth against the wall under the drawings of famous Broadway stars at Sardi's. The other private personal triumph was at Lindy's. Comics like Milton Berle, Sid Ceasar, Henny Youngman, and Phil had their own large booth there, and they were all so surprised when Mr. Lindy himself, who was usually watchful but aloof with everyone, would often come over and inquire about my health. I never knew why, I never came there alone, but Mr. Lindy always paid me individual attention. I know that doesn't sound like much, but those two tiny personal happenings meant a lot to me.

There was one personal disaster which marred those simple triumphs, as well as my memories for the rest of my life. Gene and Betsy stopped over in New York for a couple of days to see Phil's show on their way to Europe, and we met them afterwards at the Plaza Hotel for supper. The Empire Room was a magnificent dining room with a fine orchestra and large dance floor. I was starved for ballroom dancing, and delighted when Gene asked me to dance. Recognizing Gene, the other dancers moved off the floor and stood in a circle to watch as the ever showman, swung me around as he would have Cyd Charisse in one of his marvelous athletic dance routines. The band merged one number right into another in Gene's honor, and, as though my feet were divinely guided, I followed his every swirling and bending move perfectly. I was wearing a bright red crepe dress, which had a tight-fitting bodice and long sleeves with an extremely wide, flaring skirt so it was perfect for showing off Gene's brilliant choreography.

Fortunately, I was happily unaware that a stain of sweat under my arms was slowing enlarging with each graceful turn. With another color or fabric, the stain would not have been so noticeable, but with red crepe, it was a blaring black that shouted its presence to the gilded ceiling. I was too exalted and concentrated on following his steps to notice until Gene bent me gracefully almost to the floor for a theatrical finish. Then I was nose-to-nose with the awful sweat-stained horror, so to speak. The glorious moment burst into flames and I got as red in the face as my dress. No one at our table mentioned it, but I had to sit there and eat supper, my arms clenched tightly to my side, while my magical, shining fantasy time got all ugly and ashamed. I have been fanatical about using underarm antiperspirant ever since, but that couldn't change the reality of my lost opportunity for a perfect moment in time.

Sex: What Is It Really?

During my first two years in New York, I had inhaled every available cultural experience and was still a-swirl with the sheer energy and stimulation of the life I was living. It was the early 1950s. My imaginary tapestry showed many new blobs and dots of intense colors, and both intricate and free-flowing designs multiplied across its surface almost daily. I had never before felt so *utilized*. I visualized new brain cells growing in rapid bursts and each of my five senses acquiring fresh abilities to absorb and embrace ever-increasing awareness and understanding. I was getting *educated*! Heywood (Woody) Hale Broun was particularly helpful in the literary category. Woody was a slight, sandy-haired man in his early 30, who was a talented sports writer but yearned to be an actor and adored Phil. He always had an aura of apologetic vulnerability, despite his attempts to stand out by wearing loud, gangster type clothes. I loved him dearly. His parents, Heywood Broun and Ruth Hale, were both important writers and literature was his expertise, so he volunteered to make me a well-read person by loaning me books and then asking me questions about their content. Woody had more books covering all kinds of subjects in his apartment than most small town libraries. He started me off on ThorstenVeblen's *Theory of the Leisure Class*, for heaven's sake, and induced me to work my way through the Ancient Greeks, until finally I told him, "I've *had* it with Plato!" He relented enough with the hard stuff to get me into the fun stuff by authors like Austen, Eliot, Dickens, Waugh, Forster — all those 19th-century and early 20th-Century British stalwarts who are still some of my favorite authors. The best thing he did for me was to get me to start H. G. Wells' *Outline of History*, and intersperse additional books on any period that interested me. Thereby, one after the other, I fell in love with Paleontology, archeology, anthropology, Greek, Egyptian, and Chinese history, the naturalists, and finally the whole of history. It was a great way to learn. Woody then took me to the multitude of fascinating used book shops along 2nd Avenue where "I bought out the store," as the saying goes, so I could start my own collection of classical books.

Leonard Bernstein was one of my friends who continued my musical education. One day he took me way up in the Bronx to a beautiful old church to hear the *Messiah* sung by a famous choir. He told me to learn to separate out the voices of the altos, sopranos, and bass singers, and then all the different musical instruments, until I could hear just one at a time. Then when I had learned how to do that — to put them all back together again and that would add another whole dimension to my listening to music. It did.

Heywood Hale Broun got me reading the classics.

And it was such fun to be in the "mainstream" of the Broadway theater. While Phil was performing in his own show, different friends took me to opening nights of some of the marvelous shows that opened in New York in the 40s. Or we went to *avant-garde* little off-Broadway experimental theaters, which I pretended to like so as not to appear gauche. An experience that remains especially vivid in my memory is the night Michael Kidd, choreographer of *Guys and Dolls* (for which he won the Tony), took me with him to see its last dress rehearsal before opening night. We sat on the steps of the aisle of the last row in the balcony, while he made notes for the actors and checked voice levels. *Guys and Dolls*, based on Damon Runyon stories, was an innovative, brilliant musical starring Robert Alda, Vivian Blaine, and Sam Levene. Sitting there in the dark watching this piece of American Broadway history unfold, for those magical moments in my imagination I became an integral part of the real glamour, drama, and enchantment of show business. I either knew well or

had met Frank Loesser and Abe Burrows, the writers of these songs
that would be performed all over the world for decades to come, the
director, legendary George S. Kaufman, all the stars and even some
of the actors, singers, and dancers. I had known Vivian Blaine when
she was a star and I was a starlet at Fox. She had been badly under-
used there, playing third banana to Betty Grable and June Haver;
until she finally left Fox in despair. Now here she was blazing her way
to glory on Broadway just like a real Cinderella. I felt so lucky to be
even a peripheral part of all this.

One important thing I was learning, however, was that I could
never be a real intellectual. After many hard head-butts against reality,
I had finally realized that the "intellect" responded to and acted upon
reason, judgment, and serious thought — whereas I responded to and
acted upon pure emotion, sentiment, and spontaneous vehemence.
I found I could think and reason and make judgments, but it came
from my heart, not my mind. I never ceased to admire intellectuals,
both in print and in person, and eventually learned to be comfortable
with our differences.

As my tapestry grew in density with the furtherance of my chosen educational quest, my need to show off my meager learning less-
ened. Except with Blackie. The day after I married Phil, I received
a telegram addressed to "Mrs. Phil Silvers" and the message read,
"Congratulations on your marriage. I hope you will be very happy.
Please do an old friend a favor and tear up unread the letter that I
have just sent you, Always, Blackie." The letter had a return address
of *The Fort Worth Star Telegram* so I knew that he had gotten his dream
job as a journalist on a big city Texas newspaper, and I was glad for
him. I did tear up his letter unread, not so much because he asked me
to as because I was afraid that he had again reached out to me — and
again I wasn't there. A strange kind of guilt and a slender, steel, connective thread kept me bound to Blackie in a strange way for the rest
of my life. I always wanted him to know what I was doing and thinking, and, mostly, I wanted his approval. It wasn't that I was holding
on to him as an ace in the hole, I could never imagine myself living
with him as a housewife somewhere in Texas, but it was Blackie's support that had given me the courage to leave the medicine show, and
he had been the lifeline that kept me afloat during those first years in
Hollywood. I could never let go entirely of that lifeline. After Phil and
I moved to New York, I wrote Blackie letters filled with examples of

my recently acquired knowledge and cultural experiences. He wrote back his usual humorous and admiring letters, telling me that his work on his hometown paper had gained him enough recognition to be offered a top job as sports writer. And while someday he wanted to be a novelist, for now he was gaining lots of good experience and he loved it. Neither of us mentioned my married life.

But Blackie was a shadowy figure in the back of my mind. My focus was on the life I had chosen with Phil, and a determination to make it be the right choice. One Saturday, as I was in a taxi on my way downtown to meet him between shows for dinner at Sardi's, I suddenly had an unusually contented vision of being a *wife* on her way to meet her *husband*. I was suffused by the powerful emotion of *belonging* to him — a glad knowledge of being his *wife*. It was an extraordinary feeling, which stayed with me all day.

That night when we were lying in our own twin beds (in those days married couples usually slept in twin beds), both in movies and in real life (I'm not sure why), I tried to explain to Phil the wonderful experience I was having. The time was propitious: we were alone, he was quietly reading, and the radio was playing soft music.

I said, "Phil."

"Hummm?"

"Today I had a lovely feeling as I was coming down to meet you in a taxi. I had this thought that you and I were really *married*. And I was so happy that I was your wife and that we belonged together. I really enjoyed thinking that we would *be* together for the rest of our lives. It was a great feeling. You understand?"

"Ummmm."

"Well, I haven't always felt that way, and this feeling of our being really *married*, and that we … I mean, it was such a *good* feeling that we would always be together. You know?"

"Ummmm."

"Do you ever feel like that?"

Phil turned a page and didn't answer.

I lay there watching that lovely feeling shrink and disappear.

Soon after this deflating experience, I had another even worse which started with a severe pain in my lower regions. An actress friend of mine, Shirley Mitchel, had married a young doctor who was interning at New York Hospital, and he, Julian, referred me to a well-known specialist. The specialist looked to be in his 60s, squinty eyes, gray fringe around his balding head, stooping shoulders, and he quickly popped me into New York Hospital for a pelvic examination. It was my first time in a hospital and I found the goings-on very strange. That first morning, as I lay there uncomfortably naked under my skimpy hospital gown, young interns kept coming in with their stethoscopes hanging around their necks, pushing my gown up around my neck and giving me a thorough physical examination that included much prodding and touching. Embarrassed, not knowing if I was making too much of it, for after all they were *doctors,* I silently endured it. Finally, the specialist came and gave me another going over, and then under the observation of two of the interns, he forcefully inserted his fingers into my vagina and felt around my insides, squeezing here and there for an interminable time. I had always prided myself on being stoic under pain but that was by far the most excruciating experience I had ever had, and tears were streaming down my face and I was gasping out loud before he was finished.

Taking off his rubber glove, he said briskly, "Well, young lady, you have a nasty cyst on one ovary. We'll have to take that off tomorrow," and they all left.

When Phil called later, I was still whimpering from my ordeal, and when he asked what he could bring me to the hospital, I cried, "I want my dooog!"

Phil packed Budget into his covered carrying basket and sneaked him into my room at visiting hour. Budget and I hugged and cried together on my bed until after a bit a nurse came in, trying to hide her smile as she told Phil that dogs were not allowed in a hospital. It seemed that Phil's subterfuge was quickly discovered as he walked jauntily past the nurse's station, smiling his engaging con man's smile, basket under his arm, not knowing that Budget's wagging tail was sticking prominently out of one of the handle holes. Since Phil's face was famous and beloved in New York, against all the rules the nurses had let him go past for a short visit.

Fortunately, the next day, I was under full sedation when the specialist removed the cyst. And I was feeling fine two days later when I went into the specialist's office for a follow-up appointment. When I was seated, the specialist came around his desk and sat on its edge in front of me. As he leaned over and held my hands, he said softly, "Young lady, I have discovered the cause of your vaginal problem."

Dramatic pause as his squinty eyes glinted down at me, "You are oversexed."

Totally confused, I said, "Oversexed?"

With an openly salacious smile, he explained, "Your sex glands had become clogged with glandular secretions." He waggled his forefinger reprovingly at me, "Have you been having regular orgasms?"

Flooded with shame and embarrassment, I stammered, "Well, no. Not really. I mean ... I never have had an orgasm."

He rested his hand suggestively on my knee and murmured, "You know, I thought that might be the case. Now, I am also a sex therapist and I could help you with that problem." He smiled, almost licking his lips, "If you will come back after office hours, I will show you just what we can do to make you happy so you won't get clogged up again."

As his full meaning became clear to me, I jumped up and pushed him away and literally scrambled out of his office, speechless in fury.

I couldn't wait to tell Julian what a terrible time I had in his hospital and what a monster the specialist was. The degradation of the whole experience became complete when Julian kind of snickered about the internists, and said, "Well, maybe I shouldn't have told my fellow internists you were a former Miss America; obviously they just couldn't resist an opportunity like that. But forget about the specialist, I think he was just impressed with you being a Miss America, also. However, you surely don't want to get clogged up again. I tell you what I'll do, I will talk to Phil about it."

I was bitterly disappointed in Julian. I had thought we were friends, and in my book no friend would do such a thing as to tell his buddies that a Miss America body was available just down the hall. "Come one, come all, come see the show," so to speak. I felt humiliated and betrayed, and dirty, somehow, about the whole experience. I thought Julian was no better than the rest of them.

Evidently, he did talk to Phil, however, because a few nights later, Phil turned the lights out, got in bed with me and began to feel inexpertly around in my vagina, as he said, "Here, here it is. This is your clitoris. It is like a little penis. Now, if I stroke it around like this it should make you excited. Does it?"

What could I say to a question like that? True, his fingers had pressed on a knobby little part of my vagina that I had not known was there, but whatever this part of me was, the thought that I inexplicably had a little *penis* instantly shriveled my insides into a tight rejecting ball.

It was a mystery to me that Phil at thirty-six, having spent his life around women of all kinds in vaudeville, burlesque, Hollywood, and New York, was so inept in the art of making love. Except that one time in the bath tub, I had never seen his naked body in the light nor had he seen mine. He always turned the light off, and kept his pajamas on, more or less, and so did I. In the three or four times a month that Phil initiated intercourse during the five years we had been married — by the time it stopped hurting, it was over. I had never personally experienced the much-touted "foreplay," so his abrupt, scientific exploration of my "private parts," as my mother called it, was startling and repulsive. Strangely, sophisticated Phil seemed as inexperienced and clumsy about making love as a teen-age Hale Center farm boy, maybe more so, and I couldn't understand it. The humiliation and frustration and fury aroused in me by the doctors and all this mess about my sexual organs had forced me to take stock of where I was in my life, and think about where I wanted to be.

I had held firmly to my commitment to marriage, I had been faithful to Phil in word, thought, and deed, and had supported him in every way I could think of. But clearly some ingredient of marriage that was vital to its longevity was missing in this commitment. I was twenty-five now, and everything I read, heard, or saw told me that good sex was a very important part of life. I thought, "If there is beautiful music playing out there somewhere — *I want to hear it!* That music was definitely not playing with Phil, so I realized that I would have to get out and find another orchestra leader. I knew I would need all the courage of my little red hat in order to leave this financially upscale, secure, and socially fulfilling life with Phil, and the future unknown had a lot of possibly scary quantities. But I wasn't happy. If I wanted that feeling of joy I'd had as a child again, then by George, I was going to have to go look for it.

Consequently, one rare afternoon when Phil was home, instead of at *The Friar's Club* or somewhere else, I asked him to sit down with me out on the terrace for a serious talk. My stomach was in knots at the magnitude of what I was about to do, but I was determined now to undo this unhappy and unrealistic commitment while I had my nerve up.

I said, "Phil, I want a divorce."

Phil lifted his whole face up with his eyebrows, and after a pause, said haughtily, "I'm not going to give you a divorce. I'm not going to have you running all over town with other men, *sneering* at me with my own teeth!"

Of course, I broke up laughing. Phil had never even commented about the expense of paying for the four caps on my front teeth five years ago, but evidently he had not forgotten it. Even under these very serious conditions, Phil could instantly think of something ridiculously funny to say, and I would have to see the humor and laugh. I knew Phil could deflect any unwanted topic with his unique wit but I was undeterred. I said sternly, "Don't try to make me laugh, Phil, this is very serious. I want out."

Phil had the most extraordinary ability to swiftly twist his face into a series of expressions that were hilarious because they so clearly represented various exaggerated emotions. He put on one of his best, and probably honest, bewildered expressions, and said, "You have a large allowance, a maid, a mink coat, and a penthouse apartment. What more could you possibly want?"

Stalemate.

I did have a maid, who also made our meals for us, but too often I ate those meals alone with my mink coat in my penthouse apartment. Even on a Sunday when Phil didn't have to be at the theater, he was not at home. He had a multitude of excuses: the card game at *The Friar's Club* ran over, he met Joe DiMaggio at Toot Shor's restaurant and couldn't get away, he had to rehearse with a new understudy — he was extremely inventive in that way.

We did live in a penthouse apartment, but my allowance wasn't all that large compared to the salary Phil was making. However, since I never spent much money on feminine finery, it did allow me to comfortably take care of Mother's needs on a monthly basis.

And I did have a mink coat. That was one of our major bones of contention. Joe Kipness, the proud producer of *High Button Shoes* and an expensive furrier by trade, decided to custom design a mink coat for me as a bonus for Phil to celebrate the second year of the run. Joe boasted to me when I went in for a fitting that this mink coat was to be the finest ever made. Ankle length, shawl collar, puffed sleeves, with all male skins which were the most luxurious, he said. Since this coat was really a big deal, representing a lot of money both as a bonus to Phil and as a show-off piece for me to wear, I made Phil promise he would go with me to pick it up when it was completed, so I could wear it home. The big day came — Phil had to go out that morning but he promised faithfully to meet me later at the showroom. I went — the coat was truly magnificent — I loved the way I looked in it — but Phil never showed. I refused to wear the coat home and told Joe Kipness just to box it up for me. That night I draped this glory of a coat over Phil's chair at the dining table to surprise him — but he didn't show for dinner either. Furious, petulant, tearful, I put the coat back in its box and threw it out in the hall where the trash was collected and went to bed.

When Phil came home after the show I was in bed reading. Bouncing in, he sang out, "Where is my darling girl in her gorgeous new coat?"

When I told him I had thrown it out in the trash, I thought he was going to have a heart attack. I had never seen him as devastated as he was when he absorbed what I had done, and he immediately rushed out into the hallway. When he came back in the bedroom carrying the box, he was almost hysterical as he said, "Thank God, they hadn't picked up the trash yet. What in the world possessed you to do such a gawd-awful thing? Are you out of your mind?"

Phil had never expressed anger at me before, never, but I was so angry myself that it didn't touch me. It only depressed me. It made everything seem hopeless.

There was no way that we could understand each other. He could never understand why I would throw away a $10,000-dollar coat (in the 40s, that was more than some people made in a year) just because he hadn't found the time to come with me to pick it up. It was simply not in his makeup to understand why material things did not mean as much to me as emotional things. Conversely, I could never understand why he wouldn't keep his promises to me, and would rather play cards at *The Friar's Club* than be with me.

Of course, I was childishly overreacting. But it is sad, really, when two people who truly want to love each other — can't.

That afternoon on the terrace, as I tried for the last time to explain our differing priorities to Phil, I reminded him of that day when I had felt so close to him and happy to be his wife, but how that night when I was offering these tender, loving thoughts to him, he had just continued reading and didn't respond.

Uncharacteristically, Phil took me seriously and thought it over. Gently, facing me directly, he said, "If I was reading, I was reading the *Racing Form* and I didn't really hear you." After a long thoughtful pause, he said, "Josie, I have never spoken about this to anyone, but I will tell you why I don't go with you to pick up wedding rings and mink coats. It is because I am at *The Friar's Club* playing cards for a lot of money, and losing. When I don't come home for dinner it is because I have a big bet on the last race at the track. When I don't hear what you say, it is because I have placed a bet on a baseball game and I am waiting for the results on the radio. Since I was a kid I have been a compulsive gambler, and I can't stop. I hate to have to tell you this, but gambling has always come first with me; it is the most important thing in my life. More important than my career, or even my wife. I'm sorry, Josie. I didn't want you to ever know about my gambling, but that's the way it is."

I was appalled. I had no indication of Phil's addiction. In retrospect, I should have picked up on a lot of things, but I had never known a serious gambler, never gambled myself, and had nothing but contempt for gamblers. It just never occurred to me that Phil had a horrific problem: that he was a *sucker*.

I had learned on the carnival that the game of chance is *fixed!* I had seen that there are two kinds of gamblers: the card shark — and the sucker who is stupid enough to play against a marked deck. One of them makes money and the other one loses it. Everyone knows that. Obviously, Phil was the kind of gambler who loses — in so many different ways. At that time, I had no concept that gambling was as serious a physical addiction as alcoholism. I had never heard of dopamine and the irresistible rush that comes with making a bet for some people. I didn't understand the problem so I *blamed* him for this sickness, and decided that we were even more disconnected than I had thought.

I should have known a year or so before that there was something wrong when I accidentally found $10,000 dollars in $100 bills rolled up in a pair of socks in Phil's drawer as I was putting some laundry away. When I showed it to Phil, he told me it was from a big *one-time* bet he had won at the track. I believed him and, with Phil's blessing, we used the money to make a down payment on a house and furnish it for Mother in West Los Angeles. Now, however, so many things I had not understood in the past became clear. Phil's obsession with gambling explained why sex was not important to him — all his sexual passion was spent on his addiction. I had been playing second fiddle to a horse race! It clarified why Phil would rather go to the fights on our wedding night than go to bed with me. I could see that Phil's backbone as a man had been broken by this lifelong burden of deceit and obsessive craving. I knew the psychology involved in such an addiction was a killer. I had played that part as a child with the besotted drunken father in *Ten Nights in a Bar Room*, "Father, dear Father, come home with me now, the clock in the steeple strikes one …" It was pathetic and I felt sad for him, but I couldn't respect him anymore as a man, and, consequently, like the emptiness on the line after a telephone is hung up, our connection as husband and wife was broken.

I knew I would always love him for his little boy sweetness and playfulness, and for the blessing of laughter he had given me; I knew that fondness for him would never leave me and it never did. Quite likely, if Phil had understood more about the clitoris, or if he had been able to be as passionate about making love as making a bet, things might have been different. As it was, I knew I had to get a divorce.

And I was ready. During the five years I had been married to Phil, I had learned a lot. Many of the strangely-shaped pieces of my "Who am I and what do I want?" puzzle had snapped into place. I knew I was not an intellectual, but I knew that I wanted to be around people who were, and, seemingly, the gods be praised, they wanted to be around me. Having always thought I was a loner and different from everybody else, it was a new kind of pleasure to me to find how comforting and strengthening it was to feel I belonged to a group. I had this image that I was now a part of all the people in the world who loved classical music, literature, art, philosophy, and liberal thinking. As a tangible expression of who I was, I had walls full of books. I had learned through experience that outward manifestations of self like jewelry, clothes, money, social status, or even celebrity, would never mean anything important to me — I wanted people to know me by the books I read!

I had always had only one basic goal — to be as happy and peaceful as I had sometimes been as a child. I treasured the memory of that feeling of being secure and quiet and connected to something larger than myself. That state of being was always in the back of my mind as eventually my Life Achievement Award. It seemed to me that my life had been made up of a few precious moments of joy and peacefulness — followed by long periods of just waiting for them to come again. The only way I could think of to make that happen was just to forge ahead within my present circumstances, until something happened to bring that happy peaceful time back again. Provided, of course, that I had the guts to forge ahead. The year after my father's desertion and return were spent trying not to feel anything. The miraculous gift of my horse, Creampuff, brought me back the feeling of being joyfully alive. Then my life on Dr. Tate's Medicine Show, age 11 to 17 had been a wasteland of waiting, and gutting it out, until the joy of Blackie and of learning to be a happy teenager in Tyler. That period had passed like a shooting star, bringing me again to a wasteland of waiting as a starlet in Hollywood. Meeting and then marrying Phil had brought me the explosion of laughing and learning, and I don't mean to say that I did not experience extreme highs of excitement, both socially and emotionally, during those years. I did. All of it had been vastly worthwhile because of the important bits and pieces of learning and understanding garnered from some of the people I met, some of the books I read, and the art and music I was exposed to. Now, however, it had all coalesced enough to give me the courage to bolt out of my safe haven in search of that childhood basic goal of happiness — and a satisfying sex life. And, while I was at it, I thought that along with a good sex life would come a soulmate kind of love. Not right away, maybe, but soon. Since I had done my decisive homework, my guardian angel decided to help me. Divorce in New York was very difficult and messy, not so in California. Now that his show was closing, Phil accepted an offer to play in *Summer Stock* with Gene Kelly and Judy Garland at Metro. We were moving back to Los Angeles!

On the last night of *High Button Shoes*, I stood in the wings and watched Phil doing his familiar, hilarious performance with a warm/ sad nostalgia, knowing I would never again watch this talented, tortured, delightful man perform on a stage as his wife.

Ah, Sweet Mystery of Life

Eventually I found that missing piece of my sexual puzzle in all its climactic glory, but that "complete woman" experience I'd heard so much about lay many years in the future. Getting there required years of hit and miss, trial and error, fumble and stumble. For the most part, though, after the initial terror had been, ah, laid to rest, so to speak, the search was a lot of fun.

Returning to my Hollywood friends from my New York friends in the summer of 1950 was a seamless bliss as they were kind of interchangeable, it was like going from one welcoming home to another. Going from a penthouse apartment to my mother's house under these circumstances, however, was awkward as I didn't plan to stay long. We had bought Mother this two-bedroom and den house in the Trousdale development in West Los Angeles with the $10,000 Phil had won on a horse race, and it was a total joy to her. With her green thumb for gardening, she made the patio and yard overflow with beauty, and her church and club friends gathered there for potlucks and cookouts all the time. Mother had moved into the second bedroom, so Phil and I could have the large master bedroom and was all aglow to have her "children" living with her. It was good for Phil, as the house was quite near Metro and he could be at the studio in ten minutes, but within days I had found myself a "single" apartment in Beverly Hills and was ready to move out. The hard part was telling Mother.

Getting her settled on the couch, I sat beside her and said, "Mother, I have to tell you something. I am divorcing Phil."

Her face crumpled with shock and she slumped backwards, as she said sorrowfully, "Oh, Josie, is it other women?"

"No, no. It's nothing like that."

Taking my hand in hers, she said with sad understanding, "Does he drink?"

"No, Phil has sinus trouble and he never drinks."

Trying to pull me to her and looking directly into my face, she said, "Then, what is it, honey baby?"

Earnestly, daughter to mother, my deepest awful secret revealed, I said, "I just don't want to *be* with him anymore, Mother. I don't like to *sleep* with him."

With a deep sigh of relief, she let go of my hands and said, "Oh, well, Josie, that's nothing to get a divorce about. I think most women feel like that after awhile. If he is good to you and doesn't drink or mess around, then I think you are lucky to have him and should make the best of it. Be careful, Josie, think about what you're doing. You don't want to make a big mistake here."

I said, "Oh, I made that big mistake five years ago by marrying Phil, and I have already rented a small apartment on Olympic at Beverly."

Somehow I wanted to protect Phil against Mother knowing that he had a gambling obsession, so I chose sex as a reason for divorce. Though I am sure Mother was sick at heart, she held her peace as she had been trained to do, and that was that. The only pain involved for me was that I had to leave Budget temporarily with Mother, as I couldn't find an apartment I could afford that would take dogs. In many ways, Budget had been my soul companion and chief confidant during my marriage and I surely hated to leave him. I hated to leave my treasured books behind, also, but it was "onward ho" for me now, so I had to leave my book boxes stacked up in Mother's garage. I promised the books and Budget that I would be back to collect them soon, and by the time Phil came back that evening, I had already taken my clothes and was gone. I left him a note saying (coward that I was) that I was making a trial separation, and giving him my address and phone number. My yellow Buick convertible had been stored in Mother's garage when we moved to New York, and I drove off with the top down in an ecstasy of freedom, singing "Don't cry, Jo, let him go, let him go, let him go," a Sinatra favorite of the time, with great gusto. I walked into that tiny, dark, pull-down bed, $75-a-month furnished apartment with an elated feeling of ownership and pride. I made a big private ceremony of pulling off my wedding ring and dropping it in an ashtray, saying to myself in a wall mirror, "Goodbye Mrs. Phil Silvers, Miss Frigidaire — Hello, Jo-Carroll Dennison, soon-to-be Miss Sex Goddess." I felt like the past five years had vanished and I was magically 21 again and rarin' to go to learn how to kick out my inhibitions and welcome in a new exciting life for myself.

First order in this new life was to get organized, so I asked my darling friend, Ethel Chaplin, to suggest a good lawyer and a good psychologist — one to disentangle me from my marriage vows, and the other to disentangle me from my sexual hang-ups. She did suggest a lawyer, who said it would be no problem, based on Phil's earnings, to get me $1,400 a month alimony, until I remarried, plus community property. (In those days divorce courts in California were very supportive of the "little woman.") For cause, he said, all I would have to do would be to swear on the stand that Phil often didn't come home until late at night, corroborated by one witness. The inference being that it was another woman who kept him out late rather than a card game. That seemed simple enough, and Phil would not even have to appear in court.

While awaiting the drawing up of papers to this effect, two astonishing things happened: One, Phil called and said he had to have a wisdom tooth extracted and asked me to go with him to drive him home afterwards from the dentist. A nurse came to get me in the waiting room to take me to Phil after his operation was over, and as she led me down the hall I could hear Phil making the dentist roar with laughter. To my horror, however, when Phil saw me his face crumpled up and he burst into tears. Pointing his finger straight out at me, he sobbed, "You are leaving me. You are the only person I have ever loved, Josie, and you are leaving me. Don't go, Josie. Don't leave me," and he buried his face in his hands and wept.

The dentist motioned with his head for me to leave the room and, with hostile, accusing eyes, the nurse led me back to the waiting room. I wanted to say, "Don't look at *me! I* don't know where that came from. He never said anything like that *before!*"

I sat down feeling guilt, pity, and total bewilderment about what had just happened. I knew that in those days dentists used sodium pentothal, the so-called truth serum, for extractions, but this kind of emotional outburst from Phil was totally astounding and very hard for me to understand. Was it true? Did he really feel that way? Did he *love* me? It didn't seem possible as he had never before given this kind of indication that I was that important to him. I sat there in a state of suspended animation and shock until after a few minutes the doctor walked Phil out to the waiting room and I could hear him joking all the way. Phil greeted me as though nothing untoward had happened and on the drive back to Mother's he maintained his usual affable attitude. Neither of us was able to speak openly about what had happened, or what we were feeling and thinking. For me, our connection had been broken, my life with Phil was over. What Phil was really feeling under his pleasant banter was a complete mystery to me — a mystery I had no desire to solve.

The second astonishing thing was that when Phil received the divorce papers, he refused to sign them. Over the phone in a mean tone of voice I had never heard before, he said, "I don't want this divorce and I am not going to pay you any alimony. As far as community property is concerned, your lawyer has asked for my financial statement and you can tell him that I have put everything in my brother, Harry's, name so I don't have any property to be communal with, except for your mother's house. We can split that if you want. If you stay with me, I will give you anything you want, but if you leave, then I will give you nothing!"

Completely unprepared for his attitude, I said, "Phil, I am not asking you for anything more than what the law says. Considering what you have lost gambling, it seems to me you might as well split community property with me instead of giving it to the bookies."

In a fury, he said, "What I do with my money is my business. I am going to contest this divorce and if you go ahead with it, I will testify on the stand that you forced me to associate with homosexuals against my will."

I couldn't think of an answer to this ridiculous nonsense, so I just hung up. It had never occurred to me that Phil would contest the divorce. I didn't for a moment think that he would carry out his silly statement if I took him to court. It was true many of my best friends were homosexual, but then so were Phil's and I knew he would never say a thing like that on the stand. What bothered me was that he would *think* of a mean spirited thing like that. I had never heard him say a mean or prejudiced word ever before and it was surprising and depressing.

Trying to decide whether I should cry or curse, I went to see Ethel and told her all about it, asking what she thought I should do. It would be hard to find two women with more different backgrounds than Ethel and I, but over the years we had formed a powerful kind of teacher/pupil bond. Ethel was a totally generous, loving, genuine person who had all the attributes I admired. She was grounded, knew who she was, and her values and absolute certainty about right and wrong were the characteristics I most wanted to attain. I wanted to be just like her. Consequently, she was the only one I felt I could go to for this decision based completely on values.

She said, "Josie, I love you, but I love Phil, too. He must be hurting to say a thing like that. I think if I were you, I would just go ahead and get your divorce and forget about alimony or community property if he doesn't want to give it to you. You are young and able-bodied, you don't have any children, and it will do you good to get back to work."

I hadn't quite expected that advice. Without giving it much thought, I had taken for granted that Phil would give me community property and alimony, it was the law and common practice, so I had not been concerned about making a living right away. With a little cold knot of anxiety in my stomach, I thought about the old adage, "*Tis not life that matters, tis the courage you bring to it.*" Yeah, well, it was going to take a lot of that courage to get back out there right now and scrounge for a paying job or another contract without the lure of being the current Miss America — to be back on my own as I had been as a child. Being 26 now instead of 19 made me a tad long in the tooth for a starlet. However, the more I thought about it, the more I thought Ethel was right. I'd had a successful history of "taking the bull by the horns," so to speak, so I called Phil and said, "Pay my lawyer, pay off Mother's house and put it in my name, and give me $5,000 to support Mother and me until I can get started back to work, and we'll call it quits."

Phil instantly became his old jolly jocular self and hastily agreed. On my court date, my lawyer asked me if Phil often stayed out late, I said yes, and that was all there was to it. Our divorce ceremony was just about as unreal and superficial as our marriage ceremony had been, which seemed both fitting and sad. Not once in my life did I ever regret foregoing that considerable community property and the $1,400 a month alimony. I had not been able to do without more intimacy from Phil, but doing without his money always made me feel good about myself.

Ethel suggested Dr. Philip Cohen as a psychologist and she couldn't have picked one more suited to my needs and personality. Dr. Cohen had a shock of unruly hair and was sweet and funny, but I felt his understanding, support, and caring was total. It was clear that he was a good man who would not try to "cop a feel" and I was instantly at ease with him. Before we got down to the difficult childhood stuff, he wanted to know about my life as it was now. I told him that I was very secure about many things but my secret fear was that I was never sure why these brilliant friends that I liked … liked *me*.

Sitting in this dimly lit room in his comfortable armchair directly opposite the narrow couch upon which I lay, Dr. Cohen said, "Why wouldn't they like you?"

"Well, they are all so much more talented and creative than I am. And they are so much better educated and know so much about so many things, and are so sure about what is right and wrong."

"You are always welcomed to their homes and parties, with or without Phil, why do you think that is?

"I think it must be because I do numbers from the medicine show and I do a great imitation of Gene dancing. Because I come on strong like *Gangbusters*."

"*Gangbusters* is a loud, violent television show. Is that what you think you are really like?"

"Well, no, but you know what I mean. I don't think that's what I'm really like, but you asked me what my *friends* like about me and that's what I think it is."

"Do you mean that you have to be "on," as you call it, or entertaining in some way to make your friends like you?"

"Yes."

In his soft, firm voice, he said, "Now, Jo-Carroll, listen carefully to what I am about to say. *I* like you, and I know who you really are under that smokescreen you call *Gangbusters*. And so do your friends. They like you because you are *you*, not because you come on strong or are a good entertainer."

"Do you really think so?"

"I know so."

That was hard for me to believe.

However, it was an immense relief to tell this warm, sympathetic doctor about that part of my life I had kept most hidden: my father and Dr. Tate. I was eager to explain to him my inability to love and trust, and about the sexual inadequacy I was so bitterly ashamed of. Words poured out in an avalanche of rocky events as I tried to explain my life's vicissitudes and triumphs and fears, winding up with my feelings about Blackie and sex in general.

I said, "I know that the only way to overcome my fears is to learn to do by doing, but I am terrified that someone is going to try to put their tongue in my mouth. I got used to whatever that was that happened in bed with Phil, but when I think of going to bed with someone new, the memory of Dr. Tate *touching* me and *holding* me on his lap, his *smell*, that thought actually gags me.

Dr. Cohen said, "You are too smart to let something that happened to you as a child govern your life as a woman."

"I don't *feel* like a woman. I couldn't love Blackie as a woman is supposed to love, as I imagine a woman loves. I married Phil because he didn't require that kind of love. I don't have any problem with unrestricted love for animals and nature, but I can't feel it for a man."

"That is because you feel safe loving animals and nature. Animals love back unconditionally and nature is non-threatening. Tell me, how often do you masturbate?"

My face burning with embarrassment, I thought, "How often do I masturbate? I can't even say the *word*, for heaven's sake. Anyway, I thought that was something only boys did and it gave them warts or something."

Aloud, I said, "I, ah, don't. I never have."

"Why not?"

Defiantly, "Because my mother said it was nasty to touch yourself down there, and your hair would fall out if you did."

Dr. Cohen rarely smiled, but, when he did, his smile was so sweet and kindly it almost made me want to cry, as he said, "Your mother is misguided, probably by her own mother. That is a very old wives' tale, most likely started by fathers. It is not nasty to touch yourself or take pleasure in your own erogenous areas, it is natural. Nature designed our bodies for those pleasures, and, outside of abusing our bodies with *un*natural things like alcohol or drugs or sadistic pain, it is good to take enjoyment from what nature intended."

I said dubiously, "Yes, well ..."

"Don't you see, Jo-Carroll, you are a human being, and every human being is born with the capacity, the *need*, for love and sexual gratification. And the most rewarding kind of love and sexual gratification is that which a woman feels for a man in a sexual union. You don't want to miss that, do you?"

"No, I *don't* want to miss it, but I can't. I want to, but I can't."

"You can because it is naturally in you to do so. It is the same as saying you can't learn Latin. You have the ability to learn Latin if you try hard enough. You were born with the ability to think and the need to love. You don't have to learn Latin, but you do have to learn to love. You can, therefore you must."

"I think, therefore I am?"

"Something like that. But you must first understand that you don't have a special brand on your soul, that you are not cut off from the best that life has to offer because of shameful, hurtful experiences you had as a child. These experiences are much more common than you think, and they must be overcome with your same energy and confidence that has led you to read more books than most college graduates. Nothing in your past can prevent you from overcoming these kinds of unrealistic fears. All you have to do is focus that force you have within you. That force which has prevailed in the different kinds of contests you have been winning all your life."

After a thoughtful pause, he continued, "This is just one more step in triumphing over the traumas of your life. You say you want to, so now is the time to use that same determination and bravery you used to face down new school kids and Dr. Tate and find yourself a nice, attractive man and go to bed with him."

"Yechhh!"

"Try it. You'll come to like it, I guarantee it. But first you must get yourself fitted with a diaphragm. I can't believe you have never done that. This is no time to be careless. About pregnancy, I mean."

I, too, was appalled at the chances I had taken in that regard with Phil, and vowed to quickly make amends. But I knew Dr. Cohen was wrong about my friends knowing both my public and my private selves, because even *he* didn't know my private self. I didn't tell him or anyone else at that time about having seen God when I was a child, and feeling I was on a continuing spiritual quest. I never spoke about my personal connection with animals and wildlife, or about feeling that my natural element was to be found on mountain tops and in solitude. I don't know exactly why I felt compelled to keep my private self private. Partly, because I was afraid of being misunderstood or laughed at, I imagine. It was by no means the "in" thing to believe in a divine spirit with which we were all connected amongst the people I admired. It is funny even to envision Phil's face, if I had attempted to explain that I felt the divine spirit and I were *One* to him. But mostly, from childhood I had believed that I had a covenant with my God to keep my connection with Him between the two of us.

What Sex Is - Mostly

With Sydney Chaplin after tennis.

With great determination and blind obedience to Dr. Cohen, I worked away at what I thought must be masturbation, but it didn't do anything for me except make me feel foolish. At 26, I didn't even know what a diaphragm was; Phil had always mysteriously taken care of the prevention precautions, but now I hurried to obtain one. Then, diaphragm and determination at the ready, to her everlasting credit my guardian angel came up with the absolutely ideal candidate for the breaking of my ironclad barriers.

Howard Leeds was a great looking, funny, and kindhearted young man who was bright and decent and good, a combination not in great supply in Hollywood. He was a successful comedy writer, and he and his writing partner, Artie Julian, were members of the inner sanctum of the Gene Kelly group, both for their humor and their excellence at volleyball. Howie Leeds wasn't like most comedy writers who have to be "on" all the time; his humor was subtle and witty and laid-back. One thing that attracted me to him was he always looked so *clean.* He was immaculate in his looks and dress, even when he was hot and sweaty from playing volleyball. Best of all, next to Gene, Howie was the best ballroom dancer I ever knew. Divorced now from Phil, it didn't take much to find myself and Howie in my little single apartment ready to do the deed. The hugging and kissing part had gone exceedingly well (no intermingling of tongues), but then the time came to comply with Dr. Cohen's diaphragm experiment. Even having been married to Phil for five years, I still felt like a novice in the ways of sex. Shedding a few drops of blood from a punctured membrane, under the circumstances, didn't keep me from still feeling like a virgin. I was terrified by thoughts of: "Will he think I'm frigid?," "Will he think I'm not good in bed?," and "Will he talk to me about my clitoris?"

Me and Howie Leeds in Acupulco.

Not wanting to be presumptuous, I had not inserted the new diaphragm until I was sure the big moment was at hand. Consequently, crouching naked in my bathroom, my nerves came unglued and the whole romantic adventure turned into a grotesque nightmare. The prophylactic jelly was the problem. What seemed as simple as one, two, three, in the doctor's office became all but an impossibility in actual practice. For some reason, my fingers became numb and shook uncontrollably when I tried to force the jelly from the small tube into the rubber circle of the diaphragm, resulting in an excess of jelly, both on the rubber and my fingers. Therefore, when I tried to fold and insert the diaphragm as shown me by the doctor, it repeatedly spurted from my fingers and slithered around the floor or bounced off the wall, resulting in continued application of jelly, and further willful noncompliance from the slippery thing. Soon, both the bathroom and I were slathered with jelly and, to exacerbate the difficulties, I broke out in a copious sweat all over my body and felt both hot and cold at the same time. By the time I got the darn thing inserted, all I really wanted was a cool shower and to fall exhausted into bed alone. Only the thought of poor Howie waiting all this time in hopefully high expectations forced me to wash myself off as quickly as possible and go out to him with an inner attitude of holding my nose and jumping off a high cliff into a bottomless ocean.

To my delighted surprise, after a bit it *was* rather like floating in a warm, silken, rolling ocean. Possibly because of my chattering teeth and lengthy stay in the bathroom, Howie must have sensed my terror because he was slow and smooth that first night — using much the same technique as I would to soothe a spooked horse. In the weeks and months to come, he gradually initiated me into the wonders of what sex was all about. I had no idea about the amazing sensations that could be evoked in different parts of my body by knowing hands and lips. Most importantly, I never felt that I was out of my depth or in danger of losing control. Howie seemed to be having a repeatedly rewarding experience himself, may the gods be praised, and more than satisfied with me as a partner. Both my pleasure and my relief were enormous.

Howie seemed so *experienced*. Not as though he had studied a "how to" book with pictures, but as though his naturally loving and sensual nature encouraged him to explore and enjoy every possible move and sexual position. Yet, this advanced course in the extensive possibilities of sexual behavior was performed in such a non-threatening way that I couldn't remember why I had been so afraid. Also, it was quickly apparent that he was very sure of his masculinity and stamina. Important, that. Being made love to by a man who loved *making love* to a woman, a man who was both tender and passionate, quite literally took my fears away, while at the same time, his know-how relaxed every resistant thought and muscle in my body. It was the most extraordinary physical experience of my life; however it didn't bring about that "cataclysmic explosion" I had heard about, but I figured orgasms could wait until later as this was even better than riding bareback or ballroom dancing! Howie was also an ardent traveler and we took many trips in California and Mexico, dancing on beaches and making love in exotic places. We loved one another in a wholly sweet and easy way. I gleefully told Dr. Cohen that I didn't need to learn to masturbate, I had Howie!

"Loving" and "in love" are two vastly different things, however, as I found one fateful night at the Kelly's. Evelyn Keyes, a leading actress at Columbia, whom Phil had worked with in *Thousand and One Nights*, dropped in one Saturday night with Sydney Chaplin. Sydney was the knockout handsome, apparently shy, younger son of Charlie Chaplin, and after a bit, he joined my group singing at the piano. As our eyes met across the piano, we seemingly learned all the more intimate details about each other from that one long, mesmerizing look. Every cell in my body went into full alert.

Sydney phoned me the next day, and said, "You know, I've got a crush on you," and my heart gave such a convulsive flip-flop that I had to sit down or fall down. I knew as if with foreknowledge that a new and totally different experience for me had just begun. We went to dinner at the beach and talked, and walked afterwards in the sand and talked — and I learned just how funny and sweet Sydney could be — and fell wildly in love. One of my favorite authors, Knut Hamsun, said, "One of God's first actions was to create Light, and Light is Love." Surely, that was true for suddenly my whole world became brighter and gloriously vivid. Ordinary things took on an extraordinary shining light.

It is ironic that if I had not known Howie first and learned to relax my defenses, I could not have been freed to fall in love in this complete way. As it was, I had to tell Howie what had happened to me, and it was not a happy thing for either of us. I knew it wasn't fair, for although many other men may possibly be as accomplished technically speaking, it was clear to me that Howie was the best man by far to have been my first lover. But, though love surely is a many-splendored thing, it is very often not fair.

I never knew what Sydney told Evelyn Keyes, but he and I were together on a daily basis from then on. Well, for awhile at least.

Even after all these intervening years, I get all soft and nostalgic when I remember Sydney the way he was when I first knew him. Crisp, curly, black hair and large dark eyes inherited from his Spanish mother, Lita Grey, endowed with a truly marvelous sense of humor from his genius father, well over six feet with a beautiful athletic body and an engaging self-deprecating grin, at 24 Sydney was already a ladykiller *par excellence*. I think the killer part came from his not-too-well-hidden vulnerability and invigorating appeal of an enthusiastic Peter Pan, which is irresistible to most women. It certainly was to me.

Being the son of a famous and beloved man is very tough on a boy; few sons manage to grow up unscathed. Also, being sent away to a military boarding school as a child by his divorced, teenaged alcoholic mother, took a heavy toll. Being naturally funny, he had learned to use his humor in self defense, and by now laughter was the way he paid the bills and dulled the fears of his life. To me, he was funnier than his father, but they both had that "little tramp" kind of vulnerability and sweetness.

And while Howie had taught me the fun and pleasure engendered by the right moves in bed, I learned the deeper pleasures that really being in love brought to the intertwining of two bodies from Sydney. For the first time, sex was the underlying motivational force in all that I thought and did. It put zest into waking up to each new day and sizzle into the slightest touch. Sex combined with Sydney was the yeast that made my life rise up into hitherto unexplored heights.

Due to financial restrictions, I was sharing a little one-bedroom house in the Hollywood hills with Ellen Ray, a stock contract dancer at Metro. She and I shared the rent and the bills, and took turns with a friend in the bedroom when the occasion warranted. Ellen, a tall, thin, ethereal woman in her late 20s, with lovely long curly brown hair, was a truly marvelous dancer. She was going with another dancer and when she and Jimmy wanted to use the bedroom, Sydney and I went to the movies, or vice versa. If, as often happened while sitting in our favorite area of the balcony, a touch from one of us stirred our erotic imagination, and we quickly left in the middle of the movie and raced to our favorite motel in the San Fernando Valley. It was called the *Hi Ho Inn*, and had a saucy neon sign of a top hat waving back and forth in the night sky on the roof. It was kind of our "home away from home," and the memory of our driving there through the night with the top down on my yellow convertible anticipating what was to come at the *Hi Ho*, still reverberates nostalgically in my mind and body. Suffice it to say, I became quite adept at using a diaphragm.

It is interesting that some experiences which may only cover a short amount of time will extend through memory as vivid and moment-by-moment complete as though they had lasted for years, while some experiences that really did last for years can fade from our memory altogether. A sentence like "I've got a crush on you," a look across a piano, even a single momentary emotion, can be powerful enough to last a lifetime.

In those glowing memories of driving with Sydney with the top down, we were always in my car because Sydney didn't have a car. Unfortunately, to my mind, according to his mother's divorce decree, Sydney had a subsistence-level trust fund which enabled him to squeeze by financially – as long as he didn't have a car or his own apartment. Eleven years from now, at 35, he would come into a great deal of money, which gave him even less incentive to get a job. He was a very good actor when he appeared in little plays around town for nothing, but he preferred playing tennis and hanging out with ever-willing friends of one sex or another to trying for parts in movies, or any other kind of paying job. From lack of incentive and fear of failure, I thought.

But negative thoughts only lurked in the closet during those first months with Sydney. I was supporting Mother as well as myself, of course, but she had started learning at birth how to be frugal, and her lovely house was now paid for. Also, Phil continued living with her for a long time and was paying for food and some of the bills. They were an incongruous pair, but they somehow understood, amused, and adored one another. Anyway, the fact that neither Sydney nor I had much money detracted not one whit from the high-flying bliss I was feeling. The majority of the delicious times we had together didn't cost money. Southern California offered abundant opportunities for free or inexpensive pleasures: the ocean, with its sand and surf a few minutes away; mountains and lakes and sunsets in the desert a couple of hours away, or cafes on Sunset Strip where we could sit all day over coffee and people watch, either holding hands or touching in some contented sensual way. We were both sports enthusiasts and often watched or played volleyball at the beach or at the Kelly's, played tennis at Charlie Chaplin's house, or went up to Will Rogers State Park in the lovely Santa Monica Mountains to watch the celebrity polo matches. Plus, the *Hi Ho* didn't cost much, comparatively speaking, and Ellen was at work during the week, leaving the house to us for free entertainment.

Although most of our time was spent alone together, all my friends were charmed by Sydney, and I would sit and watch him interact with them in a cocoon of proud possessiveness. But I wanted more for us than just fun and games. Since neither of us had much formal education — military schools teach mostly discipline and Sydney had dropped out during high school — I decided it would be good for Sydney if we both took the *Great Books Course* that the University of Chicago had just put out. The course required only that you buy the 50 inexpensive condensed paperback books of the world's greatest literature and thinking, such as Plato, Spinos, and Shakespeare, and have a knowledgeable arbitrator for the weekly sessions of learning. Sydney's father was delighted with this development, and supplied the arbitrator, Professor Reginald Pole, and his fee.

Professor Pole in his day had been a well-known British philosopher, and was just one of the several indigent aging celebrities that Charlie Chaplin supported, including Bill Tilden, the great tennis player. Sydney and I asked six of our younger friends to join the group, and Professor Pole, this extremely thin, tall, slightly stuttering, elderly Oxford professor, did his best to inculcate at least a smidgen of knowledge about the Greek, Roman, and European cultures and ideas into our relatively blank noggins. It was a tremendous experience for all of us and opened up a lifetime of interests. I still cherish those boxes of thin, yellowing, paperbacks of learning. I was so happy while learning from them.

"Ah, well, it was swell while it lasted," as Bob Hope's theme song goes, and I am so grateful for that special time, although I can no longer remember exactly how long it lasted. In some ways, forever. When I think of that period in my life, often it is of one special moment. One time when Sydney and I were at our favorite cafe on the Sunset Strip, and when he had gone next door to the famous *Schwab's* drug store to get something, I remember watching out the front café windows as I waited for him to return. Suddenly, I was flooded with the realization that I was the most completely happy I had ever been. Or possibly ever would be. Just looking through the window and visualizing Sydney soon walking back by it in his white, unbuttoned sports shirt showing a slash of smooth, tanned skin, head a bit forward to minimize his height, characteristically walking with one shoulder higher than the other in his rather defensive way, I knew that I would never forget that exquisite moment in time of being perfectly happy.

Another kind of memory I have of that time is of my first attempts to cook. Although the oceans and the mountains and the deserts were more or less free, unless from a soup kitchen, eating out is not, and I was positively euphoric when my home-cooked steak, baked potatoes, and salad turned out well. So much so that more and more I made dinner, while Ellen set the table, and Sydney perched on a stool and kept us both laughing. I found that laughter is so different when there are sexual undertones and the erotic electricity between Sydney and me put a tang of spice in my laughter, as well as the dinner. Laughter had been vitally important to me ever since Todd, the comic on Dr. Tate's Medicine Show, first taught me the relaxation and *fun* of laughter. I had always laughed at animals and birds, but I don't remember laughing at people before Todd. I was attracted primarily to Blackie because he made me laugh, and there is no way I would have married Phil except for his constant ability to make me laugh. But while Phil could make me curl up with laughter, my laughter with Sydney was like the explosive shout of a happy child.

I was learning that there are big differences in a sexual experience, as well as laughter. Whereas, Howie, while making love, focused his expertise and attention on making *me* feel good about myself and about sex in general, I focused my own new-found expertise and attention on making *Sydney* feel good about himself. Considering his background, it was not surprising that he had sexual anxieties, and somehow that made him more dear to me. It was as though I felt that *his* sexual hang-ups were more important than mine Evelyn because I was in love with him. In my joy, I disregarded that part about my lack of orgasms, I thought that would come in due course, so to speak. In the meantime, Sydney was exciting and loving and touchy-feely, and it was my pleasure to make him feel good in every possible way.

When I wasn't laughing, though, I still had to get out and earn a living. I scrounged around and didn't have too much trouble getting parts in B movies such as Gene Autry's westerns and series like *Perry Mason, The Shadow, Dick Tracy* and others. A fun thing I did was assisting the Shdanoffs in their work as coaches to major stars. George Shdanoff had been one of my teachers when 20th sent me to the Actors' Lab, and George and his wife, Elsa, had become life-long friends. They both individually worked with the best actors in town as drama coaches. They paid me to cue or work up scenes in the films the actors were working on, or about to start. Some of those I partnered with, like Gregory Peck, Patricia Neal, and Yul Brynner, liked what I did in the scenes with them and suggested me for parts here and there. Gregory Peck and Dorothy McGuire had formed the *La Jolla Playhouse* in La Jolla as a place for actors in Hollywood to get the experience of working on a stage and Gregory gave me that marvelous part of the prostitute in *The Front Page*, starring Pat O'Brien and Michael O'Shea. All the many men's roles in the play were performed by well-known character actors, and we all stayed at the same hotel and had a blast after the show in its bar. I also performed in *The Ladies of Washington* there.

The actors I worked with in the Shdanoff's studio would sometimes suggest me for major roles, the Shdanoffs would work with me on a scene, and the director would test me – but I never got the parts. The closest I came to a major role in a major film came about through Sydney. A well-known photographer for *Photoplay* did a layout of me as a "young starlet" for the magazine that included photos taken at the beach with my dog, Budget, and at my house in informal attire. For this kind of shoot, photographers take well over 100 shots, which are printed up about 20 to a page for proofs. One was a candid shot where I was sitting cross-legged on the floor looking up at the camera. I didn't like candid shots because often I look sad and vulnerable in them, as I happened to do in this case. Sydney, however, liked it and cut it out of the proofs page and kept it in his wallet. He showed it to his father and his stepmother, Oona, and Charlie asked to meet me. As Sydney rather nervously brought me inside this Victorian-style mansion high above Sunset on San Ysidro Drive, it was so cavernous and dark in the cathedral-style entry that I almost couldn't see Oona and Charlie as they came forward to meet us.

Oona was a tall, slender woman who wore her dark hair parted in the middle and pulled back Madonna fashion. She was the famous playwright Eugene O'Neil's daughter and was eighteen when she married the 50-something Chaplin, much against her father's will. She and her father were completely estranged, but Charlie was much more than a father-replacement for her as they already had several children together. Oona was a lovely, quiet woman just three or four years older than Sydney, and he adored her.

With my picture in his hand, Chaplin asked me to sit beside him on a huge, brown-velvet couch and shooed Sydney and Oona away, so we could talk alone. Although I had never seen Chaplin around his own tennis court, I had met Charlie and Oona at the Kelly's once before. Feeling especially frisky that night, I had made Chaplin laugh with a takeoff I did on a bigoted southern senator, but that "on" girl looked nothing like the vulnerable girl in the photograph, so neither of the Chaplins recognized me. Anyway, on that first interview with Chaplin, he did all the talking and I never reminded him that we had met before. As with all his movies, he explained that he had written the screenplay and composed the music for his next film, *Limelight*, the story of an old vaudeville clown who befriends and then falls in love with a young crippled ballerina. In the movie, the clown, Chaplin, convinces the girl she can walk if she believes enough; she does, regains her ability to dance, and becomes a star while the old clown dies from love of her. It was the theme of most of Chaplin's movies: the joy and pain of love. I could see it was a sad story and, not wanting to disappoint him as I had George Cukor, I quickly told him that I had a hard time crying.

Taking my hand and looking straight in my face, he said, "It is easy to cry. Watch," and within seconds, tears were streaming down his face.

Instantly, I felt inadequate and said apologetically, "I envy you that ability, but I just don't have it. I wish I could cry like that, but I can't."

That vulnerability on my part seemed to enchant him, and he said firmly, "I can teach you." Looking from my sad picture to my face, he came to a rapid decision, and said, "I want you to play the part of the girl. I think you are just what I am looking for. You are 24, aren't you?"

"No, I am 26."

Chaplin looked thoughtful for a moment, then said, "Well, never mind. I can make you look younger. You will come five mornings a week to my private studio, and I will work with you on the part. I will put you under personal contract at $250 a week, with a bonus, of course, at the end of the picture, which will start sometime next year. My lawyer will send you the papers." Chaplin handed me a copy of the script for *Limelight* as though it was the Holy Grail, and suggested that Sydney and I meet Oona and him for dinner that night at Don the Beachcomer, the best Polynesian restaurant in town.

I was in shock. I had gone with Sydney to see the great Charlie Chaplin without having any idea why he wanted to meet me. I thought it must be because of the relationship I was having with his favorite son. Sydney and Oona were hanging over the upstairs balcony trying to hear what was happening between Chaplin and me during the interview as we afterward came into the foyer. I could see the relief and excitement on their faces, as they saw the smiles on ours. I felt numb and unreal rather than excited, but I knew they expected me to be delighted and I tried to look it.

Being a devout believer in Method Acting at the time, I soon got into an argument with Chaplin that night at dinner about whether acting is "revealing an honest emotion" versus "acting is all technique." Chaplin, this world renowned actor, named by the *America Film Institute* as "one of the best male actors who ever lived," and said by George Bernard Shaw to be "the only genius to come out of the movie industry," contended that bringing emotion to an audience was all in learned acting skills, that the audience felt the emotion not the actor. He gave an example of a famous stage actor who, during a big dramatic scene, would turn his back to the audience and shake his shoulders pretending tears in such a way that there would not be dry eye in the house. Chaplin said the actor could have been planning what to have for dinner or picking his nose while his back was turned, but the audience furnished the heartbreak they *thought* he was feeling. Clearly, Chaplin was completely wrong and I felt it my duty to explain it to him. Oona and Sydney were strangely silent throughout this lesson in acting I was giving Charlie Chaplin, but I didn't notice it at the time. Of course, the number of powerfully potent *Don The Beachcomer's* Navy Grogs which I so enjoyed probably elevated my tone of voice, but I am sure I would have argued the same way without them.

When I went for my first rehearsal with Chaplin, I had made the time to study his script and had discovered that he had given the girl the wrong attitude in the dialogue of her big scene discovering she could walk again. When I explained that to him, though, he didn't seem to get what I was saying, and when I was ready to leave, he told me not to come back the next day as planned, that something had come up and his secretary would call me to set another appointment. The secretary never called, and Chaplin's lawyer never sent me the personal contract as promised. Claire Bloom played my part in *Limelight,* and the next time I saw Charlie Chaplin was two years later in London.

I never regretted losing the part. There was no way I was the actress Chaplin was looking for, not in temperament or talent. But though I was a loudmouth about my theories about acting, I wasn't stupid. If I had subconsciously really wanted that part, there is no way I would have told the genius Charlie Chaplin that he had written a scene wrong. I still don't completely understand it, but I had a way of sabotaging myself when it came to the test of getting a major role in acting. So many times I was given the opportunity of testing for big roles on the recommendation of someone who had seen me at a party. Chaplin hadn't remembered me or that he had told me I was the best comedian in Hollywood when he had seen me doing a takeoff on Senator Bilbo that night at the Kelly's. However, it does go to show that when I was relaxed at a party, or even just walking down the street, there must have been a kind of glow, an unconscious inner light perhaps, that shone in such a way that made people think I would be a good actress. But I had realized long ago when my father had such grandiose hopes for my stardom that I didn't *want* to be an actress. Fate or circumstances had forced me to continue to make a living in show business, one way or another, and consciously I dutifully did the best I could when presented with these opportunities, but subconsciously — my light went out. Performing in one way or another when I was happy at a party lit my fire — making a test for a big part in a movie evidently put it out. I think one of the reasons was that most good actors say that they are shy about themselves and became actors because they would much rather play the part of someone else. I never felt that way. I always liked being who I was and never, ever, wanted to be someone else. Also, to be a good actor, you have to literally lose control of yourself to *become* someone else. I never wanted to lose control and that can keep one from getting truly inside another character.

I can honestly say, however, of all the big parts I was up for, the only one that I truly regretted not getting was that of the phony movie star with the horrible voice in *Singin' In the Rain*. Darling Betty Comden and Adolph Green, who had written the show, were always trying to help me get work, and, I guess because of the way I clowned around in the Kelly's living room, they thought I could play this marvelous part and arranged for me to audition for co-director Stanley Donen. They had written the screenplay with Judy Holliday in mind, but she was working in the movie of *Born Yesterday* so they gave me a script and I worked on it with the Shdanoff's and did a long monologue for Stanley. It seemed odd to be auditioning for someone I knew so well, but I gave it my best shot. He liked it well enough to set up an audition for Arthur Freed, the producer, in his office. So I performed a 10-or-15-minute scene for this famous producer, the two director/choreographers (Gene and Stanley), Betty and Adolph, the writers, and Saul Chaplin, music directors for the film. The entire creative staff, for what was later to be called, "The Best Musical Ever Made," was all grouped around as I did my best to give a good audition.

My memory of that audition is mercifully a blank. I don't remember anything about the scene, what it was about, or any of the dialogue. I don't remember it at all. Nada. When I had finished the scene, a stunned silence on the part of the assembled made it only too clear that I had bombed. Immediately, my protective psyche grabbed all relative memory and buried it beyond recovery in the darkest reaches of my consciousness. Later Betty said to me, "Oh, Josie, I am so sorry. You must feel so badly about the audition."

But I said airily, "No. No, I don't. I have just put it behind me."

Shocked, Betty said, "I wish I could do that. It would just have killed me."

I didn't tell her that I had long ago learned how to protect myself from pain and humiliation, and could literally block an unwanted incident out of my mind. For some inexplicable reason I couldn't bring myself to tell her how horribly guilty I felt for having let them down in what was evidently such a disastrous way. Unfortunately for me, *Singin' in the Rain* plays constantly on TV and really is the perfect musical. I watch it because I do love the musical numbers, but watching Jean Hagen doing "my" part is painful. I now have so many good ideas about how I *should* have done the scene, even if I don't remember how I *did* do it for the audition. Rather than going for the high comedic voice like Judy Holliday's, as Jean Hagen did, I should have gone for an extremely deep voice with a strong Texas accent. *I could have done it!* On the other hand, maybe my guardian angel/subconscious was right. If I had gotten the part and been good in it, that would have led my life in a whole new direction. One that may not have been as right for me as the direction I followed. I guess if I had my druthers, I would have gotten the part, been marvelous in it, but then continued on with my life as it has been. Impossible, of course.

Now that I was losing high-salaried jobs right and left, I realized just how nifty it had been to be under contract to Fox with that steady check coming in and having jobs given to me rather than having to look for them. Murray Feil, my longtime agent, had assigned me a lesser agent at William Morris when Fox had dropped my option and he came up with a small part now and then, but mostly I got jobs through friends. I was almost a regular on Frank Sinatra's television variety show as a "Talking Woman" in the comedy sketches; I played the part of "Breathless Mahoney" in a *"Dick Tracy"* series out at Hal Roach; a friend got her producer husband to cast me in a very low-budget terrible movie, *"Prehistoric Women;"* and through Actors' Lab, friend Hugo Haas, I got a job as the leading lady's friend in *"Pickup,"* which Hugo directed and starred in. Jobs like that were enough to get by on. But after awhile, I was irritated that I had to get up early to bring home the bacon for the scrambled eggs, while Sydney slept late and then played tennis all day. As much as I loved him, I couldn't accept Sydney for the way he was. I thought the fact that I had to learn to take care of and support myself as a child had been vital to my sense of self, and therefore Sydney's potential and self esteem would be destroyed, if he didn't begin to learn those kinds of growing-up lessons. Finally, in a fit of righteous this-is-going-to-hurt-me-more-than-it-does-you showdown, I told Sydney that I didn't want to see him anymore until he had at least *tried* to get a job!

Feeling that my "tough love" was going to be the making of Sydney, I went around in a kind of virtuous glow until after a week he called and said he needed to see me. I put on my very sexiest daytime dress and was alone in the house when he came over. As he walked in he grabbed me in a bear hug and, astonishingly, began to weep on my shoulder, gasping through his tears, "I love you, Josie. I need you."

I held him and patted his back until he was quiet, and then, pulling back and looking up in his face, I said gently, "Do you want to get back together? Is that it?"

Trying to smile and make a joke, he said, "I do."

Hand-in-hand, we moved over to the couch and Sydney lay down and put his head in my lap. I wiped away his tears with my skirt and slowly ran my fingers through his hair. After a bit, sighing deeply with his eyes still closed, he said, "I must love you because I have never been able to cry in front of anyone before."

I was struck dumb with the ramifications of such a statement. In a way, I understood completely because I had trained myself not to cry ever since my father had run off with the blonde. Boys are trained not to cry by their parents or culture, but I thought Sydney and I had trained ourselves not to cry in order not to appear vulnerable. Circumstances had taught us not to trust anyone enough to show that weakness. I wanted to weep myself when I thought of what in Sydney's past had destroyed his childhood trust. I imagined experiences of hurt and fear which he could never tell me and might not even remember. So I just held him and told him over and over that I loved him and I understood, and that everything would be all right. Nothing more was mentioned about his getting a job and we went on as before in a burst of relief on both our parts.

But our issues were not really resolved. All my life I have suffered from impatience. I admire patience greatly, but I wa,nt it *now,* as the joke goes. I do not always want the right thing, but right or wrong when I want something, I want it immediately and work hard to get it. Sydney's lackadaisical attitude toward life kept bugging me until I said he had to make some effort to *make something of himself* or I was going to New York. He didn't, so I went to New York where it was easier for me to get jobs in the burgeoning live television market, and also in the hope it would shake Sydney up enough to make him take action. Betty and Adolph were in Hollywood working on the movie *Band Wagon* and Adolph loaned me his great apartment on 51st and Second Avenue so my expenses were manageable. I got jobs here and there on television series like *Kraft Theater* and *Omnibus,* played the "Talking Woman" on *Ed Sullivan Presents* in sketches with comedians like Red Skelton and Victor Borge, and did a few live commercials. Between jobs I didn't partake of the wonders of New York City as much as I used to when I lived there with Phil. Most of my free time was spent, rain or shine, on the recessed balcony of Adolph's apartment, which faced out on midtown and the elegant, art nouveau Chrysler Building. My favorite thing was watching the spring storms thundering over the city with the lightning reflecting in the skyscraper windows, while listening to a record from Adolph's extensive classical collection like Beethoven's *Pastoral Symphony* or Wagner's *Flight of the Valkyrie.* That experience was a bringing together of nature and music that thrilled my soul.

Mostly, however, I sat on that balcony and thought about Sydney. And life. I was into metaphysics at the time and the books I was reading were opening my eyes to the extent of my own fears of wholehearted commitment and self exposure. I began to see that my fear of losing control had made me controlling. Like the grinding of rusty gears, I began the effort of looking honestly at my own defensive mechanisms, and the word "judgmental" stenciled its painful way across my forehead. I had been bargaining with Sydney: my love for his changing to fit my image. In order for him to receive my love, he had to conform to my imposed conditions. In which case, of course, I wasn't being truly loving. It was painful to realize that, while my private self was peacefully loving, open, and patient with nature and animals, my public self was restless, defensive, and impatient with people and circumstances. Patience usually lost out to instant gratification. I couldn't enjoy and accept Sydney for the person he was; I wanted him to be the person I thought he should be!

I resolved to change. I had asked Sydney to think it over and write me if he wanted to continue our relationship on the basis I demanded. I made a commitment to myself that if I ever saw him again, I would love him completely and without reservations of any kind. I became afloat with the concept of unconditional love! But I needed to hear from Sydney *first.* For months, every morning I hurried to the front door to see if there was a letter from him on the mat outside — and one morning there it was. My one and only letter from Sydney. In it he said, "I am looking for a job — I love you — I want to marry you — and I want you to have my baby. (Oh, Glory!) P.S. Don't believe what you read about me in the papers. I'll explain later." Every little corpuscle in my bloodstream seemed to do the Highland Fling, and I took the next available plane back to him.

I never read newspapers, so I was unaware that the Los Angeles papers had been full of an altercation that occurred when Kirk

Douglas had returned home unexpectedly and found Sydney in bed with his wife. On our way home from the airport, Sydney explained apologetically that he couldn't remember exactly how it had happened. He had just been playing tennis with Mrs. Douglas and one thing had led to another. I knew how attractive he was to women, and now that I had gotten my mind around not judging or condemning, I was swift to forgive and explain his actions to myself as coming out of his fear of being alone, and his need to be reassured about his worth as a man. It didn't seem to have anything to do with *us*. Anyway, I was sure it was Mrs. Douglas who had initiated it!

I threw my newly-devoted heart and soul wide open to him, eagerly explained my revelation about unconditional love, wanted to constantly touch him and admire him — and he proceeded to walk all over me with football cleats.

Sydney was living with the tennis pro at the Beverly Hills Tennis Club at the time, so I stayed with Mother. Phil had gone back to New York to work on a new Broadway show, *Top Banana*, and Mother was delighted to have my company. Oddly, she was the only one I ever knew who did not fall under Sydney's spell, and took a dislike to him. Alas, my Texas farm girl mother was more foresighted than I. Soon, Sydney seemed to be out a lot when I called him, was too busy to see me every night, and seemed distant and preoccupied when we were together. After I had been back a few weeks — he stood me up — and didn't call to explain. When I called to ask for an explanation, I overheard him tell his tennis pro roommate to say he wasn't in. *Kaboom*! I don't think a sledgehammer to the heart could have hurt me as much. As Sydney had not again mentioned his proposal of marriage or our having a baby together, neither had I. Nonetheless, his having said so hung between us like a full water balloon and presumably its weight was too heavy for Sydney. Knowing him as I did, I could understand it. What I could not understand was the way he did it. Actually, while I loved reading his proposal that we start a family together, it had never seemed real to me and I had not taken it seriously, preferring to live for the magic moment. But nothing is more painful, or more cowardly, in a relationship than for one partner to withdraw without explanation. An ending of something important deserves resolution, whether it is an argument or an affair. The end of a love affair that has a value should be honored with a dignified and defined burial. Kindness, above all, I would say. Preferably over a candlelit dinner of wine and remembrance. Otherwise, it leaves a sickening residual of questions like indigestible food. Fear of explanatory confrontation is such a spineless cop-out.

I heard later that Sydney told friends the reason for our breakup was that I wanted us to get married, but that wasn't true. I was not masochistic enough to marry him, even if he had not scared himself into withdrawal with his by-mail proposal. I knew very well that because of his appeal to women and fear of responsibility, he would break my heart every day of the week and twice on Sunday, if I made such a commitment as marriage. Now, however, having made a commitment to loving him just as he was, I found it had become a fact and I couldn't just turn it off. Once having learned the joy of fully loving, of daring to be defenseless, the adrenaline rush that gave me was as strong as Phil's addiction to gambling. But Sydney didn't want unconditional love, he wanted tough love. He had been attracted to an arrogant woman who told him what to do and snapped the whip, if he didn't jump fast enough, not an adoring wimp who said, "Hit me again, I don't mind because I love you." I was so intent on practicing unconditional love, that I forgot my father's most important axiom: "To thine own self be true." Being non-judgmental in any relationship is all well and good, but that doesn't mean that you should allow anyone to treat you unkindly or without respect. When I was much older I came to know that it all boils down to *self*-respect. First to *know* "thine own self," and then to respect that self by following its dictates and protecting it from abuse. When I went against what my inner self told me — was expedient rather than righteous — then I was no longer grounded and I lost my self respect and my way. And my guy, too.

As it was, I had tears in my eyes for a very long time, and tried to dry them with several affairs. Until one morning I woke up with a hangover and the voice of my mother saying clearly in my ear, "Josie, *think* what you're doing." Thinking, suddenly I felt like I had deliberately jumped into a tar pit and had come out all slimy and blackened, knowing I had betrayed every code of ethics I held dear. Realizing that meaningless sex is degrading and worse than no sex at all, I firmly resolved I would never have sex with someone I didn't care deeply about ever again, and I felt better. For long after, however, I had a small pang of loss whenever anyone mentioned Sydney or I saw "Sydney" written with a "y" somewhere. I had worn *Soft Shoulders* cologne because he said it suited me, and I continued to wear it for that reason for decades, like the remembered scent of a blessing. But I never laughed loud like a happy child anymore.

A Very Unusual Man

I had always been so fortunate to live in places with a view. For a time in the early 1950s, I lived in a house literally perched on a ridge-top in fabled Laurel Canyon, at the very top of aptly named Wonderland Avenue. It sat in the fork between two dirt roads, with sweeping views over Hollywood's twinkling lights and on to the sea, the air scented with eucalyptus and crickets cheering through the night. I loved it, and Russ moved in after we were first married. The Canyon became a nurturing counterpoint to my busy life in town.

The years following my divorce from Phil were tremendously exciting ones. Apart from the life-changing and body-rousing experience of Howie and Sydney, my life was buoyed high with the enchantment I felt with the Kelly's and other friends. I became more and more exhilarated with the feeling of being an active part of a crusade for justice!

The 50s were a tumultuous and dramatic time for civil rights, with marches, demonstrations, and a marvelous sense of comradeship. Almost all the people I liked were heavily involved in *our* fight against the House Un-American Activities Committee and all the rest of the bigoted bad guys.

When I told Norman Corwin, the premier writer, director, and producer of radio theater at the time, how much I admired *On a Note of Triumph,* his brilliant dramatic summation of World War II, he invited me to come by his 'open house" any Sunday afternoon. Norman was the most erudite, stimulating, and kindly man I ever knew. On his weekly dramatic radio show, his inspiring thoughts about humanity and the human spirit brought a new dimension to my social consciousness. At his home I met writers, philosophers, and people of like-mind with Corwin, and sat at their feet in awed admiration as they opened my mind to new thoughts and ideas.

Another even more radical group I became a part of was centered around Y. P. "Yip" Harburg, that delightful pixie and writer of sparkling lyrics for songs like "Somewhere over the Rainbow" and "April in Paris." A song he wrote during the Depression, "Brother, Can You Spare a Dime," summed up the period. Yip was a magnet for those in Hollywood who were passionately dedicating their lives to political and cultural change, and I was thrilled when *his* group scooped me up and made me one of their own. It amused them perhaps to incorporate a Miss America into their coterie of activists. Caught up in this cauldron of high ideals and the "Man-the-Barricades!" mentality, I was imbued with the excitement of righting wrongs and changing the world. *I believed we could do it!* It gave my life a forceful purpose, a sense of being a part of something important that I had never felt before. And to help ease the pain of heartbreak over Sydney, my ever-watchful guardian angel sent me an unusual fairy godfather.

One of the men I dated at that time was Jerry Orbach, the wealthy department store chain heir, and one night he invited me to a dinner party at his house where I was seated next to his honored guest, Matthew Fox. Mr. Fox was a short, rotund, slightly balding black-haired man, with large, brown eyes, who was, I'd been told, a bigwig New York financier and a "boy genius" in the motion picture business. He didn't look like a "boy," but I assumed that all the people at the table were deferential toward him because of the "genius" part. He didn't dress like a movie mogul either, his beautifully tailored dark charcoal suit, white-white shirt with a charcoal tie made him look more the New York financier than a studio head. Though he had a soft, pleasant speaking voice, he used it very little and I put him down as a stuffed shirt. During dinner, Jerry said jokingly, "Be careful with Jo-Carroll, Matty. She is a very unusual girl. I offered her the Newark branch and she wouldn't take it."

It was true that one night when Jerry came to take me out to dinner, he presented me with a large box containing a beautiful mink coat. The expected price for the mink coat was clear to me, of course, and I firmly refused it, saying haughtily, "I don't take presents from men!" (I never wore my own gorgeous mink coat because my new friends had taught me that wearing animal skins was sinful!) As Jerry was a very handsome, very eligible bachelor, I was rather smug about my ability without a second thought to turn down such an expensive gift and the relationship it implied. I was self-sufficient, again, and proud of it! At that time in my life I developed a system that I rigorously enforced: if I were inclined to kiss a man, I was ready to go to bed with him. If I didn't want to kiss him, then there were no bedroom activities in our future and he could take it or leave it. And I very rarely met a man I wanted to kiss. In trying to rectify the rotten way I felt about myself because of my tawdry getting-over-Sydney-affairs, this retention of control and morals was the security blanket that kept me feeling right about myself. With some of the men I went out with, I think it became a kind of game to see if they could break down my resolve about a smooch or two, but I remained adamant. In a way, my five years of marriage to Phil had given me a time out to recover from the upheaval in my life caused by winning the Miss America Pageant and the strangeness of being a Hollywood "starlet." It allowed me to grow up a little and rediscover my sense of self. A new self, no question, but mine own.

Anyway, Matthew Fox called me from New York a few days later and asked me to go to dinner with him the next time he was in California.

Astonished, I said, "How did you get my unlisted number?"

He said, "I didn't want to ask Jerry; so I called around until I found that Adolph Green was a friend of yours and I got George Abbott (that irascible all-powerful Broadway director) to get me his number, and Adolph gave me your number."

I was to learn that Matthew Fox was a very determined person and an expert at finding ways to put things together.

I said, "Well, listen, I hope you understand when I say that I am in a period of my life where I don't want to go out very much. But I am moving back to New York soon and if I change my mind, I'll call you."

He said, "When you come to New York I will know it and I will call *you*." And thus began one of the most magical relationships of my life.

I had returned to California to see Sydney and Mother; now it was time to go back to my beloved New York and pick up as a struggling-to-pay-the-rent actress. Until I could find a place of my own, I asked my friend Dellie if I could stay with her. Dellie was the actress Joan Lorring, who had been nominated for an Academy Award as best supporting actress in *The Corn is Green*, a good and loyal friend. She had told me that she was "going with" someone now, but I was in no way prepared for the date who came to pick her up on my first night at Dellie's apartment on 52nd Street and Lexington. He was without question the most gorgeous man I had ever seen — and his name was Harry Belafonte! He was singing at the *Blue Angel*, the most "in" nightclub in New York at the time, and his startling talent and good looks had bowled over even the most sophisticated New York. My best friend, Anita Ellis, the splendid jazz singer, was also appearing at the *Blue Angel,* and I was instantaneously caught up in the exciting life of what was to me this best of all possible worlds: the world of New York Show Business. To me, "roll 'em" had nowhere near the impact of "curtain up."

There had been an explosion of talent in the New York theater during the 40s and 50s. A Golden Era on Broadway never seen before or since, it was as though handfuls of stardust had been scattered over New York and fell on an unusually large number of people. Top-of-the-marquee names like Rodgers and Hammerstein, Cole Porter, the Gershwins, Betty and Adolph, Lerner and Lowe, Ethel Merman, Mary Martin, Patricia Morrison, Julie Andrews, John Raitt, Alfred Drake, Rex Harrison, Leonard Bernstein, Jerome Robbins, Agnes de Mille made musicals that will live forever. Tennesee Williams, Arthur Miller, Laurette Taylor, Marlon Brando, Jessica Tandy, George C. Scott, and others brought dramatic theater to forever unequaled heights.

I lived with the giddy feeling of being a part of this special clan of talented people. It was a feeling that was both comforting and electrifying. It seemed always to be "party time." Leonard Bernstein loved to give parties and play piano at them; Andre Previn would play piano at anybody's party, as George Gershwin did before him. In my memory, there was constant music and singing and laughter at a party going on somewhere at someone's apartment — and I was invited to sing along. In many ways it was a closed society, with creative talent being the membership fee (I was included by osmosis.) Oh, sometimes, someone from another clan would come to a party — but they were just guests, they didn't really belong.

True to his word, Matthew Fox learned that I was in New York. Somehow he got Dellie's number and called to ask me out for dinner. From what I'd heard of Mr. Fox, I naturally put him in the category of monster movie moguls, like Zanuck and Cohn, possibly combined with J.P. Morgan. The kind of men to be avoided at all costs. His ingenuity amused me, however, so I agreed; but when he suggested The Pavillion, the most expensive restaurant in town at the time, I said, "Just pick me up and I'll take you to *my* favorite place." I wanted him to know right away that I thought snazzy places like The Pavillon were boring, so I took him to a tiny Italian restaurant in Greenwich

Village tucked away in an alley. We sat in a booth with a checkered tablecloth and ate spaghetti with clam sauce with homemade crusty bread and drank Frascatti red wine. To my surprise, he loved it. Matthew Fox was full of surprises.

Throughout my life in a time of need my guardian angel had redirected my "downs" to "ups" in various ways. When I was seven she sent me a horse to heal my broken heart; when I was 16 and seriously depressed, she sent me a dog to cheer me up; at 17 she sent me Blackie to get me finally off the medicine show; Sydney for a lot of reasons; now at 27 and at a crossroads, she sent me Matthew Fox.

Growing up in Racine, Wisconsin, Matthew was a *wunderkind* in school, at age nine was working as an usher at the local movie theater, and by the time he was in his early 20s he had made a fortune setting up various deals in the motion picture business. From his office in New York, he was a prime mover in the embryonic television industry, a prescient movies-to-TV businessman who bought the RKO inventory and invented pay TV; and in Los Angeles, he was called a genius for the fantastic deals he put together to create the new Universal-International Studio from the old Universal and Republic Studios, and the way he reorganized the languishing United Artists Studio, formed by Charlie Chaplin, Douglas Fairbanks, Mary Pickford and D.W. Griffith in 1919, into a new organization altogether. Under its new management, United Artists quickly became the most financially and artistically successful studio in Hollywood.

All of this "genius" stuff I learned from others. What I learned from Matty that first night was how as a child he had loved skating on frozen Wisconsin lakes and cross-country skiing in the winter, and how he remembered the smell and beauty of the Wisconsin forests in the summer. And then he told me an amazing story. During World War II, he had quickly moved from being a private in the Army to a major assigned to General Eisenhower as his public relations officer. (I could just imagine how Matty's abilities to wheel and deal had come in handy for Eisenhower!) He had met many top dignitaries, both in the military and diplomatic corps, and among them was General Sukarno of Indonesia.

Two days after the surrender of Japan to the United States in August of 1945, Sukarno had declared Indonesian independence from the three-century rule of Dutch colonialism. The Dutch East India Company had profited from its rule and exploitation of this island nation, as the British East India Company had done in India; but now world events had emboldened the Indonesian people to start a fight to get their country back. Shortly after Matty was out of uniform and back in his New York office, a representative of Sukarno came to him with an interesting proposition. The fledgling Indonesian Independence Movement was running out of money; and Sukarno, having found Matty a sympathetic (and rich) person, was asking him for a few million dollars to finance their continuing struggle for justice and liberty for all. In return, they would sign a contract giving him *the export/import rights of the country* (which the Dutch had been enjoying for 350 years) after they had won their independence.

In astonishment, I said, "The *export/import* rights for the whole country? Good night! And did you do it? Did you give them the money?"

In his calm, soft voice, Matty said, "Oh, yes. I thought it was a good investment. And, anyway, they were desperate. The Dutch had been so brutal with them."

I was in shock. This *money man* was one of *us*. My friends and I talked a great deal about the need for independence and freedom, be it for countries or people, and loudly sang, "We Shall Overcome" at any opportunity. But here this man sitting before me had actually *done* something to help the oppressed overcome the oppressor! Since Matty was 34 now, he must have been in his late 20s when he did all that. How surprising and how delightful.

I knew that the Indonesians had won their independence the year before, and I said, "So, now do you own all the exports and imports in Indonesia?"

Without inflection, he said, "Well, no. I went there after they won their independence, and they seemed like such nice people, and badly in need of money to get their country back on its feet after such a devastating war. So I signed the rights back to the government."

"You gave it back?"

"Yes. I am not really interested in being in the export/import business, and besides, I didn't need the money and they did."

I was flabbergasted!

As Matty continued this astonishing story, my imagination took me out of the booth in Greenwich Village into an Indonesian jungle with groups of small, dark men in camouflage uniforms, black thumb marks under their eyes, a machine gun in one hand and a grenade in the other, creeping courageously forward to annihilate hordes of huge, blonde Dutchmen. In his immaculate business suit, Matty was a shadowy figure in the background surreptitiously handing million-dollar-bills to their leader. It seemed both espionage and guerilla warfare at its finest.

Matty said he never told this story as there was some kind of international law against what he had done. The Dutch government had officially complained to Truman about his financial support of Indonesia, as the *Truman Doctrine* forbid that kind of thing. However, Truman, evidently judging the country's feelings at this time about colonialism, had decided to do nothing about it. I must admit, I felt flattered that Matty would trust me about his international doings. And somehow I found myself telling him things in my own life I never talked about with anyone: my early childhood, my father's abandonment, and Dr. Tatc's attempted rape. Even about the death of my horse and my dogs and what it had meant to me.

Like a born-again person, when I left the medicine show at 17 and got on that train for Tyler, I shed my previous life like a serpent's skin. There were no memories I wanted to take with me; so, along with my tap shoes and stage costumes, I left them all behind and rarely even thought about the past. Other than singing old songs from the medicine show around the piano at the Kelly's, I never talked to anyone about anything that happened to me before I moved to Tyler. Not even Blackie, Phil or Sydney knew the details I was telling Matty. But he had shared his private persona so openly with me, had such understanding brown eyes, and was such an attentive listener, that for some inexplicable reason I poured out all those hidden memories in a torrent of self-exposure. It was such a relief to air out those painful memories to Matty, who quietly seemed to absorb them with real empathy.

I was curious to see if Matty would make "advances" to me on the way home, but he did not. At my door, he formally took my hand and said, "This evening is the best time I've had in a very long time. Thank you for it," and got in the cab. I was impressed.

Matty's gentlemanly behavior impressed me particularly because strange things had been happening to me in the "advances" regard of late. Aside from the almost daily grind of finding jobs in television or radio in order to support my mother and myself, I had an interesting social life in New York — often by myself. Things like going alone to parties or the *Blue Angel* if someone I knew was appearing there were commonplace to me, whereas I would never have gone to a nightclub alone in LA. New York was my *home* in a way that no other city ever was, and I felt completely safe and personally secure going anywhere alone.

Male companionship was available when I wanted it, I hasten to say, but back in New York as a single girl, some of my experiences were strange and unpleasant. For example, one day on the street I ran into Richard Rodgers. Through Phil, I had known him slightly for many years, but was surprised and honored when this musical giant of the theater recognized me and asked me to have a drink with him. He suggested we go somewhere near where I lived. Since he knew Adolph was still in Hollywood and had loaned me his apartment way over on 1ˢᵗ Avenue and 57th, I got the impression he would just as soon nobody he knew saw us together. I took Mr. Rodgers (as he would always be to me) to my favorite bar right around the corner from where I was staying, which had a dark, intimate Polynesian décor with recorded rain storm sounds playing intermittently. I always enjoyed that. We had a few drinks and then Mr. Rodgers suggested we have dinner at a Chinese restaurant next door. At dinner, I sobered up a bit and let myself realize that he was going to suggest something else for after dinner. Why else would one of the most important men in town, this stratospheric talent whose music was more often played than any other composer in the world, including Mozart and Beethoven, be behaving in this way?

Not wanting him to have false impressions, I said, "Listen, Mr. Rodgers, I don't want to be presumptuous, but I want to say up-front that if you have any bedroom activities in mind with me you'd best forget it, because it's not going to happen."

Needless to say, he was startled by my bluntness, but manfully admitted that bedroom activities were exactly what he had in mind.

Honestly wanting to understand, I said, "Why would you want to sleep with me when you have such a lovely wife at home?"

And he said, equally honestly, "If I see a beautiful woman and don't want to sleep with her, then I won't be able to write beautiful music anymore."

A stunner! In order to write the gorgeous love songs like "If I Loved You," from *Carousel*, "People Will Say We're in Love," from *Oklahoma*, "Some Enchanted Evening," from *South Pacific*, and on and on, this mega-talented man had to want to have sex with every pretty girl he saw? *That's* where his inspiration came from? Astounding. But at least we understood each other and could part amicably.

(Rodgers wrote music with other lyricists and for more than musicals — when he died, statistics showed that his was the most played music in the world. I wonder how many beautiful women were involved in all that beautiful music, and what the Me, Too movement would have done about it.)

Harvey Orkin, on the other hand, a comedy writer for Sid Caesar, Woody Allen, and others, whom I had also known for a long time, was *not* married and often available for movies or nightclubs. It took me awhile to convince him that I was serious about my "hands off" decision, but he finally accepted my rules with humor and we had fun together. Comedy writers were much like comedians, in that they are naturally funny and most of them have the need to be funny all the time. That was fine with me. I liked to laugh all the time. Harvey had an improvisational sense of humor that could be almost manically funny.

What was not at all funny, however, was an encounter I had similar to that with Richard Rodgers. I had never thought of Oscar Levant as highly as everyone else did. Or as highly as he thought of himself, for that matter. I agreed that he was a brilliant musician, but his famous sarcastic wit never appealed to me. Betty and Adolph thought so much of him they wrote parts for him in *American in Paris* and *Band Wagon*, but I always thought he was miscast. Well, one day Oscar called me at Adolph's to say that he was in New York for a few days to do a concert at Carnegie Hall, and could we have dinner. I was surprised because while I was friendly with his wife, I don't think I had ever said more than hello and goodbye to Oscar. I was even more surprised when, after a kind of awkward dinner, he took me back to Adolph's apartment, asked to come in for a minute, and abruptly tried to take my clothes off. Non-athletic, hypochondriac Oscar was certainly no match for me when it came to arm wrestling, and my repulse nearly dislocated his shoulder. In a fury, I said, "What in the world is the matter with you, Oscar?"

Equally furious, he snarled, carefully cradling his elbow, "Well, why do you treat me like you're a Sunday School teacher and everyone else like you're a hooker?" and he stormed out.

"A hooker!" I was at a total loss to explain both his attack and his accusation.

A pattern began to develop when Harvey Orkin called to ask me if I would like to have dinner with him and S. J. Perelman. *S. J. Perelman?* Boy, I'll say! He was one of my favorite writers and was noted as being a first-class intellectual, so I was eager indeed to meet him. Perelman, a rather small man with large glasses, was quiet during dinner, and I was disappointed that Harvey did most of the talking in his rapid-fire comedic way. It was greatly flattering when Perelman asked if he could see me home, and then asked if he could come in for a nightcap. I so enjoyed the kind of philosophical talk I used to have at Norman Corwin's and other intellectuals, so I was eager to listen to what this great mind had to say without Harvey's monologues. Once we were settled on the couch with our drinks, I began to ask him all kinds of questions concerning the meaning of life — about which he professed to know very little. Then he made clear sexual advances to me, about which he *also* seemed to know very little, saying, "Let's not talk, let's make love."

Nonplussed, I said, "You are always writing about how close you and your wife are. Why would you come on to me?"

He said rather hesitantly, "Oh, one thing has nothing to do with the other."

Drawing myself up very tall, I said, "I am very particular about whom I sleep with, but even if I wanted to sleep with you, you would have to *talk* to me first!"

Abashed, he stood up, bade me good night, and left.

I couldn't get over it. I always thought Oscar Levant was a dolt, but for S. J. Perelman I'd had great respect, and I was extremely disappointed in him. In all my years in Hollywood, I had never had to fight for my honor before, and now it was two in a row. And anyway, they had both been so *inept* about it. Richard Rodgers was at least smooth.

It turned out Perelman was a gent, however, because early the next morning I was awakened by the doorbell. Standing in the hall was Perelman. He kind of bowed and handed me a wrapped package, saying, "Since I am not really what you expected, I brought you someone I think is. And I am very glad to have met you."

The package contained Thoreau's *Walden.* On the flyleaf Perelman had written, "For lovely Jo-Carroll, here is an author who knew a lot about the meaning of life. From a friend who does not. Sid."

Walden had long been one of my favorite books, and I was touched that S.J. Perelman understood that and had brought the book as a kind of apology. Although his behavior remained a puzzle to me. That puzzle was explained to me a short time later by my friend, Anita Ellis. Over drinks one day she said, "That crazy Harvey Orkin is telling everyone that you are a nymphomaniac."

"A *nymphomaniac?* Good Night! He knows how I am about sex. Why would he do such a thing?"

She replied, "Oh, you know how Harvey is. He loves to play practical jokes."

That shattered a little chunk of my faith in mankind. I'd thought Harvey was my friend, and this wasn't funny, even as a practical joke. It was depressing, really, that he would do such an embarrassing thing, both to me and to these two sexually insecure men. I could imagine him telling other comedy writers about the funny trick he had pulled on the three of us. I could hear him saying, "Can't you just see those schmucks thrusting their hot little bodies so eagerly against "The Ice Woman Who Cometh Not?" Everyone laughing. I wondered if there had been a little revenge involved for my rejecting his own attempts at seduction, but I never spoke to him again so I never knew.

I guess it was naïve of me to be surprised that married men like Rodgers, Levant, and Perelman were out looking for an easy lay. When that Justice of the Peace read Phil and me our marriage vows, we were both too numb to really hear them, but I had seen enough wedding scenes in movies to know the vows by heart. Admittedly, the "Til death do us part" might have seemed a little extreme, but the "Forsaking all others" part was a clear commitment to me and I took it very seriously while I was married to Phil. And I was confident that Phil did, too. I understood that toads like the movie moguls in Hollywood seemed to feel they had the right and obligation to have sex with every female under contract to them (if she was pretty), but I had thought *respectable* men took their marriage vows as seriously as I did. Apparently not.

My confusion about "right and wrong" between genders was deepened sometimes by my work in live television. NBC's *Matinee Theater* was a 5-days-a-week daytime dramatic show that I worked on occasionally, and in one play I had a love scene with a young actor that wasn't going very well in dress rehearsal. During the live show, I was horrified when as he kissed me he forced his tongue in my mouth! Since this was live television I had to take it and try not to either throw up or bite his tongue off. This was only the second time in my life that a man had put his tongue in my mouth and both were men I hardly knew. "French kissing" seemed much more intimate to me than intercourse and I was insulted that this stupid actor would take such a liberty. After the show, I turned on him furiously and said, "What was *that* all about in the kissing scene?"

Sheepishly, he said, "Well, the director told me to do it. He said you needed something to stir you up in the scene."

I was shocked at the director. What had he said, "That girl is such a cold fish you need to do something to hot her up?" Or something else equally degrading? Also, it hurt my feelings that the director thought I couldn't play a love scene effectively.

My feelings were greatly different, however, when I got the part to play the lead in a documentary the New York Racing Association was making. Racing had been getting a bad rap recently because of syndicate gambling and they wanted to do a film that would show how fair, square, and above board racing really was. I was to play a girl who inherited a racing stable, without knowing anything about it, hence she needed to be shown every aspect of the racing world. The locations were the tracks at Saratoga and Belmont, and the fabulous stables of Calumet in Kentucky. Glorious locales, all. Plus, the producers bought me an expensive new wardrobe for the various scenes. But the movie was about — basically — *gambling*, and I wasn't sure I should be a part of it. I overcame my scruples, though, because it paid good money and would go a long way toward insuring Mother's monthly check and my own expenses for a bit. Mother's house was paid for, and I was living rent-free at Adolph's. Mother and I were relatively frugal with living expenses, but even so I was in a constant search for income and this was the biggest check I'd gotten in a long time. But my *feeling* was that the project was against my principles. I decided to express my disapproval by doing the scenes to the best of my ability, but privately to remain aloof from the racing scene. My principles were immediately tested on the first day when I was introduced to Alfred Vanderbilt, who was the first one to show the heiress around. Clearly, his racing stable was his biggest interest in life, and he was surprisingly easygoing and unpretentious for a scion of such immense wealth and prestige, but I remained cool and distant with him to prove my point. I wished I could tell him how much I disapproved of gambling, but it never seemed quite the right time. The acting part was easy enough, all it required was to look interested, smile, or jump up and down with excitement when her horse won. I had to admit meeting the extraordinary men who were well-known trainers and the famous jockeys was fun. Of the jockeys, mischievous, black-eyed Eddie Arcaro, who was just back from a suspension for dirty tricks on the track, and polite, quiet Bill Shoemaker were the most interesting. Talking with them made it seem impossible that these child-sized men could control and manipulate those tons of charging muscles in the chaos and tempest of a horse race several times a day. But, of course, my main attraction was the horses. Just to watch them getting a bath or walking around on an exercise lead was like seeing poetry in motion. Sometimes a trainer would let me actually pet one of the horses in its stall, and now and then, one of the horses was willing to let me put my face alongside his for a moment. It did my soul good to be in close physical contact with a horse.

On the second day of shooting at the race track in truly beautiful old historic Saratoga, between takes I was sitting on the ground under an ancient black oak reading, when a slender, freckle-faced, red-haired man leaned over me and said, "Tell me, Miss, what are you so interested in reading?"

I held the book up to show him the title, as I was a little unsure how to pronounce the author's name. The "Gide" pronunciation was a bit tricky, and I very much needed to appear cool and intellectual.

Incredulously, he straightened up and said, "*Gide?* (He had no trouble pronouncing it correctly) A pretty girl is sitting here on the grounds of the Saratoga race track reading the *Autobiography of Andre Gide?* Well, I never."

His name was James Roach, a sports writer for the *New York Times*. He sat down on the ground beside me and within minutes we became fast friends. For a big city sports writer, he was nothing like I would have imagined. Warm, unsophisticated, guileless, Jim was a home-town boy personified. In his 30s, he was boyish and unaffected and seemed to be delighted to make my acquaintance. I learned the extent of that delight when he invited me to go with him into the press box. The other sports writers instantly vehemently attacked him jokingly for bringing a female into the sacrosanct press box, a thing never before done in the annals of press boxes, they claimed. But they were a charming, hilarious, tough bunch of well-known sports writers and I was amused and flattered to be with them. The only one missing was Red Smith, the most famous sports writer of his day. Jim Palmer of the *New York Daily News* told me that it often took Red most of the day to survive his hangover and he would most likely show up soon. He told me a Red Smith story that I laugh about to this day. It seemed that one morning when Red staggered into the press box late, one of the other writers said in dismay, "Red, you look terrible. Look at your eyes."

Red said mournfully, "You should see them from *this* side!"

There was a lot of laughter in the press box, and I could see how Blackie would fit right in with those other sports writers in a Texas press box somewhere. However, now was now, and Roach was a lovely man who in a friendly way became my constant companion both in Saratoga and Belmont. Another man I became friends with was Max Hirsh, perhaps the best-known trainer of the period, who played my trainer in the documentary. He was the opposite of Jim: dour, uncommunicative, humorless, but somehow he took a liking to me and appeared interested in enlightening me into the mysteries of training a young horse to win races. I never watched the races if I could help it. I didn't like to see the jockeys use their whips, and I was terrified I would see one of the horses fall. It didn't seem right to me to run them so hard with their thin sticks for legs holding up those hundreds of pounds of flailing muscle. One day Max sought me out and surreptitiously pressed a $20 dollar bill into my hand, as he said, "Put this to win on *Doughboy*; he's a 2-year-old I'm running for his maiden race. He's a long-shot but I think he'll do good."

He was asking me to *gamble*. I was in a tizzy of indecision. I had never placed a bet in my life. Even when I had gone to the track with Phil, I never made any bets for money. I did pretty good picking winners just by looking at the horses in the paddock or when they first came on the track, but I picked one just by intuition and it gave me a horse to root for. I felt very smug when *my* horse won and Phil's didn't. But now I had to "put my money where my mouth is," as the saying goes, and it really hurt me to have to put that whole $20 on *Doughboy* to win. Of course, Max knew what he was talking about, *Doughboy* won, and I had won almost $300. I felt it was ill-gotten gains so to ease my conscience, I sent it to Mother to buy a new used car, as her old one was giving out. I was touched that Max liked me enough to give me that tip and dared to give him a big hug when we said goodbye at Belmont.

It was not goodbye for me and Jim, as we continued to see one another back in New York, and one night he almost brought me to tears by proposing to me on bent knee. That sweet, gentlemanly, gentle man didn't have a clue who I was, or what married life would be like with me, so I refused him as warmly as possible and gave him my first kiss on his cheek. Like Matty, we had never even held hands, and I honestly couldn't imagine why he would want to marry me. I thought we had nothing in common, really, and I wondered why he thought we did. Jim and I never dated again, but we always kept in touch and in the years to come he married a lovely, red-haired woman. They had several red-haired daughters, and he became the editor of the prestigious *New York Times* Sports Department. Bless his heart.

After these various brief encounters, I began to appreciate Matty all the more — although I could never quite believe his story about Indonesia. I mean, to *finance* an insurrection in your 20s in return for the *export/import rights* to a whole country, and then give the rights *back* seemed almost incredible. Incredible, that is, until one day Matty asked me to go to a luncheon given by some friends of his out on Long Island.

Now, if there was anything that bored me to tears, it was a Sunday afternoon outdoor luncheon with a big bunch of Long Island types floating around. So I said no.

Matty said, "Do come. I promise we will arrive late and leave early. I have to go and I would really appreciate it if you would come with me."

Well, it turned out to be an Indonesian Embassy affair to *honor* Matty! It was a *Great Gatsby* kind of party, as I had suspected, where there was an expansive bar and a buffet set up under a tent on the lawn that swept down to the ocean. Hordes of well-dressed people were already scattered around the tent, many of them in exotic Indonesian attire, which resembled Indian saris for the women and long Nehru jackets and caps for the men. Matty was greeted effusively upon arrival by several of the Nehru-type men, as he explained that he was sorry to be late, but we had been unavoidably detained. They pressed glasses of champagne on us, and said they had just been waiting for him to arrive for their ceremony to begin. A stand with a microphone was set up near the tent, and one of the very elegant Indonesian men who had greeted us stepped up, called for attention, and introduced himself as the Prime Minister of Indonesia. Everyone clustered around the stand as he made a long speech about what freedom meant to his country, and then he announced that this gathering was to honor the man who had made that freedom possible, and to present him with a token of his country's appreciation — their friend and benefactor, Mr. Matthew Fox.

Amid much applause and "Bravos," the Minister handed Matty a stunning sculpture representing Indonesia, with a plaque saying, "To Mathew Fox — the man who made our country possible." As an acceptance speech, Matty said, "Thank you."

Afterwards, the Minister came up to us and told me in more detail about just what Matty had meant to Indonesia. Matty shifted from foot to foot during this elegy, and told the Minister that we had to go. On the way home, I was unusually speechless at the enormity of it all. Even now it hardly seemed real.

I wasn't speechless, though, when Matty asked me to marry him. Now, mind you, Matty had not so much as tried to hold my hand all the time we had been seeing each other. I had told him that first evening at dinner about my feelings concerning love and sex, and he had respected those feelings. Now, however, he was asking to put our relationship on a whole different level. I admired Matty, particularly after learning that the Indonesian affair was all true, but I had never thought of him as a lover or in any kind of permanent relationship.

The proposals of marriage I had received in my life had been rather odd. Blackie's proposal had been an assumption, not "Will you...?" but, rather "When we..." Phil's had been made jokingly; Sydney insincerely; and my two real like-in-the-movies proposals of marriage had been made by men I had never even kissed. That ought to explain something about me, but I couldn't figure out what.

I couldn't imagine my life being forever intertwined with Matty's, for one reason because I wasn't interested in what he did for a living, plus I didn't feel we had the same values. He had taken me to dinner once at the Hotel Pierre with a banker friend and his wife from Baltimore. Evidently the two men were in the midst of some big business deal, which I didn't understand and didn't want to. The wife didn't say much to me; she just sat there counting her diamonds and eyeing me suspiciously as though I might be a call girl, while the two men talked. I could barely keep from putting my head down on the table and taking a nap. Afterwards, I told Matty how bored I was by such talk and such people, and he promised not to subject me to it again. He cajoled me once into going to The Pavillon for dinner. It was his favorite restaurant, and they kept a table there for him. I had gotten even by ordering hamburger instead of Boeuf Bourguignon or Coquelets sur Canapés. True, it was called chopped sirloin, but it was hamburger just the same, and represented my not-so-subtle-protest against this pretentious place. So, mostly, we ate alone at small Village restaurants or at Matty's apartment. His apartment was as surreal as his involvement with Indonesia.

It was a multi-storied building standing on the southeast corner at 415 Park Avenue. Matty had financed its construction, with the provision that the top penthouse floor be built to his specifications, and rent-free to him in perpetuity. A private elevator went up to the top floor, and the foyer opened into the most perfect place to live I have ever seen in New York. A lot of people I knew had expensive, sumptuous apartments and town houses with magnificent views, but Matty's apartment was one of a kind. It seemed to float like a spaceship in the air, all self-contained and disconnected from other real estate. There were solid windows on two sides overlooking his garden-like terrace, with all of Manhattan forming a backdrop. The living room, dining room, and Matty's study (which were all I ever saw of the apartment) all had this great view and were both elegant and simple. The colors of the rooms were muted earth tones, given warmth and brilliance by exotic sculptural lamps and exquisite Chinese blue and white vases always filled with fresh flowers. The living room had a grand piano and different seating areas scattered here and there, but the main focus was a grouping of big soft chairs and a couch facing the prominent view and a huge fireplace. Over the fireplace was a gorgeous almost life-size portrait of Patricia Morrison in a costume as the leading lady in *The King and I,* a part she had originated. Matty never talked about her, but obviously he had loved her very much at one time. She was a big Broadway star and a classical beauty, and I was very curious about their relationship. But Matty never talked about his business or his previous relationships, so I just had to wonder.

It's hard to remember now what we *did* talk about. Matty loved
music, especially classical music, so I know we sat and listened to his
records a lot. Matty liked to read and loved the theater, so I know
we talked about books and the theater; and for a financier, he had
surprisingly liberal views about politics. Although he was very anti-
communism. But Matty and I didn't talk about politics much; mostly I
think we talked about me. Matty had an excellent cook, and over dinner served by a man servant, or sitting in front of the wood fire and
the fairyland view of New York lights, I told him about times in my
life that I had almost succeeded in forgetting. Like being ostracized by
the PTA in Hale Center for something I didn't do; refusing to accept
Senator Mayfield's offer of making me an oil-rich woman if I didn't
marry Phil; and turning down a contract at Metro after I won Miss
East Texas because I didn't want to be on the stage any more. And
about only accepting a contract at 20th because my mother would
have to go back to shoveling ice for snow cones if I didn't. Even my
close friends never seemed to really believe that I didn't care about
money or fame, but Matty did. From what he said, I could see that he
actually understood me and why I was the way I was, even after I told
him some shameful things I had done that I had never told another
living soul. I had yearned always for someone who would and could
show such understanding, and here this man, whose past life was as
totally different from mine as could possibly be, and who wasn't even
a member of my "clan," who *did* understand the good and the bad
about me. He applauded the good and comforted me about the bad.

The night that Matty asked me to marry him was like a sudden
shot in the dark. We had never even *touched* one another. I thought
of him as a special friend but certainly not a husband. I said, "Oh,
Matty, I don't think that would work out. We want such different
things out of life."

Matty said softly, "How do you know what I want out of life?
I think we want the same thing: we want to be happy. I am happy
with what I do because I am good at it, but I could be happy doing
many other things. The main thing I want to do is make *you* happy.
You say you want to travel, well, I like to travel, too, and I would wind
up my work tomorrow and take you traveling all over the world if
that is what you want. It wouldn't cause me a moment's concern to
change my life anyway you wanted. We could do anything you like,

live anywhere you like, it wouldn't matter to me. It wouldn't matter at all because I love you."

Feeling a frantic need to explain properly, I said, "But that is the whole thing. I like you a lot, but I don't *love* you. You know how much I loved Sydney, and how much I loved loving him. Even though that didn't turn out so well, I am determined to wait until I feel that way again to get married. I married Phil without really knowing anything about love, but now that I do I want it again. I get such a thrill just *remembering* how overwhelming the feeling is, and I am going to wait to get married as long as it takes to feel that way again."

He said, "But, Jo, dear. I am afraid you will miss having the whole apple for just the stem."

I cried, Oh, Matty, I want it *all!* I want the whole apple and the stem, too. Don't you see?"

He said quietly, "Yes, I see. We will never speak of it again."

I didn't take time to weigh the pros and cons of being married to Matty. Not for one moment did I consider it, any more than I had thought to ask him to go ice skating with me. One night Matty had asked me what I had done that day. When I told him I had gone ice skating in Central Park, he said, "Why didn't you call me? I would have loved to go skating with you." It simply never crossed my mind to ask him to go ice skating with me. It never occurred to me that he would *want* to leave his office during all his mysterious business deals to go ice skating — just as it never occurred to me to ask Matty to go with me to the parties I went to, or introduce him to my friends. Matty would have been at ease at Leonard Bernstein's parties, but in my mind my relationship with Matty had its own unique sphere containing just the two of us. My party friends knew my public self, it was Matty who knew the private side of me. He was like one of those spreading black oak trees in whose branches I had felt at peace and secure as a child. With him I felt protected, taken care of. But I didn't laugh with him like I had with Phil, or shout for joy like I had with Sydney. Matty wasn't a romantic figure to me. He didn't fulfill my need for adventure or excitement.

It turned out Matty understood that, too. Not long after his rejected proposal of marriage, again sitting in front of the fire, Matty said, "Jo, I have had a great idea. How would you like to go to Europe, all expenses paid?"

I sort of went, "Glugg," at his question.

Congress had passed a bill exempting American citizens from income taxes if they worked out of the country for over 18 months. The bill's purpose was to encourage Americans to work in the Saudi oil fields, but many in the movie industry, like the Kelly group, jumped at the chance to avoid taxes and began working on various projects abroad for that extended period of time. The major studios were eager to finance films abroad in order to use up their money that had been put on hold during the war. Consequently, I had been whining that my best friends were all in Europe, and how I had always wanted to see Paris. Matty decided to fix that for me.

With more excitement than I had ever seen him show, Matty said, "You know, Jo, I have been to Europe many times. I spent quite a lot of time there when I was setting up the new United Artists, as we have offices in London, Paris, Rome, and Barcelona, and when I was in the Army working for Eisenhower, of course, we were stationed there. So I know it well and I would love to see it again through your eyes. It would give me so much pleasure to arrange a trip for you to go all over Europe, all expenses paid, and I will be a little bird sitting on your shoulder enjoying it all over again through your eyes."

My never-take-anything-from-a-man syndrome swiftly kicked in, and I said with some vehemence, "Matty, I could never possibly let you do a thing like that!"

Eagerly, he said, "I know how you feel about being 'beholden' to someone, but don't you see, this would be such fun for me as I imagine you seeing all the wonders that are there waiting for you. I couldn't get away myself now, so you would be doing *me* a favor by going in my place."

Of course, I knew that he was stretching the truth a bit about doing him a favor, but the magnitude of what he was suggesting took my breath away. After we had argued it back and forth awhile, I said, "My head is spinning, let me think about it for a bit."

I wanted to discuss it with my spiritual guru. Normally, I wouldn't need to think twice about accepting a gift of this magnitude from anyone, much less from someone I was going with, but he did put it so nicely that my mind was torn. The friend who had taken Lassie's place as my moral arbitrator was Louise Schacht, a very good painter and the most spiritually enlightened person I had ever known. I had met her in 1943 when Metro brought her out to Hollywood from New York to paint the portraits of Ronald Coleman and Marlena Dietrich, the stars of their big new extravaganza, *Kismet*. When Louise and I met, it was uncanny how she *sensed* the spiritual feelings I instinctively kept hidden. I had learned that *compassion* is the basic link between all religions when I studied comparative religions at Hunter College several years ago, but these concepts were abstract to me, Louise made them real. Though Jewish, Louise was a member of no organized religion, but she had a deep sense of the divine spirit and she actually *practiced* compassion in all that she did or thought. All my friends scornfully rejected religion as the "opiate of the masses," but Louise taught me the difference between religion and spirituality, and put her stamp of approval on my feelings that I was connected to a Universal Spirit (call it God or Buddha or whatever) and had a guardian angel looking after me. I trusted her judgment of right and wrong implicitly. When she had heard my extraordinary story about Matty's plan, without further discussion, Louise said, "Josie, from his past behavior, you have no reason to suppose that Mr. Fox has ulterior motives in giving you this marvelous experience. He obviously won't miss the money and it doesn't sound to me like he has a lot of fun, and clearly planning and implementing this trip for you would be fun for him. You must not let past experiences make you unduly suspicious of the motives of others. It is better to trust and be misled than not to trust at all. However, I feel strongly that you will not be misled in this case. Think of what he did for Indonesia. What he wants is to give you joy, so accept his offer and be joyous with him about it."

Matty was indeed gleeful when I "joyfully" told him I accepted his offer. He said, "I have it all worked out. I will see to your spending money needs, and I will contact the heads of United Artists in Europe about your trip and give you letters of introduction to them. They will take care of any of your other needs. I will tell the Paris office to arrange a car for you when you want to travel. They will buy it with French francs and when you are ready to come home they can sell it for dollars, and with the exchange it will not have cost them anything." I didn't understand any of this, but since this was a fairy tale anyway, a car sounded a lot like a golden carriage so I nodded enthusiastically at whatever he said. "I will cable Sam Spiegel, who is producing a movie in Africa just now, to leave word at the desk at the George V Hotel in Paris for you to have the use of the apartment he keeps there. And United Artists will give you the use of apartments in London, Rome, and Barcelona. You will have an open-ended round-trip ticket on Pan Am so that you can fly to any other country you choose if you get tired of driving." If he had said, "You must return promptly before midnight when you come back, however, or you will turn into a pumpkin." I would not have been surprised.

And then he came up with the *piece d' resistance*. "I have been thinking it over and I know how important it is to have someone to say, 'Oh, look at that' to, so I would like to suggest that you invite a friend of yours to go with you at my expense to share everything with. Would you like that?"

The friend I thought would benefit most from such a trip was Ellen Ray, the dancer I had lived with in the Hollywood Hills before I came back to New York, and she was thrilled out of her skin to go with me. And so it was that three weeks later, she and I were preparing to take a plane to begin the most spectacular experience of our lives. Matty gave me $5,000 in American Express traveler's checks (a lot of money in 1951), two first-class open-ended round-trip tickets on Pan American, many letters of introduction, and a new Polaroid camera that was just about to come on the market. I had bought myself a little book of *Common French Phrases* and intended to learn French on the plane trip over.

A couple of things happened just before we were to leave that I would have preferred to miss. For one, Matty insisted that he give me a farewell party and that I should invite all my friends. I had a bad feeling about that, but I couldn't dissuade him. So I invited about 20 friends to come to his party. The apartment looked marvelous, with lots of candles vying with the lights of Manhattan for best in show, fabulous food was spread on the buffet, and excellent champagne was flowing in abundance. But there was a strange atmosphere that I couldn't explain. Some of my best friends were either in Europe or in Hollywood, Betty and Adolph were still working on *Band Wagon*, Anita was dubbing the songs for Rita Hayworth in *Gilda* — but even so there were lots of other friends there. There was no gaiety, however, nobody played the piano, and the general feeling was uncommonly subdued. Dellie and Louise were the only ones who spent time talking with Matty. Lenny Bernstein and Jerry Robbins came together, but they left early. I hadn't invited Harvey Orkin but he came anyway and was almost rude to Matty. The strange atmosphere was explained when a recently arrived friend, who shall be nameless, came up to me and said, "Oh, I have been dying to meet your new sugar daddy." I felt like I had been hit in the forehead with a claw-hammer. It was not only unwarranted, it was cruel; and I wanted to slap my no-longer-friend across the face and ask everyone to go home. I was stricken with the injustice of it all, and ashamed of my friends for Matty's sake. I didn't know what to say to Matty about it so I said nothing, and prayed that he wasn't aware of my friend's lack of insight.

The other untoward thing was that the night before Ellen was to arrive from California, Matty and I went to the *Blue Angel* nightclub for our own private farewell. It was dark in the club, so I didn't know who it was at first when some tall figure loomed over our table. It was Sydney. Just dropping over to say hello, he said.

I hadn't heard he was in town, and during the time since I'd last seen him I had been doing a lot of things, and hopefully doing a lot of forgetting. The last thing I wanted was to see Sydney now. Like the song from Camelot, "Stay away until you cross my mind, merely once a day," — well, this was too soon. I had worked my way from having him constantly on my mind — to having memories and images of him cross my mind only every hour — to now *almost* thinking of him "merely once a day." In no way was I prepared for him to materialize like a genie out of a bottle right there before my very eyes. Sydney. Looking exactly the same. His voice exactly the same. My throat got very dry and my voice came out as a squawk when I introduced Matty to Sydney. My heart was pounding so hard it should have been visible through my clothes, and my stomach seemed in serious danger of exploding. Sydney had a mischievous look in his eye, which gave me the feeling that his reasons for coming over were untrustworthy. I very much didn't want to know what they were. Considering the way our relationship had ended, it wasn't kind of him to appear unexpectedly like this. And I think he knew it. After the introductions were acknowledged, Sydney said to me, "I hear you're going to Europe." I mumbled agreement, and with a brilliant smile, Sydney said, "Have a nice trip," shook hands with Matty, saying "Nice to have met you," and left.

After a long pause, Matty said, "So that is Sydney."

And I said, "Yes, that is Sydney."

Though Matty was only six years older than Sydney, the physical contrast between the two men was readily apparent: short, overweight, balding Matty and tall, fit, gorgeous Sydney were not to be compared physically. The physical way I felt about the two of them was not to be compared either. When Sydney had gone, Matty and I were left feeling a little awkward, each thinking our own thoughts.

In the cab going home, the pain of unrequited love fresh in my mind, I blurted out, "Oh, Matty, you've been so good to me, and I'm afraid I'll hurt you."

With calm decision in his voice, he said, "You leave that to me, Jo. When you come back from your trip, we won't be going out together anymore. I will always be your friend, and care about you, but that will be all."

I snapped out of my reverie at this unexpected statement. I didn't know whether to be glad or sad. The magnificence of Matty's gift to me dwarfed our friendship as it was, and I, too, could see that it couldn't continue on its present basis. I knew I should be relieved, but a cold, small ball of loss and sadness formed in the pit of my stomach nonetheless. I wondered if his decision was because of Sydney, or if he had planned it all along.

In later years, I was to wish with all my heart that I could have worn a pair of magic glasses that night to truly see the difference in character and quality between the two men. But by that time it was much too late.

Paris and All That

It seemed to me I had always dreamed of Paris. The very name held enchantment. From movies, songs, books, and postcards, I had formed a picture of Paris which ran in my mind like an animated film. For years it had beckoned seductively to me. Magically, the taxi Ellen and I picked up at the Orly Airport carried us out of the animated film of my dreams into the live action of the glorious tree-lined Champs-Élysées, and we were actually in Paris. The Arch de Triumph and the Place de la Concorde at its either end were right where they should be, and, though it was May instead of April, the chestnut trees were in blossom. The sights, sounds, and smells of Paris engulfed me as one of their own, and I fell instantly in love. As I peered eagerly out of every window of the taxi, my chest felt like it would burst with joy and fulfillment. I was somewhere over the rainbow.

A cloud appeared over the rainbow, however, as we entered our hotel. The George V was touted as being one of the finest hotels in the world, but when we walked into its lobby it seemed all wrong. Its glossy dark paneling, shiny brass fixtures, and elegant crystal chandeliers were way too similar to the lobby of the Plaza in New York — except the men behind the desk at the George V spoke better English. It wasn't different. It wasn't French! It wasn't what I had expected at all. And when the bellboy (speaking perfect English) led us to Sam Speigel's apartment, it could have been any elegant apartment on Park Avenue; it didn't even seem to be in another country. Still, we had arrived at our destination and the wild excitement of the trip began to pour out of Ellen and me like sawdust. We sank into chairs and surveyed our new abode, then decided to order some simple sandwiches, unpack our pajamas, and go to bed. Early the next morning we were taking the train for Chartres, where we would meet our friends Lois and Jeanne who would drive us to the house Betsy and Gene Kelly had rented for the year in nearby Ramboulette.

Some well-meaning but badly misguided friend had told me that when travelling in Europe, rather than hauling around several suitcases for the two of us and trying to find porters at every stop, I should buy a strong, but lightweight salesman's cardboard sample case to take instead of luggage. It would hold all our stuff, and the top fitted down over the bottom so it could telescope up if we bought more things. With handles at either end, it could be carried between the two of us, and, as I was ever eager to be self-reliant, I bought one. True, it was lightweight but it was huge, so we called it the Black Mariah. The bellboy had to just put it down in the middle of the living room floor, as the delicate luggage stands in the bedrooms wouldn't hold it. Probably it was the same friend who had told me erroneously that it was not possible to get Tampax in Europe so, to save room, Ellen and I had discarded the dozens of cardboard boxes and tucked the little paper enclosed Tampax in wherever they would fit. Presumably because of the changes of pressure within the airplane, when we pulled the lid off the Black Mariah to get out our pajamas, each little container shot out all over the room as though jet propelled. We were too tired to retrieve them all, or unpack our clothes properly, so we just dug out our pajamas and the things we would take in our small carry-all the next morning and fell into bed. The next morning we were late waking up, so we just rushed off to the station, leaving the Black Mariah and its scattered contents where they lay.

As we waited for our train to be called, seated at one of the little tables in the enormous Gare de Sud (train station for the south), an enchanting little girl of about four came up to me as though she had been looking all over for me. She leaned her elbow confidingly on my knee and began to speak to me of serious matters. In French. I was somehow astounded that this tiny child could already speak such fluent French and wished desperately that I had not waited for the flight over to start to learn to speak it myself. Eager to communicate with her in some way, I thought of my new Polaroid camera and began to take pictures of this delightful little curly-haired cherub. When the photos developed in seconds and I gave them to her, it had the desired effect — she was awed and thrilled. She looked incredulously at the pictures — at the camera — up at me — back to the photos of herself — and then ran as fast as she could over to her mother. Her mother had been closely watching her from a table nearby, and she also was suitably amazed at the magic of an instant picture. A tall, thin, anxious-looking woman, she came over to thank me, and then, explaining something indecipherable to me, she hurried away. I thought for one lovely moment that she had given Miss Adorable to me, but shortly she came back with a large sack of expensive crystal candy as a gift in return for the photographs. I have always kept some pieces of that crystal candy, and the memory of that lovely, blonde child is forever clear in my mind. It was such a perfect way to fall in love with the people of France.

As eager as Ellen and I were to explore Paris, it was first things first and like homing pigeons we were drawn to what was "home" for us. Even though they were now in a foreign country, the Kelly group (as I shall call it) was like a missing part of our overall being, and we hurried to rejoin that part. Betsy Kelly, Lois McClelland, Jeanne Coyne, Carol Haney, Ellen and I had formed a group within a group for a "girl's night," which met for years at Lois's house once a month to laugh and exchange secrets and opinions. That group was just for fun. Gene's group was for both fun and very hard work. Choreographers usually have two or three dancers who act as their assistants. One to help with choreography by acting as sounding boards, and performing the steps so the choreographer can see them in action during the planning. Another assistant takes notes and teaches the steps to the chosen dancers for the numbers, and one assistant conveys orders, runs errands, and gets coffee. In other words, they need a creative assistant, a dance assistant, and a personal assistant. Gene had met Stanley Donen when Stanley was an 18-year-old southern boy in the chorus of *Pal Joey*, the show that made Gene a star on Broadway. Gene saw Stanley's innate talent and he became Gene's creative assistant and collaborator from then on. Jeanne Coyne had studied at Gene's dance studio in Pittsburgh when she was a child, and had so impressed Gene as a dancer that he took her with him as dance assistant when he went to New York to choreograph for the *Diamond Horseshoe's* nightclub show, and she had been with him ever since. Gene had met Lois McClelland when they were both in the Navy during the war, as she was the script girl on the documentary unit Gene was assigned to direct. Lois remained Gene's devoted personal assistant for the rest of his life. Carol Haney and Ellen had both trained under the brilliant choreographer Jack Cole, a precursor to Jerry Robbins and Bobby Fosse, dancer extraordinaire. Jack's nightclub act was the absolute best erotic dancing I have ever seen. I mean it was downright pornographic, in a nice way, of course. The dancers were breathtakingly good, but also I don't think there was anyone in the audience who didn't have a splendid sexual experience while watching the act. Jack's act was comprised of three men (including himself) and three women, Carol, Ellen, and Gwen Verdon. The

act broke up when Jack signed a contract with Columbia as choreographer, primarily for Rita Hayworth (his most famous number was
Rita's "Put the Blame on Mame," dubbed for Rita by my best friend,
Anita Ellis, incidentally), and took Gwen with him as his dance assistant. Later Jack went to 20th to work with Marilyn Monroe, where
he choreographed her first dance numbers, like "Diamonds Are a
Girl's Best Friend." He taught Marilyn how to walk and sit and be, as
well as dance. She is quoted in biographies as saying, "Without Jack
Cole there would be no Marilyn Monroe." Gwen Verdon went on to
become a major star on Broadway with Bobby Fosse. Carol and Ellen
both got dance contracts at Metro, which is where they first worked
with Gene. Ellen never discussed with me the way she must have felt
when Gene singled out Carol to work more closely with him and
Stanley. I am sure it helped that when Fred Astaire came to Metro to
do *Easter Parade* after Gene broke his ankle, he chose Ellen as his dance
assistant for that movie and the succeeding ones he did at Metro. But
I know Ellen would have preferred working with Gene. As it was, as
far back as *Anchors Aweigh*, the ones who assembled in Gene's den to
work out the intricacies of the various dance numbers were Gene,
Stanley, Jeanne, and Carol. If I happened to be there that night I got
to watch. (Today, all these years later, I feel like going down on my
knees in gratitude for the privilege of seeing these incredible talents
at work. Stupidly, at the time I took it all for granted.)

Anyway, the Kelly group was like family to me and letters telling
of my marvelous miracle trip had quickly winged their way across
the Atlantic to them, and it had early been arranged that Ellen and I
would come immediately by train to see them after arrival in Paris. So
it was with much hugging and kissing and jumping up and down at
the enormity of us all being here together in France that we met Lois
and Jeanne at the Chartres train station. They explained that Betsy
and Carol were not there to meet us because Betsy was presently at
the apartment she and Gene had rented in Paris, and Carol and Gene
were at a crucial point in the choreography for Gene's new film and
would see us later. Then they led us across the square into that incredible cathedral, built in the 12th Century, that Chartres is famous for.
The moment I entered, I had an epiphany of transcendental experience that has remained unequaled for me — except in nature. It was
more than just the colors of the fabulous stained-glass windows, or
the grandeur of the architecture itself; from the moment I walked in

I experienced a spiritual exaltation similar to the time when I was five and saw God in my imagination. It was a confirmation of all I held sacred. I was certain that only an unknowable divine source could have inspired the creation of this great edifice.

Soul-satiated by our spiritual experience at the cathedral, the four of us stopped for lunch at a small inn on the way to Ramboulette and sat outside in the sunshine at a rustic table set up under a grape arbor. We ordered soup and salad, and after it came I knew that my life had been altered forever. First of all, the bread and looked like bread and butter I had eaten before, but the taste was altogether different and incredibly better. Then when I took my first swallow of the soup, my taste buds burst open with a whole new capacity for transmitting delight. I immediately asked the owner/waitress for the recipe and, with Jeanne translating (the group had all become fluent in French before they came to France), when I heard leeks, carrots, celery, potatoes, milk, and salt and pepper I knew she must be deliberately leaving out the most important ingredient because those combinations were familiar to me and they had never tasted like this. The word "ambrosia" came to mind and I thought that might be right, as this was truly a soup for the gods. The salad was picked fresh from the garden near our table and was a fitting companion for that superb soup. All my life, even though my mother was a wonderful cook, my favorite food had been milk and saltine crackers. Possibly because my grandmother's insistence on corn bread and molasses three times a day when I was 10 had so depressed my taste buds that they had gone into a coma, but this simple meal in an ordinary inn in an ordinary little town in France changed my epicurean needs and appreciation forever. Eating had always been on the bottom of my list of important things to do today, but that first real meal in France changed its position to the very top; from that moment on one of my chief anticipations and pleasures in life became: breakfast – lunch – dinner. I had eaten at good French restaurants in New York, but French cooking didn't taste the same in the U.S. I was sure it was something extraordinary in the air and soil of France, and some secret ingredient only the real French cooks knew about, that made the difference. (I later learned that it was because they used unpasturized milk. Consequently their butter, cheese, yogurt, etc., tasted a million times better than ours. To my mind, bacteria was a small price to pay for this divine taste.)

Gene and Betsy had rented a fairy tale house. It was called a "mill house" because it was built over a small river, and in the distant past had indeed been a mill, but it had been remodeled into an absolutely gorgeous four-bedroom house in the middle of a forest. The famous Forêt de Fontainebleau, no less! With its predominantly green pallet of surrounding trees, high, slanted, shingled, brown roof and moldings, this white house looked like a Monet painting. Inside, its large, many-angled rooms, furnished in Country French with its dark reds and blues, were warm and beautiful and comfortable. (Forever after I have furnished my living rooms with those colors.) Outside the river sang a bubbling, lively song, but at night it provided a suitable lullaby for sweet dreams. Gene and Betsy had rented an apartment in Paris on the beautiful Ile St. Louis, but he preferred to really live in the country while he was preparing his present massive project of Invitation to the Dance. Metro had asked Gene to make a musical in Europe in order to use some of their funds that had been frozen during the war; consequently, he had been given carte blanche to make any kind of film he wanted. Gene had studied dance all his life, and was proficient in ballet, tap, and modern dance. Before him, Fred Astaire had been the premiere male dancer in movies, Broadway, too, for that matter. But Astaire was all grace and elegance, and cool to the touch, you might say. I don't think women watching him would have yearned to go to bed with him; I never thought Ginger Rogers wanted to. But Gene, on the other hand, brought a male sexuality of exuberance and romantic tenderness to the screen that set a whole new tone, plus his athletic prowess surpassed even the great Douglas Fairbanks. Also, where Astaire's dance numbers were done almost entirely in full figure shots, Gene experimented with lighting, camera techniques, and special effects in order to achieve a true merger of film and dance. He was the first dancer to use split screen, double image, and to integrate live action with animation. And, if I do say so myself, he looked great doing it!

American in Paris was a tough act to follow, and to top it Gene was preparing a landmark musical to be done in dance and mime without any dialogue, which would cover all forms of dance. He was the writer, choreographer, director, and lead performer of a film in three sections, the only connecting link being Gene, with music composed for each section by Jacques Ibert, Andre Previn, and the late Rimsky-Korsakov. Gene had a thing about the public perception of American male dancers being effeminate. He was determined to prove, both in private and in public, that male dancers were muy macho as well as superb athletes. That night at dinner, mouth-wateringly prepared by their French cook, the talk among Carol, Jeanne, and Gene was of the kind I had been privy to so many times in the Kelly den — the always fascinating, intricate planning of a dance number. It seemed odd not to have Stanley Donen there, who had previously been co-director/choreographer of all Gene's musicals and a permanent fixture wherever Gene was, but Stanley had departed their partnership after *American in Paris* to direct his own movies, and Carol was taking his place. *Invitation to the Dance* was a bold endeavor. In the first segment of the film, Pierrot, Claire Sombert of the Ballet de l'Opera National de Paris Company was to dance with Gene; in the second, The Marine, Tamara Tourmanova; and in the third, Sinbad, Carol was his partner, simulated by animation as a young girl and a snake. The way Gene and Stanley did numbers like Gene's alter-ego dance, or his dance with a cartoon character, was that Gene and Stanley were filmed doing both parts of the dance opposite one another, and then Stanley would be taken out technically and the alter-ego or a cartoon character inserted in his place. In this case, Carol would be doing the actual dancing with Gene, and then Disney artists would superimpose a cartoon girl and snake to follow her moves. Their intense excitement as they developed these themes was a joy to see.

Gene introduced Ellen and me to the benefits of several kinds of French wine during dinner, with the result that we retired early. But the next morning, eager to get our big adventure started, Ellen and I were up and at 'em before anyone else and decided to explore another part of the forest before breakfast. We discovered a small old wooden bridge behind Gene's house that crossed the river into a thick grove of trees. Much to our delight, we soon entered a kind of meadow of pale green grass — and in the distance was a huge French Chateau, with lots of big barn-like buildings around it. It seemed unreal yet perfect to find it there. In an excess of exuberance, I began to perform one of my favorite improvisations of a physically-challenged, considerably over-weight woman who mistakenly thinks of herself as a ballet dancer of Pavlovian quality. My ecstatic twirls and leaps inspired Ellen and she began to do the same, only with elegance and grace. We were madly dancing around in the meadow when, coming at a rapid pace, a farmhand appeared in the distance with a pitchfork in his hand. Incredibly, he began shouting as he approached us, "Allez, allez vous. Allez, allez!" By this time I knew that "allez" meant "Go," so I said to him in puzzlement, "Go? Do you mean you want us to go?" I would have expected anyone watching us to burst into wild applause rather than ask us to leave, for heaven's sake, but the ferocious looking man menaced me with the pitchfork, repeating even more belligerently, "Allez vous. ALLEZ!" So, with wounded dignity, we turned and stalked off as gracefully as possible back the way we had come. At breakfast Gene told us, rather coldly I thought, that we had been trespassing on the grounds of a famous 14th Century Chateau in which formerly King Louie XVI had resided, and which presently the French Presidents used as a summer home. I thought, "14th Century? Good night, that's when Columbus discovered America, isn't it? Let's see, that's 600 years ago, right? That Chateau is old!" However, I still thought its inhabitants were rather stuffy. (I never could get the numerology straight about centuries.)

After three heavenly days at the mill house, we arrived back at the George V, and were dismayed to find Sam Speigel ensconced in his apartment, with our belongings and dozens of Tampax scattered around him in the living room. Sam, a heavyset, sandy-haired, balding man with a perennial cigar in his mouth, had just arrived and explained that business with his agent, Irving "Swifty" Lazar, had brought him back to Paris from Africa unexpectedly, where he was producing *The African Queen*, but he was delighted to continue to share his apartment with us. Since he had two bedrooms, I was giving this some thought until he aggressively pulled me down on his lap and gave my waist little squeezes while telling us that he and Swifty were taking us to dinner at La Tour d'Argent tonight. I thought to myself "Whoo, boy. Dinner, OK, just to be nice, but I'm outta here right after dinner." I would have thought that since he knew I was Matty's friend, he wouldn't have tried to come on to me, but I could tell by his lascivious attitude that instead he must have thought I, and probably Ellen also, would be willing after-dinner companions in his master bedroom. I knew his wife, Lynn Baggett, fairly well, as she had been a starlet at Fox during my time. When I knew her she was a gorgeous, sultry young woman of 20, the same age as I — but she was much more experienced than I as during some of our Les Girl's discussions she had filled us in on multiple ways to get out of sleeping with your husband. The only way I could think of to get out of sleeping with her husband was to remove myself as quickly as possible. (Sad to remember, 16 years later, divorced from Sam, Lynn killed herself.)

Hastily cramming the Tampax and our other far-flung belongings back in the Black Mariah, Ellen and I toted it into the second bedroom and got out our finest finery, as Sam had proudly told us the restaurant he was taking us to tonight was the best in the world. I had to admit La Tour d'Argent was breathtaking. The dazzling white tablecloths, the glitter of exquisite crystal under the delicate chandeliers and candles, the low ceiling of the rounded room putting attention on the walls of windows overlooking the Seine, were luxurious beyond my experience. The white tie and tails of the maitre d' shook with delight at the sight of Sam, whom he had greeted as though Sam were visiting royalty. He seated us at what appeared to be the best table by a window overlooking the Seine, and handed round enormous menus. Through the window, the passing well-lit Bateau Mouche (tourist boats), the rooftops of Paris, and the sparkling lights of Ile St. Louis created a view of my Paris that made my mouth water more than the menu. In fluent French, Sam ordered what he said had been the house specialty since the 16th Century (imagine that!) for Ellen and me: Caneton à l'Orange, Épinards au Gratin, et Pomme Double Frit, which turned out to be duckling with orange sauce, spinach with a fantastic cheesy sauce, and those blown-up fried potatoes that I had tried to get my bewildered cook to make at my first dinner party when I was married to Phil. I thought, "Of course! Double fried potatoes. Somehow the second time around makes them blow up like a balloon. I should have known that." Anyway, suffice it to say, my newly awakened taste buds were in ecstasy. Sam ordered something for himself that sounded lovely in French but turned out to be a repulsive whole almost-raw veal kidney with pathetic little crayfish clustered around it. I couldn't look, and Swifty ordered a steak and a baked potato.

I had gone to a few parties with Swifty in the distant past. One of the best agents in Hollywood, he was a small man who was considered an all-around good guy. He was an amusing escort, whom I didn't think liked women very much. Anyway, while Sam was in conference with the maitre d', Swifty regaled us with Sam's many accomplishments. He said that Sam spoke seven languages fluently, and that he and his Jewish family had escaped Poland and then France just ahead of the Nazis. Starting in the U.S. with literally nothing, Sam had made millions in the motion picture industry, and had a world famous art collection. The movie he was producing now in Africa was *The African Queen*, with Humphrey Bogart and Katharine Hepburn; the proposed movie they were here to discuss was *The Bridge On the River Kwai*. (In the next 10 years this chubby, cigar-waving man was to produce *On the Waterfront* and *Lawrence of Arabia*, among other fabulous movies. Eventually, the Academy Awards would present him with the prestigious Irving Thalberg Award. The engraving read: "To Sam Speigel, whose wit, charm, sophistication, and many contributions to art, have made him a titanic figure the movie world will not see again." Sam wound up spending his last years in Israel, and when he died, he donated his art collection to that government.) But that was long in the future and now I looked carefully at this man with such an extraordinary past, but the creative force and financial skills it took to make such motion picture masterpieces as he did were not evident to me, particularly, when he and Swifty got down to business. From then on the kind of conversation between them was exactly the same as would be taking place at many tables right now at Chasen's in Hollywood. The view was great and the food was great, but I wished heartily that Ellen and I were at some little bistro listening to some strangers speaking French.

Who should be waiting on the sidewalk in front of the George V when we got back, but Orson Welles. When Sam introduced Ellen and me, Orson barely acknowledged us and immediately launched into a production proposal for Sam. Why he had not chosen to wait for Sam inside I never knew; maybe he owed the hotel money as I had heard that his extravagant tastes and unsuccessful projects had made him hard up now. Five years earlier, he had quarreled violently with RKO about the enormous financial override and editing on what he considered his second masterpiece, *The Magnificent Ambersons*, after *Citizen Kane*. His subsequent movie, *The Lady From Shanghai*, with his recently divorced wife, Rita Hayworth, had also greatly overrun its budget, and was a flop originally. Studio bosses stick together and the boy genius had not been able to get another production financed in Hollywood, so in 1949, he left the U.S. in a well-publicized huff — and during these past three years had been finding it difficult to get financing for his many elaborate plans in Europe. He had previously done *The Stranger with Sam*, starring Edward G. Robinson and Loretta Young, and so here he was to waylay him in the effort to get Sam to produce his latest scheme. Tired already of business talk through the long hours it took to eat that heavenly four-course meal, and feeling frisky now that it was over, while singing the theme music from *American in Paris*, Ellen and I began to dance up Avenue George V toward the Champs-Elysees. It was early in the morning and the streets were empty as we leaped and twirled our way back to the two men. Glaring at me, Orson snarled contemptuously, "Hyperthyroid!" For once in my life I thought of the proper response before it was too late, and snarled back, "And don't you wish you still were!" I had never forgiven him for embarrassing me so cruelly at Toots Shor's restaurant when Phil and I were on our honeymoon and was pleased to get a bit of my own back, as my mother would say.

Leaving the two men to discuss whatever it was Orson wanted, we said good night and politely thanked Sam for a lovely dinner. At the desk of the George V, I pleaded for another room for the night. There was none. Determined not to have a sexual confrontation with Sam — I insisted. Finally, the concierge agreed to let us have a chauffeur's room, warning us it only had a single bed and was a bit small for the two of us. Never mind, I said, grabbed a bellboy, and dashed up to Sam's apartment. We had never really unpacked so all we had to do was cram the Black Mariah together (it really was a handy catch-all), look around to make sure no stray Tampax had eluded us, write Sam a hasty "thank you for the hospitality" note, and hurry out to our new digs.

Small! By the time we got ourselves and the Black Mariah crammed into the room, you had to step up on the bed to go from one side of it to the other. The low ceiling was made even lower by huge pipes that ran through it, and rumbled and hissed all night. I don't know how a chauffeur could have gotten any sleep, for we surely didn't. Consequently, we were up and dressed by 8 o'clock and ready to go find a real French place to have breakfast. As we walked toward the Champs-Elysees, someone called out, "Is that Josie?" I turned and found that Irwin Shaw was also up early, and when we described our adventures of the evening before to him, Irwin had to hold on to a wall to keep from falling down with laughter. Particularly about the Tampax. Irwin had made a lot of money on the sale of his book, *The Young Lions* (later to be made into a movie starring Montgomery Cliff and Marlon Brando), and was living in Paris because his second book, *The Troubled Air*, about the dangers of McCarthyism, had gotten him blacklisted in America. He and I were old radical buddies and I was delighted to see him. He grabbed us each by the arm, marched us up to Le Fouquets on the corner, and plied us with questions about our trip. He understood completely why I was disappointed with the George V and told us that when he was first in Paris years ago, as a starving young writer, he had stayed at an inexpensive atelier (studio) on the top floor of a small hotel off Avenue Grande Armee just beyond L'Etoile (Arch de Triumph). He assured us the personnel didn't speak English, the self-service, two-person elevator most often didn't work, and there was no telephone, TV, or room service. In other words, it was just what I was looking for. As we sat outside under the umbrellas of this famous 18th Century restaurant watching the fascinating passing parade along the Champs-Elysees, and eating our first indescribably delicious croissant, Irwin went to telephone to see if the atelier was available and returned with the excellent news that it was! He went with us to pay our overnight bill at the George V, extricate the Black Mariah, and then on to introduce us to the owners of the hotel. I was thankful we had not run into Sam while we were checking out, and indeed, I never saw him again.

I have forgotten the name of that precious small hotel but I have a photographic memory of our atelier. Whenever I see Roman Holiday with Audrey Hepburn and Gregory Peck, I get such a nostalgic pang because Peck's studio in the movie is almost exactly like the one we had, only his looks out over the rooftops of Rome while ours looked out over the rooftops of Paris. Our top floor studio had two daybed-couches, two comfy chairs and two un-comfy ones by a small round table, a bureau/closet, a chest with a two-burner hotplate, a skylight (under which I imagined starving young artists painting masterpieces) and an infinitesimal bathroom with an overhead shower. Its main attraction was one wall of French windows framing a panorama of Paris, and a tiny terrace. And there was a small bistro just around the corner that served the kind of simple French food I loved the best. The Bistro Francois's omelets were made with ambrosia, too. It was all perfect.

Like with any love affair, mine with Paris started off with everything looking brighter and better. The leaves of the chestnut trees were a more delicate and luminous green than American trees, the sunlight softer and more caressing, the exquisite clothes in the shop windows along the Champs Élysées and the scarves displayed on Rue

St. Honoré were a mixture of heretofore unseen gorgeous colors. And then there was the language. I wanted to lean my elbows on the counters of the shops and spend the day listening to the oh-so-chic salesgirls speak in their high, melodious voices, while the men spoke in this smooth-creamy-éclaire tone that melted me at the knees. When the French spoke English, their accent made me want to roll over on my back like a puppy and waggle my paws in the air. Even the birds in the trees chirped with a French accent. And I loved to watch the French eat. Americans cut up their food with the knife in their right hand and the fork in their left hand, then put the knife down, transfer the fork to their right hand and thus to their mouth. The French cut up their food like a skilled surgeon performing a delicate operation and transfer a bite to their mouth with their fork still in their left hand. It was so economical of movement, so precise. Of course, my grandfather was just as economical of movement and transferred his food with his knife. It just didn't look the same.

Paris is very accessible to the newcomer. Unlike Los Angeles with its sprawl or New York with its long straight streets, the curving major arrondissements (sections) of Paris can be covered in two days, if you don't dawdle. I know because Ellen and I did it on our first excursions, then we got our heads straight and spent a good part of each day sitting in different sidewalk bistros drinking beer (it tasted like champagne to us), café au lait, or a Kir (white wine and crème de cassis, or a Kir Royale if made with champagne), a new aperitif I had become enamored with. Of course, we saw the Louve, or parts of it, the Winged Victory on the first stairwell so blinded me with its beauty that it was hard for me to get enthralled with anything else. My favorite museum experience was the Musée de l'Orangerie, where most of the Impressionists paintings were at that time. I had become so familiar with these brilliant innovative painters from my many art books and my study of their few paintings at the Museum of Modern Art in New York, I was so overwhelmed with rooms filled with hundreds of their paintings I couldn't decide which of them to run to next. Well, I didn't run to the paintings of Picasso or Braque, I didn't even look at them if I saw them first, except for Picasso's early paintings. I thought their work was brutal and scary, and in no way compared with the willowy, serene, golden-lit pleasures of the rest of the group. Le Sainte-Chapelle with its glorious stained glass windows had nearly the same sacred effect on me as Chartres Cathedral, but it was too small and narrow for the full experience. To rest our worn-out feet, we took a carriage ride through the Bois de Boulogne, which took us clopping right back to those 1800s when everything important in Paris seemed to have happened. But after a week of being on our own, we were glad to see the Kelly group who now moved to Paris to start dance rehearsals.

Gene was well-known and much-loved in France, and the Ballet de l'Opéra Company, several members of which he was using in his film, had agreed to allow him to use their rehearsal hall for his film in the glorious Paris Opera House. The first time I turned a corner and saw the opera house itself, I was literally staggered by its majestic molded artistry. Its columns, statuary, and curlicues gave it an unreal look, like a painting. Inside, it was so ornate and gilded that I found myself talking in whispers when Lois showed us around. As Gene's personal assistant she was allowed to take us all over and give us a historical rundown. Designed in 1861 by Charles Garnier, the theater itself only had 2,156 seats, but the whole complex, with its galleries, rehearsal halls, dressing rooms, marble and onyx Grand Stairways, bars and so on, made it the largest theatrical venue in the world, imagine that! Lois introduced us to the dancers in the ballet rehearsal hall, both French and American, some of whom Ellen and I already knew. Among others, there were the delightful Zizi Jeanmaire and her dance partner, Serge Perault, Tommy Ralls, the American tap dancer featured in Gene's film and a good friend of Ellen's, and Igor Youskevitch, a wildly handsome and equally nice man, who was a marvelous ballet dancer and was a featured dancer in one of the film's three sections.

Ellen, Tommy, Serge and I formed a fast friendship and often went out ensemble, as they say. I knew that French ballet male dancers didn't make much money, so I paid the checks for Serge. (I thought Tommy could pay his own checks as he was already on salary for Gene's film.) That enabled Ellen and me to go out at night to places we were not comfortable going alone. Serge was great company although he spoke even less English than I did French, but his ability to mime, his sense of humor, and the fact that he was gorgeous, with his black hair, blue eyes, and his athlete's body, made him an all around charming companion. Black jazz musicians were all the rage in Paris then and the likes of Benny Carter (an old friend of mine), Lionel Hampton, Lester Young, and Louis Armstrong were jamming the nightclubs with enthusiasts. They were honored like royalty by the French and treated with awed respect. It was heartbreaking that these brilliant musicians had to come to a country other than their own to be fully appreciated and treated as equals. Next to American movies, the music these black artists had originated was what the rest of the world loved most about America — whereas, most Americans honored the music but wouldn't sit next to one of the musicians. The nightclub that Serge especially favored was The White Elephant, a dark, smoky, cave-like club with a miniscule dance floor, but Benny Carter's saxophone opened it up to the heavens. The nightclub that I most favored was the one where Yves Montand was singing. With other romantic singers, even Sinatra, I sighed and tenderly thought of moonlight and roses while listening to them. With Yves, I vibrated with the image of rumpled sheets and hot hands. Of course, he was extraordinarily handsome and, with his shirt open to the waist, caressing the mike as well as the words of the song with his gorgeous deep voice, Yves was the sexiest performer I have ever seen, outside of Lena Horne. I think it was the guttural way the French men roll their r-r-r-rs that did me in.

Serge was also no slouch at rolling his r-r-r-rs. One day he and I went to visit the Chateau de Chambord, that enormous French Renaissance structure King Francois I had built between 1519 and 1547 in order to be close to the chateau of his mistress, the Countess de Thoury. I was absolutely knocked out by it. Several architects were required to fulfill the king's plans to have Chambord resemble the extraordinary skyline of Constantinople, and Leonardo de Vinci was reputed to have designed the two spiral staircases that went all the way to the top of the chateau. Serge knew the Chambord so well that he was able to elude the tourist guide so that we could be alone in this vast fairyland of a place. (It was so big that the stables could house 1,200 horses!) Without a tourist guide to make it all pedantic, Serge then became a French king showing his ladylove his palace, and dancing up and down one of those fabulous staircases in the style of the 16th century with lots of flourishes and kissing of hands. Instantly, he effortlessly conjured up his country's early history in mime and dance. Now, you can't beat that for a memorable experience! Serge was great fun to be with in many ways and he and I made several trips into the French countryside together, including the Chateaus of Versailles and Fontainbleu. Even though I didn't understand half the things he said, his dancer's body in mime made the French 16th century vivid and alive for me in a way no history book could do.

Ellen and I also met some of Gene and Betsy's other friends, mostly journalists and show biz folk, the most well-known being Art Buchwald, that charming and witty columnist on the *New York Herald Tribune*, Paris Edition, and Claude Dauphin, a charming and suave French movie star whom I had met before at the Kelly's in Hollywood. Without hesitation, they took us in and helped Ellen and me learn French and how to have fun in non-tourist Paris. One day we were taken up to Montmartre to look at various art galleries, as well as the drove of would-be artists painting away in the square and side streets. We had lunch at La Mere Catherine, the restaurant where the Impressionists hung out in the 1800s, and it was there I became a laughingstock. I asked for the toilette at the bar and was pointed to a dark back room, but it was confusing because there was no sign for Madames or Messieurs, just one almost indecipherable small sign over a door saying *Toilette*. Since that seemed the only option, I opened the door, a light went on in the ceiling, and I found myself in a very small, unpainted cement room with footprints in the cement on both sides of a slight depression in the floor. It had an extremely smelly hole in its center. I stared at it for a bit and decided this must be the men's room so I went back to the crowded bar, and said to the bartender, "Excuse moi, ma je désir un toilette pour la femme," in my exceedingly elementary French. There was a burst of laughter from the surrounding patrons as the bartender gave that marvelous Gaelic shrug and again pointing, said, "c'est ça." Ashamed both of my inadequate French and my ignorance, I went back into that little cement room and gave it careful thought. Once I got my feet planted in those footprints on either side of the smelly hole, I couldn't get my underwear down. Obviously, I had to first stand flat up against the wall to have room to take my panties down, and then try again. By this time it was urgent and the fact that I saw no toilet paper could not deter me. I did see a pull chain after I had literally relieved myself, splashing my shoes and stockings in so doing, and gave it a yank. Unfortunately, I didn't think to stand aside and wound up with a wet head as well as shoes and stockings from the shower-like thing in the ceiling. I dried off my hair with my blouse as best I could and strove for dignity as I passed through the snickering bar. It was equally humiliating when I joined my friends at our outdoor table to find them all laughing uproariously at my dishevelment and wet stricken face. They knew what to expect and had been waiting for my tourist's reaction. To make up for setting me up for this most embarrassing adventure, one day we were taken for lunch at Le Pré Catelan, another 1800s restaurant, only this one was all grace and elegance, and in the Bois de Boulogne! Sitting under a colorful umbrella beneath these spreading chestnut trees, we were treated to the piéce de resistance of taste thrills — fraise de bois avec crème. The remembered taste of my first tiny French strawberries with clotted cream is right up there with my first French soup. I was also relieved to find that there was an American-made toilet in the elegantly furnished salle de bain.

Although I knew my accent was atrocious, I had determined that I would communicate only in French with the French. Ellen and I would cue each other every night in our homey atelier from our Conversational French booklet, and I had acquired about 40 words which seemed to cover every ordinary situation. Of course, I didn't discuss politics or Einstein's Theory of Relativity with anyone, but what my 40 words didn't cover I made up for with mime and a plethora of goodwill. I say with great pride that I never had a bad experience with a French person. Even the fearsome, usually hefty, concierge women sitting outside their apartment buildings, from whom we sometimes asked directions, were gracious and went out of their way to direct us. I have heard so many Americans say that the French were rude and arrogant — pas moi!

The lunch that stands out from all others, however, was brought about by my darling friend, Adolph Green. He unexpectedly came to Paris because his wife, Allyn Ann McCleary, was divorcing him and he needed love and sympathy from his American friends in Paris. Adolph took Ellen and me to meet his good friend, Peter Ustinov, who had arranged a lunch for us in Les Halles. Les Halles was the wholesale market center, nicknamed "The Belly of Paris," from which retailers of all kinds, butchers, florists, you name it, came at dawn to get their supplies for the day, and was in a rather raunchy part of Paris unknown to me. I also had never met Peter Ustinov, but I knew a lot about him. I knew he was born into a noble Russian/German family, was now a British subject, had been David Niven's batman during World War II, and was becoming well known as an actor and playwright. He had just written a successful play called, *The Love of Four Colonels*, and was also newly divorced. I knew he was fluent in seven languages and spoke several other Middle-European dialects, designed sets, costumes, and directed operas, plus being a successful book writer, lecturer and public speaker. Let's see, what else? Oh, yes, and a distinguished intellectual and celebrated wit. And he was only two years older than I! What I didn't know about him was that he was one of the most charming men alive. Meeting Ellen and me for the first time, he made us feel we were old and cherished friends whom he had just parted from the day before. He took us to an insignificant-looking restaurant in Les Halles, which Peter said had the best food in Paris. The owner, obviously an old friend of Peter's, proudly took us upstairs into a private room which had been set up especially for us. Other than the best onion soup in the world, for which the area is famous, I can't remember what other special food we had to eat and drink because I was laughing so hard and so consistently for the next five hours that laughter precluded thought of everything else. None of us had any inclination to leave our table until the apologetic restaurant owner told us we had to vacate the room so they could set up for dinner. We all knew this to be a one-of-a-kind occasion and we didn't want to break the spell by leaving. It was one of those times when two or more people, who are naturally gifted in comic improvisation, feed on each other's humor in a way that opens a vein of creative comedy that is pure genius. Fortunate indeed are those lucky enough to be present.

Over the soup, Peter and Adolph took off on current events in the language and mode of Shakespeare. Each of them was familiar enough with his plays that he could carry on a comic conversation in Shakespeare's style and manner of speaking, covering both real and imagined events. Their wealth of knowledge and erudition enabled them to ramble on for hours, each prompting the other to greater hilarious heights. For Ellen and me, our sole contribution to the hours we spent over that lunch was uproarious laughter, but then, of course, that is the fuel that feeds the flame of humor. Peter and Adolph wouldn't have been so funny had they been alone. It is not possible for me to describe the flow of humor that real comedians can sometimes achieve; it's a you-had-to-be-there kind of thing. But for myself, I found that sometimes, depending on the company and the atmosphere, a hatch opened into some well-guarded place in me and out came something funny. A line, a dance, a takeoff on something or other, would flow out like a suddenly turned on jet in a fountain, and for a few moments something spontaneous and comic would find raucous life. That inexplicable jet stream from that inexplicable source of humor remained stubbornly closed for me unless the circumstances were absolutely right; it came of its own volition and could not be summoned on demand. Ruefully, its availability only lasted a few years, and then my fountain of mirth dried up for inexplicable reasons. But while those propitious circumstances were very rare for me, for people like Peter and Adolph, they were always at the ready and their jet stream was spontaneous and inexhaustible. That lunch is one of my most cherished memories. How I wish I could relive it, at least one more time. Our paths never crossed again, Peter's and mine, but I have always thought of him as a close friend.

Other than being in the company of Serge, Peter Ustinov, and French food, when Ellen was off with some of her dancer friends, my favorite thing was to go off on my own just to sit outside at any bistro and quietly watch and listen — or stroll and sit under the chestnut trees in any of the many delightful parks and watch and listen — or sit on the banks of the Seine and watch and listen. I felt my every pore was drinking in the essence of Paris. I never could get enough of it. All my life, I have found that the most satisfying and enlightening moments in any new or natural setting came to me when I was alone. Just walking down a street or in a park, I have a completely different and richer experience in and of my surroundings when I am alone than when I am accompanied. When you are with someone your attention is divided and often superficial; it is when you are alone that all your senses can focus outward and you can see, hear, smell, and experience the moment as a whole, and then bring it inward.

As an expression of gratitude, I tried sharing these and other experiences I was having with Matty. I had made the plan that I would write Matty or at least send a postcard several times a week, particularly when we went to a new place or had a special adventure. It was fun picking out postcards of the Gare du Nord, Chartres, Ramboulette and its Chateau, little bistros, funny erotic ones of Montmartre, and of course, the rooftops of Paris. It was fun imagining him reading them.

Speaking of Matty, a strange thing happened one day when we were having lunch with Betsy in her Ile St. Louis apartment. It was the first time Ellen and I had been to their apartment, and walking across the stone bridge onto the narrow island with its lovely old trees, charming bistros, cobbled streets, and ancient buildings was to instantaneously seem back in the 18th Century I kept hearing so much about. The lovely old building in which Gene and Betsy had rented the top floor was right on the Seine overlooking Notre Dame, and was almost as awe-inspiring as the mill house in Ramboulette. For lunch, it was just Lois, Jeanne, Carol, Ellen, Betsy, and me, the same six who had gotten together once a month in Beverly Hills for "girl's night" for years. I was telling them about looking for fun postcards for Matty, and going on about how generous he had been to Ellen and me when I had not even held his hand. The strange thing was that they all snickered and cast amused glances at one another. Ellen was sitting beside me, but I could see her in a mirror as she rolled her eyes and smirked along with the others. They didn't believe me. These women, whom I considered among my closest friends, thought I was lying about my relationship with Matty. I didn't protest about it any further because I needed to get off by myself and think about their attitude, which at the moment was incomprehensible. I was dumbfounded by the feeling that the floor beneath me, which I had thought was as solid as the rock walls of this building, had suddenly turned to quicksand.

The next day I made it a point to find an opportunity to sit alone by the Seine; I had always done my most insightful thinking looking at moving water. I argued with myself, "Why would they think I would lie? I learned long ago never to do anything I wouldn't want to see on the front page of a newspaper. Not because of what other people would think about what I did, but because of what I would think. My whole sense of balance depended on doing what I thought was right, so there was no need to lie. Why didn't they know that?" The insight I came up with was painful — my friends didn't really know me. These women whom I admired above all others didn't believe I could have a relationship of this kind with a man that wasn't sexual. And they believed that I would lie about it. That led me to a more frightening understanding — I didn't really know them either. When I mulled this over, I realized that it was very heavy stuff, and I must be very careful about where it led me. These people were too important to me to doubt them, so without thinking further, I quickly buried this insight out of sight and mind. It wouldn't do to dig deeper into it. Too much depended on it. Anyway, I was having the most exhilarating adventure of my life and I wasn't going to let anything darken its shine.

After about two weeks of exploring Paris, I dutifully called the head of United Artists in Paris as I had promised Matty, and he (I have forgotten his name) asked me to come right in to see him. He said he had been trying to find me because France was having its annual Automobile Show in a few days and they wondered if I, as a former Miss America, would ride down the length of the Champs Elysees on top of the back seat of a new convertible in their pre-show parade. Well, I should say! I had always hated doing that on the streets of Atlantic City or other places as Miss Texas or Miss America; my arms got tired and my smile got numb, but this was something that would thrill me to the core. When the day came, I smiled and waved effortlessly, and with vast enthusiasm, to the mass of people lining the street. Unless they read the papers carefully I am sure they had no idea who I was, but I knew who they were — they were French!

Later, Mr. United Artists took Ellen and me to the Hillman-Minx showroom and said to pick out the car we wanted for our trip. Again I was told that they would pay for the car in French francs and that whenever I was ready to go home, UA would buy it back in U.S. dollars, and the exchange rate would make it so that it hadn't cost them anything. Or maybe it was the other way around? I never got the foreign exchange straight, but the gist of it was that we would have a new car to drive as long as we wanted and it wouldn't cost anyone anything. You can't beat that. We picked out a little red four-passenger Hillman-Minx with tan leather seats and a sliding roof that went halfway back. It was adorable. Ellen and I had gotten our international driving licenses before we left New York, so I drove "the Minx" off the showroom floor, up the Champs-Elysees, around L'Etoile (one of the more life-threatening experiences to be had), and on to our hotel without a hitch. Considering that I hadn't driven a stick shift in years, and the madness of the French drivers, particularly around L'Etoile which has six major streets converging into one circle, it took all the courage of my little red hat to do so. I was very proud.

Our new French friends helped us plan our trip with suggestions of the best places to go, and our other new best friend, the Guide Michelin, listed hotels, restaurants, and places of interest with their 5-star system, so we were all set. I paid our hotel a month's rent — I didn't want to lose our atelier before we got back to Paris, and besides,

420   *Finding My Little Red Hat*

we had to have some place to leave the Black Mariah as there was no way it would fit in The Minx. We had brought mostly "drip dry" clothes and so we were traveling light with our two new suitcases (carrying only a few Tampax) as we headed the Minx toward the south of France and Italy. One of the books I had read about Paris years ago was *Our Hearts Were Young and Gay* by Cornelia Otis Skinner, about the trip she and her friend, Emily Kimbrough, took to Paris in 1923 (the year I was born) when they were 18. Ellen and I were 28 and our trip was 28 years later, but our hearts were surely young and gay as we set off, and we thought we were the luckiest and happiest adventurers in the whole world.

Tomorrow, the World

It was with a feeling of heady excitement that Ellen and I drove our new little car out of Paris into the unknown of the French Riviera and Italy. We felt that we had conquered Paris (never mind that we had mostly been with friends who spoke English and guided us around) and were now setting out to conquer the rest of the world. The "heady" part came from being entirely on our own for the first time — and feeling we were completely prepared for it! With our approximately 40 words of French, our trusty Michelin Guide, which we called "The Mich", and boundless enthusiasm, what could go wrong?

That second week in June the French countryside seemed to be going out of its way to show off for us — the sun shining through tall, leafy-headed trees often formed glittery tunnels for us to drive through. Fields and fields of heavenly-smelling lavender alternated with the brilliant yellow of a plant they unfortunately call "rape,"and the different greens of rows of growing produce all combined to make the same palette of soft, glowing colors so often seen in Impressionist paintings. We inhaled the colors like scent and grew intoxicated with the perfume of it all.

We had reservations at the Hotel du Cap on Eden Roc near the town of Cap d' Antibes for two days hence. Our friends had told us it was the most beautiful place in all of the Riviera, so we surely had to see it. Meantime, we wanted to find and make our own choices of where, what, and when. After careful and rapturous study of The Mich we had decided to have lunch in Macon and spend the night in Orange. However, in France I started getting ready for lunch as soon as I finished breakfast, so by the time we reached the outskirts of Macon I was starving. When I spied a sign with a *"Poisson"* (fish) in the name of a restaurant in front of a picturesque building in a shady garden, I asked Ellen to turn into the parking lot. As we tried to enter the front door, we were prevented in doing so by a tall, burly man who was struggling hastily into a black jacket as he motioned us away from the door and asked us to follow him. I think. It appeared that the lovely building was where the restaurateurs *lived* — the restaurant was on top of their *garage*. Anyway, we puffed our way after him up some steep stairs beside the garage, and surprisingly found a delightful terrace all nicely setup with yellow tablecloths, big yellow umbrellas, and a magnificent view of the Saône River!

I had recently fallen in love with maps and the idea of tracing our routes on them for souvenirs, so I knew that we had been traveling alongside the river for some time, but a heavy growth of trees had obscured it from our sight until now. Here the foliage had been cleared and, as we were sitting not more than 30 yards from it, we seemed to be actually looking right down into its smoothly flowing depths from our ringside table. Lovely! I was awed by its breadth and power. Small boats were zipping up and down, and large tourist ships sailed majestically by now and then for our pleasure.

We were handed a sheet of paper with lavender writing on it for a menu, but the writing looked like it had been done by a nimble spider and I didn't recognize any of the words. I played it safe and asked the man, "*Avez vous une spécialité de la maison?*" (Irwin Shaw had told me when in doubt to ask for the special.) The waiter said, "*Mais oui!,*" and we were all set. As we were the only patrons (the French like to eat much later than Americans), we got prompt service and soon we were eating our fresh, fresh salad with that delicate dressing only the French seem to know how to make. As we were making fast work of our cold Chardonnay, we saw the brawny man had changed out of his black jacket and was now wearing knee-length boots, and over his shoulder he had a long pole with a net on one end as he marched down to the river. We assumed he was taking a break while our lunch was being prepared, but very shortly here he came marching back up to the kitchen with a full net.

What transpired a very short time later is right up there with that first soup and the *fraise de bois*. It never occurred to us that the waiter had gone down to the river to *catch* our lunch, but when he put plates of deep-fried tiny fish before us, they were clearly the *freshest* fish we had even eaten. There must have been about 30 to a plate and each plate was cleared of fish in record time. We left without knowing the name of those fish, but I have searched for their like ever since. Once in Monterey, California, I thought I had found them in a little restaurant right on the ocean, but though the fish were tiny and delicious, they were not the same. The waiter told us these fish were grunion and that their French equivalent were a different species altogether. But I didn't need to search for the equivalent of that gustatory delight Ellen and I shared on those yellow tablecloths under those yellow umbrellas, with the smell of lavender and the Saône River as air freshener. I have always kept that experience complete and vivid in my memory, and besides there *could* be no equivalent!

We had settled on Orange (pronounced *O-raunge*) as the best place to spend the night because it had been founded by the Romans in 35 BC (!) over an ancient Celtic settlement. We thought we might as well start at the beginning. The Mich said the monumental temple and forum complex in Orange was mostly in ruins, but the Roman theater that remained was the best preserved of all the Roman ruins in France. We wanted to see that. I had chosen a "been-in-the-same-family-for-generations" hotel in the old part of town that sounded like the kind of place the real French people would use, but we had a very difficult time finding it because it didn't look like a hotel. It was a part of a line of old buildings that were right on the street, and had only a small, weathered sign over its door indicating it was a hotel so we kept passing it by. Finally, we saw the sign but then couldn't find a place to park. There seemed nothing to do but park on the narrow cobbled sidewalk like the French do, but it felt illegal to me. I fully expected a parking ticket when we came back, but we figured "When in France, do as the French do," and mushed on. The foyer of the hotel was tiny, and bare of any amenities except a narrow counter as a front desk. Behind it were a wisp of a man and a formidable giant of a woman, who appeared to be man and wife and the last of the "generations of owners." The good part was that they didn't speak any English; the bad part was that they didn't seem to understand my French either.

I thought if I smiled hard enough and tried hard enough I could communicate anything, so finally I got it straight, I thought, that we wanted a room with two beds and a bath for the night, and they agreed that they had one and asked us to sign the register. I think the wispy man offered to carry our bags up the narrow stairs (there was no elevator), but I declined with many smiles and *"Merci, non,"* as I didn't like to trouble him since he was smaller than me, and we wove our way up to our assigned room feeling grateful that we hadn't brought the Black Mariah. Both it and we would never have made it up those narrow stairs.

The inadequacy of my French was brought home to us, however, when we entered our room to find a small neat room, with no windows, a small double bed and no adjoining bath. I had terrifying visions of a cement room with footprints in the floor as we searched for a bathroom, but when we found it way down the hall, to my great relief it had a regular toilet and separate shower. By now it was getting dark and I was getting hungry, so we decided to have dinner in the hotel rather than search for a restaurant. When we got down to the dining room, however, it was empty of other patrons, so we decided to eat at one of the two little tables out on the sidewalk. The metal table and chairs were a tad wobbly on the cobbled sidewalk, which was so narrow that passersby had to walk in the street to avoid bumping into us, but who was I to complain? When the wispy man brought us another sheet of paper with faint lavender handwriting for the menu, the only item I could make out was *"Tête d' veau pour deux,"* Considering the overall of our hotel, I was hesitant to order the specialty of the house, and since I knew that *"tête-a-tête"* meant a kind of intimate get together for two I thought that ought to be pretty good and ordered it. I had read that this was the area where Châteauneuf de Pape was made, so we ordered a bottle and it was indeed delicious.

Ellen and I both were martini fans, and I had never drunk wine much before, but by now we were *vino* aficionados and drank a bottle between us for both lunch and dinner. We had learned the hard way that the French make a dry martini that is undrinkable. So we were in a pleasant frame of mind from the wine, even though it did seem a long time for our order to come. Then disaster struck! With a flourish, the giant woman proudly placed in the center of the table *the whole, gray, pebbley-skinned, boiled head of a calf — which was staring at me*! Arrrgh! Belatedly, I remembered that *veau* meant veal, and that is what *tête d' veau* must mean. The whole head of a calf! Who could possibly *eat* such a thing? Sick at my stomach, embarrassed beyond measure, I managed to explain to the insulted giant woman, mostly by gestures, that we would pay for our entrée, but we couldn't *eat* it, and would she please, please take this, ah, *thing* away and bring us an omelet instead? I vowed to myself never to order anything but an omelet again without an interpreter. My exciting idea of being a world conqueror and a linguist vanished along with the horrible *tête d' veau*. Eager to get away from a place where they would *do* such a thing as boil a poor little calf's head and serve it to an unsuspecting customer, we got in the car and went to find the celebrated Roman theater.

It was indeed worth the trip as the amazingly well-preserved actual theater was dramatic and thrilling beyond our wildest imagination. On a steeply slanted hillside, the perhaps 25 rows of semi-circular smoothly-fitted stone seats faced down to a stage that was dramatically lit by invisible spotlights. The French do marvelous illuminations of their monuments at night, and sitting high in the last row of seats, if we were quiet, it was easy to hear the roar of ancient Romans that had once filled the arena. Of course, the roar I was hearing was probably more like that which the Romans gave to encourage the lions to eat the Christians than to encourage the actors to greater heights, but I could certainly hear *something* supernatural. It was transformative to think that our bottoms were in the exact same place as countless Roman bottoms had been before us. The acoustics in the amphitheater were such that even a whisper from an actor could be heard clearly in the last row, and sure enough, when I tried it, Ellen could hear me perfectly. Just imagine standing on a stage that was built around 2,000 years ago and having your whisper clearly reach someone maybe 50 yards above you without effort. I didn't see how it was acoustically possible. The stage had only a wall behind it to back up sound, and the whole amphitheater was open to the skies. There was a certain similarity to the medicine show with the backdrop behind the stage and open air seating, but you couldn't have reached the back of *those* seats in a whisper, I can tell you that.

Overawed by the enormity of the history of these stones we were sitting on, and the magic of this warm summer night under the stars, we just sat and absorbed what was reaching out to us from the past. Maybe it was the wine, maybe it was the past becoming real for us, or maybe it was the shock of the calf's head, but after we had sat quietly for a spell, Ellen began to talk. She said, "You know, Josie. I'm getting really pissed-off at the way you order me around and make all the decisions about everything."

Not understanding what she was saying at all, I said, "What?"

"Well, you are always *telling* me where we are going or what we are going to do. You never ask me what *I* want to do."

"Are you serious? I *always* ask you what you want to do!"

"No, you don't. For example, I would have liked to stay at Sam's apartment at the George V. I *liked* it there and he wasn't going to be there very long, and anyway, we could have handled him without any trouble. And he would have taken us out to good restaurants like La Tour d'Argent, which I liked a lot better than Bistro François. You didn't *ask* me if I wanted to move, you know, you just said we were moving."

"But ..."

"And *I* was the one who found Serge and I really liked him, but you came along and just grabbed him for yourself. He naturally went with you because you were paying the checks, but I saw him first. And I would have liked to stay at a nice hotel tonight. You can afford it, but without asking me, you picked that awful deathtrap we're in because (and she mimicked me in a ridiculous voice) *"I want to go where the French people go."* And tonight you didn't ask me what I wanted for dinner, you just ordered that horrible thing for both of us. You *never* ask me what I want."

"Well, I certainly didn't mean ..."

"And it isn't just now, you have always ..." Sobbing, her voice getting higher and shriller, she went on and on into the past about the times I had hurt her feelings or made decisions without asking her. I just sat there feeling stricken, until finally she got up and went back to the car and I slowly followed. Silent on the way back to the hotel, when we got there Ellen said she had to go to the bathroom, and by the time I got back to our room after my own visit to the bathroom, I found her fast asleep. I lay down beside her and considered this situation and what it meant.

Protected by my security blanket of personal ethics, I usually sailed along feeling good about myself. But if I did something to make me feel I had betrayed those ethics, like now with Ellen, I reacted all out of proportion. The devil himself could not have attacked me with pitchforks and brimstones any more vehemently that I attacked myself; I even had visions of slicing my chest with knives in penance and self-hate. Replaying many times the things Ellen had accused me of, castigating myself severely, I tried to understand the ramifications of what had just happened. Since I was practically phobic about being beholden to anyone, I thought I had been keenly aware of the position Ellen was in and had tried to mitigate any feeling of her not sharing equally in our adventure by giving her $300 in travelers checks before we even left New York. That was a lot of money in those days, but I wanted her to feel she had her own money to spend on anything extra she wanted, like clothes or something personal. I thought it was simpler for me to pay all the bills rather than try to figure out who had what for lunch or whatever. Plus, I'll admit, I thought of this as *my* fairy tale, and I thought of Ellen as just another character in it, like Cinderella's good sister or something.

But I loved Ellen and I wouldn't have hurt her or made her feel slighted for anything. Ellen was a brilliant dancer with cyclonic energy on the stage, but when she was not dancing — she was quiet and vulnerable. I knew that Ellen was what my mother would call "thin skinned." And I felt that it was her lack of self-esteem that thinned her skin, leaving little cover for some old open deep wound, or maybe lots of little wounds, from the past, and I had always felt protective of her and tried to make her feel good about herself. I thought.

As for Serge, well, Ellen hadn't told me that she really liked him and consequently I hadn't given her feelings a second thought when I scooped him up and made off with him. But he didn't mean anything important to me, certainly he was not as important as Ellen's feelings. If I could say, "Take him, I don't want him, you can have him," and magically move him into my place in bed with her right now, I would do so gladly. I was just attracted to his beautiful face and figure when I saw him dancing and thought he fitted the character of Prince Charming in my fairy tale. And I must say he played that part exceedingly well, and I enjoyed playing princess with him, but still the most important thing now was to do everything I could to be more aware of Ellen's feelings and find ways to make her feel important.

The next morning, Ellen was up bright-eyed, bushy-tailed, and full of cheer, while I could hardly see. At once I began to try to apologize for my behavior, but she didn't seem to know what I was talking about. She said gaily, "I had a bit too much wine last night and I can't remember a thing that happened. Let's just get our things and leave this awful place; we can stop for breakfast somewhere along the road." Either she had honestly forgotten it, was in deep denial, or just didn't want to talk about it. Whatever, I thought to let sleeping dogs lie was the better part of valor, but I made myself a solemn promise to be a more thoughtful and sensitive friend from here on out.

The Hotel du Cap's brochure stated: "Situated in a 9-acre private park, this 5-star Hotel is an 1870 Napoleon III structure and a mythical refuge. It is a temple of elegance where the rhythm of the dazzling Riviera pulsates, and the golden secret moments of the past merge with those created in the present." Well, I mean! Who could resist that? With no trouble, we found the simple little white sign reading Hotel Du Cap with a gold arrow pointing to our left, which led us through what surely looked to be an enchanted forest with lovely old trees and manicured bushes, of which I had never seen the like. The hotel, however, was so huge and rectangular and white, with gilt outlining all the curlicues around the columns and windows, that it reminded me of Versailles. Two young men in dark blue pants, white jackets, and perky red caps ran out to get our bags, accompanied by another man in *striped pants and a swallow-tail coat*. Right away, I knew I was in trouble. And sure enough, the lobby was about as warm and cozy as Versailles, and almost as large. It was two-stories-high and everything in it seemed to be made of marble. Even the concierge. If I'd had my druthers, I would have paid for the night and gotten out of there right then, but Ellen's eyes were as big as muffins as she looked through a wall of French glass doors to the terrace, which overlooked a truly enormous rose garden, and far below an equally enormous swimming pool, and the enormous sparkling Mediterranean, which was decorated with many enormous yachts. She loved it, and with my new-found determination to make her wishes paramount, I was stuck. To me the only good thing about the place was the Eden Roc Pavilion down beside the saltwater pool. The seaside along this part of the Mediterranean didn't have much of a beach; what there was of it was too rocky to walk barefoot without severe pain, and usually the cliff loomed up right at the water's edge.

The Eden Roc Pavilion was an exceptionally charming restaurant/spa complex built right at the edge of the cliff overlooking the ocean and the Eden Roc Harbor. The swimming pool was hacked out of the cliff rock, with tables, deck lounges, and colorful umbrellas on the heavily shellacked wooden decking around it. There were wooden steps leading down to a roped-off swimming area in the sea, and a wooden pier for the shore boats to tie up. I had to admit, with the whole complex surrounded by trees and glorious flowers, it was spectacular, and I thought to myself, "I'm going to spend all my time right here, and only go back to that monstrosity of a hotel just to sleep."

That night after dinner Ellen struck up a conversation around the pool with a silver-haired Englishman named Rodney something, and they went off to have a nightcap in the bar while I went helpfully to bed. I was not going to repeat the Serge thing with Ellen and was determined to stay out of her way. Not that it was a hard decision.

Rodney was very fashionably dressed in his casual clothes, and looked tan and fit, but his face had been so surgically stretched that he could hardly smile, which always puts me off, and I could tell right away that he was a monologist. Almost as soon as we met him, he settled back and began a story in the British colonial tone of voice, "One time when I was in Kenya on safari ..." — and I excused myself with a headache.

The next morning, Ellen told me that Rodney was a guest on the yacht of some people who were just stopping here at Eden Roc for a few days on their way to Greece. She said Rodney was a wealthy nobleman, (who didn't use his title), had an estate in England, an apartment in Paris on Avenue d' Iena overlooking the Étoile, and spent part of the year in Beverly Hills with his best friend, Edmund Gwen. Since I knew Gwen was a homosexual, I figured Ellen couldn't get into much trouble with Rodney. At breakfast, here was Rodney again and he said that he had told his hosts, the Count and Countess Ricci, about us, and they invited us to have lunch with them on their boat. He said they would send a shore boat for us at noon, but I quickly told him not to bother, that we would swim out. Then I thought, "Oops. I did it again." I had spoken without stopping to think that Ellen would probably have preferred the shore boat, but when Rodney had pointed out the Ricci yacht, it seemed only a short distance away and I didn't want a *Count*, for heaven's sake, to do me any favors. So it was agreed that we would swim out for lunch at noon, although Rodney appeared a bit perplexed.

I was always eager to learn new things — this day I learned that distances at sea can be very deceiving. The yacht appeared to me to be just out there a little way, but as we were swimming toward it, it *stayed* just out there a little way. We never seemed to be getting closer. Probably because of tap dancing and horseback riding during my formative years, I had developed strong leg and arm muscles and was a good swimmer. I hadn't thought Ellen would have any trouble because the dancers at Metro had to do the water ballet numbers with Esther Williams, and during rehearsal and shooting, the dancers were swimming in the water all day. Apparently, it is different swimming in a studio pool doing ballet movements than distance swimming in the ocean, however, because by the time we were about two-thirds of the way out to the boat, Ellen began to run out of steam. I was tired, but still had enough energy to pull her along until we reached the boat-side ladder and helping hands. I felt like a fool there in my dripping bathing suit and hair, while the Count, who was tan, tall, and gorgeous (looking a lot like German actor, Curt Jurgens), was resplendent in white pants, silk shirt, and jacket with a red silk handkerchief in the pocket. The Count also had a mischievous twinkle in his eye as he gave us a gracious welcome. I instantly had him pegged as a pincher, but his Italian accent was almost as knee-melting as the French, so I had to like him. And then there was the Countess. She had on a *dress.* It was a multi-colored chiffon almost to her ankles and she wore a big hat in the same tones. She also wore a most supercilious disapproving look on her face, and barely acknowledged us.

It was easy to imagine the Ricci's story. Arranged marriage between two aristocratic families; he slept around and did as he pleased, and she pretended she didn't know and took care of all the social and family things. The yacht itself was truly an awesome beauty, and there was an exquisitely set table for five under an awning on deck. During an elaborate lunch, which it took five servants to pull off, Rodney and the Countess were mostly silent. I thought Rodney's stories had probably been too oft-told for him to talk much, and the Countess was too stiff-necked to get many words out, but the Count and Ellen and I got along just fine. He seemed totally interested in our lives and our trip so far and found us very amusing, and then, astonishingly, invited us to come with them on their extended cruise of the Greek Islands as his guest. Ellen or no Ellen, I was not about to sign on for something like that, so I quickly declined. I was tempted to agree just to see the look on the Countess's face, but instead agreed to have dinner with them that night as long as we could eat at the Pavilion instead of the stuffy dining room in the hotel.

At dinner, Ellen and I had taken pains to dress well and comb our hair so we didn't look like the rag-a-muffins we had at lunch, but the Countess outdid us in that department, needless to say, particularly when it came to jewelry. Ever eager to prove I was not an "ugly American" and was just one of the common folk," I always struck up friendly conversations with cab drivers, clerks, and waiters in my meager French. For one thing, I was just bursting with affection for all things French, and secondly I was heavily involved with my "Up the Proletariat" prejudices. So at dinner I asked our waiter his name, where he was from, and so forth. I thought the waiter seemed a little shy so I kept beaming at him to put him at ease. After he had gone the

Countess attacked me with the viciousness of a mongoose. Pouncing her words off me like bullets, she said, "We Italians don't fraternize with servants, Miss Dennison. It shows a want of class!"

Taking a mental stance of, "En Garde!" I said, "I am in a class by myself, ah, Countess, and I do as I please."

The Count lay back in his chair roaring with laughter, and said, "She's got you there, Isabella." Then turning to me, still laughing, he reached over and put his hand on mine, saying, "Won't you reconsider being our guest for the next few weeks? The Greek Islands are lovely this time of year. I will arrange with the hotel to store your car and we will bring you back to pick it up sometime in July."

"No, thank you," I said sternly, as I snatched my hand from under his, glaring at him like an affronted spinster.

Unfazed, he said, "Well, when you get to Rome you may find it difficult getting accommodations since this is the tourist season, so just use my name at The Hassler. I will drop them a note to make sure you get a nice room."

The next day as we watched his yacht sail majestically away, I said, "That Count Ricci is a toad. He looks like a prince, but he is still a toad to humiliate his wife that way in front of us. And we certainly don't need *him* to get a reservation at a hotel." I never seem to learn not to make emphatic pronouncements, even though they so often come back to bite me, as this one shortly did.

Our next stop was Saint Tropez. Our friends in Paris had said it was the "in" place to go as of last year when Brigitte Bardot had made the hit movie *And God Created Woman* on location in St. Tropez, and liked it so much she bought a house there. It had been a small, quiet, medieval fishing village until the advent of Bardot, but now it had become the place where the "jet set" gathered by boat, private plane or Maseratti to party all night. We had been told the Hotel Byblos was a "little jewel" of a hotel and t'was thence we wended our way. Even with The Mich's directions, it was very hard to find it on these narrow, one-way, cobblestone streets. We found it, though, but not a place to park, so Ellen stayed in the car while I went in to get us a room. This time, I was truly dazzled by the lobby which had the most harmonious and beautiful décor I had ever seen. Even though it was a small hotel, huge bouquets of flowers were in abundance and the lovely furniture glowed with a polish that made you feel you could see deep inside the wood. Even the front desk appeared to be originally from a cathedral or something. Through the French glass doors, I could see outside a delightful dining terrace *under a grape arbor.* Thus it was with unalterable determination that I asked for a room for two with bath. The imposing young man behind the desk said, if I understood his French correctly, that there were no rooms without a reservation. I never tried so hard in my life to be charming as I coaxed him to change his mind. He was unimpressed and unbending. Since it seemed that only "no reservation" was the problem I refused to take "no" for an answer — but he just turned away from me and began to go through some papers. Desperate, wishing I had Count Ricci with me right now, I ran out to the car and asked Ellen to go in and force him into giving us a room. There was no way I was going to give up, *I loved this place.* Of course, Ellen didn't speak any better French than I did, and didn't have as much chutzpah, so she did what she did best — she danced. Bravely she began to do some tap steps, saying, "Gene Kelly *est mi danseur* (dance partner).

The imposing young man fell apart. *"Gene Kellee? Ahhhh! Gene Kellee! Mais oui,"* and he began indicating that he wanted to be a dancer and Gene was his idol. Ellen kept showing him Gene's steps while he bounced up and down in ecstasy, and, naturally, gave us the best room in the house. Where there's a will there's a way, I always say.

Ellen and I were wildly excited when we saw our room. With big windows overlooking the garden, right down to the smallest vase, it was the most beautifully decorated room I was ever in. Later when we read the hotel's brochure, we saw that the owner of the hotel was an antiques dealer, and she had furnished each room in the hotel in a different era's style — predominately the Louies from III to VII — and everything in the rooms was authentic, even in the bathroom, although the fixtures were all new, may the gods be praised. I wanted to roll around in the ambiance of it all like a dog when something smells wonderful to him.

Having an exquisite dinner under the grape arbor that night kept the marvelous feeling of being in another world going, and we were feeling light as bubbles as we went down to an outside bar by the harbor for a nightcap to see the night life we had heard so much about. Cointreau over ice was our cocktail of choice at the time, and we sat there in the warm night air looking at the fairy lights on the multitude of yachts in a haze of bliss, while waiting for the "jet set" to jazz up the joint. Nothing. We were the only patrons at the bar and the quay side was deserted. Obviously, we had been misinformed about the wild nightlife of St. Tropez so, as it was almost midnight, we decided to go back to our Louis VI room and make it an early night. As in a dream, as we climbed up the hill in this medieval town, the faint sound of a piano playing Cole Porter drifted down to us out of the night. The magical magnet of the sound irresistibly drew us up and around into a dimly lit cave of a nightclub, seemingly empty except for a slight young man with a cigarette hanging from his mouth playing a piano on a little bandstand in a dark corner. Dream like, we moved over and leaned on the piano, and as he smiled up at us, we began to sing along with him. The only other people in the room were a middle-aged woman with two young men seated at a table near the bandstand. Encouraged, perhaps, by her triumph with the concierge, after a bit Ellen began to dance by herself on the dance floor while the piano played on. The woman and the two men began to applaud and shout out to Ellen as she did a combination of Gene and Jack Cole — Gene with his knee slides, a little tap, and flying leaps, and Jack with his erotic tiny bumps, sensual writhing, and pole dancing. The silent guy at the piano understood the magical quality of the night and segued into the Gershwins, Rodgers and Hart, and Irving Berlin while I kept leaning on the piano singing softly. As though all part of a dream and on cue, the tables filled with patrons who watched Ellen and roared their approval. The three band members had quietly come in and sat in their chairs watching Ellen also, until after a bit, the drummer and saxophonist began to softly join the piano. Perhaps it was the applause or perhaps it was the effect of this incredible night, but Ellen became inspired. A hitherto unknown artistic creativity opened up for her and she began to dance as I had never seen her. Her long, dark hair flying in all directions, she swooshed and slithered around that dance floor in a frenzy of dazzling talent. Finally, she did a series of twirls all around the dance floor and collapsed back at the piano to riotous applause. Josephine Baker didn't wow the Parisians back in the 40s naked any more than Ellen wowed her audience that mesmerizing night in culottes and a T-shirt.

The friendly threesome came over to the piano to congratulate Ellen on her performance, and it turned out they all worked for Christian Dior in Paris, including the piano player who was from New York and still never said a word. They were here on vacation and explained to us that St. Tropez only came alive around midnight, and asked about Ellen's dance background. Then there ensued cries of delight, "Gene Kelllleee! Ahhhh," and questions to Ellen about Gene. During all this, two young men joined us to say "Bravo" to Ellen, and the tall, dark, and handsome one introduced himself to us as Francisco and his friend as Ramon. He spoke little English, but his Spanish accent was delicious. It turned out they were attachés at the Argentine Embassy in Paris, who were in St. Tropez on vacation. Francisco had the dark hair, bedroom eyes, and sexy attitude of a Rudolph Valentino, whereas Ramon had sandy-colored hair and blue eyes, and the haughty attitude of a captain in the Nazi Gestapo. Francisco asked Ellen if he and Ramon could take her and her friend out to dinner the next night, and Ellen didn't let him finish his sentence in her eagerness to accept. It was by now after 2 a.m. and I was about to turn into a pumpkin. Trying to remember all the lyrics to those songs had worn me out, and Ellen's adrenalin was expiring from excessive use, so we trundled off to bed amid roaring farewell applause for Ellen.

The next morning, Ellen lay in bed luxuriating in that best of all theatrical feelings: the aftermath of a triumph. She seemed almost a new person and I was truly glad for her. She was also in a lather of anticipation all day as visions of an everlasting Latin romance and moonlight rides over the Argentine pampas made her giddy. When we started to dress for dinner, she suggested we wear shorts. Now, Ellen had really long, lovely legs. If we stood side by side, we were the same height but her legs came up almost to my waist. My shorts were well above my knee, but Ellen's were dance rehearsal shorts that were up to her crotch and revealed all her beautiful legs. I could see she was desperate to look enticing for Francisco, but I said, "You wear shorts, I think I'll wear slacks." But Ellen begged me, saying she couldn't do it, if I didn't. Visions of Ellen weeping on the stone steps of the Roman Theatre in Orange nudged me sharply — so I agreed to wear shorts as well. *It turned out to be a very bad idea.*

When Francisco and Ramon met us in the lobby of our hotel they looked a tad startled at our attire, dressed as they were in elegant white linen pants, flowing-sleeved white silk shirts, and crimson cummerbunds, but, being diplomats, they suavely offered us their arms to lead us out into the St. Tropez night. Most towns along the French and Italian Rivera are built into cliff or hillsides and the homes and shops seem to grow right out of the rock. In the daytime, the buildings, with their contrasting colors and trims, look a lot like children's building blocks, but at night with the shops all shuttered and the street lights dim and far between, the ancient stone buildings appear to huddle together and turn their backs on passersby. Our escorts knew where they were going, however, and they led us confidently up the winding cobblestone streets until we reached a kind of high promontory upon which was perched an edifice of massive dark stones looming up into the skies. A small lantern hung over a magnificent iron gate through which we entered into a narrow stone passageway leading up a few stairs to an imposing set of wooden doors with iron fittings. I wouldn't have been surprised if Gene Wilder as Young Frankenstein had answered the big brass bell, but instead it was a slender, young woman of delicate grace and beauty, who was introduced to us as Countess Clothilde something or other. I was too stunned by her appearance to catch her last name. She was wearing a long pale-gray garment, with long sleeves and a high neckline that looked to be made of cashmere and spider webs, and which flowed around her like liquid mercury. With the utmost grace, she led us through an enormous foyer filled with suits of armor and life-sized statues and on up a couple of floors of wide staircases. The staircases were lit by candles in wall niches, mind you, and led out onto a balcony that ran the length of the house and overlooked the ocean flowing back and forth against huge rocks far below. There was a full moon which revealed that the stone balustrade around the balcony had ceramic pots of flowers interspersed with candle-lit heraldic images and statuary that made the antiquity of this — well — *castle* I guess you would have to call it, truly palpable. I felt I could reach out and touch the centuries it had weathered.

The Countess introduced us to the third member of the Argentine Embassy party as her fiancée (his name went by me in a blur) who was the reason the three young men had rented a yacht to come here for their vacation. We gave our orders for drinks to a silent, very old butler who had abruptly materialized. I wished I could have ordered a large cyanide and soda or else been instantly consumed by the flame of embarrassment that swept me from head to toe at the inappropriate way Ellen and I were dressed, but as always when feeling threatened or inadequate, I became arrogant and tried to appear in control. I sat on a lounge chair swinging my bare leg and nonchalantly said, "How old is this, ah, your home, ah..."

I had called Countess Ricci "Countess" with a sneer, but I had no sneer for this elegant, gracious young woman and couldn't think for a moment what to call her.

But she swiftly said, "Call me Clothilde, please, Jo-Carroll," and began to tell Ellen and me the origins and history of her ancestral home. I am sure it was interesting, but all I could hear was the twang of humiliation humming in my ears until the welcome suggestion by her fiancée that we get ready to leave for dinner. The Countess asked that we excuse her for a moment and within minutes returned — dressed in *shorts*! I wanted to throw myself at her feet and blubber out how gracious and kind she was to do such a thing to make Ellen and me feel more comfortable, but I was too stunned and ill-mannered myself to do so at the time. I couldn't even acknowledge the gesture. I knew what she was doing, I had heard the story about the Queen of England drinking out of her finger bowl when her unsophisticated guest had unknowingly done so, but I felt I had been turned to stone — like one of her ancient statues along the walls — and could say or do nothing but numbly trail along.

To this day, I could not tell you what the fiancée looked like or where we had dinner. I think it is the only meal I ate in France that is a blank to me. My ability to blot out that which is too painful came to my aid and I have only a dim memory of several dark caves the French had made into restaurants and nightclubs, but the only clear moment I remember is telling the boring Ramon that I didn't feel well and needed to go back to the hotel. He didn't seem to mind. I must have said good night to the others, but memory fails me. The next thing I remember about that horrible night is Ellen returning to join me at breakfast on the terrace of the hotel the next morning, still in her shorts. She never told me where she had been all night and I didn't want to know. Neither of us mentioned the Countess.

Ellen was both exhausted and ebullient: exhausted because she hadn't slept all night and ebullient because Francisco was coming to take her to lunch today, so she quickly had breakfast and went upstairs to get some beauty sleep, while I went out to explore St. Tropez. I was surprised at how few people there were on the fascinating, winding cobbled streets or in the multitude of small, almost hidden shops. True, some of the mullioned shop windows displayed the latest Paris fashions but they seemed out of place somehow, and scarcely anyone was in the shops. When I got back to the hotel for lunch, I found that

Francisco had never arrived to pick up Ellen and after we waited around for an hour or so, our new best friend, the concierge, advised us to go to the beach for the afternoon. Tahiti Beach (what a name for a French beach!) was quite a distance out of town, but when we found it, we also found out where all the people were — hordes of them were scattered along the white sands under umbrellas, sunning on large towels, in the water, buying snacks at the many food and drink stands, or playing beach volleyball. Tahiti Beach turned out to be one of the few sandy beaches along the whole Rivera and the only difference between it and the California beach in Santa Monica was there were lots more yachts anchored near it. Well, the waves were smaller and the water was a prettier color, but outside of that the only difference was that the *bikini* had arrived and the tiny tops and bottoms made our one-piece bathing suits look antique. Also, part of the beach was reserved for *topless* bathers. Now that was *French*!

As soon as they saw me, children and even adults began to point at me and laughingly yell, *"Regarde le clown."* I always wore white zinc on my nose at the beach to avoid sunburn and the French crowd thought I looked hilarious. I obligingly did a Charlie Chaplin walk around our beach towel and was rewarded with laughter and shouts of agreement. Suddenly, Ellen grabbed my arm and was doing her own pointing out to sea. She whispered hoarsely, "Look, Josie. That's *his* yacht. That blue and white one. Oh, Josie, I can't stand it. Swim out there and see if he has another girl with him on the boat. I have to know. Maybe that's why he didn't pick me up for lunch."

Apparently, she could identify Francisco's yacht because she had spent the night there, but she had been weeping off and on for the past hour and was in real distress, so like Tarzan to the rescue, off I went. The Mediterranean can be almost as flat as a swimming pool, as well as being buoyant, but in my haste to be a Girl Scout I had forgotten how distance at sea is deceiving and was really winded by the time I reached the side of the yacht. Plus, I didn't know what to say when I got there. Sure enough, the three diplomats were aboard along with the Countess and two gorgeous girls, all wearing French bikinis and looking tanned and fit while having their afternoon cocktails. Hanging on a rope alongside, I refused their startled invitation to come aboard and have a drink by saying, "Oh, no (gasp), I was just (gasp) passing by (gasp) and when I saw you (gasp) I thought I'd just (gasp) say hello. But, ah, well, ah, bye-bye for now," and I started my swim back. Now it is one thing to swim out to a yacht and have lunch; it is quite another to swim out and then immediately swim back. I was still far from the beach when I just gave out, my arms felt like lead weights and my legs refused to stay up in the water. I could see Ellen at water's edge frantically waving at me for encouragement, but I really didn't see how I was going to make it. Suddenly, as I hung there in the water unable to move further, I sensed a huge presence beneath me in the water and something soft and silky brushed swiftly by my legs. The word "shark" flashed before my eyes. Instantly enough energy to run a battleship surged through me, and I made it back to the beach in a time Michael Phelps would envy. I found out later there were no sharks in this area, but there were lots of dolphins and they loved to play with swimmers. I always felt that friendly dolphin saved my life.

Francisco came by for Ellen the next day and it turned out that when he had told her "Tomorrow, tomorrow" he had meant the day *after* tomorrow, so all was well with Ellen and she went gaily off with him while I spent the next afternoon alone at the beach. But I didn't go in the water. I greatly enjoyed my dinner alone that evening under the grape vines.

The following day the Argentines had to sail back to Paris so Ellen was happy to continue our trip, and we went first to Nice. The Hotel Byblos was like a single precious jewel, but the Hotel Negresco looked like the whole set of the Queen of England's crown jewels. With its huge paintings and elegant blue and red furnishings, each downstairs room — enormous foyer, sitting rooms, conservatory, dining rooms — was more wondrous than the next. Our bedroom had an exquisite canopy over the king-size bed and a fabulous view of the ocean from our balcony. Awesome. The Hotel du Paris in Monte Carlo was much the same, only less so. Then we were onto the Italian Riviera where the hotel in Portofino seemed quaint by comparison, but the lovely hotel in Rapallo we stayed in had been a convent and its grounds and colonnades and view high above the harbor were breathtaking. Plus, Ava Gardner and Humphrey Bogart had stayed there when they had shot the movie, *The Barefoot Contessa,* nearby and had taught the bartender to make perfect martinis. But even with the martinis, after a couple of days there, we were ready for some more excitement and decided to go back to Nice, and leave the car at the airport and fly to Rome. The mountainous roads of the Riviera were extraordinarily picturesque, but could be exhausting too. We asked the concierge at the hotel to book us a room in a good hotel in Rome, but after some telephoning, he told us the hotels at this time of year were already filled. So, reluctantly, I called The Hassler, (which the concierge told us was the best hotel in Rome) mentioned Count Ricci, and like magic we had a reservation. He *had* sent them a note about us.

The Hassler Roma Hotel was a delight. It sits at the top of the famous "Spanish Steps," and is extravagantly elegant but cozy. Its relatively few rooms made you feel part of a family in a way. Its Imago Bar was the place to be for cocktails in Rome, and their roof-top restaurant, The 7th Floor Terrace, had the best food and view in town. But when you're in love, the attractions of would-be suitors are at a distinct disadvantage. To me, the light in Paris was ethereal and luminous while the light of Rome was harsh and glaring; the most famous monuments of Paris were lovingly maintained and intact, while so many of the famous monuments in Rome were its ruins; the two cities both had rivers that ran through them, but the Seine was a sparkling pale green, the Tiber a turgid yellowy-brown. And the difference in the *food*, well, I won't go into that. I'll admit Rome tried hard, the Borghese Gardens were a lovely, cool, glory of nature where one could sit and be happy out of the brutal heat of Rome, and seeing *Madama Butterfly* in the ruins of the Caracalla Baths was an indelible experience. I had never heard of the lead singers and have forgotten their names now, but the evocative and wildly imaginative scenery on the stage of this open-air theater, similar to the one in Orange, is the setting I envision every time I listen to that music. My rising enthusiasm for Rome took a hit, however, when we tried to enter St. Peter's Cathedral and were turned away because as it happened I had on a sleeveless blouse that day. Stupid man-made rules like that are a good part of why I am against organized religion. What do bare arms have to do with the love of God, for heaven's sake? I was so infuriated I never did see Saint Peter's, or the Sistine Chapel either on that trip!

Anyway, my principle interest in Rome was not its famous sculptures and paintings, but rather its famous Emperors and the forms of government that came out of that extraordinary period in history (around 400 BC to 400 AD) that was Ancient Rome. The study of Ancient Egypt, Greece, and Rome were fascinating stops on my early pathway through the adventure of learning. My favorite Emperor was

Hadrian, whom historians called "One of the five good Emperors," and Gibbon called Hadrian's era, "The happiest in human history." According to what I had read, Hadrian was an artist, poet, humanist, epicurean, and military genius who had built the miles of 15-foot wide stone wall in the north of England as a barrier against the Barbarians, much of which remains to this day. And I admired him because of his policies as emperor and his innovations in architecture, like the Pantheon and the Castel Sant' Angelo, and particularly for his love of nature as expressed by the gardens he personally planned around his villa. I admired him for his determination to live his life as he chose — he had the obligatory wife, but made no secret of his homosexuality. I had learned a great deal about him personally from Ramsey & Stewart's fascinating book, *Hadrian's* Villa, which had detailed plans and pictures of his gardens, and one of the primary desires I had in visiting Rome was to kind of walk in Hadrian's footsteps.

I was still intrigued by that feeling I'd had sitting on those stones in the amphitheater in Orange — of being *connected* to the ancient Romans. I wanted to experience it again in some way in Rome, and had chosen Hadrian as the medium. The chaos created by the crowds and the noise of the traffic, particularly the ubiquitous ear-shattering Vespas roaring around the squares of the present center of Rome, made its antiquities look unreal, like giant picture postcards of themselves. Nary a whisper of the ancients could be heard there. But the old center of Rome, The Forum, was almost deserted at night, so I devised a plan.

In the daylight, The Forum's multitude of ruined temples, basilicas, arches and monuments spread out over the ancient heart of Rome looked pathetic — most of its marble had been removed by later Emperors to build monuments to themselves elsewhere and the shattered remnants of what had once been the glory of Rome were maintained merely as a tourist attraction. Since Hadrian had been responsible for a good many of The Forum's most magnificent buildings, I thought that if I could find his spirit anywhere it would be there — at night when all the disturbing clutter of daytime tourism had been dispersed. Thus it was that one night, Ellen and I took a taxi at midnight to the bridge over the Tiber that directly faced the majestic Castel Sant' Angelo. It had been designed by Hadrian as his tomb, and was indeed where his ashes reposed now in a splendid chapel. (Somewhat later Tom Cruise and Katie Holmes chose to get married there, but that's another story.) The huge round edifice was dramatically lit at night, as are all the antiquities in Rome, and we leaned on the balustrade of the bridge and communed with Hadrian's tomb for a long time, but all we could hear was the rumble of the river passing beneath us. Undeterred, we turned and walked back until we came to the area of the cracked and broken travertine paving of the leftover brilliance of the center of the abandoned Forum. Sitting quietly on a white marble bench in the middle of what must have been the square in front of the Senate buildings, we felt somehow that we were on sacred ground. I could never make contact with Hadrian's spirit, more's the pity, but did feel I was merging into the minds of the people whose imagination and creative force had erected these splendid symbols of their religions and aspirations. These men whose ambition and military genius had conquered and ruled almost half the then-known world — this Forum was their legacy. Speaking only in whispers, it became possible to return these ghostly white and lonely skeletons back into their original forms of beauty and meaning. In the semi-darkness, illuminated by the occasional spotlight, soon it seemed I could hear the distant arguing voices of Roman Senators. Even if they spoke with the words of Shakespeare, the voices were those of Julius Caesar and Augustus and Mark Anthony. We sat there for a long time absorbing the emanations from those topless marble columns, nose-less statues, still-standing beautifully sculptured facades of long gone buildings, and the faint pressure of past centuries. That experience alone was worth the trip to Rome.

To add to the eerie feeling, as we silently rose to leave, out of the darkness came an apparition in the form of a possibly 2-month-old black and white kitten. He pattered up to me as if we were old friends and accepted as his due my strokes and admiring comments as to what a fine feline specimen he was. I had heard that there were hundreds of feral cats around The Forum and knew this must be one of them who lived nearby. However, as we walked off he followed us across the paving keeping up a conversation as though he was giving us the story of his life. We tried to shoo him back, but he continued alongside us as though we were a family going home together. Several times, we stopped and I tried to explain the situation to him, that this is where he lived and he couldn't go home with me because there was no way I could keep him. He looked up at me with seeming understanding, but as soon as we started off he was keeping right up with us, calling "Hey, wait up." I stopped and looked at Ellen. She didn't much like cats, but agreed that this was spooky. Was this kitten a gift from the Ancient Roman Gods? Was he an omen? The last thing in the world I needed under the circumstances was a cat. The ramifications were enormous. Kitty litter! Getting him home! I hadn't owned a cat since I was a child, but if this one was sent to me by the Ancient Roman Gods, dare I refuse? Well, obviously I couldn't. Like it or not, convenient or not, the gods had spoken and I had a kitten. I decided to name him Zeus. But just as I started to pick him up and make off with him, out of the darkness streamed his mother who gave him a hard smack across the nose, and began hissing dire threats at him if he didn't get himself back home right this minute. He turned and skittered back, with her right behind him muttering what a bad boy he was to frighten his mother this way. I watched them disappear behind some columns feeling both relieved and deprived. I never forgot him, that little black and white sprite, and always have wondered what would have happened if his mother hadn't arrived at just that moment? He was such a part of that magical night.

The next day as Ellen and I were sitting at an outdoor café on the Via Veneto people watching, I was still feeling a little wistful. But that feeling was swept away by the strange little miracle that then happened. A man who had been sitting at a nearby table came over to me and said, "Are you Jo-Carroll Dennison?" Upon my admission that I was, he said he had recognized me from photographs and introduced himself as Mario (I forget his last name), the husband of Venus Ramey, Miss America of 1944. Since I never attended any of the yearly reunions of former Miss Americas, I hadn't met Venus, but I had heard she'd married an Italian theatrical agent and was now living in Rome and working in their burgeoning film industry, so I said hello and that it was nice to meet him.

Mario was a handsome, somewhat stout, man, who looked to be in his mid-40s. After asking my permission, he settled into a vacant chair and ordered fresh drinks. Like Count Ricci, he spoke English with a delicious Italian accent, and after we discussed what Ellen and I were doing in Rome, I asked after Venus.

In an offhand way, he said, "Thank you, yes. Venus is well, but she has just gone back to her farm in Kentucky for awhile."

I could tell by the expression on his face and his tone of voice that he didn't expect her to come back. But he continued affably, "Jo-

Carroll, as her agent, I got Venus a lot of work in films here in Rome. The Italian directors like to use American actors whenever they can and a lot of Americans are working now in our industry. I saw your work in *Winged Victory* and *The Jolson Story* and I know I could get you some films, too."

Hastily, I said, "Oh, no. The only Italian I can speak is on a menu."

Raising both hands, he protested, "No, no, no. You don't have to speak Italian, you just speak in English and they dub you later. Excuse me just a moment. I will be shortly back," and he rose and hurried inside the café.

At that time, more people around the world saw American films than those of all other countries put together, imagine that! You could hardly pass a movie theater marquee in any town in France or Italy that wasn't featuring large posters showing Clark Gable and Myrna Loy in a clinch, or perhaps Humphrey Bogart with a gun and a snarl. You certainly never saw posters featuring European actors outside of American theaters! Most often American actors were dubbed in the language of the country where their pictures were shown, and it was hilarious, for instance, to see John Wayne doing his cowboy thing, while delicate French words seemingly issued from his mouth. To me, a dubbed film lost all the actor's individual flavor by substituting another person's voice, and I much preferred subtitles. But after the war, there had been an explosion of neo-realistic movies from Italian directors such as Fellini, Visconti, Antonioni, Rosselini, and De Sica, and to help reach an American audience they often used American actors.

Mario, returning with a triumphant smile, said to me, "I got him! I knew Vittorio De Sica was shooting out at Cinecittá, and I spoke to him and he said he would give you a screen test."

I was astonished that a mere agent could get a famous director who had just done the marvelous *Shoe Shine* and *The Bicycle Thief* (which had received all kinds of awards, including the Oscar in America,) to speak to him on the phone just like that. You can bet George Cukor wouldn't have done it. Anyway, I said, "Oh, gosh, I'm sorry, Mario, but Ellen and I are leaving for a trip tomorrow and I'm not sure when we'll be back."

Grasping my hand and half rising, Mario said, "Oh, no, no, no. I mean right now. He is shooting a movie just now and they will fit you in for a screen test as soon as we get there."

Not comprehending, "Without seeing a script?"

"You won't need a script. He just wants to talk to you and see how you move and react on film. De Sica doesn't need for you to be playing a part in the test. They wouldn't be using your own voice in a film anyway; he just wants to see how you come across on the screen. It won't take more than a half hour. And after he sees the film, if he likes it, he might put you under personal contract like he did Venus."

I thought, "Personal contract? This Italian genius who made *The Bicycle Thief* may want to put me under personal contract!" It was Charlie Chaplin all over again, only it didn't seem real at all. It seemed perfectly logical in my fairy tale, however, and I could only think my guardian angel was just having fun, so I said, "OK. Sure. Let's go."

I asked Ellen to come along, but she said, rather stiffly I thought, "No, since you don't want to go there, I think I will go see St. Peter's and the Vatican while you're gone. I'll meet you back at the hotel."

Cinecittá wasn't as big as Fox or Metro, but otherwise it looked much the same and amazingly soon I was seated in a chair on a sound stage talking to Vittorio De Sica before a rolling camera. De Sica was about as handsome as a man should be allowed to be, and was just as charming as he was handsome. At the time, I didn't know that he had been a famous Italian movie star before the war and had only recently gone on to directing. He put me at ease immediately by saying in his musical accent that he could see how I became Miss America, and asking me how I liked Rome. Well — I did 30 minutes on my admiration of Hadrian and our ineffective effort to connect with his spirit at Castel Sant' Angelo, and our consequent continuing search for him among the ruins of The Forum in the dark and eerie night. I told De Sica about our extended vigil on the cool marble bench eventually resulting in the apparent faint murmur of arguments among lesser emperors and senators, and concluded with the apparition of the kitten and my dilemma about adopting him until his furious mother came and snatched him away. De Sica and the whole camera crew were laughing with me, and the entire screen test experience was a lot of fun. The gorgeous De Sica even gave me a hug as we parted. Mario said he thought the test went very well and tried to persuade me to stay on in Rome until after De Sica had seen the test, but I was adamant that our trip to Capri was already planned and I would call him for the results as soon as I got back to Rome. He grudgingly agreed, urging me to call him the minute I got back.

That night disaster struck once again, only this time much worse. For our last evening in Rome, I had made reservations at The 7th Floor Terrace. The large round room, which was dramatically decorated in the Early Etruscan style, had sliding glass doors on three sides which were open to the warm night air. The booth-like tables encircled a large dance floor and the tuxedo-clad musicians were very good indeed. Also, and perhaps this was the cause of our downfall, Humphrey Borgart had evidently been there often as the bartender made excellent dry martinis. Ellen and I had a few while waiting for our dinner and listening to the orchestra, wishing we had dance partners to make good use of it. We had some excellent red wine with our dinner, and suddenly Ellen felt an urgent need to once again astound the people with her dancing.

She beamed at me, "Josie, why don't you ask the orchestra leader if you can sing a song with them and I will dance."

Looking at the dance floor full of sophisticated diners swinging and swaying, I said, "Oh, Ellen, I don't think this is the time or place."

But she begged, "Please, Josie, do it for me. I can't dance if you don't sing, and I think the people would love it."

I had the thought that Ellen was feeling a tad left out of things like screen tests and such, and I like to think that the drinks had made me of unsound mind and body, because to give her the opportunity to shine I sashayed up to the orchestra leader at the end of a number and said softly, "Could I sing *Bewitched, Bothered, and Bewildered* with your orchestra?"

He leaned down to me and said, "What?"

Stomach getting a little tight, I repeated, "Could I sing *Bewitched, Bothered, and Bewildered* with your orchestra?" and stepped up on the bandstand to indicate my intention. I can still see the incredulous look on the orchestra leader's face as he turned to the orchestra and gave them the number in their repertoire for this very popular song. It was one of my favorite songs and had always been very well received when I sang it around the piano at the Kelly's, so I confidently stepped up to the microphone and waited for the down beat. There was an important item I had overlooked. At the Kelly's, Solly Chaplin or

André Previn knew what key I sang in — this orchestra didn't. From the first note, I knew I was in a lot of trouble. I found that dance music is usually played in a higher key than for singers and the *screech* that issued from my throat as I bravely tried to sing in tune with the music "I'm *wild* again, *beguiled* again" would have impressed a screech owl, but not the startled orchestra and patrons of the Hotel Hassler Roma. I mean, it was nightmare. For both of us. From my vantage point on the stage, as I struggled on screeching the lyrics, I could see Ellen caroming off the dancing couples with her flying leaps and, after disapproving first looks they all completely ignored her as she twirled and slithered among them. I think we both imagined that everyone would stop dancing to watch Ellen and applaud. They did not. But there were no two ways about it, both of us had to keep making fools of ourselves until the excruciating song was over. Neither of us could do the sensible thing and stop this humiliating travesty and slink back to our table. True performers, we stuck it out until the end, and with heads held high we tried to ignore the sound of absolutely no applause as we reached our table. I felt as though a bucket of green sticky shame had been poured over me head to toe, and I would never be able to wipe it all off, as I said quickly, "Waiter, check, please."

Neither of us ever said one word about what we had just endured to one another, and I never knew what Ellen felt about it, but for me, even now almost 60 years later, it is the most vivid and painfully humiliating experience of my life, and, unfortunately, that song is still popular and is heard regularly on the radio and the CD collections that I love to play. I cannot escape it and can only cringe and hear again in memory the screech "I'm wild again, beguiled again," and wait for the song to be over. I have rarely cared much about other people's opinion of what I do. I've had enough confidence in my own judgment that if I felt something was right for me to do, then what other people thought was not relevant. But, oh, I cared very much what each of those people in The 7th Floor Terrace at the Hassler that night thought about this ugly American. And still do.

The End of an Era

'Twas on the Isle of Capri that I decided to make a major turn in the direction of my life. The concierge at the Hassler Roma had made arrangements for a car and driver to take us to the south of Italy, with an overnight in Sorrento, Naples for lunch, and then on to Capri by ferry for two days, while the driver waited in Naples to drive us back to Rome. For years I had read about Capri; while studying Ancient Rome its name came up often as the place Roman emperors went for relaxation and to get themselves back together after the stress of the grisly infighting between political factions that was the norm in Rome. (It's pathetic to think how little things have changed in that regard for almost 3,000 years.)

More importantly, one of my favorite books was *The Story of San Michele* by Axel Munthe, a Swedish physician, who was world famous for his healing powers, and whose clientele consisted of royalty, nobility, and other high society folk in both Paris and London in the late 1800s. I admired him because he was a leading advocate of the prevention of cruelty to animals and because he had a reputation for charging exorbitant fees to the rich and nothing to the poor. A sort of animal-loving Robin Hood with lots of medical degrees. But I admired him mostly because when he got fed up with society as he knew it, he separated from his wealthy British wife in order to search for peace of mind and serenity of spirit in solitude. In 1895, Axel bought land in a tiny village at the highest tip of Capri called Anacapri and lived there for most of the rest of his life. The land included a ruined chapel from the time of Tiberius that perched right on the edge of the cliff overlooking the Gulf of Naples, and it was there he built his house. He had decided that he must use his body, mind, and spirit to their fullest in order to achieve what he sought; so, with the minimum aid of local labor, he built himself a house, loggias, and gardens that were totally according to his own vision, without the aid of designer or architect. He said, "My house must be open to the sun, to the wind, and the voice of the sea, just like a Greek temple, and light, light, light, everywhere." Now *that* is my kind of guy. The memoir he wrote in the early 1900s about his experiences became a bestseller in 45 different languages, and it had a powerful influence on my thinking ever since I first read it in the 40s. (It is even now available almost 100 years later in both hard-cover and paperback.)

I had been a bit scattered in my thinking of late, and the disaster at Hotel Hassler Roma restaurant had left me feeling in truth bewitched, bothered, and bewildered. Something was simmering inside me, some kind of disease, that I felt must soon be dealt with. Even though this trip had been the most consistently exciting and rewarding time of my life, or maybe even *because* of that, I felt somehow I was changing. It was as though I was topsy-turvy for some reason. I had an intuitive idea that on Capri I could find some of Munthe's peace and serenity and get myself back together like the Ancient Romans did.

Sorrento was as charming and picturesque as the song "Come Back to Sorrento" says, and I very much wish I could go again. Our hotel was small, with a great view of the Gulf of Naples and a delightful outdoor restaurant with tables surrounding a dance floor, and a small orchestra. Even now I can clearly visualize our superlative fresh seafood and spaghetti entree and reexperience the surprising delight of its taste. I can also clearly see the image of our driver. Piero was a small young man with a pock-marked face and a slumped body, whose shyness and minimal English made him a poor choice for a guide. But I felt sorry for him and in an effort to make him feel appreciated, I invited him to be my guest for dinner that night, during which I did my gregarious best to engage him in friendly conversation. After dinner, Piero, staring down at his empty dessert plate, asked me to dance. He was a stiff and graceless dancer who was silent as he walked me around the floor, until suddenly he mumbled, "Do you want to sleep with me?"

Thinking I must have misunderstood his meager English, I said, "What?"

He repeated his invitation even more softly and with still averted eyes, "Do you want to sleep with me?"

Appalled, I assured him, "Oh. Ahhh ... no. No. But, grazie. Grazie just the same."

The look of profound relief that spread over his face amuses me still. His whole body language brightened. Poor boy, he had felt so unwillingly forced to defend his Italian masculinity by singing for his supper, and I realized belatedly, that he would have been so much happier to have had dinner on his per diem somewhere alone. That taught me something. Not enough, but something.

In Naples we had lunch at a seaside restaurant and reveled in the taste of the *cioppino* fish soup that truly rivaled the *bouillabaisse* of France. The amount of boat traffic in the huge harbor made it look like the Grand Central Station of the sea. When we took a quick tour of Pompeii, I learned a surprising and possibly shameful thing about myself. Looking at the casts of the people, young and old, preserved as they were killed by the flaming ash which had trapped them during the volcanic eruption was interesting, like looking at sculpture in any other museum, but seeing the cast of the agonized death of a chained dog made me cry. Subsequently, throughout my life I have realized that man's inhumanity to man revolts me mentally, but man's inhumanity to animals breaks my heart. I wonder why that is?

In the late afternoon we caught the ferry to Capri. The Gulf of Naples was a tranquil, gloriously greeny-turquoise, enhanced by the majesty of deadly Mount Vesuvius and other major island outcroppings. We arrived just at sunset, which gave Capri the magical qualities I'd read about. Our hotel was small, like in Sorrento, and also had a fabulous view. Later, seated on our hotel terrace with a cooling Cointreau over ice, we could see that the town of Capri after dark was as lovely as the sunset. Its cobble-stoned, cypress-lined main street wound serpentine-like up a hill, with lit-up shops of all kinds lining either side. Ellen was enchanted with the shops. Since I detest shopping and Ellen loves it, we arranged that the next day she could shop to her heart's content and I would take a box lunch and a taxi up to Anacapri to see if I could find what Axel Munthe had found there. In a way, I did.

Anacapri is well over 2,000 feet above Capri itself, and is reached by a road clinging to the cliff side that is so hazardous the faint-of-heart dare not look out the windows, but for the brave it is a spectacular view beyond compare. Of course, in Munthe's time there was no road. Laborers building the villas of the Roman Emperors, and later his house, had to climb 665 steps cut out of solid stone to carry up the supplies on their backs, or on the backs of their tiny donkeys. During the time of the Roman Emperors, some of the laborers had decided just to stay on top and thus was established the original village of Anacapri. Arriving comfortably by taxi 50 years later, however, I found that Munthe's house and garden was a bigger tourist attraction even than the ruins of villas belong to Augustus and Tiberius. Although the view from his long loggia could bring peace to the most troubled soul, his wonderful house was so jammed with tourists that Munthe's spirit was surely hiding out somewhere in the stratosphere until the tourists had all gone. So I left the house as well and went in search of a tranquil spot to have my lunch and commune with the gods of old.

I found an ancient olive tree above the gardens which over-looked the vast expanse of the Gulf of Naples and sat on the grass beneath it to enjoy my simple lunch. Physical hunger satisfied, I tried to sink into a contemplative state that would bring me the answers I was looking for. After quite a long spell of trying to clear my mind of all extraneous interference, like watching the ferries in transit on the Gulf, or the buzz of the egoistic conscious mind that is always trying to drown out the subconscious, the thought appeared in my mind with the plunk of solid truth: *I have lost my way.* My inner compass revealed clearly to me that I was off course. I believe we all have a tiny personal compass in the center of our chests which fluctuates according to how we live our life. Let's say it points true north when we are moving in the direction that is right for us, that direction in which we can best achieve the fulfillment of our innate potentials for self-knowledge, self-expression, and joy in living. When we get a few points off true, we may either be exploring a direction which will teach us something that is important for us to know in order to get further along true "north," or it could be that the course we are on will eventually take us all the way "South" to defeat and despair. Too many people give in to either inertia or fear and stay on "east" to "lead lives of quiet desperation," as Thoreau says. "West," — well, I imagine that direction takes one to a rip-roarin' good time, but on one-level life. I felt my hard, cold, ball of anxiety as I tried to figure out in which direction I was presently heading.

The most important force in my life was the miracles that my guardian angel had dropped on me at the times I needed them most. I recalled how the rancher in Texas, which bred champion palominos, just *happened* to come by while I was pretending to ride a horse. This stranger miraculously sensed that here was a lonely little girl in need of a horse — and he gave me one of their culls.

I imagined that my guardian angel looked a lot like Billie Burke, the Good Witch of the North in *Wizard of Oz,* as she provided miracles large and small for me throughout my life. Well, of course the experience of seeing God when I was five was the miracle that affected my whole life the most. My belief in that connection was what had always guided me toward true north, you might say. It was the feeling that God had my back that gave me my courage. Over those miracles I had no control, they just happened. But when I felt I was on the wrong track or had a serious decision to make for myself, I could always get very still in some place, preferably with a vista, and, after I had given the situation much consideration, ask my inner voice what I should do — and get the right answers. That inner voice never led me wrong. Never. Of course, my loquacious outer voice had to shut up and listen first and that was the biggest roadblock. But something on this trip to Europe, perhaps listening to new people, experiencing different cultures, or just having the opportunity to watch and absorb the individuality and universality of another part of the world had silenced my outer voice enough to let my inner voice get through. Sitting there under that tree, looking out over this most glorious of views, from the stillness of the moment it finally spoke. I thought of myself now as "Jo" or "Josie," the names given me by the friends I'd made in Hollywood, but my inner voice spoke as my real name, and our dialogue went something like this:

Jo/Josie: "I think maybe I'm on the wrong track somehow."

Jo-Carroll: "Do you know why?"

"No."

"Well, clearly it's because you have again forgotten your golden rule of 'This above all, to thine own self be true.' You know perfectly well that it wasn't right for you to go out to dinner in St. Tropez inappropriately dressed or to force your way onto a stage in that classy hotel to sing a song off-key that nobody had asked for. It is one thing to be kind and caring for a friend, but that has nothing to do with doing what you know is wrong."

" Yeah, well ..."

"You have been off your course for some time. You are not a *joiner.* A groupie. You always prided yourself on being different. But now you seem to have forgotten the most important lesson of your life. After Dr. Tate tried to rape you and your mother wouldn't/couldn't protect you, you learned that with *spiritual guidance you could take care of yourself,* even at the age of 12. The thing that has made you most right with yourself has been your ability to think for yourself and to dance to the sound of your own drummer. Of late you have been dancing, yes, but to the sound of *other people's* drummers."

"But I have *learned* so much from these "other people." Do you think I would have learned about art and music and philosophy the way I have from the people I knew on the medicine show or in Hale Center? Or Tyler, either for that matter. It is these "other people" who have taught me to *read and think*, for heaven's sake."

"It was your father who taught you to read. And it was something inborn in you that gave you the gift of the desire to learn and think. True, your recent friends have helped you immeasurably to enhance and enlarge your knowledge and understanding, but it was your own eagerness that led them to do so, and enabled you to *absorb* that knowledge, don't you see that? I am not denigrating the worth of some of the excellent things they have exposed you to; learning about music from a musician like Leonard Bernstein and art and literature from others of equal knowledge was an unparalleled experience. I am only saying that for some of the people you admire, infidelity and promiscuity is the norm; for some fame and fortune is their goal, for others anger is the torch they carry, but none of that is *your* way so why do you think you want to be like them? Like them, yes, but *be* like them, no. You were so upset when Betsy and the others didn't believe your trip wasn't payment for sexual favors rendered to Matty because you think *differently* from the people you so much want to be like. You want to be the same as they are because you are grateful that they *like* you, and that is not a good enough reason. Appreciate them, admire them — fine. But don't want to *be like* them, because you are not."

"But I *am* like them, I care deeply that the House Un-American Activities Committee and McCarthyism are destroying the lives of so many people just for political gain. I want to take up arms against the people who are cruel to animals or ruining the forests, and take a bullwhip to Sheriff Bull Connors and all the others who won't let the Negroes vote. I love feeling a part of the fight against all that."

"Terrific. *Care* about all those things. *Do* something about it. But do it because *you* think it is right, not because of what other people think. Remember when you were on that protest march in New York shouting vehemently, 'Pass the Federal Fine Arts Bill,' and a friend pointed out to you that the signs you were both waving stated, 'Pass the Federal *Finance* Bill,' not 'Fine Arts' Bill. You were just marching because your friends were. You didn't even know what the protest was about."

"Well, I'll admit that was a tad embarrassing, but I just misunderstood what they were saying. And, anyway, Fine Arts are important, too."

"And how about the time you were with a bunch of your radical friends and you took offense at something Stalin was doing, and said you thought the ends did not justify the means. Remember how they all got angry and made fun of you? And you backtracked and said you agreed with them. How about that? You lied about what you really thought because you were afraid they would think ill of you if you stood up for what you believed in. Be honest, do you really think the ends justify the means? Don't you really think that *how* you fight for Civil Rights is just as important as *what* you are fighting for? Would you honestly rather any one of your radical friends were running the country? Isn't the way those people think and behave just another form of hatred and intolerance?"

"Well, maybe. But *we liberals* are right and the conservatives are *wrong!*"

"OK, then. You feel righteous and purposeful on marches but are you ready to sacrifice for what you say you believe? Remember how horrified you were when Robert Capa told you about the massacres and atrocities he saw when he was in Spain in the late thirties with the Lincoln Brigade taking photographs for *LIFE* magazine? If you care so much about injustice, why are you planning to go to Spain and contribute your money to Franco's economy?"

"Well, ah, I don't know. Matty planned it, and I would like to see the El Grecos in the Prado in Madrid, and that fabulous architecture in Barcelona."

"So — are you anti-fascist, or not?"

"Oh, all *right* ! All right."

"And another thing."

"*Another* thing?"

"Do you really want to be an actress? Is that what you want to do with your life?"

"Well, nooo. Not really."

"Then why did you make that screen test for De Sica?"

"Oh, well, Marco asked me and it was just a fun thing to do. I don't think he would really want to put me under contract."

"Well, what if he does? Do you really want to live in Rome and do 'pretty girl' parts with someone else's voice in Italian movies? Is that who you really are? You're almost twenty-nine and you have to make a serious decision about what you want to do with your future. We're talking potential here. Most of the people you know are fulfilling the potential they were born with. Gene *is* a dancer. Lenny Bernstein *is* a musician. Irwin Shaw *is* a writer. That is what they are by nature and they are fulfilling their potential. What is *your* potential?"

"Well, I … I guess I don't really know what my potential *is*."

"What are you good at? When were you the happiest? There is where your potential lies."

Thinking hard, "What am I good at? Well, I've been good at learning lots of new stuff. I've been good at making the people I most admired like me. Laugh at me. And I've been happy dancing at the Kelly's, playing volleyball, with Sydney, and, yes, feeling a part of a group!"

"So what are you saying, that you think your potential is to be a comedian? A volley ball pro? An intellectual? A toady so that your friends will like you?"

"A toady! *That* I am not."

"No?"

"Well, I guess I see what you're getting at. But a 'toady?' That's pretty unfair."

"Until these last few years you always had the courage of your own convictions. Even if those convictions were arrived at from reading Zane Grey and the behavior of Lassie. But now you are trying to emulate the convictions of other people you admire and that is a sure way to lose admiration for yourself. You will never reach your full potential that way."

"How can I reach my potential when I don't even know what it is?"

"Well, I'll tell you. I think your inborn potential and strongest personal ability is to be connected with nature and to grow spiritually. I think the times in your life you have been completely happy were when you were alone with nature. You were happiest during those times when you felt connected to something bigger than yourself. For some reason you are unwilling to talk about your spiritual feelings. Are you afraid your friends will think you are naïve — 'religion is the opiate of the masses' and all that? But what are you doing here at

Anacapri if it is not to get some of Axel Munthe's spiritual peace and serenity to rub off on you? You have been having a rip-roarin' good time heading all the way 'West,' but that is the wrong direction for you, and you know it. The reason you are sitting here alone on top of this cliff is that you are trying to find your way back to the time when you felt most right about yourself and what you were doing. Don't you see that you have been rarely privileged to have made a real connection between nature, your 5-year-old self, and the divine spirit? That connection is what has given you your strength and understanding to do what you know is right for you — like leaving the medicine show to try to learn how to be a *secretary*, for heaven's sake, then turning down all that money Senator Mayfield offered you, and knowing all that time in Hollywood that being an actress was not what is really right for you. That *connection* is what shows you your way to the peace and serenity you are looking for, don't you see that? Your potential is the ability to evolve into an ever *closer* connection, and therein lies your true happiness. But it is a long time since you have done anything to strengthen that connection and that is why you are feeling uneasy."

"Are you are saying I have to give up my life as it is now and do something to make a better *connection*?"

"Yes."

"Whoo, boy. Well, I don't know, that's a tall order. I'll have to think about it for awhile."

All of a sudden I felt very small and alone looking out over the immense Gulf of Naples and the immensity of my thoughts. But for the first time in a long time I had a clear memory of the peace and contentment of being connected to nature and to the Divine Spirit.

The twists and turns of the road were nothing compared to the swivels my mind was making as the taxi carried me back down the hill to Capri and the unknown. Contemplating what my inner voice was telling me to do was earth-shattering and scary. As we sped around a particularly life-threatening curve, suddenly a quote from a book I had been reading flashed through my mind. In *The Unquiet Grave*, British literary critic Cyril Connolly (called "the most brilliant mind of the 20th Century") said, "As we grow older we discover that the lives of most human beings are worthless except in so far as they contribute to the enrichment and emancipation of the spirit. The more I see of life the more I perceive that only through solitary communion with nature can one gain an idea of its richness and meaning." When I read that quote it electrified me like a lightning strike of truth. Now, since that was exactly what my inner voice was saying, I thought, "If that sophisticated world traveler/literary critic Connolly and that world-famous writer/physician Munthe agree with the inner voice of a girl off a medicine show — then go for it! Whatever *it* turns out to be."

That night at dinner I told Ellen that I didn't want to go to Spain as planned because the country was too fascist. I thought it was a better idea that we would just go on to Florence and Venice after we picked up the car in Nice and go on back to Paris.

Instantly, Ellen teared-up, "Do you mean we won't get to see Barcelona or even go to Madrid?"

Remembering my inner voice's admonitions, I said, "I just don't want to spend money to support Franco's regime."

Voice a'tremble, Ellen pleaded, "But their civil war is over. Nobody is fighting there now."

"I don't care, it is the principle of the thing. I am just not going to support Franco."

"But *he* won't know whether we are there or not."

Determined no longer to give in to the threat of tears, I said firmly, "We are *not* going to Spain, Ellen."

While I was burning bridges, I went to the desk and put in a call to Marco in Rome. He told me with great excitement that De Sica had liked the test and wanted to put me under personal contract immediately. I felt kind of bad for his sake when I told him that something had come up that forced me to get back to the States as soon as possible. There was no point in trying to tell him what I was really thinking of doing. Or that it was my divine spirit who was calling the shots!

In Florence a funny thing happened. Well, kind of funny. We had a nice, comfortable room in the Hotel della Signoria and a window which overlooked the Piazza della Signoria, in which *Michelangelo's David* was on full display. (Oh, how I do love a splendid athletic male body!) But the funny and horrid thing that happened was that the day of our arrival, again in tears, Ellen told me that she had contracted crabs. *Crabs?* I didn't even know what that was, although I gathered it was some kind of venereal disease. Ellen explained, looking anywhere but at me, that it wasn't as horrible as syphilis or gonorrhea, but rather it was sexually transmitted tiny insects that looked like crabs, which lived in the pubic hair and itched and burned. Yeeuck! I automatically backed up a bit. Ellen begged me to go to a doctor there in Florence for her, saying she was too embarrassed to ask for medication herself. Well, like an idiot I did it. I got the name of an English-speaking doctor from the concierge and went to see him. He was a silver-haired majestic-looking man who sat back in his chair and looked at me cynically as I tried to explain, first the problem itself, and then that the problem belonged to a *friend* of mine. Not knowing either the medical English or Italian word for crabs, I explained the situation by sideways motion of my fingers. He said he understood the condition I meant, but his disbelieving look about my "friend" curled my insides and made me feel like a total fool. I paid for the little bottle of pills he gave me and slunk out.

On the way back to the hotel I stopped at an outdoor café to pull myself together because, unpleasant though it was, what the doctor thought didn't really matter. I would never see him again. But I felt besmirched somehow, a feeling that reinforced the conviction of my inner voice that I had let myself get on the wrong track. Of course, I had an inner giggle at the thought of Francisco, the elegant Argentine diplomat with the cummerbund, grandly giving the gift of crabs (i.e. lice, which seemed most appropriate) to an adoring and pliant Ellen. But actually, it all seemed so sordid. How had I gotten mixed up with *crabs* anyway? As I tried to puzzle through why I hadn't insisted that Ellen pay the piper by going to the doctor herself, the thought of an old quote from the writer Hendrik van Loon came to me: "*The terrible tyranny of the weak.*" Since Ellen's insecurities and weaknesses were so pervasive, I, the stronger one, gave in to her — because I was afraid if I didn't, she would fall apart. Her tears were the threat that prevailed over my own will. Her inner fragility overcame my own inner sense of right and wrong, or even my own pleasure. We think of tyranny as coming from someone strong and overbearing, but it ain't necessarily so. It was a startling thought, but I could suddenly see its validity and it changed my feelings toward Ellen. We had shared so much laughter in the past, and we had helped one another through so much pain, but ever since I saw her roll her eyes when I was explaining my relationship with Matty that day at Betsy's apartment in Paris, I felt the tentacles of our relationship releasing their hold.

Florence became my favorite European city next to Paris. You had only to walk out the door and you were in the midst of glorious art. In Paris you had to go to a specific place for works of art; in Florence there was some man-made beauty wherever you looked. It had fabulous museums like the Uffizi, of course, but just walking down the street you would see mesmerizing bronze sculpture on a *door*, for heaven's sake, or on the marble façade of a house. I could stand for a half hour lost in wonder on almost any street corner. Most of the art had a spiritual content and, as in Chartres Cathedral, and I was again in awe of the great art inspired by man's connection to a divine spirit. We stayed in Florence for several days and each was more enchanting than the last. I promised myself I would come to Florence again and again. (*And I did.*)

Venice, that magical, mystical, floating/sinking bejeweled sandcastle of architectural fantasy, seemed unreal and a tad disappointing after Florence. I did enjoy the small balcony in our hotel room overlooking the Grand Canal, but looking down into the water to see the grapefruit and cantaloupe halves, deceased rats, and I dared not think what else, floating by in the brown, turgid water put me off a bit. One morning I found I was ready to go "home" to Paris.

All the time we'd been gone, I was yearning to get back to Paris. When we returned to the atelier, it was like returning to a *home* that I had loved and lived in for years. I felt like a long-distance runner who finally finished her run, came in first, and could now relax and take a breather. I wanted to go serenely around Paris hugging and kissing all the now familiar places that I loved. But there was something else I had to do before I could serenely do anything, so I brought my relationship with Ellen to a head a few days after our return. Ellen and her dancer friend, Pat Sazuki, had just come back to the atelier after having been out for lunch. Maybe they'd had a bit too much wine with lunch which put them in a frivolous mood, for as they were discussing how long we were going to stay in Paris. Ellen said in a sneering tone, "Well, I guess it depends on Daddy Warbucks."

I exploded.

For Ellen, of all people, to make fun of Matty by comparing him to that comic millionaire who had taken care of *Little Orphan Annie*, after he had been so good and generous to both of us was intolerable. All the tension that had been building up between Ellen and me flashed before my eyes like a rocket propelling Apollo 13, and as though I had been planning these exact words for a long time, I said, "Ellen, we have had a great time together on this trip and I have loved it all, but I think it is time for us to separate. I need to be alone now for awhile. You have your first class return plane ticket home, and you should have enough money left to see you through. If you want to stay longer, you can room with Pat and change your first-class ticket to second-class for cash."

Both Ellen and Pat were staring at me with a stunned expression, as Ellen said, her big eyes tearing, "Listen, Josie, if it's because of what I said about Matty, I didn't mean anything by it. You know I ..."

But I interrupted, "Oh, it's not just that, although I think calling him "Daddy Warbucks" is the pits. It is just that I don't think it is good for us to be together anymore. Our trip is really over, and now we both can do what we want. I don't want to talk further about it, but it's something I've been thinking about for a long time. I am going out for the afternoon now and I hate goodbyes so I very much hope you will have taken your things and left by the time I return." If Ellen was going to fall apart, this time I didn't want to be there to see it.

When I got back she was gone, and I was greatly relieved. Once I had understood "the terrible tyranny of the weak," syndrome, I wouldn't let myself feel guilty as I thought she had already had her money's worth during this nearly 3-month trip. Mostly, however, it was that I needed to be alone to think so many things through – and times they were a 'changin'. I didn't call any of the friends I had made in Paris, not even Serge, I just walked the streets and thought, spent hours looking into the Seine for guidance, and sat in front of my French windows gazing out over the rooftops of Paris trying to sink down inside myself to make decisions. I thought about how most everyone I admired played by rules that said it was OK for Harvey Orkin to play nasty practical jokes, or for men like Richard Rodgers and Oscar Levant, among a multitude of others, to cheat on their wives. (As long as they were talented, of course.) Perhaps it had started with my own father's infidelity, or perhaps I was just naïve, but I realized that it wasn't OK with me. And, the more I thought about it, the prevailing relaxed attitude about one-nighters, like Ellen's behavior in St. Tropez, wasn't OK with me either. I decided that I was sitting in the wrong pew, as my mother would say, and finally came to a momentous conclusion. *I was in the wrong business. I would never work as an actress again.*

I was sobered by the rightness of that decision, and I felt good about it. Well, not *good* exactly, just that it was inevitable. Writing that letter to Dr. Tate when I was 11 was the end of my father's era.

Taking that train to Tyler was the end of the Dr. Tate era.

This now was the end of the era that included Mr. Johnson of the Citizens National Bank stopping me on the street and asking me if I would be "Miss Citizens National Bank" in the coming Miss Tyler contest. That question had led to the Miss America Pageant, Hollywood, Phil, the Kelly group, Matty, and now these months of travel, which were proving to be so pivotal for me. Well, they say travel is broadening and now it was time for me to broaden out into a new era. But I knew deep in my heart that this past decade had been my "Golden Years." Surely they were the brightest and shiniest years that would ever be. *And the fun of it all!* I wanted to weep at the thought of losing the fun of it all. To rebel at the thought that the party would be over. But — if I was to listen to my inner voice and get back to trying to fulfill my potential — whatever *that* was — then this era was over and I must get ready to begin an era that would move my compass heading back to my North Star. And finally I was ready.

As I was leaving Paris in the taxi on the way to the airport, I looked at everything we passed like a besotted lover saying farewell to the beloved while leaving to fight a war, devoutly promising with brimming eyes and heart, "I shall return. Wait for me."

Once on the plane, I dried my eyes and started to plan my attack on the future. I wasn't concerned so much about finding a job which would support Mother and me as I was about fulfilling my destiny. My "potential." But I was going to leave that up to my guardian angel, since it was her idea.

Feeling I needed written instructions, though, on a little piece of paper, I drew up a list of my own ten commandments to hold me up and help me accomplish my mission. Some quotes were from admired others, some from my own heart and experience:

1. "Fear not, fair lady." — Shakespeare
2. "'Tis not life that matters; 'tis the courage one brings to it." — Hugh Walpole
3. "Life is real, life is earnest, and the grave is not its goal."— Longfellow

4. "I am the Master of my fate, I am the Captain of my soul."
   — WB Henley
5. It is better to trust, even though sometimes deceived, than not to trust at all.
6. "Honesty is the best policy."
7. "Be brave and mighty forces will come to your aid." — Goethe
8. "The mark of a happy man is Zest!" — Bertrand Russell
9. "All of us have our feet in the gutter, but some of us are looking at the stars." — Oscar Wilde
10. "This above all, to thine own self be true." — Shakepeare

I kept this little piece of paper in my wallet and read it almost daily for many years. It was the manual which helped me win my coming wars.

Growing Pains

Matty met me at the airport and I never stopped babbling about our magnificent trip and my magnificent plans for my magnificent future as he took me back to Adolph Green's apartment. I still had the key because Adolph was in Hollywood finishing up *Singin' in the Rain*, but he would be coming back to New York soon so as well as starting a whole new way of life, I had to start looking for a place to stay.

It was 1951, and I hit the floor running when I got back to New York, though I didn't know yet where I was running *to*. My guardian angel had suggested that, since I had not enjoyed the work I had been doing, I should figure out what I *did* enjoy doing. I thought, "Reading. I enjoy reading. So I should look for something to do with books? Editing, maybe, or publishing in some way, so I must first put the word out to all my friends about my quest and see what turns up."

My writer friend, Arthur Laurents, introduced me to the news editor of the *San Francisco Chronicle*, who was in town for a few days. He was slight man, with a bit of sandy-colored hair and freckles of the same color on his scalp. A darling man. After listening intently to my burst of virtuous decisions and desires, he offered me a job. He didn't know what job it would be, he said, but he was going back to San Francisco in a couple of days and I should just follow him on out there and we would find something suitable. I was thrilled, I had always wanted to live in San Francisco.

Unfortunately, the next day, he called to say that his publisher had suddenly died, his son had taken over, and he'd been fired. Whoops! I was sorry for both of us but I figured, "Easy come, easy go," and prepared to mush on.

My friend, John Crosby, was a well-known columnist at the *Herald Tribune*, and regarded as the leading television critic in the early 1950s, so I figured him for a good source and put my case before him. Sure enough, he called later and asked if I'd like to go to Connecticut for the weekend to the home of Richard Simon (of Simon and Schuster Book Publishers). He said all kinds of people from publishing would be there. Opportunities abounded.

Determined to take full advantage of those opportunities, I was quick to regale anyone in sight with my resume and my mission of somehow fulfilling my potential. Among those I met were Gardner

"Mike" Cowles, owner/publisher of the successful *Look* Magazine and his wife Fleur, owner/editor of the new upscale *Flair* Magazine. I had the bountiful, slightly condescending attitude of a movie star asking for a job as a sales clerk as I told them that, because of my background, I wasn't sure what kind of a job I was best suited for, but I knew that any job I really enjoyed I would be good at. When I had finished my spiel, Fleur said to her husband, "Mike, we must find a job for this girl."

At his request, I called Mike's office the next week and made an appointment to see him. The *Look* building was at 488 Madison Avenue on the corner of 50th (later to be dubbed a historical monument), and Mike Cowles was a very relaxed, laid-back man with dark-rimmed glasses, who again listened patiently to my resume of experiences and my reasons for making this extraordinary shift in my life's work. When I slowed down, he told me Fleur wanted to see me later,but in the meantime his office manager would take me all around the magazine's offices to see what department I thought I would best fit into.

There weren't any. I could not see myself enjoying the work, as I understood it, in marketing, advertising, photography, and so on. So the prune-faced manager took me back to his office, sat me down and said, "Well, I can't see anything for you here, except a secretarial position. Are you good at typing and dictation?"

Struggling to remember some statistics from my aborted studies at Federal Institute, I said, casually, "I can type about 160 words a minute and take dictation about 90 words a minute."

With a slight smile, he said, "Since that qualifies you to be a court stenographer, I think you would be wasted here."

I replied hastily, "Oh, well, maybe it is the other way around. It's been a long time since I've worked as a secretary, but I'm sure I could work it out. I must tell you, though, that I have to make at least $40 a week because I have to support my mother and we couldn't live on less than that."

With the attitude of having arrived at a conclusion, he half-rose and said, "Miss Dennison, there are many skilled girls who live at home with their parents who would love to work at *Look* for $25 a week, so I'm afraid there is nothing for you here."

Remembering what Mike had said about Fleur wanting to see me, and not liking his attitude, I said, "What do you want to bet?"

Startled, he said, "What?"

"What do you want to bet I can't get a job here? I'll bet you $5 I can."

"What?"

"Mike said to tell you Fleur wants to see me when we're finished here."

Mike Cowles' office, while large, was quite dark, with only one window overlooking Madison Avenue, Fleur Cowles' office, on the other hand, had the penthouse and was huge, with windows all around and a fabulous view of New York City. Seated behind her massive antique desk when we were shown in, Fleur swept around the desk to give me a little hug, saying, "Well, here you are at last. How have you been getting on?"

While Mike's essence was laid-back and soothing like a small running creek, Fleur's was like a string of firecrackers continuously going off. I fought being intimidated as I answered her questions as well as I could.

She quickly interrupted me, however, and sitting back behind her desk, said, "Yes, well listen, I have been thinking and have come up with the perfect thing. My theater critic's assistant is pregnant and will be leaving in a couple of months so you can take her place. For now, you can start on Monday getting to know how my magazine works."

I said, "OK," and I had a job.

Outside her office, the surly manager tried to hand me a $5-dollar-bill, but I said, "No, no. I couldn't take your money. I knew it was a sure thing," (*For the rest of my life, I have enjoyed getting the best of that officious manager.*)

I was victoriously humming to myself going down in the elevator as the door opened and John Fearnley got on. Johnny was the general manager of Rodgers and Hammerstein Productions, arranging road tours, auditioning new players as replacements in their several companies, and so on. He was a tall, lanky man with a sweet smile whom I had known slightly for some years. He greeted me with a little hug, and said, "Hey, Jo, what are you doing here?"

I was in the middle of telling him about my new life plan, and my adventure with Mike and Fleur as we reached the ground floor, so he invited me to a bar next door for a drink.

When I had brought him up to date, he said, "Jo, how would you like to come work for me? There is an office secretary, but my workload has been increasing lately and I need a secretary of my own. Our office is right here in the *Look* building and I think you would like working with us. Don't take the job at *Flair*, come work with me at Rodgers and Hammerstein."

Flattered, I said I would think it over and let him know the next day.

Even as self-confident as I was, I'd thought it would take me longer than a couple of weeks to get a good job, yet already I had three offers, counting the failed San Francisco one, so I was feeling high in the clouds as I thought it over. I appreciated Fleur's confidence in me, but I didn't know anything about magazine publishing, and *Flair* was not the kind of magazine I would read, anyway. Plus, Fleur was kind of unknown and intimidating while both Rodgers and Hammerstein were known and comfortable.

I hadn't seen Oscar Hammerstein II (writer of lyrics and book for *Oklahoma, Carousel, South Pacific, The King and I, Sound of Music* and many other hit musicals) since I was sitting on his bed about five years ago in 1946. My fellow starlet at Fox, Susan Blanchard, had asked me to go to New York with her to stay with her mother and stepfather, Oscar Hammerstein II! They had invited her to come to NY to see the new revival of his 1927 big hit, *Show Boat*. Susan was a slender blonde with a pretty, soft face, who had a serious attitude toward life and a liberal political outlook, so we got along great. I needed a little respite from the tension of *Marriage 101*, and anyway, it was common in those days for folks in Hollywood to go to New York periodically to see the new Broadway shows, so I accepted. I felt sure Phil needed a respite as much as I did.

Dorothy and Oscar Hammerstein II lived in a lovely town house on 1st Ave overlooking the East River, and it was luxury indeed to spend those four days with them. As well as the glorious *Show Boat*, while we were there, Oscar got tickets for us to see a different show every night and asked us to come up to their bedroom when we got back from seeing a show to tell them how we liked it. Like an oft-remembered dream, the vision of Susan and me in this luxurious bedroom on the foot of the bed of these sophisticated, wildly-extraordinary people in their jammies, so to speak, enthusing about a show we'd just seen remains vivid in my memory. Austrian-born Dorothy Blanchard was Oscar's second wife, a thin, elegant woman who was a well-known interior designer and socialite. Oscar was a tall, bear of a man with a pock-marked face and warm, perceptive eyes. I was greatly in awe of him because from somewhere inside him he found lyrics like these:

"The corn is as high as an elephant's eye" (from *Oklahoma),* and
"You have to be carefully taught before it's too late,
"Before you are six or seven or eight, to hate all the people your relatives hate" (from *South Pacific)*

Before Oscar, musicals were songs, dances, and sketches, performed by celebrities. He was the first to write socially significant plays with songs and dances which furthered the plot and character development with regular performers. A huge advance in the musical.

(In 1950 Susan Blanchard married Henry Fonda, she was 21, he was 45. In their divorce in 1956 Susan described herself as "a geisha wife.")

I had thought of Rodgers and Hammerstein as kind of comfortable family, so the next day I called Fleur Cowles and said thank you very much, but I am going with R & H, and called John Fearnley and said I was looking forward to working for him. He was pleased, and there was evidently no problem about the $40 a week, so next week I would be off on my quest to find my potential.

To add to my feeling of exultation, Heywood Hale Broun, author, sports writer, commentator, actor, and my friend who had long been my main guide to book learning, called to say he had found me an apartment — in *Greenwich Village!* That fine actor Colin Keith-Johnson was going on the road tour of the perennial play *Journey's End* and I could sublease his apartment at 10 Downing Street in Greenwich Village for a reasonable sum. Nothing could have suited me more. While the Bronx and Brooklyn housed Jewish, Italian, Irish, and German ethnic groups, the Village was without ethnic identity. After World War II, in the early 50s, young artists of all cultural backgrounds — writers, musicians, painters, and actors — were drawn to the Village for the low rents and the camaraderie of the new "Beat Generation." That period was the pregnancy of the Gay and LGBT civil rights movement, the avant guard folk, country and western music, and the rebellion against the status-quo that was fully birthed in the 60s. The place attracted many about-to-be-famous people: Bob Dylan, Maya Angelou, and Robert De Niro.

My new apartment was tiny compared to where I had been living at Adolph's, but I felt like Goldilocks for it fitted the new me just right. Downing Street was only a block long, but it ran into the center of Bleeker Street with its produce stalls and bakeries, inexpensive restaurants, and sidewalk cafes within walking distance, and just a couple of blocks from the subway entrance at Washington Square Park. I felt bold knowing that if I went all the way up to the front of the subway to board, I could exit at 50th Street, just two doors down from the Look building. And that way I could give a cheery greeting to the train engineer and feel like a real on-my-way-to-work New Yorker.

There was nothing cheery about my nine-to-five job, however. Blinded by the splendor of my intentions, it was with great confidence that I showed up for work that Monday, and found that nothing in my past experience at Federal Institute or easy-going Senator Mayfield's office had prepared me for the actuality of a secretarial job at Rodgers and Hammerstein. I'd imagined sitting at Johnny's elbow taking notes in the theater as we auditioned performers for the road tours and replacements. Wrong! It turned out my job was to take dictation, type letters, and file. My memory of shorthand allowed me to frantically scribble marks on my secretarial pad — if Johnny talked real slow — but when I went to transcribe it, the scribbles turned into unintelligible hieroglyphics between "Dear Sir," and "Sincerely Yours." I could still type fast, but in the days before Spell Check, backspace, and delete making a clean copy was agony — and I always spent way too much time going through the alphabet from the top to find the right letter to start looking up correct spelling. It got so bad that Johnny was dictating like this: "... Jo, that's 'c-o-m-p-l-i-c-a-t-i-o-n'" in order to get his letter finished more quickly. It all shook my self-confidence to its foundation.

The office comprised a general manager and his secretary, an Office Manager and her secretary, a book keeper, and production manager, John Fearnley — my new boss. I was sadly mistaken when I expected to be welcomed with open arms by everyone in the office. I hardly ever saw the withdrawn, busy General Manager and his secretary. The office manager, Mrs. Roberts, was a tiny red-haired, middle-aged-woman, who I immediately found to be a cool, strict disciplinarian. Nary a warm welcome there. Her secretary, Margaret, a giant of a woman who turned out to be a snake in the grass, gave me a warm welcome but did everything in her power subsequently to make me quit or get me fired.

For example, she encouraged me to take all the time I wanted for lunch, or if Johnny wasn't in the office, I should take off early. I stupidly ate my brown-paper-bag-lunch at my desk and took an hour or so off to walk up to Central Park for a release of tension, and take off early gladly. Before long, Mrs. Roberts called me into her office and lectured me so severely about the requirements of arriving, leaving, and lunch periods, or else, that I was reduced to tears. I was stunned at Margaret's treachery; the people I'd known in show business had not been as underhanded as that. Also, Margaret brought a tiny peevish Yorkshire Terrier to work with her, who yapped at me every time I came near her desk. It was the only dog I ever met that I didn't like. They made a perfect pair.

I could survive Mrs. Roberts and Margaret, however, it was Johnny who done me in. He was so sweet and patient with me while I failed him abysmally as a secretary day after day. Desperate, I started going to Secretarial School three nights a week, but found it to be soul-deadening drudgery. I couldn't quit, of course; my self-respect was at stake — I couldn't let Margaret win without a fight.

My soul needed all the music I could get, as my days at the office were agony for mind and body. Day work at the office, night work at school, and bedtime study in spelling made me feel inadequate, stupid, muddle-headed, and miserable, but I had to persevere. I couldn't quit because I had made a commitment to all my friends and myself. To quit meant to abandon all self esteem and self respect. More than any previous time in my life, I needed to win. So, I persevered. I wanted to win.

From the agony of my employment to the comfort and relaxation of the beautiful music, my salvation was walking into my cozy little apartment and choosing the first sublime record of the night, possibly Ella Fitzgerald or Puccini, to change my worlds with. I had learned as a child to enjoy being alone and I could sit and eat my canned spaghetti and meatballs while listening to music in relaxing bliss. Soon, though, I met a young man, Danny Stern, to share evenings and weekends with. He was a classical cellist, trained at Julliard, and had read and understood every book I loved. We had good times together discussing books and listening to music. The

Musician's Union had a strangle-hold on jobs so it was well-nigh impossible for young musicians to find work in shows or orchestras, so neither of us could afford paid-for entertainment, but Manhattan had a plethora of freebies.

Matty called one day and said, "How would you like to go to Israel?" "I-S-R-A-E-L?," I said. I had always wanted to go there and many of my friends were Jewish or had connections in the country. He was putting together a TV series to be funded by the Weizmann Institute of Science and made at the studios in Israel. At the time there was a very successful TV series in the US based on a detective, shot all over the country. The new show would be a takeoff on that, with a detective solving crimes all over the Middle East instead. The producer said I could have a job as his assistant. Maria Riva, the daughter of Marlena Deitrich, would star. The director was to be Gerald Mayer (a former boyfriend of mine)! The other core staff and some of their children would be along as well.

I was so thrilled when I went into Jonny Fernley (at Rogers and Hammerstein) to tell him. He said "No, don't do that. I'm about to leave my current position and become a producer. You need to come with me." Well, Israel was the real draw, but I was so touched that he thought so well of me.

I needed some money to get going, but payday was a ways off. So, I asked Phil to loan me $200. He said, "Will you come back to me if I give you the money?" No thank you! I called another friend who helped me, no strings attached.

I was to travel on the maiden voyage of the *SS Jerusalem*, Israel's first cruise ship large enough to make the trans-Atlantic trip. Given the occasion, the crew was allowed to bring their families. Many famous people, such as Al Hirschfeld, the marvelous Broadway cartoonist, were aboard.

One of my first duties was to acquire the tickets, passports, and visas for the trip: this included documents for the whole executive team. I was to assemble the cameras and other equipment and take it all by ship and obtain first class plane tickets for the others.

In those days, passports that were stamped "Israel" were banned from entrance in most Middle East countries. Since we planned to shoot in Syria, Jordan, and Egypt, all warring countries to Israel, the way around this restriction was to get a new passport and separate visa for those countries in addition to Israel rather than a stamp in the official passport. I boarded the *SS Jerusalem* full of vivid anticipation. I'd never been on a big ship before and was delighted with my cozy cabin and being at sea. The captain was a tall, lean Hungarian, who saw himself irresistible and quickly offered me his body. He was indignantly outraged at my even quicker refusal, and was rudely condescending with me for the rest of the nearly week-long trip.

The SS Jerusalem.

I soon found first class to be kind of boring. The only passenger I recognized was Hirschfeld. I knew writer S.J. Perelman was a good friend of his and since he was also a good friend of mine, I thought we would have a lot in common. Sadly, he didn't seem to agree and was rather distant. Quickly, I found that the fun place was down with the crew in second class. As the ship was coming on its maiden voyage, the owners gave free passage to the spouses of the crew and they were a merry group. Most of them spoke Yiddish, my favorite language, as well as Hebrew and English. I loved their Jewish humor and delighted in learning to sing and dance the Hora, and other Jewish songs and dances. Most importantly, I loved their sense of purpose. They were so proud of what they were doing in Israel and of what they were building.

The merriment ended for me, however, when, on the 5th day out, I learned heart-stopping news. I was telling the purser about our plans, when he said: "Jo-Carroll, you can't stay in Israel and visit these other countries because you have stamps in your passport." The purser could not have stunned me more, if he had informed me I had a fatal illness. Upon examination, sure enough, he was right. Incredibly, plain as day, the offending Israeli Visa was stamped right in my passport.

I had been meticulous about double-checking the passports and visas for the cast and crew, but evidently I had failed to check my own. I said "Do we stop anywhere there is an American embassy between here and Tel Aviv?" He said "We may port in Marseille in two days, and I'm sure they have an embassy, but we only stay for four hours. You couldn't get a new passport in that length of time, if you could get one at all."

Now desperate, I began to plan how to remedy my horrifying situation. I found out that there was indeed an Israeli embassy in Marseille, and I wanted them to have someone from the Weizmann Institute meet me when we docked — with a car. I was going to get a new passport and three new visas! Abraham, from the Institute was young, amiable, and willing, though incredulous. He was game to try and help me.

The supercilious captain told me I could never make it, and not to think that he would hold back the ship if I were one minute late. Undeterred, I leapt into Abraham's car, and we were off and running. That whole four hours remains a blur to me. I have no clear image of Marseille or its embassies. I remember speeding up hills and rushing into the embassy to give the performance of my life, pleading to various faceless people, including invading the American Ambassador's lunch, that my life depended on their help. I only remember the look of my new passport #100 and arriving back at the ship to see a lot of the other passengers lining the railing looking for me. The gangplank was already up, and I had to climb up the rope ladder to board. Symbolically thumbing my nose at the disappointed captain, all my life I have thought of things like owner Vincent always giving me a good table at Sardi's, the engineer holding the train at the New York subway for me, and getting a new passport in Marseille, as among my greatest achievements.

I arrived in Tel Aviv's Haifa Port with a joyful heart and eager mind. A man named Sam, who was assigned to me from the Weismann Institute as guide/driver for the remainder of my stay, met me at the ship and took over the task of getting the equipment safely to the movie studio, and me to the Sharon Hotel. The Sharon was one of the best hotels in Israel, located a ways out of the city, right on the Mediterranean.

I was delighted to find that Harold Clurman was also staying at the Sharon. He was a director/producer/co-founder of the prestigious "Group Theater" in New York, a group of prominent liberal actors like John Garfield, writers like Clifford Odets, and directors like Elia Kazan. Harold came to Israel once a year to direct a play with local talent, and his immediate job was to look for locations and actors for our series. We became good friends and would often sit on the beach at sunset and have wide-ranging conversations. One time I asked him a question: "You know, sometimes it's so boring to be at a dinner table with someone you don't know. How do you make conversation in situations like that?" He said, "Oh that's easy, just

Me working on Lux Video Theater.

ask about their childhood." It was great advice that served me well in the future.

Since the rest of the company was not arriving for another four days, Sam began to take me to various kibbutzim to scout location. Sam was a tall, dark, quiet Russian Jew, who proved eloquent in explaining the actions and goals of the burgeoning new Israel. He showed me how many Jewish orphans were being raised to achieve their full potential and meet the emotional as well as physical needs. An adult pair, with or without children, were assigned four or five children of various ages who became their "family unit." They all lived in their own "home" together, and the children were given the sense of security and belonging they needed in their own home. The whole community, the kibbutzim, ate together, however, and collaborated in the running of the kibbutz, their own farm, and cultivated fields. They grew their own food, wove their own clothes, and in general were self-sufficient. The children were given an excellent education in the arts and sciences as well as the solid basics. Along the way, they learned self-defense and how to use a gun. There was the constant threat of sniper fire from across the Syrian border.

We went to Capernaum on the sea of Galilee, and across the sea was a well-known kibbutz, Ein Gev. I fell instantly in love with the kibbutz, particularly with how they educated children.

I thought I'd swim in the sea, but it was very shallow. Having lunch with Sam at a little cafe after my "dip", I said, "The sea is so shallow here." He agreed and said, "Sometimes it's so shallow you can almost walk across." It was hilarious.

I absorbed the super vitality and invigorating enthusiasm of the Israeli people for their country and future like fresh sunshine, and wished that I could live there forever — but it was not to be. After trying to dolly our cameras on the uneven floor of the Israeli studio, and work around the horrific fact that it was so hot outside — the film in the cameras melted if shooting was attempted between the hours of 11 a.m. and 4 p.m. — the project was abandoned. Matty called me to say he had another TV series starting up in Paris, so I should wrap it up and come on to Paris.

An unexpected event intervened. Harold asked me to go back to New York as his personal assistant on the new musical he was planning. Wow, the thought of working as the assistant in the theater was alluring indeed. (He assured me there would be a production secretary to take dictation.) Clurman was charming and erudite, and though he was married to the famous acting coach Stella Adler, he was known as a bon vivant man about town. I consulted my guardian angel and in a quiet voice she whispered, "Beware," so I decided to head to Paris.

There was a huge pan-European strike, so I had to travel to Paris via Germany. I was disgusted with the Germans because of the Holocaust, but it was an adventure. In Frankfurt, I got a car and driver and asked to see some particular sights that I was interested in. Instead, the driver took me to the places bombed out by the Americans: hospitals, schools, and neighborhoods. I didn't fall for his guilt trip, and asked him to return me to my hotel.

At the hotel, I went to the lady's room. A heavy-set Germanic lady hovered near the door. I was still flustered by the taxi driver and didn't impose on her. As I proceeded to leave, she gruffly blocked the door and said something in German which I gathered was a request for a tip. I said "No, you didn't do anything for me; I'm not tipping." She pushed a button. A manager appeared and explained in English that a tip was required. When I came out to the restaurant the waiters were snickering. That was enough. I canceled my reservation, took a cab to the airport, and went to Paris on the next flight. I've never been back to Germany.

Through Matty I quickly got a job as a production assistant on an upcoming TV series, *Paris Precinct*, with Louis Jourdan. Until that is, his wife Berthe heard about it and said to him, "No." I had met the Jourdans at Gene Kelley's several times. I had seen how Mrs. Jourdan was fiercely eagle-eyed about protecting her matrimonial rights. But it was easy come, easy go, and I soon had a similar job on a new "Buck Rogers" series in Berlin.

It had been clear when I talked with the producer that this was their first TV project and they didn't know what they were doing — but they thought I did! So I again consulted my guardian angel while sitting on the floor.

I said, "Because of my background, they think I know more about TV production than I actually do. It also seems like it's going to be a long strike, so I was thinking maybe I shall go back to Hollywood instead and talk to people I know in TV production and pick up some pointers. I could exchange my open ended 1st class ticket for a round-trip 2nd class one and come back when the strike ends. I should go see my mother anyway."

My guardian angel said, "That's a good idea," so that's what I did, but it turned out to be a long time before I used that return ticket.

Curtain rises on the best job I ever had.

To show her approval of my return to Hollywood, my guardian angel arranged for me to meet the production assistant for *Lux Video Theater*, the first live TV drama. Lux had been on TV in New York for a couple of years with their half-hour dramatic show based on their popular *Lux Radio Show*, which took old movie classics and reworked them on the radio. With a new cast, they had decided to take it to a one-hour video show and move to Hollywood, both for respect for the scripts and the proximity of top Hollywood stars.

It was the production assistant's job to interview and choose her replacement, and — the gods be praised — she chose me. She explained the duties of the position were to break down a new script — to list special props, determine the number of extras for each scene, hold the scripts during rehearsals for cues, and to figure out prompts, deletions, additions, and timing. The tricky part was to time the dress rehearsals from the control room and then go off by myself to an empty room to "back-time" during the live shooting and tell the director whether he needed to speed up or slow down to make the show come off on time. I'd never learned much math in school. Adding 4 and 4 was OK, but 4 and 5 was questionable. So, I was unsure. In any case, I had to meet the director.

I was *good* at production and it was exciting. It was the best job I ever had. My director, Richard Brooks, was a gifted, innovative man with whom I became lifelong friends. He was secure enough to often take my eager suggestions about script and acting. I was good at seeing how other people should play a scene, and we got along great.

I had never been star-struck. To me, actors in movies or on stage were just colleagues of the actors I had grown up with in the medicine show — they were like family. From top to bottom actors wanted to work on Lux Radio or Video. Top-rated shows were good publicity, plus the fun of playing famous parts in famous movies. And it was great fun to watch them do it.

The delightful James Mason was our host. He kept cast and crew amused all day with his witticisms and ribald humor. As an actor he was very serious, but as a man he was hilarious. His humor did him in, however. One night, he was introducing the cast for the following week and while reading from a teleprompter, he said, "Our leading lady will be none-other than that beautiful, fine, renowned actress of stage and screen." He paused and continued in a horrified tone of voice, "Miss Arlene Dahl!" The incredulous contempt made all of us in the booth laugh, as Dahl's ineptitude as an actress was well known, but the bigwigs at Lux fired him that night. Making fun of a famous actress was frowned upon. We gave him a big farewell.

Fate stepped in one day during the 3rd year I was on the show. I went to see Marian Reese about something. Marian joined Lux as a production assistant at the same time I did and we were very close friends. There were two units of Lux, where Marian and I alternated weekly. One unit was in the office with casting, while the other was rehearsing for the show. (In later years Marion became a top producer of many TV shows and won many awards, including a Peabody.) When I found Marian on the set, she said excitedly, "Have you met the new assistant director?" I hadn't, so she took me to the conference room saying "Now remember, I saw him first!" When I saw this neatly dressed, classy, handsome man in his early 30s sitting at the console, he knocked my socks off and all bets were off.

His name was Russell Stoneham and I was eager to work with him on my show next week. On the day of the rehearsal, I put on my most enticing behavior, so I was much gratified when he asked me into the control room as we went off the air and said, "So do you have a date after the show?" I responded, "Why no, it just happens that I don't tonight." To this he said, "Well, I do, so would you run this sheet of music down to scheduling for me?"

Disappointed and offended I said curtly, "What are you, some kind of Princeton type fellow?" I made more money than he did and this was his errand girl's job. He was also offended as he had gone to Yale. We got over our tiff, however, and were married 5 months after. We had two children, Peter and John, and were married for 24 years.

Producing live television drama is hard. I recall one climactic scene where Margaret Sullivan is driving fast at night and passes a sign saying "Bridge Out." The audience sees it, but she doesn't. She stops just in time. It was very complicated to coordinate and shoot the action — cutting from the woman's face to the speeding car — but

I figures it out. Everyone applauded me and the producer sent me flowers. That was a moment of deep satisfaction for me.

Another triumph was when the producer of a television daily matinee heard how well I had done and called to offer me a job as one of his directors. In those days, soap operas would typically have two or three directors. "Would you like the job?", he said. I said "Thank you, but no." I had recently married Russ, and he was an assistant director. For one thing I didn't really want the pressure, but secondly I knew Russ would not take it well if I made director before he did. What a shame — I would have been the first woman director in live television. However, those two incidents were the high point of my five years on Lux. I left Lux in November of 1956 to give birth to Peter two weeks later. I left because of my belief that a child needed its mother to be at home to take care of it. He laughed and said, "Oh, Jo, I always knew that." They gave me a marvelous farewell party, where I sed to Ken Carpenter, "Now that I'm leaving, I have to admit that I never could add." He laughed and said, "Oh Jo, I always knew that."

Marriage was stultifying after having been such a free spirit. I would have to submerge myself in my husband's needs and attitudes. The mantra of the day was that "A woman's place is in the home."

I don't regret being married for 23 years because I feel that John and Peter had to be born and nurtured. If I had chosen to leave Russ or had chosen to stay in Europe, the boys wouldn't have been born, and I wouldn't have my three grandchildren.

Life's choices are so extraordinarily important.

Going All The Way

Leonardo de Canal, in Idyllwild.

I met Leonardo de Canal on my first trip to San Miguel de Allende in 1976, but soon returned to Los Angeles for my son John's high school graduation. Over the next two years I repeatedly returned to my beloved writer's house in the magical Mexican town, and started on a second draft of my first book "Going All the Way," because I knew I hadn't "gotten it" yet. As literature, it wasn't well done, and there was much more to say. I knew that I had deep wells of feelings that had not been expressed in the first draft, and I hadn't written in a sufficiently descriptive way or in a way that I felt would be pleasing to the serious writers I knew. I wanted to be proud of it, not only in terms of what I had learned emotionally, but also to show my respect for the medium by doing it justice. I didn't have publishing in mind; I was writing for self-analysis. So, I picked up with page one and once again took off from there.

Living in San Miguel was enchanting. Everything was different: the language, the look of the environs, the culture, and me. I was making good headway when one day in my post office box, I found a letter addressed to Leonardo. I had a strange feeling in the pit of my stomach, knowing that I would have to call him in Mexico City in case it was important. However, I got a sinking feeling in my knees as I placed the call, and when it was answered in this soft voice, "Bueno," my knees threatened to give out all together. I stammered, "Hello Leonardo, ah it's Jo — ah — Jo Carroll — ah — in San Miguel."

Warmly, he answered, "Hola Jo, how nice to hear from you."

"Yes, well, ah — I'm at the post office and there's a business letter here for you."

"I see. All right, I'll come down on Wednesday to get it."

"Yes, well — ah — would you like for me to fix you lunch while you're here?"

"That would be lovely."

I said goodbye, hung up the phone with sweaty hands, and slumped against the wall of the post office thinking, "What just came over me?"

As I was preparing the meal, for reasons that were inexplicable to me, my hands shook, my knees shook, and my heart shook, as I picked vegetables from the garden and extended my every effort to make a simple but fine lunch. By the time he arrived, I had the table all set and flowers all around the house.

When we were seated, Leonardo came up behind me and began massaging my tight neck muscles as he was saying "Jo, I can tell that you need some pampering." And I thought, hmmm, "Pampering. That's just what I need. A lot of pampering." But, I was so nervous that I was relieved when the meal was over. Leonardo told me that he needed to be back in town the next weekend and would like to take me out to dinner then.

I picked a lovely restaurant with a fountain in the patio, which I was disappointed to find wasn't running. As we entered, the owner made a big fuss over Leonardo. I was exhilarated at the ambrosial taste of the Langosta (lobster) and I loudly exclaimed that it was the best I'd ever had. Seemingly embarrassed at my outburst, Leonardo looked around, saying: "Well, I don't think it's as good as all that."

And all of a sudden, I found myself back in the sadly familiar state of my husband Russ putting me down. I said to him: "Listen, I am excessive and excited and enthusiastic and I try not to be, but that's the way I am. And if you don't like that, fuck off." I did not ordinarily use four-letter words, but this occasion seemed to demand it. There was a long pause, and he put his napkin on the table and walked away. I thought to myself, "well I don't care. That's the way I am, and that's the way I want to be from now on." He came back and said, "I'm so sorry Jo, I went to ask the owner to turn on the fountain as a way to apologize. But he tells me it is broken. In any case, I apologize deeply and will never do that again." As attracted as I was to him, I'd been there and done that and wasn't going to repeat the pattern. This was the beginning of a major change in my life.

I recalled that when we'd first met he had said that he and his wife, Julia, were separating. I felt that infidelity was abhorrent, demeaning, and undermining. I had high standards for myself in this way.

Me and Leonardo in San Miguel de Allende, Mexico.

But it had happened. It was there. We were deeply attracted, even though he was eleven years younger than I. At first I looked very critically at myself in the mirror: sags and bags screamed out at me that I was an "older woman," but Leonardo was soon able to convince me that we were the same "age." We shared so much. He'd read every book that I loved. He listened to Cole Porter and Mozart. And we laughed a lot, and thus began the most sexually satisfying time of my life.

He took me to special places all over the town and surrounds, and I remembered as he was describing one of these places, he would often stand behind me with his hands over my breasts as he told me the history of this particular cathedral. It was a feeling I didn't know how much I'd missed. Both totally stimulating and relaxing at the same time. He knew so much about his country and loved sharing it with someone who was eagerly interested.

He came down to San Miguel most weekends. And we both experienced the peacefulness and excitement of unconditional love to its fullest. He said that we created bonds of steel that could never be broken and one day brought me a present of a silver chain link bracelet as a reminder that I was always connected to him.

One day when I was typing away at the story of my life, I came again to the part where my father abandoned me and my mother. In the past, I had skimmed over it saying that "He left with a blonde and I never forgave him," but I had been too fearful to try and re-experience the depth of emotions that experience had wrought on my life. I wrote that a month or so later my father returned, alone. These reflections hit a long-buried nerve and I burst into tears. The tears were so cleansing. That's the first time I was able to replace the image of my father's abandonment with the image of the sorrow and guilt my father had returned to us with. I could see him clearly, for the first time, since the original experience of pain and rejection. I could see him as a man who wanted one last chance at the brass ring. A man who was feeling old and a failure at life. And so he reached out once more, for youth really, but he didn't find it, and so he was back with his tail between his legs, and wishful for the love of his wife and his child. Suddenly, wiping away tears, rather than merely being immersed in my own feelings, I could imagine and empathize with what my father had been feeling. The understanding and sympathy I could not give him at that time ... the feeling of forgiveness and real love washed away the anger. Breathtakingly, the next time Leonardo and I were together, the sexual barriers that I had built up when my father returned were washed away. The clamps unclamped. The glands

opened. And I was able for the first time to fully and fearlessly partake in total giving and receiving. Leonardo was so proud of himself.

The relationship between Leonardo and me continued and
flourished for the next twelve years. I traveled back and forth between
Los Angeles and San Miguel. He wanted us to go and live together in
Ensenada, Mexico, where he planned to build some houses.

I met him there and spent a week to see which way the wind
blew. He was wined and dined there, as though he was a celebrity.
Everyone knew him. The Mariachis always came first to our table. It
was all very giddy and fun, but at the end of the week, after a great
deal of thought, I realized I needed to be alone and in my own country. I told him I just couldn't stand the Mariachi music, trying to put
some humor into a hard situation. This made him laugh.

Top of the World - 1979

My view, my way - Idyllwild.

I knew about Idyllwilld, California, because when we lived in the Pacific Palisades some neighbors of ours had a great weekend house there. Russ, a city boy, didn't like the mountains, but Peter, John, and I, and sometimes just me and my dog, loved it and often spent weekends there. Louis and Jane Jacobson had no children and kind of adopted me. Many years later, this relationship was to make a momentous difference in my life when they left me the gift of a generous inheritance. The Jacobsons (may their souls rest in peace) allowed me to have all the comforts I needed in my old age – and I didn't have to be a burden on my sons! I would be grateful to them every single day.

In 1979, I was in the process of divorcing Russ and couldn't afford to live in Los Angeles or New York. Idyllwild is a small mountain town at 6,000 feet elevation, high above Palm Springs, and I had developed a great attraction to it by this time. In 1979, I rented a house there to see how it would feel. Within two weeks I knew it was the place for me. I started looking for a house to buy: two bedrooms and two bathrooms with a big vista for under $100,000. All the realtors laughed at me. But, in the window of the last realtor's office, I saw a picture of exactly what I was looking for. This was the house I was headed toward all my life. I bought it.

On my way home I stopped at the grocery store to check the bulletin board for ads for a dog. Sure enough, there he was, five months old. Mostly border collie, with one blue eye. I called the number and said, "I'll take him." The lady said, "Don't you want to meet him first?" "No, I'm sure, but I have to wait until I can move into the new house."

"Don't do it," my friends said, "You can't live alone in a dinky village in the mountains far from civilization, you'll never make it. What would a city girl like you do in a place like that? Who would you talk to? Adjustment is not easy for a 55-year-old-newly-divorced housewife under the best of circumstances. Don't bury yourself where you don't know anyone. Stay here where your family and friends are, where you can be active in the theater. It's too tough otherwise."

It's true, divorce after a 26-year-long marriage requires a certain amount of derring-do, but the real test is to forge ahead. I had learned at my father's knee in vaudeville performances to "Fake it til you can make it, vamp til ready." So I was determined to do that by following a childhood plan to someday live in the mountains. The only one who encouraged me in this impractical endeavor was my younger son, John. Trying to imagine what it would be like to live alone in the mountains, I began to get cold shivers and confessed to him that I was sometimes afraid the bears would get me, and he said, "But Mom, you like bears!" That settled it.

At first the 'bears' were all darling. I bought the perfect little house with the perfect big view and, as it was not within screaming distance of human ears. I got a perfect dog and cat to support and protect me. I found talking to the trees to be singularly satisfying, and I loved it during my first year when the worst snow storm in fifteen years totally covered up my car. It was proof of my survival fitness that I could climb up over the snow drifts at my door and uncover the wood pile for the fuel supply with which to both warm myself and to cook my food in the fireplace when the electricity went off for two days.

But with spring the big, bad 'bears' came out of hibernation and were savage indeed. They were of the "what if" species and attacked regularly at 3 AM with: what if I fall off a rock while walking in the forest and break my leg and starve to death. What if I have a stroke and can't reach the telephone? What if I make bad investments and can't make the house payments? What if I really can't make it alone? Fear makes the worst sort of bed fellow.

During daylight hours, I followed Rodgers and Hammerstein's advice to "whistle a happy tune," but the pretense didn't fool the nighttime bears. One day, fear incarnate came out to warm itself on my doorstep. I was rushing into the house to answer the phone — and nearly stepped on a bundle of coiled rattlesnake. The shrilling of the distant phone somehow added urgency to the menace of the astonishingly loud, steady drum roll of his rattle.

Instantly, the outer edges of existence focused on a space no larger than this glistening, five-foot black and grey diamond-backed primeval serpent. Sound and dimension took on an underwater slow-motion quality as I grasped my dog's collar and slowly backed away. A foreordained certainty about this confrontation precluded my calling for help — a neighbor, the sheriff, God — I knew the snake was there because I had to kill him. There was no hope that he would just go away; he would always be there in one form or another. The decision was only: I must kill him — or learn to live in fear of him.

Pulling my dog, I dream-walked to the back door, got a shovel, and went inside to put on my armor of rain boots. It was a problem getting them on as my body's behavior was oddly beyond my control, perspiration streamed from every pore, and my hands and feet twitched and jerked to a rhythm of their own.

Boots finally zipped, I stood for a moment in an agony of indecision. Then, as though in response to a bugle of fate, some hitherto unused source of strength crystallized to stiffen my spine and force forward motion. Perspiration dried, shaking stopped, stomach quieted as I gently slid the screen door back, ignored the renewed rattle and took a deep breath, poked to make him strike, and drove the shovel into his body just behind his head.

With a power that seemed impossible in such a fluid body, the snake's entire length lashed out and up, coiled and uncoiled, as I desperately pressed my full weight on the shovel. I daren't raise it for a second chop, so I had to grind him against the wooden step, even though my heart almost stopped when his rapidly thrashing tail wrapped itself around my leg. It felt cool and smooth, with a desperation of its own that gradually weakened as I stood astride his head and with all my strength twisted the point of the shovel back and forth. He appeared to be looking directly up at me, his forked tongue flickering. Incredibly, I felt a wave of pity for him, but then the shovel snapped through, and his head fell off the step.

I didn't feel triumphant, just drained. I couldn't bear to watch the headless body continue to flail and writhe about with renewed violence, so I grabbed it and flung it as far as I could into the forest. Then I dug a hole and buried the gaping head deep so the animals couldn't eat it.

Later I went to find the body so I could cut the eight rattles off to keep as a symbol. But I didn't really need them; the only bears who come to visit me now — including actual bears — are friendly.

Thus began the most idyllic time of life possible for a human being to have. I had grown a lot, mentally and emotionally, in San Miguel de Allende, but now I found it was time to concentrate on growing spiritually. I felt clean, somehow, wiped clean of bad experiences and jumbled emotions. I decided to take a year off. I'd concentrate on being myself and learning what that really meant. From having written the book, I felt I had the tools to enable me to grow. I was happily alone, and self-sufficient. My companions were the trees, the birds, and the animals, which was all conducive to letting worldly thoughts and activities go until I could become more at one with nature, and closer to the sacred.

Me and Boss in Dark Canyon.

Looking back, I felt that I'd spent my life surrounded by too much talk, such that everyone I had known was eventually saying the same things over and over. I wasn't-clear minded. I felt that now was the perfect time for me because it was so quiet. The dominant sounds were from the wind and the birds. My home, at mile above sea level, overlooked five mountain ranges to the ocean and the enormity, the magnitude of the forces of nature were right there before my eyes.

In the mornings, there was a huge boulder in front of my house overlooking my world. I would sit on this rock and watch the sun rise over the valley, bringing a new life to me as well as a new light.

My dog, Boss, and I took long walks in the forest, rain or shine. A cat inadvertently wandered into my life as well. For that year, it was just me and my animal friends. I didn't reach out to people in the neighborhood. My house was not within screaming distance of a neighbor's house, except for rare weekenders. So I found very little to distract me from my goal of improved self-knowledge.

Me and Boss hiking in Idyllwild.

Since I had been a part of the Kelly group when I was 21, martinis had become very important to me, and I couldn't envision a life without at least two or three of them during a ritual that always began at around 5 o'clock each evening. I found, however, that the best time of day to take a walk with my dog was around that time, and so I couldn't take a walk and come back and have a martini because I was too hungry at that point. So, almost without a decision, I stopped drinking.

In those days (the early 1980s) the phrase "have a good day" had come into vogue. One day sitting on my rock in the early morning with my cup of tea, I realized, "I'm having a good day. I'm really having a GOOD day!" An overwhelming experience came one day when I went for a long walk, and there was one area, between hills, where there was a little creek that ran through a meadow-like area. There was a big, big boulder on the side where I was sitting with my dog, and, involuntarily, I gave a huge sigh of complete satisfaction. I said to myself, "I'm a successful person. All my life I have had the goal of being happy. And I am now fully happy." Finally.

The trip getting there had been a lot of fun, too, but no experience I'd ever had was as full of contentment and peace and a sense of joy. I felt that I'd gotten where I was always headed. And Boss was my perfect companion. We were bonded in a special way. We shared in a special way. And we loved in a special way.

Friends came to see me periodically. And Leonardo sometimes came for four or five days. He said at one point, "I'd be a happy man if you loved me the way you love your dog." He (the dog) was indeed my best friend. He shared all my secrets, including my longings and my joys. Part way down the mountain was a big creek, in a special place called Dark Canyon. Whenever I felt blue or anxious, I'd say "c'mon Boss, let's go." We'd walk up the creek and sit on boulders in the middle of the rushing water. It was particularly beautiful when the fragrant wild azaleas and dogwood would bloom in early spring. We'd just listen to the water and really get the feeling of being immersed in the place. It was special; a wonderful time of my life.

I had 30 years of long walks in the forest, often with Boss, being a part of nature, sitting on my back deck, looking out over the vast valley below. Sometimes I think I can see even farther, into the mysteries of the meaning of life — almost.

I was so grateful for my life that I felt I should give something back.

In order to do that I had to make friends. I began to look around me for people with similar interests and enthusiasms. I participated in events at the Idyllwild School of Music and the Arts (ISOMATA). The first people I found that were kindred spirits were Carol and Roy Mills. Carol was a wonderful abstract-expressionist artist and fine illustrator, and Roy was a retired businessman with a philosophical view on life. Carol and I became close friends, and I participated in weekly meditation sessions led by monks from the Idyllwild's Mountain Zen Center in the art studio at her home. Through Carol, I met others who helped me find ways to broaden my perspective and to be of use to my community while being true to my ideals. For example, I started Idyllwild's first Democratic Club. There had been a flourishing Republican Club, but nothing for the Dems. I was appalled that this community was so conservative. I thought it would be a good idea to work with school children. Mondale was running against Reagan. I asked the principal of the school if they had any political education. I suggested that the Republican and Democratic clubs each send speakers to the school to discuss election issues, and to then have the students vote in a mock election. To my great delight, this conservative community's children voted for Mondale.

Many of my close friends were Jewish, and I was astonished that there was no temple or gathering place. With Phil, I had been to several Seders in the past, sometimes at Edward G. Robinson's house. I rented the hall at Camp Maranatha in the village. Carol and Roy helped me find the other Jewish people in town, and we had the town's first community Seder.

I started looking for more to do with and for the community and found Hospice. Hemet (a small town at the foot of our mountain) had a program but needed support in Idyllwild. I took the volunteer training. That experience was very meaningful, and I heard that another nearby hospice was looking for a community relations coordinator. I went down and spoke with the director. I thought it would be a great thing to do. I felt a new sense of purpose and satisfaction in helping others through a process that was so full of meaning. They saw that I was good with people, speaking, and fundraising. Arlene said "What aren't you good at?" I said," I'm not a very good secretary." She said, "OK, we'll work around that!"

When I had won the Miss America Pageant and toured the military camps and assembly plants, I always felt a bit of a fraud when the soldiers cheered for me. But, when working directly with hospice, I felt that I was fulfilling that purpose and using the Miss America title in a far better way. I worked with them for 11 years. I learned so many vitally important things about human beings. I learned that dying can be a peaceful and graceful thing. I learned a lot about beauty: physical and spiritual. One of the volunteers whose husband had died (this was somewhat common) was one of the most beautiful women I had ever known. Her face looked like a proverbial prune. Everything was baggy. Hair white. But her spirit shone through so vividly. Her laughter was graceful. Her attitude was cheerful. Her living was joyous. She was the most beautiful woman that I had ever seen. In contrast, at a local department store, was a young girl in her early 20s, with striking physical beauty. Her face, her eyes, her complexion, her hair, was all what every model wanted. But her inner attitude was so morose and self-centered that as I looked at her, I compared her outer with her inner beauty. I had been through my own "sex symbol" period. If only kids knew when they were young what true beauty was, and to look for it inside rather than outside.

One time, a local paper asked to do a story on a hospice patient. I asked the nurses for suggestions. They said Betty Lou is the one. So I went to visit her in her mobile home. Pain was clearly on her face, but her attitude was excellent. She said that her greatest problem was that she'd dream that her cancer was gone, and then she'd wake up to find it wasn't true. She said "When I die I want all my friends to come to my house for a party, with a big cake saying It's Been Fun." I took a minute to think about it because it was the most beautiful expression of acceptance and strength of the human spirit.

I had another patient who lived in Hemet, also in a mobile home. Her husband and daughter lived with her as well. When I arrived she'd be up, in her dress, and sitting looking out the window. She never spoke. Her husband and daughter spoke about her as though she wasn't there. They treated her like a piece of mute furniture. They enjoyed talking to me, but I was there to talk to her.

I looked around and saw pictures of a dog on the wall, and I said to her, "Was this your dog?" I told her about my dog, Boss. I asked if she would like me to bring my dog to visit her. She looked straight at me and nodded her head. I came back another day with Boss. I was a little nervous because Boss didn't like his face touched. She was sitting outside in her wheelchair when I arrived. She smiled at Boss and held out her arms. He brought his face right up into her hands, and let her fondle his nose and ears without complaint. He knew. She smiled and smiled and hummed. I can truthfully say that this woman, who was only waiting to die, when given direct attention and encouragement by me and my dog began to talk about dogs and other things, and before long she got so much better that she went off hospice. How we treat each other really matters. If I hadn't come there and treated her as a complete person, she would indeed have gone ahead and died before her time.

Bob was another special hospice patient. I saw him frequently, and I asked his wife, Edith, to call me if she thought Bob were dying and she wanted me to be with her. So, one day she called and said just that.

The face of the man in the bed had been reduced to a basic beauty of bone and cartilage, the pale skin and delicate veins fitting tightly over the high forehead, cheeks, and prominent nose. "Bob" didn't suit him, somehow, "Akhenaton" would have been more appropriate. That falcon-faced Egyptian Sun God's spirit had a better claim on him. He had a Pharaoh's dignity, and removed stillness, too, as he turned his eyes from the ceiling in my approximate direction and allowed me to hold his almost transparent, long, elegant fingers for a moment before withdrawing them and returning his gaze to the ceiling.

I knew from hospice that the last thing to go with a dying person is hearing; even though patients can't speak, they can hear and often will respond by squeezing your hand. When I arrived, Bob was alone in his room, and his children were out on the deck talking with Edith. So, I went to him and took his hand. I said that I was there and that I loved him and asked if he would squeeze my hand if he could hear me. He tightened his grip, so I rushed out to the family and explained about the hearing and that he shouldn't be left alone. They didn't believe it, but came in perhaps to humor me. I took Bob's hand and again told him who I was and asked him to respond and the family could indeed see that he tightened his grip. They gathered around and spoke of their love for him. I felt I could go.

He did die that day, and often when I went to the post office or grocery store, I would run into Edith, and she never failed to tell me how grateful they were for those moments. And I realized more fully the power and purpose of hospice.

How the difference in attitude can affect those who are dying was made so very clear to me by two friends who happened to be dying of cancer at the same time. One had pancreatic cancer and lived in the Pacific Palisades, and the other had lung cancer and lived in Idyllwild. My friend in the Palisades chose to die at home with her music, relatives, and friends to brighten her day. I went to see her often and took her books and tapes, and one day when I came in her daughter told me her pain was getting worse, but when my friend and I began to talk, she was all excited about a book I had brought her previously and began to tell me how much she enjoyed a certain portion. It had to do with the difficulty of a man taking off his pants in a passionate hurry, and she could scarcely describe it while laughing big, hearty belly laughs. Although in pain, she could still laugh fully at the comedy of life.

My other friend chose to die in the hospital, and when I went to see her she was gasping for each breath, terrified to go to sleep. There was nothing I could say or do to even make her smile. All she could do was speak of her pain and hold onto me desperately.

I puzzled over the difference between the ways my two friends were facing death.

Finally, I realized that my Palisades friend could laugh and be joyous because she was not afraid to die. And she was not afraid to die because she had never been afraid to live. My Idyllwild friend was too frightened to laugh because she was too afraid to die. And I knew that she had been afraid to live all her life.

We all must die, but we don't have to die afraid if we have learned to live without fear, and how to laugh at ourselves and the human comedy. It's a funny thing, but it's very hard to find any jokes about death, that forbidden subject, even among comedians. I liked to tell a joke or two when I gave presentations. I even called friends of mine who were comedy writers and asked them to help me, but to no avail.

It's all in the way you look at a situation which makes it funny, or not.

After 11 years, I retired from Hospice (a better person), and decided to build upon the book I had written so long before. The first book "Going All the Way" stopped at age 18, as I set out for Hollywood. Through the writing process, I had found my little red hat of courage at that point, and wasn't interested in going further. Through friends, I got the book read by top editor Michael Korda of the *New Yorker* and one whose name I can't recall at *Harpers*. They both liked it and were interested in publishing, but said it must include the Hollywood "chapter" of my life. However, I was tired of the process, and my successful "writing therapy" had achieved what I wanted. Many years later I set out to write another book incorporating parts of the first one, while bringing my life up to the present. That eventually became the present volume.

Organizing a "Memory
Walk" with Hemet Hospice.

I was well into the writing process in 2012, when disaster struck. After almost a year of not feeling well and multiple misdiagnoses I collapsed at the hospital only to be diagnosed with Stage-4 colon cancer. They operated the next day and removed two feet of colon and intestine. Imagine! The surgeon said that a number of my lymph nodes had metastasized, and that I was terminal. Dreadful word. But I never for one moment believed him, ever, and jumped at the chance when he offered three kinds of chemotherapy. I spent many hours — four days a week over three months — in the therapy room at Eisenhower hospital, in Rancho Mirage, near Palm Springs, focusing all of my will on visualizing the orangy-pink cloud moving slowly back and forth in my stomach — healing me. I had studied yoga and practiced meditation for many years, and I used every ounce of what I had learned toward this goal. Flowing steadily through my mind was my mantra, "I can do this, I can do this." Also of great help, my years of walking in the forest had strengthened my body and a connection with nature that nourished my spirit. I was ready.

Well, 3 months later, my final exam CAT scan showed me to be disease-free! During all that time, the oncologist repeatedly told me that I was terminal. Now he said that he hadn't cured me; I had done it myself with my positive attitude. I thanked him. For 9 years now, I have been cancer free, but a case of COPD has slowly put me in hospice care.

The Final Curtain - 2021

Me at 89, and at 18 drawn by the famous cartoonist Alex Raymond — creator of Flash Gordon — at the Miss America pageant. The pair of pictures provide a poignant comparison for me at a time when I was unhappy (then) and at a time that I was happy. Raymond later created a cartoon with me as a princess character.

Having found my little red hat, these days I sit out on my deck trying to deal with the mystery of death. My goal is to do it gracefully; I don't want to leave scratch marks.

I think about the purpose of life. My life. I read once that the Persian prophet Zoroaster, said that the purpose of life was to evolve into a oneness with God. Makes sense to me, although I am far from achieving that now. I do, however, somehow believe that our individual spirits are eternal. Watching my mother die, I definitely felt something leave her body.

My tender sweet little hope is that my ashes will be buried in my backyard among the daffodils and the graves of my deceased dogs and cats. There is a giant, luxurious Coulter pine that I've raised from a baby, down a ways into the forest west of the house, that has a great view over all. My plan is that my own eternal spirit and that of my dog Boss will live among its branches happily ever-after, looking out over my beloved vista together. That's my plan, anyway.

My tale is surely in part about the lot of women in this land. While elements of the disrespect of women that prevailed when I was born nearly a century ago persist, I take heart in the great progress I've seen. More and more, humanity's inner face is merging with its outer face — and I so much wish I could live to see what women's faces will look like when that merger is complete. But the tale is also one of some wonderful men, and of being a human and sorting out all of the things one encounters in life, some serendipitous, others more calculated.

Some telling things emerge as I take stock. Every impulse I acted on that came from anger or fear turned out badly. Every time I acted from love or courage turned out wonderfully. As a case in point, as a child, anger at my father for leaving us had the effect of cutting me off from others who loved me. Forgiving my father so many years later allowed me to be reborn as a fuller person, and as a woman.

My ten commandments have evolved. While the original set reflected my aspirations and drew mostly upon the words of others, the current set reflects what has been validated through personal experience and is forged mostly in my own words:

1. Be grateful.
2. Trust.
3. "Be brave and mighty forces will come to your aid." — Goethe
4. When I say "I can do this, I can do this," over and over to myself − I can.
5. The devil hides inside fear.
6. Look − really see − everything about you wherever you are. And don't forget to look up.
7. Life is not always the party we hoped for, but while we are here we should dance.
8. If you think something nice about anyone − *tell them.*
9. Don't forget to look at both sides of the "mine & theirs" coin before you form an opinion.
10. To thine own self be true. — Shakespeare

Looking back, I can see that so-called "fame and fortune" never made me happy. Friends, and the fulfillment of my children brought me all that is truly meaningful now.

I'm finding at the end it is necessary to search for purpose. Aside from the fact that I believe Peter and John needed to be born, when asking myself "Am I leaving the world a better place?," it eases my mind to remember that from time to time someone has told me something I said or did made them a better person. It is deeply satisfying to me and I take pride in knowing that I tried never to hurt anyone's feelings. All of my life I made it a point not to do so.

I believe that if everybody behaved as Lassie did, Lassie who was forgiving, loving, honest, loyal, benevolent, and eager to help others, and had a very high moral character. Not to mention well-groomed.

End of the pathway I had built in front of my magical Idyllwild home, with five mountain ranges to the sea.

I used to imagine my life as a large abstract, unfinished medieval tapestry, portraying each thing I learned from reading the classics, each moment of seeing and understanding art, ballet, classical music, and philosophy. Every joyous moment in my life is represented in blotches, woven into the tapestry of color, representing the importance of my experiences and feelings. I'm curious how it will look when it is finished. I know the last threads will be a soft orangy-pink color in the shape of slowly moving clouds like those I visualized in healing myself in the endless hours of chemotherapy — that worked brilliantly.

Besides enabling me to find my little red hat of courage again, this trip down memory lane has been a joy ride. For the most part. While my memory is selective, some years even are a total blank, I found that these events that were most formative to me are vivid still in all respects. Revisiting those memories through the writing of this book has been much like experiencing them for the first time. So much so that now and then I yearn for my guardian angel to pick me up and drop me back into the actual experiences. I want one more flying-free ride on Creampuff, a night of dancing at the Mayfair, eating my first meal in Paris again, one more Saturday night at the Kelly's, and one more hike up Dark Canyon to sit on the big rock with Boss listening to the creek. Sounds greedy, I know that, but oh how I would love it.

Speaking of wishes, I wish I knew what it would have been like married to Blackie. For me, he is the song unsung, whose melody I can almost hear.

There is something seductive about negativity, something alluring about sinking into the depths, passively letting go of effort and releasing into the soothing lullaby of inaction and depression. Holding close the thought that all the dark forces are irresistible in the end and it is best to just succumb to the siren song of inertia and acceptance. But, as my present goal is to stay positive, when negative thoughts come, I quickly clasp to my bosom the memory of some of my life's high points:

- Becoming one with nature and animals
- The joy of travel
- The many occasions of full-bodied laughter that still ring out inside me
- The immense satisfaction of learning from books, the arts, and life
- Discovering my connection with God
- Always getting a good table at Sardis
- The engineer holding the New York subway train for me

- The producer asking me to be the first woman director in live television
- Getting a new passport in Marseille

And, most importantly, I hold close that feeling I sometimes got while sitting on a rock in the forest that I was a success as a person.

I wouldn't have missed a minute of it. Despite the adversities, life tends to offer much to be grateful for — but care should be taken to allow oneself to be grateful rather than squandering the joys of gratitude. Something that helps in all these regards is to try and *see*, really see, what's around you — faces, nature, everything.

I have few regrets, but to mention one: I wish I'd been kinder. More sensitive to other people's feelings. But — most of all — all in all, I am proud that, as the song famously sung by Sinatra says: I did it my way. Now at 97, I play it everyday as I do my exercises. It makes me feel strong and proud.

My Way[1]

And now, the end is near
And so I face the final curtain
My friend, I'll say it clear
I'll state my case, of which I'm certain

I've lived a life that's full
I've traveled each and every highway
But more, much more than this
I did it my way

Regrets, I've had a few
But then again, too few to mention
I did what I had to do
And saw it through without exemption

I planned each charted course
Each careful step along the byway
And more, much more than this
I did it my way

1 Songwriters: Claude Francois, Gilles Thibaut, Jacques Revaux, and Paul Anka

Yes, there were times, I'm sure you knew
When I bit off more than I could chew
But through it all, when there was doubt
I ate it up and spit it out
I faced it all and I stood tall
And did it my way

I've loved, I've laughed and cried
I've had my fill my share of losing
And now, as tears subside
I find it all so amusing

To think I did all that
And may I say — not in a shy way
Oh no, oh no, not me
I did it my way
For what is a man, what has he got
If not himself, then he has naught
To say the things he truly feels
And not the words of one who kneels
The record shows I took the blows
And did it my way

Yes, it was my way!

Acknowledgments

This book is my tapestry, and I offer my everlasting gratitude to Evan Mills who has been a valued discussant and editor, helping me weave together and tighten so many of the threads. He performed miracles as a text and photo editor, and sometimes scribe.

Marcia Krull and Marcia Gawecki provided eagle-eyed copy editing, for which I am grateful.

Speaking of gratitude, granddaughter Elizabeth, makes me think of the many right choices I made in my life, including those that led to bringing about her being born. Choosing to dare to leave the medicine show, led directly to the Miss America Pageant. Choosing to stop being an actress and becoming a working woman led directly to choosing not to work for Harold Clurman and the Israeli Station Head, both of which would have put my life on a totally different path. Choosing to leave Paris, instead of working in Germany, led directly to working on *Lux Video Theater* ... hence to having a family. It fascinates me to imagine all those branching paths, leading to such a fortuitous outcome. Fate, maybe.

Although most of my beloved best friends are gone, I still have enough of them left to make life a thing of beauty, with their love and support. Best friends and neighbors, Ron and Marcia, Therese, and Janice warm me with showers of love and chicken soup. Sabrina, a faraway friend, reminds me to laugh. Pete strengthens and inspires me with love and intellectual support.

My family — Peter, Scottie, John and Emily, Elizabeth and husband Kushan, grandsons William and Russell, my cousins, and the whole Burnett family — and my caregivers, Val, Marcia, and Arjuna are all helping me complete the tapestry's weaving.

Filmography, Television, Stage

Movies

1976 *Everybody Rides the Carousel* - Stage 5 (voice, as Jo-Carroll Stoneham)
1951 *A Millionaire for Christy* - Nurse Jackson (uncredited)
1951 *Pickup* - Irma
1951 *Secrets of Beauty* - Jo-Carroll Dennison
1950 *Prehistoric Women* - Nika (as Jo-Carroll Dennison)
1950 *Beyond the Purple Hills* (Gene Autry) - Mollie Rayburn (as Jo Dennison)
1946 *The Jolson Story* - Ann Murray
1946 *The Missing Lady* - Gilda Marsh (as Jo-Carroll Dennison)
1945 *State Fair* - Girl (uncredited)
1944 *Winged Victory* - Dorothy Ross
1944 *Something for the Boys* - Minor Role (uncredited)
1944 *Ladies of Washington* - Frieda (uncredited)
1943 *The Gang's All Here* - Minor Role (uncredited)
1943 *The Song of Bernadette* - Young Nun (uncredited)

Television

2005 *Sinatra: Dark Star* (TV Movie documentary, as Jo-Carroll Dennison)
1997 *Biography* (TV Series documentary, as Jo-Carroll Dennison) - Phil Silvers: Top Banana ... (as Jo-Carroll Dennison)
Late 1950s *NBC's Matinee Theater*
1953 *The Abbott and Costello Show* (TV Series) - The Actors' Home ... Ice Cream Customer (as Jo-Carroll Dennison)
1953 *The Adventures of Kit Carson* (TV Series) - Jennie Bailey - Bad Men of Marysville ... Jennie Bailey (as Jo-Carrol Dennison)
1952 *Hollywood Opening Night* (TV Series) - Prison Doctor
1951 *Adventures of Wild Bill Hickok* (TV Series) - Kathy York - Ex-Convict Story ... Kathy York (as Jo-Carroll Dennison)
1951 *Stars Over Hollywood* (TV Series) - Prison Doctor
1950 *Dick Tracy* (TV Series) - Breathless Mahoney - Dick Tracy and the Stolen Emeralds ... Breathless Mahoney (as Carroll Dennison) - Episode #1.2
Early 1950s *Perry Mason*
Early 1950s *The Frank Sinatra Show*
Early 1950s *Ed Sullivan Presents* - Talking Woman
Early 1950s *Kraft Theater and Omnibus* (hosted by Allistar Cook)
Early 1950s *New York Racing Commission Documentary*

Stage

1940s/50s - *The Front Page* - La Jolla Playhouse
1940s/50s - *Ladies of Washington* - La Jolla Playhouse
1950s - *Various* - Actors' Lab, Hollywood

Index

Dietrich, Marlene 216, 279
DiMaggio, Joe 302, 319, 342
Donen, Stanley 261, 367, 401, 405
Don The Beachcomer 365
Douglas, Kirk 370
Dunbar, Dixie 315
Dunne, Irene 325

E

Elements of Style (William Strunk Jr.) 26, 105

F

Fabray, Nanette 333
Fast, Howard 2
Fearnley, John 468
Federal Institute 155, 157, 164, 464, 468
Feil, Murray 202, 203, 204, 205, 368
Filmography 507
Flash Gordon 11
Florence, Texas 1, 40, 250, 456, 457, 458
Flynn, Errol 164, 273
Fonda, Henry 274, 467
Ford, Glen 274
Ford, John 274
Fox, Mathew ("Matty") 376, 379, 380, 381, 389, 390, 391, 392, 393, 394,
    395, 396, 397, 398, 406, 417, 418, 419, 452, 453, 457, 458, 459,
    460, 463, 470, 474, 475
France 103, 110, 116, 173, 226, 401, 402, 403, 407, 412, 419, 420, 421,
    423, 436, 443, 449
Francis, Kay 216
Freed, Arthur 367

G

Gable, Clark 164, 254, 274, 443
Garbo, Greta 2, 185, 269, 278
Gardner, Ava 294, 324, 438
Garfield, John 214, 215, 247, 285
Garfield, Robbie 261
Garland, Judy 262, 264, 346
Garrett, Betty 309
Garson, Greer 217

Made in the USA
Middletown, DE
24 September 2021

48265651R00295